Takamitsu Muraoka

Classical Syriac

PORTA LINGUARUM ORIENTALIUM

Neue Serie

Herausgegeben von Werner Diem und Franz Rosenthal

Band 19

1997

Harrassowitz Verlag · Wiesbaden

Takamitsu Muraoka

CLASSICAL SYRIAC

A Basic Grammar with a Chrestomathy

With a Select Bibliography
Compiled by S. P. Brock

1997
Harrassowitz Verlag · Wiesbaden

Cover Illustration: Herzog August Bibliothek Wolfenbüttel Cod Guelf. 3.1.300 Aug. 2°, 215 r.

Die Deutsche Bibliothek – CIP-Einheitsaufnahme

Muraoka, Takamitsu:
Classical Syriac : a basic grammar with a Chrestomathy /
Takamitsu Muraoka. With a select bibliogr. comp. by S. P. Brock. –
Wiesbaden : Harrassowitz, 1997
(Porta linguarum orientalium ; N.S., Bd. 19)
ISBN 3-447-03890-X

Manufactured by Hubert & Co., Göttingen
Printed on permanent/durable paper.
Printed in Germany
ISSN 0554-7342
ISBN 3-447-03890-X

In memory of my dear teacher

and

a true gentleman

Chaim Rabin ז"ל

(1915-96)

Professor of Hebrew

The Hebrew University, Jerusalem

CONTENTS

PREFACE

One need not perhaps look very far for a reason or two why the Syriac language still holds some fascination for not a few people. Among the Semitic languages it is one of the most richtly documented besides Arabic, Akkadian and Hebrew. Though we do possess some amount of secular Syriac writings, the bulk of Syriac literature, including one of its oldest documents, namely the Syriac Bible in its various versions, attests to the fact that this is the tongue of the Syriac-speaking church. Thus the knowledge of Syriac is an important key for investigating and appreciating the culture deposited in documents penned in this dialect of Aramaic over a period of more than a millennium. Although we are deeply indebted to Payne Smith and Brockelmann for the solid foundations they laid in the field of Syriac lexicography, and to Nöldeke for his still unsurpassed reference grammar, there still remains much to claim the attention of Syriac philologists. Especially on matters of syntax, there are issues to which Nöldeke has paid insufficient, if at all, attention, and some questions need to be investigated with a new perspective and methodology, as has been demonstrated during the past few decades by scholars such as Avineri, Goldenberg, Joosten, Khan, Van Rompay, and the present writer.([1])

The present work is meant to replace C. Brockelmann's *Syrische Grammatik*, in comparison with which our grammar shows similarities and dissimilarities alike.

Ours is also an introduction to the Classical Syriac language and its literature.

Brockelmann introduced some of his original insights in the phonology section, whilst the morphology and syntax, the latter in particular, were rather brief. We like to believe that in all compartments of grammar we have attempted to present a more detailed description of the language, incorporating results of more recent studies on the language, with special reference to syntax, which is an area where Syriac, with its only deceptive simplicity, appears to be capable of expressing rather intriguing subtleties and niceties.

[1] On the *status quaestionis*up to the late thirties of this century, see an excellent overview in Rosenthal 1939: 179-211.

Unlike Brockelmann's our approach has been essentially descriptive and synchronic, diachronic and comparative details, if presented at all, being mostly relegated to footnotes.

Generations of students of Syriac have valued the chrestomathy of considerable extent in Brockelmann's grammar. We also follow this pedagogically commendable tradition. One important difference, however, is that each piece of text in our chrestomathy is more or less fully provided with notes, mostly of grammatical and lexical nature with frequent cross-references to relevant paragraphs in the grammar. Another difference is that, whereas the pieces selected by Brockelmann are almost without an exception ecclesiastical in nature, our anthology, it is hoped, shows that in this language one can also find texts of secular nature which can be interesting. In Brockelmann's chrestomathy all the three Syriac scripts are equally represented, whilst we have shown partiality to the oldest of them, the Estrangela, not only in the chrestomathy, but also in the grammar section. This can be justified by the growing tendency to use this script in the recent scholarly publications. We have made this choice, though the wordprocessing software at our disposal has presented some technical difficulties in cases where a vowel sign and a diacritic dot or dots, for example, need to be applied simultaneously. In some such cases we have dispensed with one or more of such dots. It is hoped that this will not be found by the user too difficult or confusing. To minimise such a difficulty and in the interest of pedagogical effectiveness, transliteration in the Latin alphabet has been extensively used in the phonology and morphology section and likewise in the chrestomathy. Out of the same pedagogical consideration, the Verb Paradigms have also been provided with transliteration.

We would state at this point that we have taken the maximum care to indicate the twofold pronunciation of the six, so-called Beghadhkephath plosives. This is contrary to the practice followed in many text-editions, even in elementary grammars.

The texts in the Chrestomathy are arranged in a roughly chronological order of composition.

Another universally acclaimed boon of Brockelmann's grammar has been its "Literatur." Here again we follow in his steps, and to this end we have been able to secure the friendly service of Dr. Sebastian

Brock of Oxford, who has compiled a most up-to-date bibliography for which one can only be grateful. It is not meant to be exhaustive in the strict sense of the word, but it does present a source of information to which any serious student of Syriac would often like to turn. The section entitled "Grammatical studies" is designed to be exhaustive.

Being the author of *Classical Syriac for Hebraist*, also published by Harrassowitz (1987; reprinted 1996), I feel obliged to say a few words over the relationship between it and the present work. My general approach to Syriac grammar remains the same, though the present work incorporates some new ideas and details, and is as a whole somewhat fuller in the presentation of the grammar of the language. This time no previous knowledge of Hebrew is assumed, so that even the basic notions peculiar to Semitic languages are fully explained. Needless to say, such a knowledge would considerably facilitate and accelerate the study of Syriac, and for the benefit of such students we have mentioned some phenomena and examples related to other cognates such as Hebrew and other dialects of Aramaic. No chrestomathy text is common to both grammars. The Bibliography is, of course, a new feature. So are a set of basic language exercises with a key to them. Following an earlier edition of Brockelmann's grammar a list of proper nouns occurring in the chrestomany texts has been appended.

It remains to express my sincere thanks to the editors of the reputed series, *Porta Linguarum Orientalium*, Profs. F. Rosenthal and W. Diem, who did me an inestimable honour by asking me to contribute this volume to the series. I have also benefited from several reviews published on my *Classical Syriac for Hebraists*, and suggestions and corrections to it made known to me through private correspondence by Prof. B. Zuckerman of California, and especially Mr O.J. Schrier, M.A., of Amsterdam. My gratitude goes also to Mr. M. Langfeld of Otto Harrassowitz for his encouragement and patience.

October, 1996.

Takamitsu Muraoka
Department of Near Easterm Studies,
Leiden University,
The Netherlands.

Literature cited in the grammar and chrestomathy sections([1])

Aro, J. 1964. *Die Vokalisierung des Grundstammes im semitischen Verbum*. Helsinki: Societas Orientalis Fennica. [Studia Orientalia 31]

Beyer, K. 1966. "Der reichsaramäische Einschlag in der ältesten syrischen Literatur." *ZDMG* 116:242-54.

Birkeland, H. 1947. "The Syriac phonematic vowel systems," *Festskrift til Professor Olaf Broch på hans 80 Årsdag*, pp. 19-39. Oslo.

Blau, J. 1969. "The origin of the open and closed *e* in Proto-Syriac." *Bulletin of the School of Oriental and African Studies* 32:1-9.

Bonnet, M. 1903. In R.A. Lipsius and M. Bonnet, *Acta Apostolorum Apocrypha* II.2. Leipzig: Hermann Mendelssohn.

Boyd III, J.L. 1982. "The development of the West Semitic Qal Perfect of the double-ʿayin verb with particular reference to its transmission in Syriac." *Journal of Northwest Semitic Languages* 10:11-23.

Brock, S.P. 1981. "Genesis 22 in Syriac tradition," in P. Casetti et al. (eds), *Mélanges Dominique Barthélemy* (Göttingen), pp. 2-30.

Brockelmann, C. 1908-13. *Grundriß der vergleichenden Grammatik der semitischen Sprachen*. 2 vols. Von Reuther & Reichard:Berlin.

__. [2]1928. *Lexicon Syriacum*. Max Niemyer: Halle.

__. [9]1962. *Syrische Grammatik mit Paradigmen, Literatur, Chrestomathie und Glossar*. Leipzig: Enzyklopädie.

Budge, E.W. Wallis. 1897. *The Laughable Stories Collected by Mâr Gregory John Bar-Hebræus... The Syriac Text Edited with an English Translation*. London: Luzac and Co.

Charlesworth, J.H. 1977. Ed. and tr., *The Odes of Solomon*. Missoula: Scholars Press.

Dalman, G. [2]1905. *Grammatik des jüdisch-palästinischen Aramäisch*. Leipzig: J.C. Hinrichs.

Drijvers, H.J.W. 1965. *The Book of the Laws of Countries. Dialogue on Fate of Bardaiṣan of Edessa*. Assen: Van Gorcum. [a Syriac text with an English translation]

__. 1972. *Old Syriac (Edessean) Inscriptions. Edited with an Introduction, Indices and a Glossary*. Leiden: E.J. Brill.

Fassberg, S.E. 1990. *A Grammar of the Palestinian Targum Fragments from the Cairo Genizah*. HSS 38. Atlanta:Scholars Press.

Gibson, M.D. 1911. *The Commentaries of Ishoʿdad of Merv, Bishop of Ḥadatha* etc. Luke and John. [Horae Semiticae no. 7, vol. 3, Syriac

[1] For information on abbreviations used here, see pp. 146-47.

text; no. 5, vol. 1, Translation]. Cambridge: Cambridge University Press.

Goldstein, J.A. 1966. "The Syriac bill of sale from Dura-Europos." *JNES* 25: 1-16.

Guidi, I. 1903. *Chronica minora.* [CSCO. Syr. 1]. Paris: Carlolus Poussielgue and Leipzig: Otto Harrassowitz.

Hallier, L. 1893. *Untersuchungen über die edessenische Chronik.* Texte und Untersuchungen IX, 1. Leipzig: J.C. Hinrichs'sche Buchhandlung.

Harris, R. and A. Mingana. 1916-20. *The Odes and Psalms of Solomon* etc. Manchester, London, New York: Manchester University Press, Longmans, Green & Company, and Bernard Quaritch.

Janson, A. and L. Van Rompay. 1993. *Efrem de Syriër. Uitleg van het boek Genesis. Ingeleid, vertaald en toegelicht.* Kampen: J.H. Kok.

Jespersen, O. 1937. *Analytic Syntax.* Repr. Holt, Rinehart and Winston, Inc.: New York, 1969. [originally published in Copenhagen: Munksgaard]

Joosten, J. 1989. "The function of the so-called davitus ethicus in Classical Syriac." *Or* 58: 473-92.

__. 1992. "The negation of non-verbal clause in Early Syriac." *JAOS* 112: 584-88.

__. 1996. *The Syriac Language of the Peshitta & Old Syriac Versions of Matthew. Syntactic Structure, Inner-Syriac Developments & Translation Technique.* [Studies in Semitic Languages and Linguistics 22]. Leiden: E.J. Brill.

Joüon, P. and T. Muraoka, 1993. *A Grammar of Biblical Hebrew.* 2 vols. Roma: Pontifical Biblical Institute Press.

Klijn, A.F.J. 1962. *The Acts of Thomas. Introduction - Text - Commentary.* Leiden: E.J. Brill.

Lagarde, P. de. 1889-91. *Übersicht über die im Aramäischen, Arabischen und Hebräischen übliche Bildung der Nomina nebst Register und Nachträgen.* Göttingen: Dietrich. Repr. Otto Zeller: Osnabrück, 1972.

Lattke, M. 1979-80. *Die Oden Salomos in ihrer Bedeutung für Neues Testament und Gnosis.* Bd I, Ausführliche Handschriftenbeschreibung, Edition mit deutscher Parallel-Übersetzung etc., Bd Ia: Der syrische Text der Edition in Esṭrangelā, Faksimilie des griechischen Papyrus Bodmer XI. [Orbis Biblicus et Orientalis 25/1, 25/1a]. Freiburg: Universitätsverlag and Göttingen: Vandenhoeck & Ruprecht.

Lewis, A.S. 1910. *The Old Syriac Gospels or Evangelion da-Mepharreshê* etc. London: Williams and Norgate.

Martin, J.P. 1872. *Œuvres grammaticales d'Abou'lfaradj dit Bar*

Hebraeus, Tome I. Paris: Maisonneuve et Comp.
Mingana, A. 1905. *Clef de la langue araméenne ou Grammaire complète et pratique des deux dialectes syriaques, occidental et oriental.* Mossoul: Imprimerie des pères dominicains.
__. 1935. *Encyclopædia of Philosophical and Natural Sciences as Taught in Baghdad about A.D. 817 or Book of Treasures by Job of Edessa.* Cambridge: W. Heffer & Sons.
Moberg, A. 1907-13. *Buch der Strahlen. Die grössere Grammatik des Barhebräus. Übersetzung nach einem kritisch berichtigten Texte* etc. Leipzig: Otto Harrassowitz.
__. 1922. *Le Livre des splendeurs. La Grande grammaire de Grégoire Barhebraeus. Texte syriaque édité d'après les manuscrits* etc. Lund: C.W.K. Gleerup etc.
Morag, Sh. 1962. *The Vocalization Systems of Arabic, Hebrew and Aramaic.* 's-Gravenhage: Mouton.
Muraoka, T. 1976. "Segolate nouns in Biblical and other Aramaic dialects." *JAOS* 96:226-35.
__. 1977. "On the Syriac particle *ʾiṯ*." *BO* 34: 21-22.
__. 1985. "A study in Palestinian Jewish Aramaic." *Sefarad* 45: 3-21.
__. 1987 [repr. 1996]. *Classical Syriac for Hebraists.* Wiesbaden: Otto Harrassowitz.
Naveh, J. 1982. *Early History of the Alphabet.* Jerusalem: Magnes Press.
Nöldeke, Th. 1966. *Kurzgefasste syrische Grammatik.* [2nd ed. of 1898 with an appendix by A. Schall]. Darmstadt: Wissenshcaftliche Buchgesellschaft.
Parisot, J. 1894-1907. *Aphraatis Demonstrationes.* Patrologia Syriaca, Pars prima, 1-2. Paris: Firmin Didot et Socii.
Pierre, M.-J. 1994. *Les Odes de Salomon. Traduction, introduction et notes.* Turnhout: Breplos.
Rosenthal, F. 1939 [repr. 1964]. *Die aramaistische Forschung seit Th. Nöldekes Veröffentlichungen.* Leiden: E.J. Brill.
Segal, J.B. 1953. *The Diacritical Point and the Accents in Syriac.* Oxford University Press: Oxford.
__. 1970. *Edessa 'The Blessed City.'* Oxford: Oxford University Press.
Selb, W. 1990. *Sententiae syriacae. Eingeleitet, herausgegeben, deutsch übersetzt* etc. [Österreichische Akademie der Wissenschaften. Phil.-hist. Klasse. Sitzungsberichte, 567. Band.] Der Österreichische Akademie der Wissenschaften: Wien.
Strothmann, W. 1976. *Jakob von Sarug. Drei Gedichte über den Apostel*

Thomas in Indien. [Göttinger Orientforschung. 1. Reihe: Syriaca Bd. 12.] Wiesbaden: Otto Harrassowitz.
Tonneau, R.-M. 1955. *Sancti Ephraem Syri in Genesim et in Exodum commentarii*. [CSCO Syr. 71-72]. Leuven: Peeters.
Wright, W. 1869. *The Homilies of Aphraates the Persian Sage*. London:
__. 1871. *The Apocryphal Acts of the Apostles*. 2 vols. London/ Edinburgh: Williams and Norgate.

Abbreviations

abs.	absolute (state)
act.	active
adj.	adjective
adv.	adverb
Akk.	Akkadian
BA	Biblical Aramaic
BH	Biblical Hebrew
caus.	causative
conj.	conjunction
CPA	Christian Palestinian Aramaic
cst.	construct (state)
dir.	direct
emph.	emphatic
f.	feminine
fem.	feminine
Gk	Greek
Heb.	Hebrew
Impv.	Imperative
Impf.	Imperfect
Inf.	Infinitive
ind.	indirect
intr.	intransitive
Lat.	Latin
lit.	literally
m.	masculine
masc.	masculine
MH	Mishnaic Hebrew
n.	footnote
obj.	object
pass.	passive
pl.	plural
prep.	preposition
ptc.	participle
sg.	singular
st.	state
suf.	suffix
Syr.	Syriac
tr.	transitive

Some practical suggestions

1. The following may be considered as useful pedagogic strategy:

   a. Study the following matters thoroughly:
      1) the Estrangela form of the alphabet (§ 2),
      2) the pronunciation of the letters of the alphabet (§ 3),
      3) the "Nestorian" vowel signs to go with it (§ 4c),
      4) some graphic signs (§ 5)
      5) some phonological rules (§ 6 A, B, F, H, I, J, K, L)
      6) the basics of morphology: pronouns (§§ 9-12, 13, 15), declension of nouns and adjectives, and conjugation of verbs (§§ 17, 18, 21, 24, 27, 30, 31, 40-43, 46, 48-57, 61-68).

   b. Do the appropriate exercise as you go along, studying the above-mentioned points.

   c. Footnotes, especially lengthy ones, may be initially ignored.

2. Start working through the chrestomathy. The texts nos. 1 and 3 may be best left for a later stage of study. Begin with nos. 4 and 5, both from the Bible.

3. In studying the texts in the chrestomathy, make good use of the accompanying footnotes. Cross-references to the grammar ought to be studied carefully. Start studying simultaneously the paragraphs of the grammar section not mentioned above, including the Morpho-syntax and Syntax section.

PART ONE

WRITING AND PHONOLOGY

§ 1 **General.** Syriac is a language which belongs to the Aramaic branch of the Semitic language family. It is attested in written form by inscriptions which date from the first few centuries of the Christian era and originate from Edessa and its environs.([1]) The language of these inscriptions still shows some affinity with Aramaic of the earlier phases, and is thus distinct from the fully developed literary idiom of the subsequent centuries.([2]) Along with the Aramaic idiom of the Babylonian Talmud and the idiom used by another Christian com-munity, Mandaic, this developed form of Classical Syriac represents Eastern Aramaic in contradistinction to Western Aramaic represented by idioms such as Palestinian Jewish Aramaic of documents like the Palestinian (or: Jerusalem) Talmud and some midrashim, Samaritan Aramaic, and Christian Palestinian Aramaic.

The growth and development of Classical Syriac is closely bound up with the spread of Christianity in North Western Syria and subsequently the whole of Mesopotamia, and even further eastwards. It bloomed into a lively, literary means of expression during the third to seventh centuries. Over the centuries, a vast amount of literary works was produced in this language, covering the entire gamut of intellectual curiosity and creativity during the Late Antiquity and the immediately following period. Syriac-speaking scholars are also rightly credited with having served as conservers and transmitters of classical scholarship and as tutors and mentors for emerging, but still largely unlettered Islamic leadership. After the emergence of Islam in the region the language gradually began to decline, though its use as a literary idiom was kept alive well into the thirteenth century.

As a result of the famous Christological controversy during the fifth century the Syriac-speaking church split into two camps: the dyophysite

[1] A useful collection of such inscriptions is Drijvers 1972.

[2] On this, see Beyer 1966.

East Syrians (Nestorians) on the one hand, who came under the Persian sphere of influence, and the monophysite West Syrians (Jacobites) on the other, who remained within the Roman sphere of influence. These ecclesiastical developments came to leave some traces at language level as well in that each branch began to develop its own form of alphabet and there are some differences in phonology between the two dialects.

It now appears that Syriac, in a variety of vernacular forms, managed to survive down to the modern times. Towards the end of the 19th century attempts were made by Western missionaries to create modern literary idioms on the basis of Classical Syriac, and these vernaculars achieved a remarkable measure of success. Not only are a number of distinct Syriac idioms today in actual use as oral means of communication in pockets of the Middle East and communities of Modern Syriac speakers settled in various parts of the Western world including Australia, but there also exists a considerable amount of literary output.

§ 2 **Alphabet**. Like other indigenous Semitic scripts, the Syriac alphabet is essentially consonantal.([3]) Each of its twenty-two letters was originally designed to represent a single consonantal phoneme. However, already the earliest inscriptions show that some letters had begun to be used to mark vowels, notably the letter Waw for *o* or *u* and the letter Yod for *i* or *e*. Moreover, the first letter of the alphabet, Alaf, had ceased to be pronounced under certain conditions, and thereby appeared to be a vowel letter by default. These three letters then are bivalent, being either consonantal or vocalic or having no phonetic value, the latter applying to Alaf. All the remaining letters are consonantal.

The Syriac alphabet is known in three distinct forms: the earliest is called Estrangela, and the above-mentioned split within the Syriac church led to the emergence of two distinct scripts, Serto or Serta in use among the Jacobites, and the Nestorian in the east.

[3] The earliest known form of the Syriac script appears to be related to the cursive Palmyrene ductus developed in Northern Mesopotamia towards the closing centuries of the pre-Chrisitan era. See Naveh 1982: 143-53.

Table of the alphabet

Name	Estrangela: Unattached	Estrangela: Joined to the right	Estrangela: Joined to the left	Estrangela: Joined to the right and left	Serto: Unattached	Serto: Joined to the right	Serto: Joined to the left	Serto: Joined to the right and left	Nestorian: Unattached	Nestorian: Joined to the right	Nestorian: Joined to the left	Nestorian: Joined to the right and left	Hebrew
Alaf	ܐ	ܐ			ܐ	ܐ			ܐ	ܐ			א
Beth	ܒ	ܒ	ܒ	ܒ	ܒ	ܒ	ܒ	ܒ	ܒ	ܒ	ܒ	ܒ	ב
Gamal	ܓ	ܓ	ܓ	ܓ	ܓ	ܓ	ܓ	ܓ	ܓ	ܓ	ܓ	ܓ	ג
Dalath	ܕ	ܕ			ܕ	ܕ			ܕ	ܕ			ד
He	ܗ	ܗ			ܗ	ܗ			ܗ	ܗ			ה
Waw	ܘ	ܘ			ܘ	ܘ			ܘ	ܘ			ו
Zai(n)	ܙ	ܙ			ܙ	ܙ			ܙ	ܙ			ז
Ḥeth	ܚ	ܚ	ܚ	ܚ	ܚ	ܚ	ܚ	ܚ	ܚ	ܚ	ܚ	ܚ	ח
Ṭeth	ܛ	ܛ	ܛ	ܛ	ܛ	ܛ	ܛ	ܛ	ܛ	ܛ	ܛ	ܛ	ט
Yodh	ܝ	ܝ	ܝ	ܝ	ܝ	ܝ	ܝ	ܝ	ܝ	ܝ	ܝ	ܝ	י
Kaf	ܟ	ܟ	ܟ	ܟ	ܟ	ܟ	ܟ	ܟ	ܟ	ܟ	ܟ	ܟ	ך, כ
Lamadh	ܠ	ܠ	ܠ	ܠ	ܠ	ܠ	ܠ	ܠ	ܠ	ܠ	ܠ	ܠ	ל
Mim	ܡ	ܡ	ܡ	ܡ	ܡ	ܡ	ܡ	ܡ	ܡ	ܡ	ܡ	ܡ	ם, מ
Nun	ܢ	ܢ	ܢ	ܢ	ܢ	ܢ	ܢ	ܢ	ܢ	ܢ	ܢ	ܢ	ן, נ
Semkath	ܣ	ܣ	ܣ	ܣ	ܣ	ܣ	ܣ	ܣ	ܣ	ܣ	ܣ	ܣ	ס
ʿE	ܥ	ܥ	ܥ	ܥ	ܥ	ܥ	ܥ	ܥ	ܥ	ܥ	ܥ	ܥ	ע
Pe	ܦ	ܦ	ܦ	ܦ	ܦ	ܦ	ܦ	ܦ	ܦ	ܦ	ܦ	ܦ	ף, פ
Ṣadhe	ܨ	ܨ			ܨ	ܨ			ܨ	ܨ			ץ, צ
Qof	ܩ	ܩ	ܩ	ܩ	ܩ	ܩ	ܩ	ܩ	ܩ	ܩ	ܩ	ܩ	ק
Resh	ܪ	ܪ			ܪ	ܪ			ܪ	ܪ			ר
Shin	ܫ	ܫ	ܫ	ܫ	ܫ	ܫ	ܫ	ܫ	ܫ	ܫ	ܫ	ܫ	ש
Taw	ܬ	ܬ			ܬ	ܬ			ܬ	ܬ			ת

Note the following points applicable to all the three scripts:

a) Certain pairs of letters need to be carefully kept apart from each other:([4])

[4] For the purpose of illustration, we use the Estrangela script.

ܒ (Beth)([5]) : ܟ (Kaf)
ܕ (Dalath) : ܪ (Resh)
ܚ (Heth) : ܝܝ (double Yodh)
ܢܝ (Nun + Yodh)
ܢܢ (double Nun)
ܠ (Lamadh) : ܥ (ʿE)
ܢ (Nun) : ܝ (Yodh)

b) Syriac is written from right to left, the general direction of writing strokes is from top to bottom and from right to left.

c) Certain letters are never joined to the left: Alaf, Dalath, He, Waw, Zai(n), Ṣade, Resh, and Taw.

d) When a letter is joined to the left or to the right, or both, very minor adjustments need to be made.

e) In the Serto script the sequence of Lamadh followed by Alaf is written ܠܐ, whilst Alaf followed by Lamadh is written ܐܠ. Furthermore, where a word ends with Lamadh and the following word begins with Alaf, the combination may be spelled ܠ ܐ. In the Nestorian script a word-final sequence of Taw followed by Alaf may be written ܬܐ instead of ܬܐ.

§ 3 Pronunciation. The following description can be only approximative, and it is more than likely that in the course of the history of the language there occurred some changes. Moreover, there are, as stated above, some differences between the Western and Eastern dialects. It is widely believed that Eastern Syriac has preserved at many points a more archaic form of Classical Syriac. Hence we shall mostly follow here the Eastern tradition.

Consonants. The six plosives, namely ܒ, ܓ, ܕ, ܟ, ܦ, ܬ, are pronounced, as in the Tiberian traidition of Hebrew, in two different ways: /b g d k p t/ and, with spirantisation, /v g̱ ḏ ḵ f ṯ/: /g̱, ḏ, ṯ/ being the equivalent of the Arabic *Ghain*, /ḏ/ of *th* of the English *that*, /ḵ/ of *ch* of Scottish *loch* or German *Bach,* and /ṯ/ of *th* of *thing* respectively.([6])

Alaf (ܐ) is a glottal stop, heard in many varieties of English as in

[5] When a Syriac technical term is mentioned as such, we shall use, in this grammar, a simplified spelling, and not its phonetically transliterated form. For instance, "Beth," and not "Beeṯ."

better /bɛ́ʔə/ for the standard /bɛ́tə/.

Ḥeth (ܚ) is an unvoiced fricative pharyngeal.

Ṭeth (ܛ), Ṣadhe (ܨ), and Qof (ܩ) are said to be an "emphatic" equivalent of Taw (ܬ), Semkath (ܣ), and Kaf (ܟ) respectively. However, in practice, little distinction is made between the two series, the emphatic series often being "deemphasised." Many pronounce Ṣadhe as if it were /ts/ as in Engl. *cats*.

ʿE (ܥ) is a voiced fricative pharyngeal, forming a pair with Ḥeth.

§ 4 Vowels and their notation. Syriac knows three sorts of vowel notation. They differ from each other in conception.

a) Diacritical dot. The first is a simple dot placed above or below a word where two or three sequences of identical consonants differ phonetically, and consequently in meaning. Thus ܡ̇ܢ /maan/ 'What?' or /man/ 'Who?' vs. ܡ̣ܢ /men/ 'from'; ܩ̇ܛܠ /qaaṭel/ 'killing' (participle), or /qaṭṭel/ 'he murdered' vs. ܩ̣ܛܠ /qṭal/ 'he killed'; ܡ̇ܠܟܐ /malkaa/ 'king' vs. ܡ̣ܠܟܐ /melkaa/ 'counsel'; ܗ̇ܘ /haw/ 'that' (demonstrative pronoun) vs. ܗ̣ܘ /hu/ 'he'; ܗ̇ܢܘܢ /haannon/ 'those' vs. ܗ̣ܢܘܢ /hennon/ 'they.' Sometimes this diacritical dot came to indicate a grammatical distinction. Thus serving initially to distinguish ܒ̇ܗ /baah/ 'in her' from ܒܗ /beeh/ 'in him,' it subsequently came to be used to mark a third person feminine suffix irrespective of its phonetic shape in contrast to its masculine counterpart: ܩܛܠܬܗ̇ /qṭaltaah/ 'you killed her' as against ܩܛܠܬܗ /qṭalteeh/ 'I killed him,' but also ܩܕܡܝܗ̇ /qdaameeh/ 'before her' (but ܩܕܡܘܗ̄ܝ /qdaamaw/ 'before him.'

This is manifestly a rather crude system of vowel notation, the dot being no exact notation of particular vowel quality, but rather meaningful only in cases of homographs and providing a convenient and quick guidance for those who already know the language reasonably well.

At a later stage the system was further refined by allowing the use of a second or even third dot to distinguish, for instance, between ܥܒ̇ܕܬ /ʿevdet/ 'I made' and ܥܒܕܬ̇ or ES ܥܒܕܬ݂ /ʿevdat/ 'she made.' ([7])

b) Vowel letters. From the above-mentioned use of Alaf as vowel letter by default there developed its use as a genuine vowel letter for *a*:

[6] The use of double slashes, / /, is not meant to be phonemic notation, but a mere expedience.

e.g. ܕܘܓܡܐܛܐ δόγματα. This has spread also to indigenous Syriac words: e.g. ܛܐܠܐ for ܛܠܐ /ṭallaa/ 'dew.'

Yodh and Waw are mostly used to indicate a historically long *i* and *u* respectively.([8]) Thus ܒܝܫ /biš/ 'bad' and ܢܩܘܡܘܢ /nqumun/ 'they shall get up,' but occasionally also for a historically short *i* or *u*, e.g. ܓܝܫܪܐ /gišraa/ 'bridge'; ܓܘܫܡܐ /gušmaa/ 'body'; ܐܝܙܓܕܐ /ʾizgaddaa/ 'emissary.'

Yodh and Waw are also used to indicate /ee/ and /o/ resulting from the contraction of an original diphthong /ay/ and /aw/ respectively: ܒܹܝܬ /beeṯ/ 'the house of' and ܝܘܿܡ /yom/ 'the day of.' These are therefore historical or etymological spellings.

Furthermore, almost every *u* or *o* is indicated by means of a Waw. Common exceptions are ܟܠ /kol, kul/ 'every' and ܡܛܠ /meṭṭul, meṭṭol/ 'on account of, ' which are often defectively spelled in early periods, and regularly so in late manuscripts.([9])

c) Vowel signs. Two distinct sets of vowel signs are in use: the earlier developed Nestorian system and the later Jacobite system. The former consists of single or double dots, whereas the latter makes use of letters of the Greek alphabet. The two systems are set out below as attached to the consonant ܣ, and given the pronunciation of the syllable along with the indigenous names of the vowel signs. Whereas the dots of the Nestorian system have fixed positions, the Greek letters of the Jacobite system may be positioned indiscriminately either above or below the consonant letter concerned, or sometimes obliquely. The vowel symbols of the latter system are turned through 180^0 when they are placed below: thus ܣܱ ܣܷ ܣܻܝ ܣܾܘ ܣܴ.

[7] For a description of historical development of vowel notation in Syriac, see Segal 1953.

[8] There is no indication that Classical Syriac knew a quantitative distinction between /ū/ and /u/ on one hand, and between /ī/ and /i/ on the other. Hence, contrary to the common practice, which is diachronically informed, we shall not transliterate ܢܣܝܡܘܢ as /nsīmūn/, but as /nsimun/.

[9] Defective spellings, namely without the use of vowel letters, esp. for historically short vowels, are fairly frequently attested in early inscriptions: see Texts nos. 1 and 3 in the chrestomathy.

Nestorian (ES = Eastern Syriac)			Jacobite (WS = Western Syriac)		
/saa/	ܣܵ	(zeqapa)	/so/	ܣܳ	(zeqofo)
/sa/	ܣܲ	(petaḥa)	/sa/	ܣܰ	(petoḥo)([10])
/si/	ܣܝܼ	(ḥevaṣa)	/si/	ܣܺܝ	(ḥevoṣo)
/su/	ܣܘܼ	(ʿeṣaṣa ʿalliṣa)	/su/	ܣܽܘ	(ʿeṣoṣo)
/see/	ܣܹ	(revaṣa karya)			
/se/	ܣܸ	(revaṣa arri*k*a)	/se/	ܣܶܝ / ܣܶ	(revoṣo)
/so/	ܣܘܿ	(ʿeṣaṣa rewiḥa)			

The two notation systems clearly represent two distinct phonological systems of vowels resulting from dialectal developments.

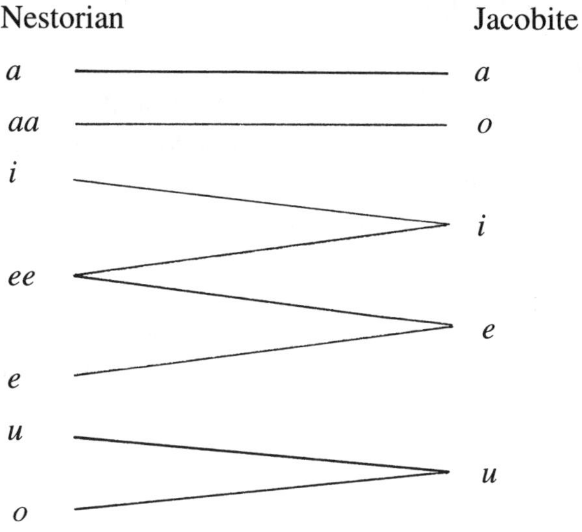

The above figure represents an inventory of the vowel phonemes in the two dialects, and a line indicates etymological, diachronic correspondences. The use of identical vowel letter does not necessarily imply identical phonetic articulation. Thus the Jacobite *o* was most likely pronounced differently from the Nestorian *o*([11]), for otherwise the correspondences in question would be difficult to understand.([12])

[10] For the notation "zeqapa," and not "zeqaafaa," and the like, see n. 4 above.

[11] A vowel quality considered to be comparable to the American English pronunciation of *so*ft.

[12] On the complicated two-way correspondence between the Nestorian *ee* and Jacobite *i/e*, see Blau 1969.

Many scholars believe that the ES represents at many points an earlier phase of Classical Syriac vowel system, although details are still debated—for instance, whether the distinction between /saa/ and /sa/ was purely one of length—and actual manuscripts attest to a considerable degree of fluctuation.([13]) Especially the WS /i/ and /u/ corresponding to the ES /ee/ and /o/ respectively are considered to be secondary.([14])

There are manuscripts which show a mixture of the two systems. Furthermore, some manuscripts and printed editions of the Bible make simultaneous use of the diacritical point and vowel signs, where the use of the former is redundant.

§ 5 Other graphic signs.

a) A dot is placed above ܒ ܓ ܕ ܟ ܦ ܬ to indicate their "hard" (plosive) pronunciation, /b g d k p t/—called ܩܘܫܝܐ /quššaayaa/ 'hardening'—and below those same letters to indicate their "soft" (fricative) pronunciation—called ܪܘܟܟܐ /rukkaakaa/ 'softening.' For instance,

[13] See Birkeland 1947: 19-39 and Morag 1962: 45-59.

The repetition of a vowel letter as in /saa/ instead of the use of a macron (/sā/) is merely a technical expedience, and it does not suggest that we consider such a vowel as a sequence of two identical vowels.

[14] There is some theoretical difficulty also about the interpretation of the vowel /o/. Unlike the vowels *a* and *e* there is only one vowel sign. Whereas a long *a* or *e* is not liable to deletion, many *o*'s are liable to such a deletion— e.g. ܩܕܘܫ /qdoš/ 'sanctity' vs. its emphatic state form ܩܘܕܫܐ /qudšaa/; ܢܩܒܘܪ /neqbor/ 'he shall bury' vs. ܢܩܒܪܘܢ /neqbrun/ 'they shall bury'—but some are undeletable as in *ܩܛܘܠ /qaaṭol/ 'murderer' vs. its emph. form ܩܛܘܠܐ /qaaṭolaa/ and noun patterns with a suffix /-on/ such as ܓܠܝܘܢܐ /gelyonaa/ 'revelation' and ܐܠܗܘܢܐ /ʔalaahonaa/ small god.' Should one interpret the latter as *morphophonemically* long? Moreover, there are cases in which one cannot find a short or long counterpart in neat paradigmatic opposition: e.g. pronouns such as ܐܢܬܘܢ 'you' (m.pl.), ܗܢܘܢ, ܐܢܘܢ 'they' (m.), ܗܢܘܢ 'those' (m.) or the *o* contracted from /aw/ as in ܝܘܡ 'day,' which does not occur in any other form of the noun (otherwise always /yawm-/). Whereas the vowel *i* remains constant, *u* is sometimes deleted: e.g. ܩܘܕܫܐ /qudšaa/ vs. its st. abs. form ܩܕܘܫ /qdoš/ 'sanctity.' All in all, it appears that deletability is a *consequence* of the historical brevity of vowels, but cannot be made a criterion for interpreting them to be short. The fact that native speakers of the language did not find it necessary to devise separate symbols for long and short varieties of *i*, *u*, and *o* ought to be made to carry due weight.

ܡܠܟ݂ܐ /malkaa/ 'king'
ܕܗܒ݂ܐ /dahvaa/ 'gold'([15])

In ES the letter Pe with a rukkaka is also pronounced hard, /p/.([16]) Moreover, East Syrians pronounce some Pe's following a vowel like Waw, which fact is indicated by means of a semi-circle under such a Pe: e.g. ܐܲܦ̮ܫܵܬ݂ܵܐ /ʔawšaataa/ 'raisins,' ܢܲܦ̮ܫܵܐ /nawšaa/ 'soul,' ܢܸܦ̮ܬܲܚ /newtaḥ/ 'he (or: we) shall open.'([17])

b) Another diacritical device of ancient origin, called *seyame*, is a double dot indicating the plural form of a noun which was often impossible graphically to distinguish from its singular form: e.g. ܡܠ̈ܟ݂ܐ /malkee/ 'kings' vs. ܡܠܟ݂ܐ /malkaa/ 'king'; ܡܠ̈ܟ݂ܬ݂ܐ /malkaataa/ 'queens' vs. ܡܠܟ݁ܬ݂ܐ /malktaa/ 'queen.' The use of the seyame sign was subsequently extended to cases where no ambiguity existed: e.g., ܐܡ̈ܝܢ /ʔammin/ 'cubits,' ܥܢ̈ܐ /ʕaanaa/ 'small cattle' (collective noun), ܛܵܒ̈ܢ /ṭaavaan/ 'are good' (fem. adj. pl. used predicatively, but not masc. ܛܵܒ݂ܝܢ /ṭaavin/), ܟ݁ܬ݂ܲܒ̈ /ktav/ 'they (fem.) wrote,' ܢܸܟ݂ܬ݁ܒ̈ܵܢ /nektvaan/ 'they (fem. pl.) shall write,' ܬܪ̈ܝܢ /treen/ ܬܪ̈ܬܝܢ /tarteen/ 'two.'

c) One sometimes finds a horizontal stroke—called *linea occultans* 'hiding line' or *marheṭana* 'hastener'—over([18]) a non-word-final consonant which is not immediately followed by a vowel as in ܦ̄ܠܓ݂ /plaḡ/ 'they were half' vs. ܦܠܓ݂ /palleḡ/ 'they divided; ܠܚܡ̄ܝ /laḥm/ 'my bread.' More often the sign indicates that the consonant so marked is not pronounced (syncope), e.g. ܡܕ݂ܝ̄ܢܬܐ /mdittaa/ 'city,' ܗ̄ܘܐ /waa/ 'was,' ܐ̄ܢܐ /naa/ 'I,' ܐܢ̄ܬܘܢ /ʔatton/ 'you (masc. pl.)'; ܒܪ̄ܬ݂ /baṯ/ 'daughter of' as against ܒܪܬ݂ܐ /bartaa/ 'daughter.'

The same horizontal stroke, when placed below a consonant, may indicate that it is to be pronounced clearly with some sort of helping vowel. Called *mehaggeyana* 'articulator' it occurs where more than

[15] In Greek loanwords with π, the dot is placed inside the letter (ܦ݂)—or a double dot above (ܦ̈)—to indicate its pronunciation without aspiration as in Dutch *pen* as against Engl. *pen*.

[16] A phenomenon attested as early as the 10th century: Nöldeke 1966:313.

[17] For a fuller list, see Mingana 1905:3.

[18] In late manuscripts or some printed editions the sign may aso be found *below* the letter in question.

two consonants are clustered together as in ܚܶܟ݂ܶܡܬ݂ܳܐ /ḥeke̲mt̲aa/ for /ḥek̲mt̲aa/ 'wisdom.'

d) Syrian scholars, like their Tiberian counterparts for Hebrew, developed a set of cantillation symbols, accents, applied to biblical texts, in order to ensure their solemn, liturgical recitation.([19])

e) The system of punctuation marks is rather poorly developed and their use is not governed by rigid rules. Of the more common marks are a dot similar to the English full period, a combination of four dots (⁘), and a sign similar to our colon.

§ 6 Some remarks on phonology

A) **Vowel deletion rule**. The vowels /a/, /e/, and /o/ which come to stand in an unaccented open syllable, namely a syllable ending in a vowel, are regularly deleted. This process can be clearly observed where the addition of an inflectional ending or a suffix pronoun leads to the originally closed final syllable becoming open and the accent shifting forward: e.g., ܒܰܪ /bar/ 'son' (or: 'the son of') → ܒܪܳܐ /braa/ 'the son' (< */baraa/); ܐܳܟ݂ܶܠ /ʾaak̲el/ 'eating' (masc. sing.) → ܐܳܟ݂ܠܺܝܢ /ʾaak̲lin/ (masc. pl.) (< * /ʾaak̲elin/); ܐܶܟ݂ܘܽܠ /ʾeek̲ol/ 'I shall eat' → ܬܶܐܟ݂ܠܺܝܢ /teek̲lin/ 'you (fem. sing.) shall eat' (< */teek̲olin/).

This rule can account for the morphological process whereby both the basic form ܨܠܶܡ /ṣlem/ 'image' and its variation with the definite article, ܨܰܠܡܳܐ /ṣalmaa/, can be derived from the underlying form /*ṣalem/: /*ṣalem/ → /ṣlem/ and /*ṣalemaa/ → /ṣalmaa/.([20]) As can be seen from the last example, where two short open syllables precede stress (Cv̆Cv̆Cv́)([21]), it is the first short open-syllabic vowel that is deleted: thus /*dahavaa/ > /dahvaa/ ܕܰܗܒܳܐ 'gold' as against /*kaat̲evaa/ > /kaat̲baa/ ܟܳܬ݂ܒܳܐ 'writing' (f.sg.). On the other hand, the structure Cv̆CvC changes to CCvC: /*kat̲av/ > /kt̲av/ 'he wrote'; /*qanayyaa/ > /qnayyaa/ ܩܢܰܝܳܐ 'reeds.'

B) /e/ → /a/ before /r/ or a guttural. Examples are: ܫܳܡܰܥ /šaamaʿ/

[19] For details, see Segal 1953: 58-150.

[20] Forms such as ܐܶܟ݂ܰܠ /ʾek̲al/ 'he ate,' ܐܱܟ݂ܘܽܠ /ʾak̲ol/ 'Eat!,' and ܝܺܕܰܥ /yid̲aʿ/ 'he knew' show that the initial vowel developed after this rule had ceased to operate.

[21] C= consonant; V = vowel; v̆ = short vowel.

'hearing' for /*šaameʿ/; ܫܒܚ /šabbaḥ/ 'he praised' for /*šabbeḥ/; ܕܒܪ /daavar/ 'leading' for /*daaver/.

C) A word-initial glottal stop (Alaf) is always followed by a vowel as in ܐܣܪ /ʾesar/ 'he bound,' ܐܠܗܐ /ʾalaahaa/ 'god.' However, the other gutturals are not subject to such a rule: thus ܚܡܪ /ḥmaar/ 'donkey'; ܥܪܩ /ʿraq/ 'he ran away.'

D) A word-initial /y/ which by analogy would have no vowel is regularly provided with a congenial /i/ vowel, often spelled ܐܝ: e.g. ܝܒܫ /iveš/ 'was dry' (cp. ܠܒܫ /lveš/ 'he was clothed'; ܐܝܕܐ /i<u>d</u>aa/ 'hand.'

E) There is no genuine diphthong, but a combination of a vowel followed by /w/ or /y/, such as /aw/ in ܝܘܡܐ /yawmaa/ 'day' and /ay/ in ܒܝܬܐ /baytaa/ 'house.'([22])

F) A syllable may begin with a single or double consonant, and end with a vowel (*open syllable*) or consonant or double consonant (*closed syllable*). Thus ܕܒܪ /daavar/ = /daa-var/; ܕܒܪ /dvar/ (monosyllabic); ܩܒܠ /qabbel/ = /qab-bel/. A form such as ܬܐܟܠܝܢ /tee<u>k</u>lin/ is best analysed as /tee<u>k</u>-lin/, though it is a variant on /tee<u>k</u>ol/ = /tee-<u>k</u>ol/, but rather in view of a form such as ܢܐܪܬܘܢ /neertun/ 'they shall inherit,' a variation of ܢܐܪܬ /neera<u>t</u>/. A doubly closed syllable occurs only at the end of a word form: e.g. ܬܚܬ /taḥt/ 'below'; ܫܒܩܬ /švaqt/ 'you forsook'; ܠܚܡܝ /laḥm/ 'my bread.' A sequence of two identical consonants at the end of a syllable is simplified: e.g. /*ʾant/ > /*ʾatt/ (with the assimilation of the /n/) > /ʾat/ ܐܢܬ 'you'; ܩܒܠ /qabbel/ 'he received' > ܩܒܠܬ /qabla<u>t</u>/ 'she received.'

G) WS has abandoned the doubling of consonants, which is however preserved in ES: thus ܩܒܠ 'he received' = WS /qabel/, ES /qabbel/. Where a short vowel is followed by another vowel, the consonant in between may be considered to be doubled: e.g., ܢܦܩ /nappeq/ 'he (or: we) shall bring out' vs. ܢܦܩ /naafeq/ 'coming out'; ܪܒܬ /rebba<u>t</u>/ 'she was great' vs. ܪܒܬ /raava<u>t</u>/ 'she clamoured'; ܡܠܬ /mella<u>t</u>/ 'the word of.'

Even in ES the doubling seems to have been given up when the doubled consonant with no vowel is followed by another consonant:

[22] The diphthong /aw/ is represented in ES always as /aaw/, so ܝܘܡܐ.

e.g. ܡܠܬܐ /mel<u>t</u>aa/ 'word' rather than /mell<u>t</u>aa/ as against ܡܠܬ /mella<u>t</u>/ 'the word of.'

A doubled consonant is not normally spelled twice. Common exceptions are ܣܡܡ̈ܐ /sammee/ 'drugs'; ܥܡܡ̈ܐ /ʿammee/ 'peoples'; ܓܠܠ̈ܐ /gallee/ 'waves.'([23])

H) The spirantised pronunciation of the six plosives ܬ ܦ ܟ ܕ ܓ ܒ (§ 5: 1) occurs when these consonants are immediately preceded by a vowel or they follow a vowelless consonant at the beginning of a syllable. Thus ܟܬܒ /kaa<u>t</u>ev/ 'writing'; ܟܬܒ /k<u>t</u>av/ 'he wrote,' but ܡܟܬܒܢܐ /ma<u>k</u>tvaanaa/ 'author' (the syllabification of the word is: /ma<u>k</u>-tvaa-naa/).

This rule may also operate across the word boundary, thus ܝܬܝܪ ܡܢ ܬܠܬܡܐܐ ܕܝܢܪ̈ܝܢ /yattir men tlaa<u>t</u>maa <u>d</u>eenaarin/ 'more than three hundred denarii.'

The /w/ and /y/ of diphthongs are considered to be consonantal in this regard: thus ܡܘܬܐ /mawtaa/ 'death' and ܒܝܬܐ /baytaa/ 'house'; ܗܝܕܝܢ /haaydeen/ 'then.' ܐܝܟ 'like, as' is pronounced /ʾa<u>k</u>/.

Classical Syriac, however, seems to represent a stage further advanced than suggested by the above-described conditioning of spirantisation, and there are signs of incipient phonematisation of spirantised, originally allophonic consonants. This is seen in cases of minimal pair contrast as in ܓܪܒܐ /garbaa/ 'leper' vs. ܓܪܒܐ /garvaa/ 'leprosy'; ܩܫܬܐ /qeštaa/ 'bow' vs. ܩܫܬܐ /qeš<u>t</u>aa/ 'stubble'; ܚܕܝܬ /ḥ<u>d</u>it/ 'you (masc. sg.) rejoiced' vs. ܚܕܝܬ /ḥ<u>d</u>i<u>t</u>/ 'I rejoiced'; ܣܟܝܬ /sakkit/ 'you (masc. sg.) expected' vs. ܣܟܝܬ /sakki<u>t</u>/ 'I expected.'

I) Four frequent one-letter particles, ܒ 'in,' ܕ 'that, which, of,' ܘ 'and,' and ܠ 'to, for,' are proclitics, forming a close phonetic unit with the immediately following word, and are spelled as part of the latter: e.g., ܒܒܝܬܐ /bvaytaa/ 'in the house'; ܘܒܝܬܐ /wvaytaa/ 'and the house.' It can be seen that the above-given rule of spirantisation applies here.

Where the first consonant of the word following one of these particles lacks a vowel of its own, a helping vowel /a/ is added to the proclitic particle to facilitate the pronunciation: e.g., ܒܫܡܝܐ /bašmayyaa/ 'in the sky.'([24]) This rule applies also where two or more

[23] These are considered to be historical spellings in which there was earlier a vowel between the two identical consonants.

proclitic particles follow one after another as in ܠܕܒܫܡܝܐ /la<u>d</u>vašmayyaa/ 'to that which is in the sky.'

J) A word-initial /ʔ/, /h/ or /ḥ/ is often deleted when such a word, usually grammatical function word, forms a close phonetic unit with the immediately preceding word. Such are (i) the /ʔ/ of the independent personal pronouns in the first and second persons (ܐܢܐ /ʔenaa/ 'I,' ܐܢܬ /ʔat/ 'you [m.sg.],' ܐܢܬܝ /ʔat/ 'you [f.sg.],' ܐܢܬܘܢ /ʔatton/ 'you [m.pl.],' ܐܢܬܝܢ /ʔatteen/), (ii) the /h/ of the third person singular pronoun ܗܘ /hu/ 'he, it' and ܗܝ /hi/ 'she, it', and the Perfect tense of the verb ܗܘܐ /hwaa/ 'he was, there was,' and (iii) the /ḥ/ of the first person plural independent pronoun ܚܢܢ /ḥnan/ 'we.'

The consonants thus elided may be left out in writing as well: e.g. ܩܒܠܢܐ /qaavelnaa/ 'I complain' for ܩܒܠ ܐܢܐ.

In the last example, not only the Alaf but also the accompanying vowel have also been elided. In the case of ܗܘ or ܗܝ, the vowels are preserved when the preceding word ends with a consonant, but they become /w/ and /y/ respectively when they are preceded by a vowel: e.g. ܐܢܬ ܗܘ ܡܠܟܐ /ʔattu malkaa/ 'you are the king'; ܐܢܬܝ ܗܝ ܡܠܟܬܐ /ʔatti malk<u>t</u>aa/ 'you are the queen'; ܡܠܟܐ ܗܘ ܕܘܝܕ /malkaw daawi<u>d</u>/ 'David is king.'

A similar aphaeresis of Alaf is observable also in ܐܢܫ /naaš/ 'man, people'; ܐܚܪܢܝܢ /ḥreen/ 'other'; ܐܚܪܝܐ /ḥraayaa/ 'last.'([25])

K) Elision of /ʔ/ in sequence <CʔV>. If an Alaf preceded by a vowelless consonant is elided, its vowel is then taken over by the preceding consonant: e.g., *ܡܐܣܝܐ /mʔassee/ 'healing' > ܡܐܣܝܐ /massee/. This also applies to cases of proclisis (# **I** above): ܒ + ܐܪܥܐ /ʔarʿaa/ 'land' > ܒܐܪܥܐ /barʿaa/ 'in the land.'([26])

[24] This explanation is neater than to postulate with Brockelmann (1962: § 74) /*waqaṭal/ > ܘܩܛܠ /waqṭal/ 'and he killed': unless one further postulated an analogy of the particles ܘ and ܠ, the preposition ܒ would remain problematic, since it is agreed to go back to /*bi/, not /*ba/.

[25] In the following cases the phonetic process is complete, leaving no graphic trace of the original Alaf: ܚܕ /ḥa<u>d</u>/ 'one,' ܚܪܬܐ /ḥar<u>t</u>aa/ 'end,' ܚܬܐ /ḥaa<u>t</u>aa/ 'sister,' ܕܝܢ /deen/ 'then' (cf. Biblical Aramaic: אֱדַיִן). Likewise the imperative of the verbs ܐܬܐ /ʔe<u>t</u>aa/ 'to come' (e.g. ܬܐ /taa/) and ܐܙܠ /ʔezal/ (e.g. ܙܠ /zel/).

L) Elision of /ʾ/ in sequence <Vʾ C>. Examples are: ܢܐܟܘܠ /neek̲ol/ 'he (or: we) shall eat' (< /neʾkol/); ܬܐܡܪ /teemar/ 'you (m.sg.) (or: she) shall say' (< /*teʾmar/).([27])

M) Assimilation of consonants. In the case of two verbs of physical movement, the /l/ as their component is assimilated when the preceding sibilant closes a syllable, i.e. has no vowel. Thus with the verb ܐܙܠ /ʾezal/ 'to go' : e.g. *ܐܙܠܬ /ʾezlat̲/ 'she went' > ܐܙܠܬ /ʾezzat̲/; *ܐܙܠܝܢ /ʾaazlin/ 'going' > ܐܙܠܝܢ /ʾaazzin/. Likewise ܣܠܩ /sleq/ 'to ascend,' though, unlike ܐܙܠ, the Lamadh is never written([28]): e.g. *ܠܡܣܠܩ /lmeslaq/ 'to ascend' > ܠܡܣܩ /lmessaq/; *ܐܣܠܩܬ /ʾasleqt/ 'you brought up' > ܐܣܩܬ /ʾasseqt/.

The /ʾ/ as the first consonant of a verb root is assimilated sometimes to the Taw of the preceding reflexive pattern prefix: so always in the reflexive pattern Ettafal corresponding to the causative pattern, Afel (see below, § 49) — ܐܬܬܩܪܒ /ʾettaqrav/ < *ܐܬܐܩܪܒ /ʾet̲ʾaqrav/ 'was fought'; Ethpeel ܐܬܬܚܕ /ʾettḥed̲/ 'was shut' < *ܐܬܐܚܕ /ʾet̲ʾeḥed̲/; Ethpaal ܐܬܬܢܚ /ʾettannaḥ/ 'he groaned' < *ܐܬܐܢܚ /ʾet̲ʾannaḥ/.

The /n/ as the first consonant of a verb is regularly assimilated to the following consonant with the exception of /h/ when such an /n/ closes a syllable: e.g. ܢܦܘܩ /neppoq/ 'he will go out' < *ܢܢܦܘܩ (as against, for instance, ܢܦܩ /nfaq/ 'he went out' or ܢܦܩ /naafeq/ 'going out'); ܐܦܩ /ʾappeq/ 'he brought out' < *ܐܢܦܩ /ʾanpeq/; ܐܬܬܦܩ /ʾettappaq/ 'he was brought out' < *ܐܬܬܢܦܩ /ʾettanpaq/. Cf. ܢܢܗܪ /nenhar/ 'it will be bright' (from ܢܗܪ /nhar/).([29]) On ܢܬܠ /nettel/ 'he shall give' from the no longer used *ܢܬܢ /nt̲an/, see below § 67.

[26] Occasionally reflected in spellings such as ܡܠܦ /mallef/ for *ܡܐܠܦ /mʾallef/; ܒܝܫ /biš/ 'evil' (cf. BA בְּאִישׁ), ܒܬܪ /baat̲ar/ 'after' (prep.), < ܒ 'in' + ܐܬܪ /ʾat̲ar/ 'place,' also shows a lengthening of the vowel /a/: /baʾ/ > /baa/ (cf. BH לֵאלֹהִים < * לֶאֱלֹהִים). Some printed editions, apparently on account of the ES tradition, do not adhere to this rule, though the ES tradition itself is not consistent in this regard.

[27] Cf. BA יֵאמַר; BH יֹאכַל, לֵאלֹהִים. This is also a historical explanation for words such as ܒܐܪܐ /beeraa/ 'fountain' (cf. Heb. בְּאֵר); ܕܐܒܐ /deevaa/ 'wolf' (cf. Heb. זְאֵב).

[28] This is because the phenomenon predates the development in Syriac.

[29] Nöldeke 1966: § 173A mentions an exception, ܐܢܚܦ /ʾanḥef/ 'to go bare,' which actually occurs at Dt 8.4.

A similar assimilation occurs with nouns and pronouns as well: e.g. ܡܕ݂ܝܢ݈ܬܐ /m<u>d</u>ittaa/ 'city' as against ܡܕ݂ܝܢܬ݂ /m<u>d</u>ina<u>t</u>/ 'the city of'; ܙܒ݂ܢ݈ܬܐ /zbattaa/ 'time (of frequency)' vs. ܙܒ݂ܢܝܢ /zavnin/ 'times' (pl.); ܣܦ݂ܝܢ݈ܬܐ /sfittaa/ 'ship' vs. ܣܦ݂ܝܢܬ݂ܐ /sfinaa<u>t</u>aa/ 'ships'; ܫܢ݈ܬܐ /šattaa/ 'year' vs. ܫܢܬ݂ /šna<u>t</u>/ 'the year of.' Such a Nun may be written only in part of the inflection: e.g. ܠܒ݂ܢ݈ܬܐ /lvettaa/ 'brick' vs. its pl. ܠܒ݂ܢ̈ܐ /levnee/. See also ܐܢ݈ܬܬ݂ܐ /ʔattaa/ 'woman'; ܐܢ݈ܬ /ʔat/ 'you (m.sg.); ܐܢ݈ܬܘܢ /ʔatton/ 'you (m.pl.).'

The dental /t/ of the prefix of the reflexive pattern assimilates to a following /t/ or /ṭ/: ܐܬ݂ܛܫܝ /ʔeṭṭašši/ < /*ʔe<u>t</u>ṭašši/; ܐܬ݂ܬܒܪ (also spelled ܐܬ݂ܬ݂ܒܪ, ܐܬܬ݂ܒܪ) /ʔettabbar/ 'was smashed.' A /d/ also, if followed by a vowel, follows the same rule: ܢܬ݂ܕܟ݂ܪܟ݂ /nedda<u>k</u>raa<u>k</u>/ 'he shall remember you.' Such a /d/ not followed by a vowel assimilates to the preceding /t/: ܐܬ݂ܕܟ݂ܪ /ʔe<u>t</u>d<u>k</u>ar/ > /ʔett<u>k</u>ar/ > /ʔet<u>k</u>ar/ 'he remembered.' A similar assimilation may be assumed also when a proclitic particle (see above # **I**) is followed by a vowelless /d/ or /t/, which is in its turn also followed by another dental: ܘܕܕܡܐ /waddaamee/ 'and that which is similar' < /*wa<u>dd</u>aamee/; ܘܬ݂ܕܘܨ /wattuṣ/ 'and you shall rejoice' < /*wa<u>td</u>uṣ/; ܘܬ݂ܛܫܐ /wattaššee/ 'and you shall conceal' < /*wa<u>t</u>taššee/.([30])

A dental /ṭ/ or /d/ is assimilated to the following /t/ of an inflectional suffix: e.g. ܥܒܝܛܬܐ /ʕabbittaa/ derived from ܥܒܝܛ /ʕabbiṭ/ 'dense'; ܠܛܬ /laat/ 'you cursed' from ܠܛ /laaṭ/; ܥܕܬ݂ܐ /ʕeettaa/ 'church' vs. ܥܕܬ݂ܝ /ʕee<u>d</u>a<u>t</u>/ 'my church'; ܥܒܕܬ /ʕvat/ 'you did' from ܥܒܕ /ʕva<u>d</u>/; ܐܒܗܬܬܢ /ʔavhettaan/ 'you shamed us' < /*ʔavhe<u>t</u>taan/. Note also ܚܕܬ݂ܬ݂ܐ /ḥdattaa/ 'new' (f.sg.emph. of ܚܕܬ݂ /ḥ<u>d</u>a<u>t</u>/), ܚܕܬ݂ܐ /ḥa<u>tt</u>aa/ (m.sg.emph. < /*ḥa<u>dt</u>aa/), ܚܕܬ̈ܐ /ḥa<u>tt</u>ee/ (m.pl.emph. < /*ḥa<u>dt</u>ee/).

N) Assimilation and metathesis.([31]) In the reflexive verb patterns the /t/ of their prefix seems to swap its position with the initial consonant of a given verb root when the latter begins with a sibilant, one of the set /s, z, ṣ, š/. Thus Ethpeel ܐܣܬܪܩ /ʔestreq/ 'to be combed' < /*ʔe<u>t</u>sreq/ (root ܣܪܩ); Ethpaal ܐܫܬܡܫ /ʔeštammaš/ 'to be served' < /*ʔe<u>t</u>šammaš/ (root ܫܡܫ). When the first consonant of a verb root is /z/ or /ṣ/, the /t/

[30] There is no doubling of a spirantised plosive.

[31] For another possible interpretation of the feature discussed here, see Joüon - Muraoka 1993: § 17 *b*.

of the prefix is further assimilated partially to the preceding /z/ or /ṣ/, namely to /d/ (assimilated to the voiced /z/) and to /ṭ/ (to the emphatic /ṣ/): e.g. Ethpeel ܐܙܕܒܢ /ʾezdven/ 'to be bought' < /*ʾeṯzven/ (root ܙܒܢ) and Ethpaal ܐܨܛܒܥ /ʾeṣṭabbaʿ/ 'to be decorated' < /*ʾeṯṣabbaʿ/ (root ܨܒܥ).

O) **Word stress**. Here also differ ES and WS: ES always stresses the penultimate vowel, whereas WS stresses the final syllable when it is closed, but the penultimate when it is open, thus ܟܳܬܶܒ /koṯév/ 'writing' (m.sg.), but ܟܳܬܒܳܐ /kóṯbo/ (f.sg.). Both, each in its own way, seem to represent a later, secondary development, whilst the general penultima stress can be postulated for the early Classical period.([32]) In any event, the stres does not appear to have phonemic status.

[32] For a reconstruction of a historical development of the Syriac accent, see Brockelmann 1962: § 71-79.

PART TWO

MORPHOLOGY

§ 7 As a Semitic language, Syriac shares with its cognates certain important features in its morphology.

a) A word consists of a root composed of mostly three, but sometimes two, four or more consonants, and this root is furnished with vowels and/or a prefix or suffix, which latter also consists of a consonant or consonants and a vowel or vowels. A given root may have a number of words derived from it, all sharing a certain meaning content borne by the root. All actual words of a given root show the root consonants or its radicals in identical sequence. For example, the root √p-s-q (ܦܣܩ) may be realised as the following words: /psaq/ 'he cut'; /pesqaa/ 'part'; /psaaqaa/ 'dissection'; /paasoqaa/ 'section'; /paasiqtaa/ 'decision'; /paasiqaay/ 'short'; /psiqutaa/ 'separation'; /pusqaanaa/ 'decree'; /ʾetpseq/ 'it was cut'; /metpasqaanutaa/ 'section'; /passeq/ 'he chopped'; /pussaaqaa/ 'chopping' etc.

b) It is customary to classify roots into strong and weak roots. Weak roots are those one radical, namely root consonant, of which is Waw or Yod or the last two radicals are identical.

In addition to these weak root patterns, those with Nun as the first radical or a guttural, especially Alaf as the first radical, cause some deviations in inflection, and it is also customary to speak of First-Alaf, First-Nun, First-Yodh, Second-Waw/Yod, Third-Yodh, geminate roots etc.([1])

c) Certain categories of words do not share the above-given features: they are pronouns, prepositions, conjunctions and such like particles.

[1] One also uses Latin terms such as 'primae Alaf,' 'mediae Waw/Yodh,' 'tertiae Yodh,' 'geminatae,' meaning roots whose first radical (*littera* 'letter') is Alaf, second radical is Waw/Yodh, third radical is Yodh, and second radical is identical with the third respectively.

§ 8 In the case of geminate roots, the first radical is geminated where it is preceded by a prefix: e.g., from the root √ܓܙܙ, /ʾeggoz/ 'I shall clip'; /negzun/ (= /neggzun/) 'they shall clip'; /maʿʿaallee/ 'entrance' (√ܥܠܠ). As can be seen from the last example, the gemination of the identical second-third radical is restored the moment it is followed by a suffix, whether a vowel or a consonant: cf. § 6 F.

Pronouns

§ 9 Independent personal pronouns. These are pronouns used mostly as subjects or predicates. Most of them have a shortened, enclitic form.

		Separate		Enclitic	
sg. 1		ܐܸܢܳܐ	/ʾenaa/	ܢܳܐ ,ܐ̱ܢܳܐ	/naa/
	2m.	ܐܲܢ݇ܬ݁	/ʾat/	ܬ݁	/t/
	f.	ܐܲܢ݇ܬ݁ܝ	/ʾat/	ܬ݁ܝ	/t/
	3m.	ܗܽܘ	/hu/	ܘ, ܗ̄ܘ	/w/ or /u/ (§ 10)
	f.	ܗܝ	/hi/	ܗ̄ܝ	/y/ or /i/ (§ 10)
pl. 1		ܚܢܲܢ	/ḥnan/ (ܐܢܚܢܢ)(2)	ܢܲܢ	/nan/
	2m.	ܐܲܢ݇ܬ݁ܘܿܢ	/ʾatton/ [WS ܐܰܢ݇ܬ݁ܽܘܢ]	ܬ݁ܘܿܢ	/tton/ [WS ܬ݁ܽܘܢ]
	f.	ܐܲܢ݇ܬܹ݁ܝܢ	/ʾatteen/	ܬܹ݁ܝܢ	/tteen/
	3m.	ܗܸܢ݁ܘܿܢ	/hennon/ [WS ܗܶܢ݁ܽܘܢ]	ܐܸܢ݁ܘܿܢ	/ʾennon/ [WS ܐܶܢ݁ܽܘܢ]
	f.	ܗܸܢܹ݁ܝܢ	/henneen/	ܐܸܢܹ݁ܝܢ	/ʾenneen/

§ 10 The enclitic forms are used mostly as weakened subjects of nominal clauses: e.g. ܡܲܠܟ݁ܳܐ ܐ̱ܢܳܐ /malkaanaa/ 'I am king.' The third person singular enclitics confer varying degrees of prominence to the immediately preceding clause constituent: e.g. ܐܲܢ݇ܬ݁ ܗ̄ܘ ܡܲܠܟ݁ܳܐ /ʾattu malkaa/ 'it is you who are the king'; ܬ݁ܲܡܳܢ ܗ̄ܘ ܚܙܹܝܬ݂ܹܗ /tammaanu ḥzeeṯeeh/ 'it is there that I saw him.' The third person plural enclitic pronouns are also used as direct objects of a verb form other than a participle: e.g. ܫܲܕ݁ܪܹܬ݂ ܐܸܢܹ݁ܝܢ /šadreṯ ʾenneen/ 'I sent them (f.).'

The enclitic forms in the first and second persons may be spelled together with the immediately preceding word, resulting in further

[2] This long variant form, /ʾenaḥnan/, occurs only in old manuscripts.

phonetic simplification: ܟܵܬܹܒ݂ ܐ̄ܢܵܐ or ܟܵܬܹܒ݂ܢܵܐ /kaaṯevnaa/ 'I write'; ܓܵܠܹܐ ܐ̄ܢ̄ܬ /gaale ʾat/ or ܓܵܠܹܝܬ /gaaleet/ 'you(m.sg.) reveal'; ܟܵܬܹܒ݂ ܐ̄ܢ̄ܬ /kaaṯev ʾat/ or ܟܵܬܒ݂ܵܬ /kaaṯvat/; ܫܲܦܝܼܪܲܬ /šappirat/ or ܫܲܦܝܼܪ ܐ̄ܢ̄ܬ /šappir ʾat/ 'you are beautiful'; ܟܵܬܒ݂ܝܼܢܲܢ or ܟܵܬܒ݂ܝܼܢ ܢܲܢ (ܟܬܒܝܢ ܐܢܚܢ), all pronounced /kaaṯbinnan/; ܟܵܬܒ݂ܝܼܬܘܿܢ or ܟܵܬܒ݂ܝܼܢ ܐ̄ܢ̄ܬܘܿܢ /kaaṯbitton/ 'you (m.pl.) write.'

ܗܘܿ followed by an enclitic shows a dissimilation: ܗܘܿܝܘܿ /huyu/ 'it is he that ...'

§ 11 Suffixed personal pronouns Possessive pronouns and pronouns which complement prepositions are attached directly to the latter. The forms which follow vowels slightly differ from those which follow consonants:(3)

		after consonants		after vowels	
sg. 1		ܝ (silent)(4)		ܝ	/y/(5)
	2m.	ܵܟ݂	/aak̲/	ܟ݂	/k̲/
	f.	ܹܟ݂ܝ	/eek̲/	ܟ݂ܝ	/k̲/
	3m.	ܹܗ	/eeh/	ܗ̄ܝ	/y/
	f.	ܵܗ̇	/aah/	ܗ̇	/h/
pl. 1		ܲܢ	/an/		
	2m.	ܟ݂ܘܿܢ	/k̲on/ [WS ܟ݂ܘܿܢ]		
	f.	ܟ݂ܹܝܢ	/k̲een/		
	3m.	ܗܘܿܢ	/hon/ [WS ܗܘܿܢ]		
	f.	ܗܹܝܢ	/heen/		

§ 12 Personal pronouns attached to verbs. These differ from the above-given forms only in respect of the 1 sg., 3m.sg., and 3pl.

3 The forms attached to masculine plural/dual nouns and some prepositions are slightly different. They may be found in § 40.

4 With two of the prepositions and the noun ܟܠ /kul/ 'all' it *is* pronounced: ܒܝ /bi/ 'in me'; ܠܝ /li/ 'to me' (but not ܕܝܼܠܝ /dil/ 'mine, my'); ܟܠܝ /kulli/ 'all of me.'

5 E.g., from the noun ܐܒ /ʾav/: ܐܵܒ݂ /ʾaav/; ܐܲܒ݂ܘܼܟ݂ 'ʾavuk̲/; ܐܲܒ݂ܘܼܟ݂ܝ /ʾavuk̲/; ܐܲܒ݂ܘܼܗ̄ܝ /ʾavuy/; ܐܲܒ݂ܘܼܗ̇ /ʾavuh/; ܐܲܒ݂ܘܼܢ /ʾavun/.

	after consonants—		after vowels—	
sg. 1	ܰܢܝ	/an/	ܢܝ	/n/
2m.	ܳܟ	/aak/	ܟ	/k/
f.	ܶܟܝ	/eek/	ܟܝ	/k/
3m.	ܶܗ	/eeh/	ܝܗܝ, ܘܗܝ /y/; ܘܗܝ	/w/
f.	ܳܗ	/aah/	ܗ	/h/
pl. 1	ܰܢ	/an/	ܢ	/n/
2m.	ܟܽܘܢ /kon/ [WS ܟܽܘܢ]			
f.	ܟܶܝܢ /keen/			

3m., f. The enclitics ܐܶܢܽܘܢ (WS ܐܢܽܘܢ) and ܐܶܢܶܝܢ are used: § 10.

The direct object of the 1sg. with an infinitive may take the form ܝ- as well as ܢܝ-: e.g. Mt 8.2 ܡܶܫܟܰܚ ܐܢ̱ܬ ܠܡܕܰܟܳܝܽܘܬܝ /meškaḥ ᵓat lamdakkaayut/ 'you can cleanse me.'

§ 12a Reflexive pronouns. The noun ܢܰܦܫܳܐ 'soul' in conjunction with an appropriate suffix pronoun is used like a reflexive pronoun: e.g. Mt 8.4 ܚܰܘܳܐ ܢܰܦܫܳܟ ܠܟܳܗ̈ܢܶܐ /ḥawwaa nafšaak lkaahnee/ 'Show yourself to the priests.' Similar, though less frequent, is the use of ܩܢܽܘܡܳܐ /qnomaa/.

§ 12b Reciprocal pronouns. The notion of "each other, one another" is expressed by the repetition of the numeral ܚܰܕ 'one': Mt 24.10 ܘܢܶܣܢܽܘܢ ܚܰܕ ܠܚܰܕ ܘܢܰܫܠܡܽܘܢ ܚܰܕ ܠܚܰܕ 'and they will hate one another, and betray one another' (the Lamadh indicates the direct object); Lk 2.15 ܡܰܠܶܠܘ ܪ̈ܳܥܰܘܳܬܳܐ ܚܰܕ ܥܰܡ ܚܰܕ 'the shepherds spoke with one another.' Hebraic is the use of ܐܰܚܳܐ 'brother' as in Gn 37.19 ܐܶܡܰܪܘ ܓܰܒܪܳܐ ܠܰܐܚܽܘܗܝ 'they said to one another.'

§ 13 Demonstrative pronouns.(6)

a) For that which is nearer: "this, these"—

sg.m. ܗܳܢܳܐ /haanaa/ (rarely ܗܳܢ /haan/)
f. ܗܳܕܶܐ /haadee/
pl.c. ܗܳܠܶܝܢ /haalleen/

In conjunction with the enclitic ܗܘ, the demonstrative changes its form: ܗܳܕܶܐ ܗܘ /haadaay/. The m. form with an enclitic becomes ܗܳܢܰܘ /haanaw/.

[6] On the syntax of the demonstrative pronouns, see below §§ 91: 2-4

b) For that which is more distant: "that, those"—

sg.m. ܗܿܘ /haw/ pl.m. ܗܳܢܽܘܢ /haannon/ [WS ܗܳܢܽܘܢ]
f. ܗܳܝ /haay/ f. ܗܳܢܶܝܢ /haanneen/

§ 14 Interrogatives

ܡܰܢ /man/ "Who?"; with an enclitic—ܡܰܢܽܘ /manu/ "Who is it that ...?'

ܡܳܐ /maa/, ܡܳܢ /maan/, ܡܳܢܳܐ /maanaa/, ܡܽܘܢ /mon/, all meaning "What?"; with an enclitic—ܡܳܢܰܘ /maanaw/ "What is it that ...?"

ܐܰܝܢܳܐ /ʾaynaa/ sg.m.; ܐܰܝܕܳܐ /ʾaydaa/ f.; ܐܰܝܠܶܝܢ /ʾayleen/ pl.c. "Which?"

ܐܰܝܟܳܐ /ʾaykaa/ "Where?"; with an enclitic—ܐܰܝܟܰܘ /ʾaykaw/ "Where is it that ...?"

ܐܶܡܰܬܝ /ʾemmat̲/ "When?"

ܠܡܳܢܳܐ /lmaanaa/ "Why?"

ܐܰܝܟܰܢܳܐ /ʾaykannaa/ "How?" (less commonly ܐܰܝܟܰܢ /ʾaykan/)

ܟܡܳܐ /kmaa/ "How much?"

§ 15 Relative pronoun. Syriac uses a proclitic ܕ as an indeclinable relative pronoun. As a matter of fact it is a linking word of vague nature, and is also used, either on its own or in conjunction with another particle, in various other ways. See below at § 77.

§ 16 Independent possessive pronouns. By adding an appropriate suffix pronoun to ܕܺܝܠ one obtains an independent possessive pronoun: e.g. ܡܰܠܟܳܐ ܕܺܝܠܰܢ /malkaa d̲ilan/ 'our own king' as against ܡܰܠܟܰܢ /malkan/ 'our king.' These pronouns can also be used substantivally: ܕܺܝܠܰܢ ܗܽܘ ܗܳܢܳܐ /dilanu haanaa/ 'this is ours.' See below at § 91: 6.

Declension of Nouns and Adjectives

§ 17 Nouns and adjectives are declined in respect of three grammatical categories: number, gender, and state. The declension takes place mostly by way of adding an appropriate ending to the stem. The number and gender are each twofold: singular and plural, masculine and feminine.([7]) The state is three in number: absolute, construct, and emphatic (or:

determinate): the meaning of these terms will be explained below.

The declensional endings are as follows:

	sg.			pl.		
	st. abs.	cst.	emph.	abs.	cst.	emph.
m.	—	—	/-aa/	/-in/	/-ay/	/-ee/
f.	/-aa/	/-at̲/	/-taa/ or /-t̲aa/	/-aan/	/-aat̲/	/-aat̲aa/

and as applied to the adjective ܒܝܫ /biš/ 'evil'—

	sg.			pl.		
	st. abs.	cst.	emph.	abs.	cst.	emph.
m.	ܒܝܫ	ܒܝܫ	ܒܝܫܐ	([8])ܒܝ̈ܫܝܢ	ܒܝ̈ܫܝ	ܒܝ̈ܫܐ
	/biš/	/biš/	/bišaa/	/bišin/	/bišay/	/bišee/
f.	ܒܝܫܐ	ܒܝܫܬ	ܒܝܫܬܐ	ܒܝ̈ܫܢ	ܒܝ̈ܫܬ	ܒܝ̈ܫܬܐ
	/bišaa/	/bišat̲/	/bištaa/	/bišaan/	/bišaat̲/	/bišaat̲aa/

§ 18 The absolute state is an unmarked form, whereas the construct state is the form of a noun logically dependent on the immediately following noun. The emphatic state was originaly roughly equivalent to the form of a noun with the definite article. In Classical Syriac, however, the abs. state is used only in certain syntactically defined environments (§ 71), and the construct state is often replaced by means of an analytic structure with the proclitic particle ܕ linking the two nouns (§ 73). The emph. state has lost its original function and has become the normal, unmarked form of a noun: cf. § 72. Apart from adjectives, many nouns are not attested in their abs. or cst. state form, but only in the emph. state form.

§ 19 A small number of nouns have two variant stem forms in the singular: one for the st.abs. and/or cst., and the other for the st. emph., which is the case with nouns having a diphthong, /ay/ or /aw/: e.g.,

[7] The dual number is virtually extinct, confined to ܬܪ̈ܝܢ /treen/, ܬܪ̈ܬܝܢ /tarteen/ 'two' and ܡܐܬܝܢ /mat̲een/ 'two hundred.' Syriac has no neuter gender as a morphological category. Cf. § 69.

[8] The seyame point is not used when a m.pl. adjective is, in st. abs., used predicatively: see § 5 b.

st.cst. ܒܝܬ /beet/, emph. ܒܝܬܐ /baytaa/ 'house'(9); abs. ܠܝܠܝ /laylay/, emph. ܠܠܝܐ /leelyaa/ 'night'; abs. ܝܘܡ /yom/, emph. ܝܘܡܐ /yawmaa/ 'day.' See above (§ 6H) on the contraction of diphthongs.

A variation in the following cases of Third-Yodh roots is only apparent: abs. ܫܛܐ /šaaṭee/, emph. ܫܛܝܐ /šaaṭyaa/ 'fool' where the vowel deletion rule (§ 6A) is at work; abs. ܩܫܐ /qšee/, emph. ܩܫܝܐ /qašyaa/ 'hard' (ditto, the underlying stem being /*qašey/).

§ 20 Some nouns insert an extra /y/ before the feminine ending. This applies to all nouns having such suffixes as /-aan/, /-on/: e.g. ܡܩܒܠܢ /mqablaan/ 'receptive; recipient'—f.abs. ܡܩܒܠܢܝܐ /mqablaanyaa/; cst. ܡܩܒܠܢܝܬ, emph. ܡܩܒܠܢܝܬܐ /mqablaaniṯaa/, pl.abs. ܡܩܒܠܢܝܢ, cst. ܡܩܒܠܢܝܬ, emph. ܡܩܒܠܢܝܬܐ. Likewise ܡܠܟܘܢܐ /malkonaa/ 'kinglet'—f.emph. ܡܠܟܘܢܝܬܐ; ܡܣܟܝܢܐ /meskeenaa/ 'poor'—f.abs. ܡܣܟܝܢܐ, pl.emph. ܡܣܟܝܢܬܐ; ܙܥܘܪ /zʿor/ 'small' (except sg.emph. ܙܥܘܪܬܐ) —f.abs. ܙܥܘܪܝܐ /zʿoryaa/, cst. ܙܥܘܪܝܬ, pl.abs. ܙܥܘܪܝܢ /zʿoryaan/, emph. ܙܥܘܪܝܬܐ; sg.emph. ܕܘܟܬܐ /dukṯaa/ 'place'— pl.emph. ܕܘܟܝܬܐ /dukyaaṯaa/; ܕܘܢܒܬܐ /dunbṯaa/ 'tail'—pl.emph. ܕܘܢܒܝܬܐ /dunbyaaṯaa/ (also ܕܘܢܒܬܐ /dunbaaṯaa/).

§ 21 A small number of nouns, mostly short, have /ayyaa/ as the pl.m.emph. ending.(10) E.g. ܒܪ /bar/ 'son'—ܒܢܝܐ /bnayyaa/; sg.emph. ܫܢܬܐ /šattaa/ 'year'—ܫܢܝܐ /šnayyaa/; ܙܢܐ /znaa/ 'sort'—ܙܢܝܐ /znayyaa/; ܬܕܐ /tdaa/ 'breast'—ܬܕܝܐ /tdayyaa/; ܐܝܕ 'hand'—ܐܝܕܝܐ /ʾiḏayyaa/ (beside ܐܝܕܐ /ʾiḏee/); ܐܦܝ /ʾappay/ 'curtain' (used as sg.)—ܐܦܝܐ /ʾappayyaa/.

This is further the rule with words of Third-Yodh roots, the m.sg.abs. form of which is spelled in the m.sg.abs. and cst. with Alaf instead of Yodh: e.g. sg.m.abs. ܩܫܐ /qšee/ (< /*qašey/) 'hard' (emph. or f.sg.abs. ܩܫܝܐ /qašyaa/)—pl.m.emph. ܩܫܝܐ /qšayyaa/; ܫܛܐ /šaaṭee/ 'fool' —ܫܛܝܐ /šaaṭayyaa/; ܡܫܪܝ /mšarray/ 'paralytic'—ܡܫܪܝܐ /mšarrayyaa/; sg. emph. ܓܕܝܐ /gaḏyaa/ 'goat'—ܓܕܝܐ /gḏayyaa/; ܩܢܝܐ /qanyaa/ 'reed' —ܩܢܝܐ /qnayyaa/; ܡܥܝܐ /meʿyaa/ 'intestines'—ܡܥܝܐ /mʿayyaa/.

9 The st.abs. ܒܝ /bay/, occurring already in Old Aramaic, is a secondary development.

10 A more archaic form.

Likewise with nouns always used in the plural (pluraia tantum): ܡ̈ܝܐ /mayyaa/ 'water'; ܫܡ̈ܝܐ (also without seyame) /šmayyaa/ 'sky'; sg.emph. ܓܘܪܝܐ /guryaa/ 'whelp'—ܓܪ̈ܝܐ /grayyaa/; ܕܡ̈ܝܐ /dmayyaa/ 'price'.

§ 22 Types of nouns dealt with in § 21 have /-in/ as their pl.m.abs. ending: ܓܪ̈ܝܢ, ܡ̈ܝܢ, ܕܡ̈ܝܢ, ܩܢ̈ܝܢ. But adjectives end in /-een/: ܡܥܝܢ, ܫܠܝܢ, ܡܫܪ̈ܝܢ.

In the pl.st.cst. we find /-ay/ with nouns—ܕܡ̈ܝ /dmay/, ܫܡ̈ܝ, ܡ̈ܝ, ܫܢ̈ܝ —but /-yay/ with adjectives and participles—ܩܫ̈ܝܝ /qašyay/, ܪ̈ܥܝܝ /raaᶜyay/ 'shepherds'; ܡܚܘ̈ܝܝ /mḥawyay/ 'showing.'

§ 23 Some nouns show /-aanee/ as the pl.m.emph. ending, often as an alternative to the standard /-ee/: e.g. ܐܒܐ /ʾebbaa/ 'fruit'—ܐܒ̈ܢܐ /ʾebbaanee/; ܣܡܐ /sammaa/ 'drug'—ܣܡ̈ܢܐ; ܒܣܡܐ /besmaa/ 'perfume' —ܒܣܡ̈ܢܐ; ܪܝܚܐ /reeḥaa/ 'smell'—ܪ̈ܝܚܢܐ; ܡܫܚܐ /mešḥaa/ 'ointment' —ܡܫܚ̈ܢܐ; ܫܠܝܛܐ /šalliṭaa/ 'ruler'—ܫܠܝ̈ܛܢܐ; ܪܒܐ /rabbaa/ 'teacher' —ܪ̈ܒܢܐ.

§ 24 Feminine nouns and adjectives of Third-Yodh or -Waw roots restore([11]) the consonantal value of the Yodh or Waw respectively:

sg.abs.	ܬܫܥܝ /tašᶜi/ 'story'	ܡܠܟܘ /malku/ 'kingdom'
cst.	ܬܫܥܝܬ /tašᶜit/	ܡܠܟܘܬ /malkut/
emph.	ܬܫܥܝܬܐ /tašᶜitaa/	ܡܠܟܘܬܐ /malkutaa/
pl.abs.	ܬܫ̈ܥܝܢ /tašᶜyaan/	ܡܠܟ̈ܘܢ /malkwaan/
cst.	ܬܫ̈ܥܝܬ /tašᶜyaat/	ܡܠܟ̈ܘܬ /malkwaat/
emph.	ܬܫ̈ܥܝܬܐ /tašᶜyaataa/	ܡܠܟ̈ܘܬܐ /malkwaataa/

The st.abs. and cst. of adjectives of Third-Yodh roots, however, show /-yaa/ instead: e.g. ܕܟܝܐ /dakyaa/ 'pure,' ܕܟܝܬ /dakyat/, but otherwise regularly—sg.emph. ܕܟܝܬܐ /dkitaa/, pl.abs. ܕܟ̈ܝܢ /dakyaan/, emph. ܕܟ̈ܝܬܐ /dakyaataa/.

Note the following common, but slightly irregular forms: ܐܣܝܘܬܐ /ʾaasyutaa/ 'cure'—pl. ܐܣ̈ܘܬܐ /ʾaaswaataa/ or ܐܣ̈ܝܘܬܐ /ʾaasiwaataa/; ܕܡܘܬܐ /dmutaa/ 'image'—ܕܡ̈ܘܬܐ /demwaataa/; ܨܒܘܬܐ /ṣvutaa/ 'matter'—ܨܒ̈ܘܬܐ /ṣevwaataa/; ܚܝܘܬܐ /ḥayyutaa/ 'animal'—sg.cst. ܚܝܘܬ /ḥaywat/, pl. ܚܝ̈ܘܬܐ /ḥaywaataa/; ܚܕܘܬܐ /ḥadutaa/ 'joy'—abs. ܚܕܘܐ

[11] "Restore" is a synchronic description. Cf. Lagarde 1889-91:146-50.

/ḥaḏwaa/, cst. ܚܕܘܬ /ḥaḏwaṯ/; ܨܠܘܬܐ /ṣloṯaa/ 'prayer'—sg.cst. ܨܠܘܬ /ṣloṯ/, pl. ܨܠܘܬܐ /ṣlawaaṯaa/; ܡܚܘܬܐ /mḥoṯaa/ 'blow'—sg.abs. ܡܚܘܐ /maḥwaa/, pl.emph. ܡܚܘܬܐ /maḥwaaṯaa/; ܡܢܬܐ /mnaaṯaa/ 'portion'—pl.emph. ܡܢܘܬܐ /mnawaaṯaa/; ܡܘܡܬܐ /mawmaaṯaa/ 'oath'— pl.emph. ܡܘܡܬܐ /mawmaaṯaa/ (same as sg.)([12]); ܚܬܐ /ḥaaṯaa/ 'sister' —pl.emph. ܐܚܘܬܐ /ʼaḥwaaṯaa/.([13])

§ 25 A fair number of masculine nouns ending in ܝܐ /yaa/ form their pl. by means of the ending ܘܬܐ /awaaṯaa/([14]): ܐܪܝܐ /ʼaryaa/ 'lion'—ܐܪܝܘܬܐ /ʼaryawaaṯaa/ (with the retention of /y/); ܚܕܝܐ /ḥaḏyaa/ 'breast'—ܚܕܘܬܐ /ḥḏawaaṯaa/; ܚܘܝܐ /ḥewyaa/ 'snake'—ܚܘܘܬܐ /ḥwawaaṯaa/; ܟܘܪܣܝܐ /kursyaa/ 'throne'—ܟܘܪܣܘܬܐ /kursawaaṯaa/; ܠܠܝܐ /leelyaa/ 'night'—ܠܝܠܘܬܐ /laylawaaṯaa/; ܪܥܝܐ /raaʿyaa/ 'shepherd' —ܪܥܘܬܐ /raaʿawaaṯaa/; ܐܣܝܐ /ʼaasyaa/ 'physician'—ܐܣܘܬܐ /ʼaasawaaṯaa/; ܡܪܝܐ /maaryaa/ 'master'—ܡܪܘܬܐ /maarawaaṯaa/.

The same pl. ending occurs also with nouns which do not end in /-yaa/: ܐܬܪܐ /ʼaṯraa/ 'place'—ܐܬܪܘܬܐ; ܚܝܠܐ /ḥaylaa/ 'power'—ܚܝܠܘܬܐ (also ܚܝ̈ܠܐ); ܠܒܐ /lebbaa/ 'heart'—ܠܒܘܬܐ /lebbawaaṯaa/ (also ܠܒ̈ܐ /lebbee/); ܢܗܪܐ /nahraa/ 'river'—ܢܗܪܘܬܐ. These are all masculine nouns.

The ending /waaṯaa/ is attested with some feminine nouns: ܐܘܡܬܐ /ʼumṯaa/ 'nation'—ܐܡܘܬܐ /ʼemwaaṯaa/; ܐܬܐ /ʼaaṯaa/ 'portent'—ܐܬܘܬܐ /ʼaaṯwaaṯaa/; ܢܘܪܐ /nuraa/ 'fire' —ܢܘܪܘܬܐ /nurwaaṯaa/ (also ܢܘܪܐ); ܣܦܬܐ /sefṯaa/ 'lip'—ܣܦܘܬܐ /sefwaaṯaa/.([15])

§ 26 In addition to /w/, Syriac inserts also /h/ in order to expand the plural stem of some nouns, especially monosyllabic nouns: ܐܒܐ 'father'—ܐܒܗܬܐ /ʼavaahaaṯaa/; ܐܡܐ /ʼemmaa/ 'mother' —ܐܡܗܬܐ;

[12] This identity is explicable, under the assumption of the original root /w-m-ʼ/: sg.emph. /*mawmaʼtaa/ > /mawmaaṯaa/, and pl.emph. /*mawmaʼaaṯaa/ > /mawmaaṯaa/. The lengthening of /aʼ/ to /aa/ is also attested in ܥܢܐ /ʿaanaa/ 'sheep' < /*ḍaʼnaa/, and ܒܬܪ /baaṯar/ 'after' < /*baʼṯar/. The other two sg. forms of the noun in question allow of similar explanation: sg.abs. ܡܘܡܐ /mawmaa/ < /*mawmʼaa/ < /*mawmaʼaa/, and sg.cst. ܡܘܡܬ /mawmaaṯ/ < /*mawmaʼt/.

[13] On the loss of the initial Alaf in the sg., see above, § 6 J.

[14] See another kind of ending, namely /-ayyaa/, typical of this group of nouns: § 21.

ܐܡܬܐ 'maid-servant'—ܐܡܗܬܐ; ܫܡܐ 'name'—ܫܡܗܬܐ.

§ 27 Whereas adjectives always display complete match between their gender and their morphology, there are many cases of mismatch. Some examples are:

1) Masc. nouns with the typically fem.pl. ending— ܝܘܡܐ 'day' —ܝܘܡܬܐ (also ܝܘ̈ܡܐ); ܐܒܐ 'father'—ܐܒܗܬܐ; ܫܡܐ 'name'—ܫܡܗܬܐ
2) Fem. nouns with the typically masc.sg. ending— ܐܘܪܚܐ 'way'—ܐܘܪܚܬܐ; ܐܪܥܐ 'land'—ܐܪܥܬܐ; ܢܦܫܐ 'soul'—ܢܦܫܬܐ([16])
3) Fem. nouns with the typically masc.sg. and pl. ending— ܐܝܕܐ 'hand'—ܐܝܕܝܐ /ʾidayyaa/ or ܐܝ̈ܕܐ; ܐܬܢܐ /ʾattaanaa/ 'she-ass'—ܐܬܢ̈ܐ; ܟܐܦܐ /keefaa/ 'stone' —ܟܐ̈ܦܐ; ܥܢܢܐ 'cloud'; ܨܦܪܐ /ṣepraa/ 'bird'([17])
4) Fem. nouns with the typically fem.sg. but mas.pl. ending— ܡܠܬܐ /melṯaa/ 'word'—ܡ̈ܠܐ /mellee/; ܐܡܬܐ 'cubit'—ܐܡ̈ܝܐ; ܫܥܬܐ 'hour'—ܫ̈ܥܐ; ܫܢܬܐ /šattaa/ 'year'—ܫ̈ܢܐ; ܡܥܪܬܐ /mʿarṯaa/ 'cave'—ܡܥܪ̈ܐ; ܥܢܒܬܐ /ʿenbṯaa/—ܥܢ̈ܒܐ /ʿenvee/; ܬܬܐ (or: ܬܐܢܬܐ) /teettaa/ (< /*teentaa/) 'fig'—ܬܐ̈ܢܐ; ܓܦܬܐ /gfettaa/ (< /*gfentaa/) 'grape'—ܓܘܦ̈ܢܐ; ܠܒܬܐ /lvettaa/ 'brick'—ܠܒ̈ܢܐ.([18])

[15] The ending with /a/, /-awaaṯaa/, is not confined to masculine nouns: see ܨܠܘܬܐ /ṣlawaaṯaa/, pl. of ܨܠܘܬܐ /ṣloṯaa/ 'prayer,' and ܡܢܘܬܐ /mnawaaṯaa/, pl. of ܡܢܬܐ /mnaaṯaa/ 'portion' (§ 24). Such a short vowel in unstressed, open syllables conflicts with the vowel deletion rule (§ 6 A): it appears to be a secondary development.

[16] In some cases there is a semantic opposition: ܥܝ̈ܢܐ 'eyes' vs. ܥܝ̈ܢܬܐ 'fountains' (both from ܥܝܢܐ; cf. Heb. עֵינַיִם 'eyes' vs. עֲיָנוֹת 'springs [of water]), but no opposition is discernible between ܪ̈ܘܚܬܐ and ܪ̈ܘܚܐ 'winds, spirits' or between ܝܘܡܬܐ and ܝܘ̈ܡܐ 'days' (from ܝܘܡܐ).

[17] An extensive list of feminine nouns with no characteristic endings in the singular may be found in Nöldeke 1966: § 84.

[18] The declension of the noun ܫܒܬܐ /šabṯaa/ 'sabbath; week'—sg.abs. ܫܒܐ, pl. ܫܒܝܢ, ܫ̈ܒܐ shows that the final /t/, which belongs to the root (< Heb. שַׁבָּת), was misinterpreted as a feminine morpheme.

§ 28 A very small number of nouns, all of Third-Yodh roots, attest to the archaic feminine morpheme /-ay/: ܓܘܓܝ /gwaag̱ay/ 'spider'; ܕܝܘܝ /dayway/ a kind of bird (kite?); ܚܐܦܝ /ḥeefay/ 'gnat'; ܛܘܥܝܝ /ṭuʿyay/ 'error'; ܛܘܫܝܝ /ṭušyay/ 'secrecy'; ܟܘܟܒܝ /kukvay/ some kind of bird; ܣܠܘܝ /salway/ 'quail'; ܬܢܘܝ /tanway/ (ES /tenway/) 'condition.'

§ 29 The grammatical gender and the natural sex largely overlap when a noun denotes a human being. Thus ܐܒܐ 'father,' ܒܪܐ 'son,' ܐܚܐ 'brother,' ܚܡܪܐ /ḥmaaraa/ 'he-ass,' and ܡܠܟܐ 'king,' for instance, are masculine in gender, whereas ܐܡܐ 'mother,' ܒܪܬܐ 'daughter,' ܚܬܐ 'sister,' ܐܬܢܐ 'she-ass,' and ܡܠܟܬܐ 'queen' are of feminine gender.

Also of feminine gender are nouns of the following categories: animals—ܥܢܐ 'sheep'; ܥܙܐ /ʿezzaa/ 'goat'; ܥܢܐ 'small cattle'; ܥܩܪܒܐ 'scorpion'; ܨܦܪܐ 'bird'; ܩܛܘ 'cat'; parts of the body, esp. those which go in pairs—ܐܕܢܐ 'ear'; ܒܘܪܟܐ 'knee'; ܚܘܦܢܐ 'handful'; ܛܦܪܐ /ṭepraa/ 'fingernail'; ܝܡܝܢܐ 'right hand'; ܟܒܕܐ 'liver'; ܓܦܐ 'wing'; ܟܪܣܐ 'belly'; ܟܬܦܐ /kaṯpaa/ 'shoulder'; ܢܦܫܐ 'soul'; ܥܝܢܐ 'eye'; ܥܩܒܐ 'heel'; ܨܒܥܐ /ṣevʿaa/ 'finger'; ܩܪܢܐ 'horn'; ܪܓܠܐ /reg̱laa/ 'foot'; ܫܢܐ /šennaa/ 'tooth': nouns for vessels and tools—ܐܠܦܐ 'boat'; ܟܘܬܝܢܐ 'linen garment'; ܦܬܘܪܐ 'table'; ܡܓܠܐ 'sickle'; ܡܚܛܐ 'needle'; ܥܪܣܐ 'bed'; ܦܕܢܐ /paddaanaa/ 'yoke'; ܪܚܝܐ /raḥyaa/ 'mill.'

Unclassifiable, but feminine are: ܐܪܥܐ 'earth'; the four points of the compass—ܓܪܒܝܐ 'N,' ܡܕܢܚܐ 'E,' ܬܝܡܢܐ 'S,' ܡܥܪܒܐ 'W'; ܐܘܪܚܐ 'way'; ܚܩܠܐ 'field'; ܟܐܦܐ 'stone'; ܡܠܚܐ 'salt'; ܢܘܪܐ 'fire'; ܥܢܢܐ 'cloud'; ܥܪܦܠܐ 'fog'; ܓܘܦܢܐ, ܓܦܬܐ /gfettaa/ 'grape.'

The gender of some nouns fluctuates: ܒܥܝܪܐ 'cattle'; ܚܘܛܪܐ 'stick'; ܚܟܐ 'palate'; ܣܝܦܐ 'sword'; ܟܢܬܐ 'colleague'; ܣܗܪܐ 'moon'; ܫܡܫܐ 'sun.'([19])

In conclusion, the gender of many nouns is unpredictable. Thus, not every noun denoting a body part, even those in pairs, for instance, is feminine. ܚܕܝܐ 'breast' and ܬܕܝܐ 'breast, pap' are both masculine.

[19] A fuller list may be found in Nöldeke1966: § 87.

Nouns and adjectives: their formation patterns

§ 30 Nouns and adjectives can be classified in accordance with the ways in which vowels and/or affixes are added to their consonantal roots. Thus one may speak of a noun of *qaṭl* or *maqṭal* pattern or of an adjective of *qaṭṭil* pattern. The following is intended as an inventory of major patterns only, and we shall focus mainly on those patterns which require some attention in the declension of nouns and adjectives belonging to them.([20])

§ 31 Pattern *qvṭl*, namely nouns or adjectives which show a short vowel after the first radical, but no vowel between the last two radicals in their stem when a declensional ending or a possessive pronoun is removed, e.g. ܡܰܠܟܳܐ /malkaa/ 'king,' ܡܰܠܟܰܢ /malkan/ 'our king.' Among nouns and adjectives of this pattern the following sub-patterns may be recognised:

a) Those which show the shape *qṭel* or *qṭol* in the sg.abs. or cst.: e.g., ܡܠܶܟ /mlek/ 'king' (emph. ܡܰܠܟܳܐ /malkaa/); ܪܓܶܠ /rgel/ 'foot' (ܪܶܓܠܳܐ /reglaa/); ܩܕܳܫ /qdoš/ 'sanctity' (ܩܘܽܕܫܳܐ /qudšaa/).([21])

Nouns of this sub-pattern whose third radical is one of the six plosives, ܬ ܦ ܟ ܕ ܓ ܒ, regularly take a *quššaya* with the radical in question in all their forms other than those of the st.abs. or cst.: e.g. ܡܰܠܟܳܐ /malkaa/, ܥܰܒܕܳܐ /ʿavdaa/ 'slave,' ܟܶܣܦܳܐ /kespaa/ 'silver,' ܒܘܽܪܟܳܐ /burkaa/ 'knee.'([22])

With nouns whose third radical is a guttural or Resh, the /e/ changes to /a/ (§ 6 B): ܬܪܰܥ /traʿ/ 'gate' (ܬܰܪܥܳܐ); ܦܓܰܪ /pgar/ 'corpse' (ܦܰܓܪܳܐ).

With nouns whose first radical is Alaf, the latter takes a full vowel (§ 6 C): ܐܶܓܰܪ /ʾegar/ 'wage' (ܐܰܓܪܳܐ); ܐܰܪܰܥ /ʾaraʿ/ 'earth' (< /*ʾareʿ/) (ܐܰܪܥܳܐ); ܐܘܽܪܰܚ /ʾuraḥ/ 'way' (ܐܘܽܪܚܳܐ). On the second vowel, /a/, see the preceding paragraph.

With nouns whose first radical is Yodh, the rule § 6 D is at work: ܝܺܪܰܚ /yiraḥ/ 'month' (ܝܰܪܚܳܐ)'; ܝܺܠܶܕ /yiled/ 'child' (ܝܰܠܕܳܐ).

[20] For a fuller listing, though admittedly not exhaustive, one may consult Nöldeke 1966: §§ 93-145, and Brockelmann 1962: §§ 117-51.

[21] These can be traced back to the Proto-Aramaic or Proto-Semitic *qaṭl*, *qiṭl*, and *quṭl* pattern respectively.

b) There are feminine nouns corresponding to those described under the above sub-pattern: ܡܠܟܬܐ /malkṯaa/ 'queen' (cst. ܡܠܟܬ, pl.abs. ܡܠܟܢ, emph. ܡܠܟܬܐ); ܢܨܒܬܐ /neṣbṯaa/ 'plant'; ܕܚܠܬܐ /deḥlṯaa/ 'fear'; ܒܘܪܟܬܐ /burkṯaa/ 'blessing.' However, there are nouns which show a vowel after the second radical in their sg. emph. form: ܪܓܠܬܐ /rḡelṯaa/ 'rivulet' (but pl. ܪܓܠܬܐ /reḡlaaṯaa/); ܥܓܠܬܐ /ʿḡelṯaa/ 'calf' (but cst. ܥܓܠܬ); ܓܦܬܐ /gfettaa/ (< /*gfenṯaa/; pl. ܓܘܦܢܐ).

c) Nouns of the second *qvṭl* sub-pattern show /a/ in their sg.abs./cst. form, and if their third radical is one of the six plosives (ܒ ܓ ܕ ܟ ܦ ܬ) it is provided with a *rukkakhaa*: ܕܗܒ /dhav/ 'gold' (emph. ܕܗܒܐ /dahvaa/); ܐܠܦ /ʾelaf/ 'ship' (emph. ܐܠܦܐ /ʾelfaa/); ܕܩܢ /dqan/ 'beard' (ܕܩܢܐ); ܙܒܢ /zvan/ 'time' (ܙܒܢܐ); ܓܡܠ /gmal/ (ܓܡܠܐ); ܫܦܠ /šfal/ 'lowly' (ܫܦܠܐ); ܣܟܠ /sḵal/ 'foolish' (ܣܟܠܐ).([23]) Although their sg. abs. /cst. form is not attested, the spirantised pronunciation of the third radical of the following nouns may allow us to infer that they also belong here: ܚܠܒܐ 'milk,' ܓܦܐ 'wing,' ܟܪܟܐ 'city,' ܥܪܒܐ 'raven,' ܪܛܒܐ 'humidity,' ܪܕܦܐ 'bread.'

A phenomenon analogous to ܪܓܠܬܐ mentioned above occurs here also: ܢܫܡܬܐ /nšamṯaa/ 'soul' (abs. ܢܫܡܐ, pl. ܢܫܡܬܐ) as against ܛܢܦܬܐ /ṭanpṯaa/ 'unclean' (pl. ܛܢܦܬܐ /ṭanfaaṯaa/) and ܙܕܩܬܐ /zeḏqṯaa/ 'alms' (pl. ܙܕܩܬܐ /zeḏqaaṯaa/).

d) In practical terms, in studying nouns belonging to the above

[22] Some exceptions occur in the plural: ܥܣܒܐ /ʿesbaa/ 'grass' but ܥܣܒܐ /ʿesvee/; ܓܘܢܒܐ /gunbaa/ 'theft' but ܓܘܢܒܐ /gunvee/; ܐܠܦܐ /ʾalpaa/ 'thousand' but ܐܠܦܐ /ʾalfee/. It is considered to go back to an earlier plural form with a vowel after the second radical such as /*gunavee/: cf. Heb. מְלָכִים and מַלְכֵי. On the other hand, forms such as ܟܬܦܐ /katpaa/ (ܟܬܦ) 'shoulder' (Heb. כָּתֵף) and ܟܒܕܐ /kavdaa/ (Heb. כָּבֵד), both of the original *qaṭil* pattern, indicate that when the /i/ or /e/ vowel of this pattern had been elided, the spirantisation rule was still in force, and the /a/ vowel in the same syllabic position of the pattern *qvṭal* pattern had not yet been deleted, which explains the spirantised /v/ in ܕܗܒܐ /dahvaa/ 'gold' (< dahavaa/): on this question, see Muraoka 1976:232f. Compare ܟܪܟܐ /karḵaa/ 'town' with ܟܪܟܐ /kerkaa/ 'volume, tome.'

[23] In the case of nouns with /r/ as their third radical, only comparison with cognate languages could assign them to this sub-pattern: ܕܟܪ /dḵar/ 'male' (ܕܟܪܐ: cf. Heb. זָכָר); ܒܣܪ /bsar/ 'meat' (ܒܣܪܐ: Heb. בָּשָׂר). In some other cases also a comparison with cognates confirms this analysis: Heb. זָקָן, גָּמָל; Arb. /safal/.

sub-patterns one needs to know two allomorphs of their stem: e.g. /sfar/ of the sg.abs. and cst. on the one hand, and /sefr-/ of the rest of the declension as appears in, for instance, sg.emph. ܣܦܪܐ 'book,' pl.emph. ܣܦܪܐ, + 1pl. ܣܦܪܢ 'our book.' From these two allomorphs one may postulate the archmorpheme of the stem as /*sefar/, from which the application of the vowel deletion rule (§ 6 A) generates the actually occurring two allomorphs.

§ 32 Nouns and adjectives of the pattern *qaaṭvl* such as ܥܠܡ /ʿaalam/ 'eternity' with sg.emph. ܥܠܡܐ, pl.abs. ܥܠܡܝܢ, emph. ܥܠܡܐ are subject to the vowel deletion rule (§ 6 A).([24]) The feminine sg. emph. of this pattern retains the short vowel: ܐܟܠ /ʾaak̲el/ 'eating,' f.sg.abs. ܐܟܠܐ /ʾaak̲laa/, but ܐܟܠܬܐ /ʾaak̲elt̲aa/.

§ 33 *Qṭaal.* Examples: ܓܙܪܐ /gzaaraa/ 'decision,' ܥܒܕܐ /ʿvaad̲aa/ 'work,' ܩܪܒܐ /qraavaa/ 'battle,' ܐܫܕܐ /ʾešaad̲aa/ 'outpouring' (§ 6 C), ܐܝܩܪܐ /iqaaraa/ 'honour' (§ 6 D).

§ 34 *Qṭil, Qṭeel, Qṭayl.* Examples: ܟܬܝܒ /kt̲iv/ 'written'([25]), ܐܡܝܪ /ʾamir/ 'said' (§ 6 C), ܝܠܝܕ /ilid̲/ 'born' (§ 6 D); ܪܬܝܬܐ /rt̲eet̲aa/ 'trembling'; ܥܠܝܡܐ /ʿlaymaa/ 'lad.'([26])

§ 35 *Qṭul, Qṭol.* Examples: ܪܚܘܡܐ /rḥumaa/ 'loved,' ܠܒܘܫܐ /lvušaa/ 'clothings'; fem. ܒܬܘܠܬܐ /bt̲ultaa/ 'maiden,' ܟܢܘܫܬܐ /knuštaa/ 'synagogue'; ܓܕܘܠܐ /gd̲olaa/ 'plaits of hair,' ܣܓܘܠܐ /sḡolaa/ 'bunch (of grapes).'

§ 36 *QvṭṭVl* (the second vowel may be short or long). The very presence of a short vowel in the first syllable implies, in the light of the vowel deletion rule (§ 6 A), that the second radical is doubled, namely the first syllable is a closed one. This is further reinforced by the hard pronunciation of the second radical when it is one of the set <ܒ ܓ ܕ ܟ ܦ ܬ>. Thus ܨܦܪ /ṣeppar/ 'bird,' emph. ܨܦܪܐ, ܐܕܪ /ʾeddar/ 'threshing

[24] In this context, the short vowel marked as v̆ , is either /a/ or /e/, but not /i/ or /u/.

[25] This is a pattern for the passive participle of a triradical root in its basic pattern, Peal: § 50.

[26] This last represents a pattern for diminutives.

floor.'([27])

Qaṭṭaal is a common pattern for nouns denoting professional activities or permanent qualities: e.g. ܓܢܒܐ /gannaavaa/ 'thief,' ܚܝܛܐ /ḥayyaaṭaa/ 'tailor,' ܟܕܒܐ /kaddaavaa/ 'liar'; ܙܟܝ /zakkaay/ 'innocent, victorious,' ܩܝܡ /qayyaam/ 'abiding.'

Quṭṭaal is a pattern for action noun derived from verbs in the Pael pattern: e.g. ܙܘܗܪܐ /zuhhaaraa/ 'warning,' ܕܘܒܪܐ /dubbaaraa/ 'conduct,' ܫܘܐܠܐ /šuʾʾaalaa/ 'questioning.' Some colour terms also belong here: ܐܘܟܡ /ʾukkaam/ 'black,' ܣܘܡܩ /summaaq/ 'red,' ܝܘܪܩ /yurraaq/ 'green,' ܨܘܚܪ /ṣuḥḥaar/ 'reddish,' ܐܘܪܓܐ /ʾurraaḡaa/ 'multi-coloured.'

Qaṭṭil is highly productive with adjectives including verbal adjectives indicating states: ܐܪܝܟ /ʾarrik/ 'long,' ܚܟܝܡ 'wise,' ܣܓܝ /saggi/ 'many,' ܥܡܝܩ 'deep,' ܪܟܝܟ /rakkik/ 'soft,' ܥܫܝܢ 'mighty,' ܫܦܝܪ 'beautiful'; ܢܦܝܩ 'gone out,' ܐܙܝܠ /ʾazzil/ 'gone,' ܐܒܝܕ /ʾabbid/ 'lost,' ܝܬܝܒ /yattiv/ 'seated.'

§ 37 Patterns with four or more radicals. Syriac knows quite a few such nouns and adjectives (some verbs as well). The expansion from the basic three-radical root is often achieved by repeating the last radical or the last two radicals, or by the addition of an affix such as /t-/, /s-/ or /š-/: e.g. ܩܘܒܠܠܐ /quvllaa/ 'countenace' < √ ܩܒܠ 'to face,' ܫܠܡܠܡ 'complete' < ܫܠܡ 'whole,' ܣܩܒܠ /saqbel/ 'to go towards' < √ ܩܒܠ, ܫܘܥܒܕܐ /šuʿbaadaa/ 'subjugation' < √ܥܒܕ 'to serve'; ܬܘܠܡܕܐ /tulmaadaa/ 'instruction' < √ ܠܡܕ 'to learn.'

§ 38 Patterns with prefixes and suffixes.

a) There are countless nouns prefixed with /m-/: ܡܫܟܢ /maškan/ 'tent,' ܡܣܒ /massav/ 'taking' (< √ ܢܣܒ); ܡܪܟܒܬܐ /markavtaa/ 'vehicle,' ܡܫܬܝܐ /maštyaa/ 'drink,' ܡܘܬܒܐ /mawtvaa/ 'session' (< √ ܝܬܒ), ܡܪܕܝ /mardi/ 'journey' (< √ܪܕܝ), ܡܐܟܘܠܬܐ /meekultaa/ 'food.'

b) Also common is the prefix /t-/: ܬܛܠܝܠܐ /taṭlilaa/ 'roof,' ܬܟܬܘܫܐ /taktušaa/ 'fight,' ܬܫܡܫܬܐ /tešmeštaa/ 'service,' ܬܫܥܝܬܐ /tašʿitaa/ 'tale.'

c) Rare are /ʾ-/ and /y-/: ܐܒܘܒܐ /ʾabbuvaa/ 'flute' (< √ ܢܒܒ);

[27] In view of BA אִמְּרִין (< Akk. /immeru/) the Syr. equivalent ܐܡܪܐ 'lamb' also belongs here.

ܝܚܒܘܪܐ /yaḫburaa/ 'dense smoke.'

d) /-aan/, or less frequently /-on/, is extremely common as a suffix: ܡܘܬܢܐ 'pest,' ܦܘܩܕܢܐ /puqdaanaa/ 'order,' ܒܢܝܢܐ /benyaanaa/ 'building,' ܢܣܝܘܢܐ /nesyonaa/ 'trying experience'; simultaneously with a prefix—ܡܣܩܢܐ /masqaanaa/ 'ascent' (< √ܣܠܩ); also common with adjectives—ܐܪܥܢ /ʔarʕaan/ 'earthly,' ܫܡܝܢ /šmayyaan/ 'celestial.'

This suffix is also added to the feminine morpheme /t/: ܚܡܬܢ /ḥemṯaan/ 'angry' (< ܚܡܬܐ 'anger'), ܢܩܒܬܢ /neqbṯaan/ 'feminine' (< ܢܩܒܬܐ 'female').

It is further exploited to generate actor nouns (§ 51) from all active or reflexive participles with the prefix /m-/: ܡܫܒܚܢܐ /mšabḥaanaa/ 'adorer' (< Pael ptc. ܡܫܒܚ), ܡܪܓܙܢܐ /margzaanaa/ 'one who angers' (< Afel ptc. ܡܪܓܙ).

e) /-aay/ is a highly frequent suffix used to derive an adjective from a noun(28): ܐܠܗܝܐ /ʔalaahaayaa/ 'divine,' ܒܝܬܝܐ /baytaayaa/ 'homely, domestic,' ܝܗܘܕܝܐ /ihuḏaayaa/ 'Jewish.' Some such adjectives are derived from the plural stem, always irregular plural formation: ܢܫܝܐ /neššaayaa/ 'womanly' (< ܢܫܐ, pl. of ܐܢܬܬܐ), ܐܒܗܝܐ /ʔavaahaayaa/ 'fatherly' (< ܐܒܗܬܐ, pl. of ܐܒܐ), ܫܡܗܝܐ /šmaahaayaa/ 'nominal' (< ܫܡܗܬܐ, pl. of ܫܡܐ), ܩܘܪܝܝܐ /quryaayaa/ 'rural' (< ܩܘܪܝܐ, pl. of ܩܪܝܬܐ).

f) Pedantic Syriac loves multiple suffixes: ܢܦܫܢܝܐ /nafšnaayaa/ ψυχικός 'pertaining to the soul,' ܪܘܚܢܝܐ /ruḥaanaayaa/ πνευματικός 'spiritual,' ܥܕܬܢܝܐ /ʕeettaanaayaa/ 'ecclesiastical.'

g) Some feminine nouns are formed by adding /-i/ as suffix: e.g. ܕܒܘܪܝܬܐ /debboriṯaa/ 'bee,' ܣܢܘܢܝܬܐ /snuniṯaa/ 'swallow.'(29)

h) Many masculine abstract nouns are formed by adding /-y/: e.g. ܚܛܘܦܝܐ /ḥṭufyaa/ 'taking by violence,' ܐܣܘܪܝܐ /ʔasuryaa/ 'incarceration,' ܗܦܘܟܝܐ /hfuḵyaa/ 'overturning.'

i) Another highly common suffix for abstract nouns, this time of feminine gender, is /-uṯ/: ܡܠܟܘܬܐ /malkuṯaa/ 'reign,' ܡܫܘܚܘܬܐ

[28] The term*nisbe*, borrowed from the Arabic philology, is often used.

[29] These nouns ought not to be confused with such as ܬܫܥܝܬܐ 'tale,' where the /i/ is derived from the third radical, which is /y/.

/maayot̲ut̲aa/ 'mortality,' ܛܰܝܒܽܘܬ݂ܳܐ /ṭaybut̲aa/ 'grace,' ܕܰܟ݂ܝܽܘܬ݂ܳܐ /dak̲yut̲aa/ 'innocence.'

§ 39 Diminutives. A number of suffixes are used to generate nouns denoting small objects: /-on/—ܡܰܠܟ݂ܘܿܢܳܐ /malk̲onaa/ 'kinglet,' ܟ݂ܬ݂ܳܒ݂ܘܿܢܳܐ /kt̲aavonaa/ 'booklet,' ܟܺܐܦܘܿܢܺܝܬ݂ܳܐ /keefonit̲aa/ 'pebble' (< ܟܺܐܦܳܐ stone')([30]); /-os/—ܢܘܿܢܘܿܣܳܐ /nunosaa/ 'small fish' (< ܢܘܿܢܳܐ), ܓܰܢܘܿܣܬ݂ܳܐ /gannost̲aa/ 'small garden' (< ܓܰܢܬ݂ܳܐ).

§ 40 Attachment of the suffixed personal pronouns. In § 11 above we have given a set of personal pronouns suffixed to nouns and some prepositions. That set (Set A) is actually used with nouns in the singular, both masculine and feminine, *and* feminine plural nouns. There is, however, another slightly different set (Set B) to be used with *masculine plural* nouns and some prepositions.

sg. 1	ـܰܝ	/-ay/	pl.	ـܰܝܢ	/-ayn/
2m.	ـܰܝܟ	/-ayk/		ـܰܝܟܘܿܢ	/-aykon/
f.	ـܰܝܟܝ	/-ayk/		ـܰܝܟܶܝܢ	/-aykeen/
3m.	ـܰܘܗ̄ܝ	/-aw/		ـܰܝܗܘܿܢ	/-ayhon/
f.	ـܶܝܗ	/-eeh/		ـܰܝܗܶܝܢ	/-ayheen/

N.B. 1. Unlike in Set A, the Yodh of the 1sg. *is* pronounced.

2. The Kaf of the 2nd person, both sg. and pl., is pronounced hard in contrast to Set A.

3. Note the peculiar form of the 3m.sg. form.

4. "his" in Set A sounds the same as "her" in Set B, though there is in the latter a Yodh before the final He: e.g. ܡܶܠܬ݂ܶܗ /melt̲eeh/ 'his word' vs. ܡܶܠܶܝܗ /melleeh/ 'her words,' or ܡܰܠܟܶܗ /malkeeh/ 'his king' vs. ܡܰܠܟܶܝܗ /malkeeh/ 'her kings.'

5. When we speak of "masculine" or "feminine" here, we are speaking of the characteristic masculine or feminine form. Thus, though ܡܶܠܬ݂ܳܐ /melt̲aa/ is a feminine noun, its plural shows the characteristically masculine endings: ܡܶܠܺܝܢ /mellin/, ܡܶܠܶܐ /mellee/. Therefore, for the purpose of the attachment of possessive suffix pronouns, its plural is regarded as masculine, requiring Set B: thus ܡܶܠܰܘ̄ܗܝ /mellaw/ 'his words.'

[30] On the infix /i/ as fem. morpheme, see above, § 28.

Conversely, since the plural of a masculine noun ܫܡܐ /šmaa/ is ܫܡܗ̈ܢ /šmaahaan/, ܫܡܗ̈ܬܐ /šmaahaataa/, the noun requires suffixed pronouns of Set A: ܫܡܗ̈ܬܗܘܢ /šmaahaathon/ 'their names.'

§ 41 The two sets are given below, attached to the noun ܕܝܢܐ /dinaa/ 'judgement.'

Set A		Set B		
sg. ('my judgement,' etc.)		pl. ('my judgements' etc.)		
ܕܝܢܝ	/din/	ܕܝܢܝ̈	/dinay/	my
ܕܝܢܟ	/dinaak/	ܕܝܢܝ̈ܟ	/dinayk/	your (m.sg.)
ܕܝܢܟܝ	/dineek/	ܕܝܢܝ̈ܟܝ	/dinayk/	your (f.sg.)
ܕܝܢܗ	/dineeh/	ܕܝܢܘ̈ܗܝ	/dinaw/	his
ܕܝܢܗ̇	/dinaah/	ܕܝܢܝ̈ܗ̇	/dineeh/	her
ܕܝܢܢ	/dinan/	ܕܝܢܝ̈ܢ	/dinayn/	our
ܕܝܢܟܘܢ	/dinkon/	ܕܝܢܝ̈ܟܘܢ	/dinaykon/	your (m.pl.)
ܕܝܢܟܝܢ	/dinkeen/	ܕܝܢܝ̈ܟܝܢ	/dinaykeen/	your (f.pl.)
ܕܝܢܗܘܢ	/dinhon/	ܕܝܢܝ̈ܗܘܢ	/dinayhon/	their (m.)
ܕܝܢܗܝܢ	/dinheen/	ܕܝܢܝ̈ܗܝܢ	/dinayheen/	their (f.)

§ 42 In attaching these possessive suffix pronouns the following points ought to be remembered:

a) The pronouns are attached to the stem of the noun which can be obtained by removing the emphatic state ending.

b) Their addition to nouns in the plural, whether masculine or feminine, is the simplest:

ܐܠܗ̈ܐ /ʾalaahee/ 'gods' > ܐܠܗ̈ܘܗܝ /ʾalaahaw/ 'his gods'

ܐܒܗ̈ܬܐ /ʾavaahaataa/ 'fathers' > ܐܒܗ̈ܬܢ /ʾavaahaatan/ 'our fathers.'

c) If the sg. stem ends in -CvvC([31]), -CvCC or -CvC=C([32]), in other words, if the last consonant is preceded by a long vowel or another consonant, whether identical or not, attach the suffix to it:

ܪܝܫܐ /reešaa/ > ܪܝܫܗ̇ /reešaah/ 'her head'

ܕܗܒܐ /dahvaa/ > ܕܗܒܟ /dahvaak/ 'your (m.sg.) gold'

[31] The symbol "vv" signifies any one of the vowels /aa, ee, i, u, o/, namely all vowels other than short /a, e/, which latter are deletable (§ 6 A).

[32] C=C means that the last two consonants are identical, or gemination of a consonant.

ܦܳܬܽܘܪܳܐ /paat̲uraa/ > ܦܳܬܽܘܪܶܗ /paat̲ureeh/ 'his table'

ܠܶܒܳܐ /lebbaa/ > ܠܶܒܶܟܝ /lebbeek̲/ 'your (f.sg.) heart'

Here the feminine morpheme /-t/ counts as final consonant:

ܡܰܫܪܺܝܬܳܐ /mašrit̲aa/ > ܡܰܫܪܺܝܬܶܗ /mašrit̲eeh/ 'his encampment'

ܝܳܠܶܕܬܳܐ /yaalet̲taa/ > ܝܳܠܶܕܬܳܗ /yaalet̲taah/ 'her mother'.

d) If the sg. stem ends in -CvvCC or -CCC, a vowel needs to be inserted between the last two consonants when the suffix for 1sg., 2pl. or 3pl. is added.([33]) When the last consonant is the feminine ending /-t/, the vowel to be inserted is /a/. Otherwise, it is unpredictable.

ܡܰܠܟܬܳܐ /malkt̲aa/ > ܡܰܠܟܬܳܗ /malkt̲aah/ 'her queen'
but ܡܰܠܟܰܬܗܽܘܢ /malkat̲hon/ 'their q.'

ܚܰܘܒܬܳܐ /ḥawbt̲aa/ > ܚܰܘܒܬܳܟ /ḥawbt̲aak̲/ 'your debt'
but ܚܰܘܒܰܬܝ /ḥawbat̲/ 'my d.' ([34])

ܕܽܘܟܬܳܐ /dukt̲aa/ > ܕܽܘܟܬܳܗ /dukt̲aah/ 'her place'([35])
but ܕܽܘܟܰܬܟܶܝܢ /dukkat̲k̲een/ 'your p.'

ܡܰܫܟܢܳܐ /mašknaa/ > ܡܰܫܟܢܶܗ /maškneeh/ 'his tent'
but ܡܰܫܟܰܢܟܽܘܢ /maškank̲on/ 'your t'
ܡܰܫܟܰܢܝ /maškan/ 'my t.'

ܪܳܚܡܳܐ /raaḥmaa/ > ܪܳܚܡܶܗ /raaḥmeeh/ 'his friend'
but ܪܳܚܶܡܗܽܘܢ /raaḥemhon/ 'their f.'

e) A small number of biconsonantal nouns whose stem is CC is also subject to the same rule as given under (**d**):([36])

ܫܡܳܐ /šmaa/ 'name'— ܫܡܶܗ 'his name,' but ܫܶܡܝ /šeem/ 'my name'

[33] Historically speaking, this /a/ has been secondarily dropped as a result of the vowel deletion rule: e.g. /malkt̲aah/ 'her queen/ is derived from /*malkat̲aah/. This *a* has been preserved in the st. cst. form, /malkat̲/. As a matter of fact, there is some fluctuation and uncertainty in this regard: ܛܳܒܬܝ /ṭaavt̲/ 'my good thing' vs. ܛܳܒܰܬܗܽܘܢ /ṭaavat̲hon/ 'their good thing'; ܡܳܪܬܝ /maart/ 'my mistress' vs. ܥܳܩܰܬܝ /ʿaaqat̲/ 'my distress.'

[34] The /w/ or /y/ of the diphthong /aw/ or /ay/ respectively is regarded here as consonantal.

[35] Though the ending is pronounced /kt̲/, morphophonemically it is /kkt̲/: see § 6 G.

[36] Though biconsonantal, words such as ܡܳܪܳܐ /maaraa/ 'master' and ܩܳܠܳܐ /qaalaa/ 'voice' naturally do not belong here, for their initial vowel is not deletable, their base form being /maar/ and /qaal/ respectively.

and ܫܡܗܘܢ 'their name'

ܕܡܐ /dmaa/ 'blood,' but ܕܡܟܘܢ 'your (m.pl.) blood'

ܒܪܐ /braa/ 'son'—ܒܪܗ 'his son,' but ܒܪܝ /beer/ 'my son'

ܙܢܐ /znaa/ 'kind'—ܙܢܗ 'her kind,' but ܙܢܟܘܢ /zankon/ 'your (pl.m.) kind'

§ 43 Some common irregular nouns.

		abs./cst.	sg. + suf.	pl.
father	ܐܒܐ	?	ܐܒܝ, ܐܒܘܟ, ܐܒܘܗܝ etc.[37]	ܐܒܗܬܐ / ܐܒܗܐ
brother	ܐܚܐ	?	ܐܚܝ ܐܚܘܟ, ܐܚܘܗܝ etc.	ܐܚ̈ܐ
sister	ܚܬܐ	?	ܚܬܝ etc.	ܐܚ̈ܘܬܐ
other m.	ܐܚܪܢܐ	ܐܚܪܝܢ		ܐܚܪ̈ܢܐ
f.	ܐܚܪܬܐ	ܐܚܪܢܝܬ		ܐܚܪ̈ܢܝܬܐ
woman	ܐܢ̄ܬܬܐ[38]	ܐܢ̄ܬܬ	ܐܢ̄ܬܬܝ, ܐܢ̄ܬܬܗ etc.	ܢܫ̈ܐ
son	ܒܪܐ	ܒܪ	ܒܪܝ, ܒܪܟ, ܒܪܗܘܢ	ܒ̈ܢܝܐ
daughter	ܒܪܬܐ	ܒܪܬ /bat/	ܒܪܬܝ ܒܪܬܟ etc.	ܒ̈ܢܬܐ
house	ܒܝܬܐ	ܒܝܬ /beet/	ܒܝܬܝ /bayt/, ܒܝܬܟ etc.	ܒ̈ܬܐ[39]
hand	ܐܝܕܐ	ܐܝܕ/ܝܕ[40]	ܐܝܕܝ, ܐܝܕܟ etc.	ܐܝܕ̈ܝܐ[41] / ܐܝܕ̈ܐ
night	ܠܠܝܐ[42]	?	ܠܠܝܗ[43]	ܠܠ̈ܘܬܐ
lord	ܡܪܝܐ / ܡܪܐ[44]	ܡܪܐ[45]	ܡܪܝ, ܡܪܗ etc.	ܡܪ̈ܢܐ[46]
city	ܡܕܝܢܬܐ	cst. ܡܕܝܢܬ/ܡܕܝܢܬ	ܡܕܝܢܬܝ, ܡܕܝܢܬܟ etc.	ܡܕ̈ܢܐ[47]
field		abs. ܡܪܐ		
year	ܫܢ̄ܬܐ /šattaa/	ܫܢܬ		ܫ̈ܢܝܐ

[37] Pronounce /ʾaav/, /ʾavuy/: similarly ܐܚܘܗܝ 'his brother'; ܚܡܝ /ḥeem/ 'my husband's father.'

[38] Pronounce: /ʾattaa/, and cst. /ʾatta͟t/.

[39] Pronounce: /baatayyaa/. Cf. Heb. בָּתִּים.

[40] /ya͟d/ in prepositional phrases like ܒܝܕ /bya͟d/; /ʾi͟d/ 'hand of.'

[41] Pronounce: /<i͟dayyaa/.

[42] Alternative spellings: ܠܠܝܐ, ܠܠܝܐ, ܠܠܝܐ.

[43] So at Jonah 4.10.

[44] /maaryaa/ of the God of Israel and Christ.

[45] The status abs. is not attested.

[46] Alternatively: ܡܪ̈ܐ, ܡܪ̈ܘܬܐ.

§ 44 Numerals

a) Cardinals

	m.	f.		m.	f.
1	ܚܕ	ܚܕܐ	2	ܬܪܝܢ	ܬܪܬܝܢ
3	ܬܠܬܐ	ܬܠܬ	4	ܐܪܒܥܐ	ܐܪܒܥ
5	ܚܡܫܐ	ܚܡܫ	6	ܫܬܐ / ܐܫܬܐ	ܫܬ
7	ܫܒܥܐ	ܫܒܥ	8	ܬܡܢܝܐ	ܬܡܢܐ
9	ܬܫܥܐ	ܬܫܥ	10	ܥܣܪܐ	ܥܣܪ

11 m. ܚܕܥܣܪ
f. ܚܕܥܣܪܐ, ܚܕܥܣܪܐ
12 m. ܬܪܥܣܪ
f. ܬܪܬܥܣܪܐ, ܬܪܬܥܣܪܐ /tartaʿesree/
13 m. ܬܠܬܥܣܪ /tlaṯaʿsar/
f. ܬܠܬܥܣܪܐ, ܬܠܬܥܣܪܐ
14 m. ܐܪܒܥܬܥܣܪ, ܐܪܒܥܣܪ, ܐܪܒܬܥܣܪ
f. ܐܪܒܥܣܪܐ, ܐܪܒܥܣܪܐ (ܐܪܒܬܥܣܪܐ)
15 m. ܚܡܫܥܣܪ, ܚܡܫܬܥܣܪ
f. ܚܡܫܥܣܪܐ, ܚܡܫܥܣܪܐ
16 m. ES ܫܬܬܥܣܪ, ܫܬܬܥܣܪ, WS ܫܬܥܣܪ
f. ES ܫܬܬܥܣܪܐ, ܫܬܬܥܣܪܐ, WS ܫܬܥܣܪܐ
17 m. ܫܒܥܬܥܣܪ, ܫܒܥܬܥܣܪ (ܫܒܥܣܪ)
f. ܫܒܥܣܪܐ, ܫܒܥܣܪܐ (ܫܒܥܬܥܣܪܐ)
18 m. ܬܡܢܬܥܣܪ (ܬܡܢܥܣܪ)
f. ܬܡܢܥܣܪܐ, ܬܡܢܥܣܪܐ
19 m. ܬܫܥܬܥܣܪ, ܬܫܥܬܥܣܪ, ܬܫܥܣܪ
f. ܬܫܥܣܪܐ, ܬܫܥܣܪܐ
20 ܥܣܪܝܢ 30 ܬܠܬܝܢ 40 ܐܪܒܥܝܢ 50 ܚܡܫܝܢ
60 ܫܬܝܢ, ܐܫܬܝܢ 70 ܫܒܥܝܢ 80 ܬܡܢܝܢ (ܬܡܐܢܝܢ)
90 ܬܫܥܝܢ
100 ܡܐܐ(48) 200 ܡܐܬܝܢ 300 ܬܠܬܡܐܐ

[47] Apparently singular used collectively. Note further pl. st. cst. ܡܕܝܢܬ; + suf., ܡܕܝܢܬܝ or ܡܕܝܢܬܝ, ܡܕܝܢܬܗ 'his cities,' ܡܕܝܢܬܗ 'her cities,' ܡܕܝܢܬܗܘܢ or ܡܕܝܢܬܗܘܢ 'their cities.' There also exists a Grecised plural form: ܡܕܝܢܣ or ܡܕܝܢܘܣ.

[48] St. emph. ܡܐܬܐ; pl. abs. ܡܐܘܢ, emph. ܡܐܘܬܐ.

1000 ܐܠܦ, pl. ܐܠܦܝܢ, ܐܠܦܐ 2000 ܬܪܝܢ ܐܠܦܝܢ or ܬܪܝܢ ܐܠܦܐ
10.000 ܪܒܘ, pl. ܪ̈ܒܘܬܐ

Forms designated as masculine are used with a masculine noun, and those designated as feminine with a feminine noun: e.g., ܬܠܬܐ ܒܢܝܢ ܘܬܠܬ ܒܢܢ 'three sons and three daughters.'

A composite number shows the descending order as in English: 7337 = ܫܒܥܐ ܐܠܦܝܢ ܘܬܠܬܡܐܐ ܘܬܠܬܝܢ ܘܫܒܥܐ.

ܬܪܥܣܪ̈ܬܐ 'the twelve (apostles)" and ܥܣܪ̈ܬܐ 'the decade" are cases of substantivised numerals.

b) Ordinals

1st ܩܕܡܝܐ, also ܩܕܡܐܐ, st.abs. ܩܕܡܝ
2nd ܬܪܝܢܝܐ, f. ܬܪܝܢܝܬܐ, also ܬܢܝܢܐ, f. ܬܢܝܢܬܐ
3rd ܬܠܝܬܝܐ 4th ܪܒܝܥܝܐ 5th ܚܡܝܫܝܐ
6th ܫܬܝܬܝܐ (WS ܫܬܝܬܝܐ) 7th ܫܒܝܥܝܐ
8th ܬܡܝܢܝܐ 9th ܬܫܝܥܝܐ 10th ܥܣܝܪܝܐ

An alternative and favourite mode is the use of the particle ܕ followed by a cardinal numeral, which latter must agree in gender with the noun concerned: Gn 1.19 ܝܘܡܐ ܕܐܪܒܥܐ 'fourth day,' Dt 26.12 ܒܫܢܬܐ ܕܬܠܬ 'in the third year.'[49]

The first five days of the week are indicated by using the stem of the cardinal numerals: Sunday ܚܕܒܫܒܐ([50]), Mo. ܬܪܝܢ ܒܫܒܐ, Tu. ܬܠܬܐ ܒܫܒܐ, We. ܐܪܒܥܒܫܒܐ, Th. ܚܡܫܒܫܒܐ, Fr. ܥܪܘܒܬܐ, Sa. ܫܒܬܐ.

The days of the month for the 2nd to the 19th are given by the masc. emph. form of the cardinals: 'on the 2nd' ܒܬܪܝܢܐ, 'on the 3rd' ܒܬܠܬܬܐ([51]), 'on the 4th' ܒܐܪܒܥܬܐ etc., 'on the 11th' ܒܚܕܥܣܪܐ etc.

c) Fractions. ܦܠܓܐ 1/2, ܬܘܠܬܐ 1/3 (ܬܘܠܬܐ 'three-year old'), ܪܘܒܥܐ 1/4, ܚܘܡܫܐ 1/5, ܬܘܡܢܐ 1/8, ܥܘܣܪܐ 1/10.

§ 45 The cardinals from 2 to 9 can take a suffix pronoun: e.g. ܬܪܝܟܘܢ 'you (m.) two,' ܬܪܬܝܗܝܢ 'they (f.) two ܬܠܬܝܗܘܢ 'they (m.)

[49] This must be distinguished from cases such as Jn 21.37 ܕܬܠܬ ܙܒܢܝܢ 'for a third time.'

[50] On ܫܒܐ 'week,' see above § 27.

[51] /batlaattaa/ < /batlaattaa/.

three.'([52]) The rest, with the 3m.pl. suffix, are: ܐܪܒܥܬܝܗܘܢ, ܚܡܫܬܝܗܘܢ, ܫܬܬܝܗܘܢ /štaatayhon/, ܫܒܥܬܝܗܘܢ, ܬܡܢܝܬܝܗܘܢ, ܬܫܥܬܝܗܘܢ, ܥܣܪܬܝܗܘܢ.

§ 46 The **prepositions** take the pronouns they govern in the form of suffix pronouns: thus ܠܡܠܟܐ 'to the king' vs. ܠܗ 'to him.' The following prepositions, however, take the suffix pronouns of Set B:

ܥܠ: ܥܠܘܗܝ 'on him/it,' ܥܠܝܗܘܢ 'upon them'

ܚܕܪ /ḥdaar/ 'around'; ܬܚܘܬ /tḥot/ 'under'; ܨܝܕ /ṣeed/ 'with, towards'; ܩܕܡ /qdaam/ 'ahead of; before, in the presence of'; ܚܠܦ /ḥlaaf/ 'instead of'; ܒܠܥܕ /belʿaad/ 'without'; ܠܥܝܢ /lʿeen/ 'in front of.'

With a suffix pronoun we find ܡܛܠܬ /meṭṭolaat/ for ܡܛܠ /meṭṭul, meṭṭol/: e.g. ܡܛܠܬܗ 'on his account'.

The following are subject to the vowel deletion rule (§ 6 A):

ܒܣܬܪ /bestar/ 'behind'—ܒܣܬܪܝ, ܒܣܬܪܟ, but ܒܣܬܪܗܘܢ etc.

ܒܬܪ /baatar/ 'after'—ܒܬܪܝ, ܒܬܪܗ, but ܒܬܪܟܘܢ etc.

ܠܘܩܒܠ /luqval/ 'opposite, against'—ܠܘܩܒܠܟ but ܠܘܩܒܠܗ, ܠܘܩܒܠܗܘܢ.

The preposition ܐܝܟ /ʾak/ has an allomorph to be used with a suffix pronoun: ܐܝܟ ܡܠܟܐ 'like a king,' but ܐܝܟܘܬܗ 'like him.'

The particle of existence ܐܝܬ /ʾit/ and that of non-existence ܠܝܬ /layt/, when they take a suffix pronoun, take one of Set B: ܥܒܕܐ ܐܝܬܘܗܝ ܒܩܪܝܬܐ /ʿavdaa ʾitaw baqritaa/ 'the servant is in the field'; ܠܝܬܝܗ ܒܗܝܟܠܐ /layteeh bhayklaa/ 'she is not in the temple.' Likewise ܒܠܚܘܕ /balḥod/ 'alone': ܒܠܚܘܕܘܗܝ /balḥodaw/ 'he alone, on his own.'

§ 47 **Adverbs**. /-aaʾit/ is a productive ending for forming an adverb from any adjective or noun: e.g. ܫܪܝܪ /šarrir/ 'true' > ܫܪܝܪܐܝܬ /šarriraaʾit/ 'truly'; ܐܠܗܐ 'god' > ܐܠܗܐܝܬ 'divinely.' A far less produc-tive suffix is /-at/: e.g. ܥܪܝܬ /ʿaryat/ 'in naked condition'; ܪܒܬ /rabbat/ 'greatly'; ܚܝܬ /ḥayyat/ 'in living form'; ܫܘܝܬ /šawyat/ 'simultaneously'; ܚܪܝܬ /ḥraayat/ 'lastly'; ܩܕܡܝܬ /qadmaayat/ 'firstly.' Here we may include also ܛܘܬ /ṭwaat/ 'without eating'([53]); ܫܘܬ /šwaat/ 'simultaneously';

[52] The hard /t/ of the middle Taw is due to an assimilation: /*tlaatatayhon/ > /tlaattayhon/, where the /-ay-/ is due to the analogy of /trayhon/ 'they two.' The /-aattay/ thus produced seems to have influenced all the following numerals. So Brockelmann 1908:488.

ܬܢܝܢܘܬ /tenyaanut̲/ 'for a second time'([54]); ܬܠܝܬܝܘܬ /tlit̲aayut̲/ 'for a third time.'

Verb

§ 48 The Syriac verb is conjugated in respect of "tense," pattern (or: binyan, pl. binyanim), person (1st, 2nd, 3rd), number (sg. and pl.), gender (m. and f.), and voice (active, passive, and reflexive). The conjugation takes place through the addition of suffixes and/or prefixes, the modification of vowel patterns([55]) and/or the doubling of the middle radical.

Syriac knows three "tenses," traditionally termed perfect, imperfect, and participle, the last of which is often nominalised. In addition there are the imperative and the infinitive.

§ 49 Syriac has six **patterns**, traditionally named after the root ܦܥܠ:

Pᵉal	Et̲pᵉel
Paᶜᶜel	Et̲paᶜᶜal
ʾAfᶜel	Ettafᶜal([56])

The semantic or functional opposition between these six patterns is still a matter of debate. The three Eth-prefixed patterns are partly reflexive, passive or ingressive, the last of which indicates entry into a new state or taking on of a property or characteristic. Each of the three

[53] Note the same form in BA, Dn 6.19.

[54] Note the same form in BA, Dn 2.7.

[55] Unlike in Hebrew and Arabic, for instance, the vowel pattern, except in Peal, remains constant throughout the conjugation. For instance, the vowel sequence /a-e/ characterises the entire conjugation of Pael: Perfect and Imperative ܩܰܒܶܠ /qabbel/, Imperfect ܢܩܰܒܶܠ /nqabbel/, Participle ܡܩܰܒܶܠ /mqabbel/. The Infinitive ܡܩܰܒܳܠܽܘ /mqabbaalu/) deviates slightly: see below § 52. The only important exception here is the Imperative of Ethpeel: ܐܶܬ݂ܩܰܒܰܠ /ʔet̲paᶜl/ (spelled also ܐܬ݂ܦܥܰܠ or ܐܬ݂ܦܥܠ with a marheṭana), which thus contrasts with the Perfect ܐܶܬ݂ܦܥܶܠ.

[56] Partly in accordance with the widespread practice and partly for simplicity's sake, we shall hereafter refer to these patterns as Pe(al), Pa(el), Af(el), Ethpe(el), Ethpa(al), and Ettaf(al).

Eth-patterns corresponds to the one in the first column: e.g. ܟܬܰܒ /ktav/ 'to write'([57]) vs. ܐܶܬܟܬܶܒ /ʾetktev/ 'to be written,' or ܩܰܒܶܠ /qabbel/ 'to receive' vs. ܐܶܬܩܰܒܰܠ /ʾetqabbal/ 'to be received.' Afel is often causative: ܥܪܰܩ /ʿraq/ 'to take to flight' vs. ܐܰܥܪܶܩ /ʾaʿreq/ 'to put to flight.' Its Eth-pattern, Ettafʿal, is relatively little used. Instead, not a few Afel verbs show their *Eth*-pattern as Ethpe or Ethpa: e.g. ܐܰܟܪܶܙ /ʾakrez/ 'to preach' vs. ܐܶܬܟܪܶܙ /ʾetkrez/ 'to be preached'; ܐܰܫܠܶܡ 'to deliver' vs. ܐܶܫܬܠܶܡ 'to be delivered'; ܐܰܗܶܠ /ʾahhel/ (√ ܗܠܠ) 'to mock' vs. ܐܶܬܗܰܠܠ 'to be mocked.'

There are a small number of causative verbs whose prefix is either /š/ or /s/. These latter are, however, far less productive than /ʾ/: ܫܰܟܠܶܠ 'to perfect,' ܫܰܥܒܶܕ 'to subjugate,' ܣܰܩܒܶܠ 'to go towards.' These patterns may be called Shafel and Safel respectively. Their *Eth*-patterns show metathesis (§ 6 N): Eshtafal ܐܶܫܬܰܟܠܰܠ 'to be perfected.'

There are a considerable number of verbs with four, sometimes five, radicals, among which one may include the above-mentioned Shafel and Safel. Their conjugation is analogous to that of Pael and Ethpaal: ܒܰܠܒܶܠ /balbel/ 'to confuse,' ܐܶܬܒܰܠܒܰܠ '/ʾetbalbal/ to be confused,' ܗܰܝܡܶܢ /haymen/ 'to believe,' ܐܶܬܗܰܝܡܰܢ /ʾethayman/ 'to be entrusted,' ܫܪܰܓܪܶܓ /šragreg/ 'to display fanciful thoughts,' ܐܶܫܬܪܰܓܪܰܓ /ʾeštragrag/ 'to indulge in fantasies.'

Not every verb is attested in all the six patterns, and many were most likely never used in all those six patterns. Where the tradition of vocalisation is not certain, one is not always able to determine with certainty the pattern of a particular verb form.([58])

§ 50 The **passive voice** is partly indicated by the *eth*-patterns. In other words, all the three non-*eth*-patterns are active. The participle of these three active patterns has a passive pattern indicated by a vowel pattern different from that of the active pattern, which we may call internal passive as against *eth*-prefixed external passive:

[57] As on the foregoing pages, we shall quote a verb as a lexeme in its simplest form, namely Perfect, 3m.sg., but gloss it, for convenience' sake, as an infinitive: here "to write," not "he wrote, he has written, he had written."

[58] Hence the occasional, non-commital designation "Ethp." in Brockelmann 1928.

	Active		Passive	
Peal	ܟܳܬ݂ܶܒ	/kaatev/	ܟܬ݂ܺܝܒ	/ktiv/
Pael	ܡܟܰܬܶܒ	/mkattev/	ܡܟܰܬܰܒ	/mkattav/
Afel	ܡܰܟܬܶܒ	/maktev/	ܡܰܟܬܰܒ	/maktav/([59])

Where an internal passive participle is attested side by side with an external, *eth*-prefixed one, the former stresses a result, the latter a process: ܟܬ݂ܺܝܒ '(already) written' vs. ܡܶܬ݂ܟܬܶܒ 'in the process of being written'; ܒܢܶܐ 'built' vs. ܡܶܬ݂ܒܢܶܐ 'under construction.'

§ 51 The **participle** is, in all the patterns except Peal (ܟܳܬ݂ܶܒ), characterised by a prefix /m-/([60]), and is conjugated in the manner of nouns and adjectives.

Pa: ܡܟܰܬܶܒ /mkattev/; Af ܡܰܟܬܶܒ /maktev/; Ethpe ܡܶܬ݂ܟܬܶܒ /metktev/; Ethpa ܡܶܬ݂ܟܰܬܰܒ /metkattav/; Ettaf ܡܶܬ݁ܰܟܬܰܒ /mettaktav/.

Morphologically affiliated with the participle is **nomen agentis**, a noun denoting a person who executes the action indicated by the verb. Except in Peal, which shows a pattern ܟܳܬ݂ܽܘܒ /kaatov/, all the remaining, "derived," patterns build their nomen agentis by adding /-aan/ to their active participle: ܡܩܰܒܠܳܢ /mqablaan/ 'receiver' from Pa. ܡܩܰܒܶܠ /mqabbel/ (with vowel deletion); ܡܒܰܪܟ݂ܳܢ /mvarkaan/ 'one who blesses' from Pa. ܡܒܰܪܶܟ݂; ܡܰܣܟܠܳܢ /masklaan/ 'sinner' from Af. ܡܰܣܟܶܠ /maskel/. For the feminine, of these nomina agentis, see above, § 20.

By extension, a nomen agentis may be used adjectivally: ܕܳܪܳܐ ܡܚܰܒܠܳܢܳܐ 'a corrupt (lit. corrupting) generation'; ܦܽܘܡܳܐ ܐܳܟ݂ܽܘܠܳܐ 'a voracious (lit. eating) mouth'; ܨܠܰܘܳܬ݂ܳܟ݂ ܡܦܰܪܩܳܢܝܳܬ݂ܳܐ 'your saving prayers.'

§ 52 The **infinitive** is always prefixed with an /lm-/ or /lam-/([61]), and, in all the patterns except Peal, ends with /-CaaCu/: Pe ܠܡܶܟܬܰܒ /lmektav/; Pa ܠܰܡܟܰܬܳܒܽܘ /lamkattaavu/; Af ܠܡܰܟܬܳܒܽܘ /lmaktaavu/; Ethpe ܠܡܶܬ݂ܟܬܳܒܽܘ /lmetktaavu/; Ethpa ܠܡܶܬ݂ܟܰܬܳܒܽܘ /lmetkattaavu/; Ettaf ܠܡܶܬܰܟܬܳܒܽܘ

[59] The vowel deletion rule (§ 6 A) neutralises the voice distinction when an inflectional ending is added: e.g. ܡܟܰܬܒܳܐ can be either a Pa. active or passive feminine participle. With some weak roots, however, the distinction remains intact: Af. act.m. ܡܰܪܺܝܡ 'lifting,' f. ܡܰܪܝܡܳܐ, pass. m. ܡܪܳܡ 'lifted,' f. ܡܪܳܡܳܐ.

[60] We give the basic, i.e. m.sg., form: for details, see Paradigm I below.

[61] The choice between the two is governed by the rule § 6 I.

/lmettaktaavu/.

§ 53 Conjugation classes.

The above-described general scheme of conjugation applies to the regular, triconsonantal verb. There are, however, verbs which deviate from this scheme to varying degrees. These irregular verbs consist of those with Alaf, Yodh, Waw, Nun as one of their radical or those whose second and third radicals are identical: thus Second-Alaf verbs, Third-Alaf verbs, First-Nun verbs, First-Alaf verbs, First-Yodh verbs, Third-Yodh verbs, Second Waw or Yodh verbs, and Geminate verbs. Some of the deviations from the regular pattern can be explained in terms of one or other of the phonetic rules, but not all.

§ 54 The following **inflectional affixes** are applicable irrespective of pattern and conjugational class (§ 53) with the exception of Third-Yodh verbs, on which see below, § 64.

Perfect

sg.	3m.	-	pl. ܘ- (silent) [-, ܘܢ-]([62])
	f.	ܬ- /-at/	- [ܝ- (silent); ܝܢ-]
	2m.	ܬ- /-t/	ܬܘܢ- /-ton/ [WS: ܬܘܢ /tun/]
	f.	ܬܝ- /-t/	ܬܝܢ- /-teen/
	1c.	ܬ- /et/	ܢ- /-n/, ܢܢ- /-nan/

Imperfect([63])

sg.	3m.	ܢ-	pl.	ܢ ... ܘܢ	/n ... un/
	f.	ܬ-([64])		ܢ .... ܢ	/n ... aan/
	2m.	ܬ-		ܬ .... ܘܢ	/t ... un/
	f.	ܬ.. ܝܢ /t ... in/		ܬ ... ܢ	/t ... aan/
	1c.	ܐ-		ܢ-	/n- /

[62] Rare forms are enclosed within the square brackets.

[63] The prefix consonants may be followed by a vowel: /a/, /e/ or /ee/, or no vowel at all. The choice is determined by pattern (Pe, Pa etc.) and/or conjugation class (regular, First-Alaf etc.).

[64] In WS a silent Yodh is often added at the end to distinguish the form from that of the 2m.sg. The Yodh common with the Pf. 3f.pl. in late WS texts serves to distinguish the form from that of the 3m.sg. (except in Third-Yodh verbs).

Imperative

sg. m.	-	pl.	ܘ- (silent) [ܘܢ-]
f.	ܝ- (silent)		ܝܢ̈- [ܝ- (silent)]

Participle

sg. m.	-	pl.	ܝܢ- /... in/
f.	ܐ- /... aa/		ܢ̈-([65]) /... aan/

§ 55 **Triconsonantal regular verb**. (Paradigm I)

Whereas Paradigm I presents the complete conjugation of a regular verb ܟܬܰܒ /k̲tav/ 'to write,' the basic pattern, Peal, has the following sub-patterns in respect of the stem vowel, a vowel following the second radical:

	Perfect	Imperfect and Imperative
1.	*a*	*o*([66])
2.	*a*	*e*
3.	*a*	*a*
4.	*e*	*a*
5.	*e*	*e*
6.	*e*	*o*
7.	*e*	*e*([67])

Whereas the type to which a given verb belongs is not always predictable—such information may be found in standard dictionaries as well as in the Glossary at the end of this work—the following observations may be made.

a) Type 1 (*a-o*) is by far the commonest: e.g. ܟܬܰܒ /k̲tav/, ܢܶܟܬܘܿܒ /nek̲tov/.

b) Type 2 (*a-e*) is attested by two regular verbs—ܥܒܰܕ /ʿvad̲/ 'to

[65] Where the short and long forms are given, the former are the older. The imperative forms other than that for the m.sg. retain the middle vowel, as in BA, showing that these are affiliated with the shorter, so-called jussive forms, which are distinct from the normal imperfect forms from which the middle vowel is deleted in accordance with the vowel deletion rule.

[66] This vowel, also of type 6, appears as /u/ in WS.

[67] Two verbs attest to the vowel pattern /o-o/: ܣܡܘܿܪ 'to bristle' and ܐܟܘܿܡ 'to be black.'

make,' ܢܥܒܕ /neʿbed̲/; ܙܒܢ /zvan/ 'to buy,' ܢܙܒܢ /nezben/—as well as by some First-Nun verbs like ܢܦܠ /nfal/ 'to fall,' ܢܦܠ /neppel/; ܢܦܨ /nfaṣ/ 'to shake,' ܢܦܨ /neppeṣ/.

c) Type 3 (*a-a*) is frequent with Third-Guttural verbs, but not confined to them: e.g. ܫܡܥ /šmaʿ/ 'to hear,' ܢܫܡܥ /nešmaʿ/, but also ܫܠܛ /šlaṭ/ 'to rule,' ܢܫܠܛ /nešlaṭ/; ܥܡܠ /ʿmal/ 'to toil,' ܢܥܡܠ /neʿmal/.(68)

d) Type 4 (*e-a*), intransitive *par excellence*, is rather common: ܕܡܟ /dmek̲/ 'to sleep,' ܢܕܡܟ /ned̲mak̲/; ܣܠܩ /sleq/ 'to ascend,' ܢܣܩ /nessaq/ (with the assimilation of Lamadh: §§ 6M, 61); ܪܚܡ /rḥem/ 'to love,' ܢܪܚܡ /nerḥam/, ܫܠܡ /šlem/ 'to be at peace,' ܢܫܠܡ /nešlam/.

e) Type 5 (*e-o*) is attested only by ܢܚܬ /nḥet̲/ 'to descend,' ܢܚܘܬ /neḥḥot̲/ (the Nun assimilated: § 61); ܣܓܕ /sḡed̲/ 'to worship,' ܢܣܓܘܕ /nesgod̲/; ܩܪܒ /qrev/ 'to draw near,' ܢܩܪܘܒ /neqrov/; ܫܬܩ /št̲eq/ 'to keep silent,' ܢܫܬܘܩ /neštoq/.

f) Type 6 (*e-e*) is confined to ܝܬܒ /yit̲ev/ 'to sit,' ܢܬܒ /nettev/ (see below § 63).(69)

§ 56 Both stem vowels of each of the seven sub-patterns described in the preceding paragraph are subject to deletion (§ 6 A), except in the Imperative, which retains the stem vowel even with the addition of an ending, not only silent consonant (see n. 65 above): e.g. ܟܬܘܒ, ܟܬܘܒܝ, ܟܬܘܒܘ, ܟܬܘ̈ܒܝ (all pronounced /kt̲ov/), ܟܬܘܒܝܢ.

The distinction in the Perfect between *a* sub-pattern and *e* sub-pattern is retained except in the 1sg. and 3f.sg.—

3sg.m.	ܩܒܪ	/qvar/	'he buried'	ܩܪܒ	/qrev/ 'he drew near'
f.	ܩܒܪܬ	/qevrat̲/		ܩܪܒܬ	/qerbat̲/
2sg.m.	ܩܒܪܬ	/qvart/		ܩܪܒܬ	/qrevt/
1sg.	ܩܒܪܬ	/qevret̲/		ܩܪܒܬ	/qerbet̲/
3pl.m.	ܩܒܪܘ	/qvar/		ܩܪܒܘ	/qrev/

§ 57 Beghadhkephath (§ 6H).

a) A plosive, one of the six consonants, Beghadhkephath, is

68 Unlike in Hebrew, Third-Guttural verbs may have an *o* in the Imperfect: e.g. ܢܛܒܘܥ 'he shall immerse.'

69 For a comparative Semitic description, see Aro 1964.

pronounced soft when it occurs as the second member of a consonant cluster—CCv—at the beginning of a word or a syllable: ܫܒܰܩ /švaq/ 'he abandoned'; ܡܒܰܪܶܟ݂ /mvarrek̲/ 'blessing'; ܐܶܬ݂ܩܒܰܪ /ʾet̲qvar/ 'he was buried.'

b) In Peal a Beghadhkephath as third radical becomes hard in Pf. 3f.sg. and 1sg.: ܩܪܶܒ /qrev/ 'he drew near,' but 3f.sg. ܩܶܪܒܰܬ݂ /qerbat̲/ and 1sg. ܩܶܪܒܶܬ݂ /qerbet̲/.

c) In the Peal participle, a Beghadhkephath as third radical is pronounced hard if an ending is added: ܢܳܩܶܦ /naaqef/ 'consorting,' but f. ܢܳܩܦܳܐ /naaqpaa/.

d) In Ethpeel, a Beghadhkephath as third radical is pronounced hard when a helping vowel *a* is inserted([70]) after the first radical, which happens in Pf. 3f.sg. and 1sg., Impf. 2f.sg., 2 and 3 pl., all forms of the participle except the m.sg., and the Impv.: e.g. ܐܶܬ݂ܪܰܕܦܰܬ݂ /ʾet̲rad̲pat̲/ 'she was persecuted,' ܬܶܬ݂ܪܰܕܦܺܝܢ /tet̲rad̲pin/ 'you (f.sg.) will be persecuted,' ܐܶܬ݂ܗܰܦܶܟ݂ /ʾet̲hafk/ 'Change!'

e) In Afel, a Beghadhkephath as second radical is always pronounced hard: e.g. ܐܰܟܦܰܪ /ʾak̲par/ 'to compel to renounce faith' (with *e* to *a* before *r* : § 6 B).

f) In Pael and Ethpaal, a plosive as second radical is always pronounced hard: ܩܰܒܶܠ /qabbel/ 'to receive,' ܐܶܬ݂ܩܰܒܰܠ /ʾet̲qabbal/ 'to be received,' Pa., inf. ܠܡܩܰܒܳܠܽܘ /lamqabbaalu/.

In these two patterns the third radical, if a plosive, is always pronounced soft. Hence the distinction between Ethpe. Ptc. f.sg. ܡܶܬ݂ܥܰܒܕܳܐ /met̲ʿavdaa/ 'being made' and Ethpa. Ptc. f.sg. ܡܶܬ݂ܩܰܪܒܳܐ /met̲qarvaa/ 'approaching.'

g) In Pael Impf. 1sg. the first radical is always doubled, hence pronounced hard, if it is a plosive: ܐܶܒܰܪܶܟ݂ /ʾebbarrek̲/ 'I shall bless.'

§ 58 The <*e* to *a*> rule (§ 6B) is regularly applied to Peal Ptc., Pael, Afel, and Ethpeel: e.g., Pe. Ptc. m.sg. ܩܳܒܰܪ /qaavar/ 'burying' < /*qaaver/; Pa. Pf. ܫܰܕܰܪ /šaddar/ 'he sent' < /*šadder/; Ethpe. Pf. ܐܶܬ݂ܩܒܰܪ /ʾet̲qvar/ 'he was buried' < /*ʾet̲qver/. This has the effect of neutralising the

[70] Perhaps more correct to say that this *a* is original: /*ʾet̲paʿel/ > /ʾet̲pʿel/ (vowel deletion).

distinction between the active and passive participles in Pael and Afel: thus ܡܫܰܕܰܪ /mšaddar/ can mean either 'sending' (act.) or 'sent' (pass.).

§ 59 Second-Alaf verbs.

The phonological rule (§ 6K) governs the conjugation of a common verb ܫܐܠ: Pe Pf. ܫܶܐܠ /šel/ < /*šʔel/ 'he demanded'; Impf. ܢܶܫܰܐܠ /nešal/ < /*nešʔal/; Inf. ܠܡܶܫܰܐܠ /lmešal/ < /*lmešʔal/; Ptc. pass. ܫܺܐܝܠ /šil/ < /*šʔil/; Ethpe Pf. ܐܶܫܬܶܐܶܠ /ʔeštel/ < /*ʔeštʔel/ (with metathesis: § 6N).

§ 60 Third-Alaf verbs.

A very small number of verbs are conjugated as if their final Alaf were still a genuine guttural, though it is actually a silent letter, and thus the phonological rule § 6K applies. The most common of this group is ܒܝܐ 'to comfort': Pa. Pf. ܒܰܝܰܐ /bayya/ (as if < /*bayyeʔ/ (§ 6B), but 1sg. ܒܰܝܶܐܬ݂ /bayyet̲/ (§ 6K); Pa. Impf. ܢܒܰܝܰܐ /nvayya/; Pa. Ptc. act. and pass. ܡܒܰܝܰܐ /mvayya/. So also ܛܰܡܰܐ /ṭamma/ 'to defile.'([71])

§ 61 First-Nun verbs.

A vowelless Nun is assimilated in Peal Imperfect, Afel and Ettafal. This Nun is absent in the Imperative of most verbs of this type.([72]) Otherwise the conjugation is regular: e.g. Pe. Ptc. m.sg. ܢܳܦܶܩ /naafeq/ 'exiting.'

	/a-o/	/a-a/	/a-e/
Peal Pf.	ܢܦܰܩ /nfaq/ 'to exit'	ܢܣܰܒ /nsav/ 'to take'	ܢܦܰܠ /nfal/ 'to fall'
Impf.	ܢܶܦܦܽܘܩ /neppoq/	ܢܶܣܣܰܒ /nessav/	ܢܶܦܦܶܠ /neppel/
Impv.	ܦܽܘܩ /poq/	ܣܰܒ /sav/	ܦܶܠ /pel/
Inf.	ܠܡܶܦܦܰܩ /lmeppaq/	ܠܡܶܣܣܰܒ /lmessav/	ܠܡܶܦܦܰܠ /lmeppal/

Afel: Pf. 3m.sg. ܐܰܦܶܩ 'he took out', 1sg. ܐܰܦܩܶܬ݂; Impf. ܢܰܦܶܩ, ܢܰܦܩܽܘܢ; Ptc. ܡܰܦܶܩ; Impv. ܐܰܦܶܩ; Inf. ܠܡܰܦܳܩܽܘ.

Ettafal: Pf. ܐܶܬܬܰܦܰܩ /ʔettappaq/ 'he was taken out,' 3f.sg. ܐܶܬܬܰܦܩܰܬ݂.

Exceptions to the assimilation rule are verbs whose second radical

[71] The majority of original Third-Alaf verbs have gone over to the Third-Yodh class (§ 64).

[72] Exceptions include ܢܕܽܘܪ 'Make a vow!,' ܢܟ݂ܽܘܬ݂ 'Bite!,' verbs which retain the Nun in the Impf. such as ܢܗܰܪ 'Be bright!,' and verbs which are also of the Third-Yodh class like ܢܨܺܝ /nṣi/ 'Quarrel!'

is /h/ (or /ḥ/): e.g. ܐܢܗܪ 'to illuminate'; ܐܢܚܦ 'to be barefoot,' but ܢܚܘܬ 'he will descend' (< ܢܢܚܬ) and Af. ܐܚܬ 'he made to descend' (< *ܐܢܚܬ).

An important verb Impf. ܢܬܠ /nettel/ with Inf. ܠܡܬܠ /lmettal/ belongs here. For the other parts of the conjugation, a different root, ܝܗܒ, is used: § 63 c.

Another common */e-a/* verb ܣܠܩ 'to ascend' may be assigned here: Pf. ܣܠܩ /sleq/, Impf. ܢܣܩ /nessaq/, Impv. ܣܩ /saq/, Inf. ܠܡܣܩ /lmessaq/, Af. ܐܣܩ /ʾasseq/ etc.

§ 62 First-Alaf verbs.

a) In accordance with § 6C, the initial Alaf takes a full vowel: /e/ in Pe Pf. and in the whole of Ethpe, and /a/ in Pe. Ptc. pass. and Pa. Impf. 1sg.—ܐܟܠ /ʾek̲al/ 'he ate, ܐܬܐܟܠ /ʾet̲ek̲el/ (§ 6L) 'it was eaten,' ܐܟܝܠ /ʾak̲il/ 'eaten,' ܐܒܕ /ʾabbed̲/ 'I shall destroy.'

b) In Ethpe. and Ethpa., § 6L applies: ܐܬܐܟܠ /ʾet̲ek̲el/ < *ܐܬܐܟܠ 'was eaten'; ܐܬܐܠܨ /ʾet̲allaṣ/ < *ܐܬܐܠܨ 'was oppressed.' The same rule accounts for ܢܠܦ /nallef/ Pa Impf. < *ܢܐܠܦ 'he shall teach,' Ptc. ܡܠܦ /mallef/ < *ܡܐܠܦ. Note also ܐܠܨ /ʾalleṣ/, which is Pa. Pf. 'he oppressed' as well as Pa. Impf. 1sg. (< *ܐܐܠܨ).

c) The prefix vowel /e/ of the Pe. Impf. and Inf. coalesces with the initial Alaf into /ee/: ܢܐܒܕ /neevad̲/ 'he shall perish'; ܢܐܡܪ /neemar/ 'he shall say'; ܢܐܟܘܠ /neek̲ol/; ܠܡܐܡܪ /lmeemar/ 'to say.' This also applies to verbs which are simultaneously Third-Yodh: ܐܬܐ 'to come'—ܢܐܬܐ /neet̲ee/, ܠܡܐܬܐ /lmeet̲aa/.

The prefix vowel in question is spelled with ◌ܶ in ES, but in WS with ◌ܰ when the stem vowel of the Impf. is /a/ and with First-Alaf/Third-Yodh verbs, but with ◌ܶ when the stem vowel is /o/ (or rather /u/ in WS):

ES	WS	
ܢܐܡܪ	ܢܐܡܪ	'he shall say'
ܢܐܙܠ	ܢܐܙܠ	'he shall go'
ܢܐܦܐ	ܢܐܦܐ	'he shall bake'
ܢܐܚܘܕ /neeḥod̲/	ܢܐܚܘܕ	'he shall seize'

When the Pe Impf. stem vowel is /o/, the Alaf of the Impv. takes /a/, but /e/ if the former is /a/:

	Impf.	Impv.
	ܢܶܐܟܽܘܠ	ܐܶܟܽܘܠ
	ܢܶܐܡܰܪ	ܐܶܡܰܪ
Irregular:	ܢܺܐܙܰܠ	ܙܶܠ from ܐܶܙܰܠ 'to go'([73])

d) In Afel and Ettafal the initial Alaf appears as Waw: ܐܰܘܟܶܠ /ʾawkel/ 'he fed' < ܐܶܟܰܠ 'to eat'; ܐܰܘܒܶܕ /ʾawbed̲/ 'he destroyed' < ܐܶܒܰܕ 'to perish'; Ettaf ܐܶܬܬܰܘܟܰܠ 'he was fed.' The important exception is: ܐܰܝܬܺܝ /ʾayti/ 'he brought' (from ܐܶܬܳܐ 'he came'), Impf. ܢܰܝܬܶܐ /naytee/, Ptc. ܡܰܝܬܶܐ /maytee/, Inf. ܡܰܝܬܳܝܽܘ /maytaayu/. Cf. below, § 63.

e) In Ethpeel some verbs assimilate the initial Alaf to the preceding /t/: ܐܶܬܬܚܶܕ (also spelled ܐܬܚܕ) /ʾetḥed̲/ 'was captured, shut' (< ܐܶܚܰܕ 'to capture, shut'); ܐܶܬܬܰܣܰܪܬܽܘܢ 'you (m.pl.) were bound.' Also once in Ethpa ܐܶܬܬܰܢܰܚ /ʾettanaḥ/ 'he sighed' (< ܐܢܚ).

f) In Pael Impf. 1sg., note the deletion of the prefix vowel /e/: ܐܰܠܶܦ /ʾallef/ < /*ʾeʾallef/ (cp. ܐܶܩܰܒܶܠ 'I shall receive') 'I shall teach.'([74]) In the case of this particular and common verb, the Alaf is not written at all under similar circumstances, not only in this particular form: Ptc. ܡܰܠܶܦ /mallef/; Impf. ܢܰܠܶܦ 'he shall teach'; Inf. ܡܰܠܳܦܽܘ /mallaafu/; nomen agentis ܡܰܠܦܳܢܳܐ /malfaanaa/ 'teacher.'

g) The following is a synopsis in tabular form:

Peal

Pf. ܐܶܟܰܠ, ܐܶܟܠܶܬ, ܐܶܟܰܠܘ /ʾek̲al/

Impf. ܢܶܐܟܽܘܠ, ܬܶܐܟܽܘܠ, ܬܶܐܟܠܺܝܢ, 1sg. ܐܶܟܽܘܠ; ܢܶܐܡܰܪ, ܬܶܐܡܰܪ, ܬܶܐܡܪܺܝܢ, ܐܶܡܰܪ

Impv. ܐܶܟܽܘܠ ܐܶܟܽܘܠ; ܐܶܡܰܪ, ܐܶܡܰܪ

Inf. ܠܡܶܐܟܰܠ; ܠܡܶܐܡܰܪ

Ptc.pass. ܐܟܺܝܠ; ܐܡܺܝܪ

Ethpeel

Pf. ܐܶܬܐܶܟܶܠ, 3fs. ܐܶܬܐܶܟܠܰܬ; Impf. ܢܶܬܐܶܟܶܠ, ܢܶܬܐܰܟܠܽܘܢ; Impv. ܐܶܬܐܰܟܰܠ

Inf. ܠܡܶܬܐܰܟܳܠܽܘ /lmet̲ek̲aalu/; Ptc. ܡܶܬܐܶܟܶܠ ܡܶܬܐܰܟܠܳܐ /met̲ak̲laa/

[73] The Infinitive is regular: ܠܡܺܐܙܰܠ /lmeezal/.

[74] The form is accidentally identical with Pf. 3m.sg. 'he taught.' In Peal this verb is First-Yodh: ܝܠܶܦ 'to learn.'

Pael

Pf. ܐܰܠܶܨ 'to compel'; Impf. ܢܰܐܠܶܨ, 1sg. ܐܰܠܶܨ; Impv. ܐܰܠܶܨ
Ptc. act. ܡܰܐܠܶܨ, pass. ܡܰܐܠܰܨ; Inf. ܠܡܰܐܠܳܨܽܘ

Ethpaal

Pf. ܐܶܬ݂ܐܰܠܰܨ; Impf. ܢܶܬ݂ܐܰܠܰܨ; Impv. ܐܶܬ݂ܐܰܠܰܨ; Ptc. ܡܶܬ݂ܐܰܠܰܨ; Inf. ܠܡܶܬ݂ܐܰܠܳܨܽܘ

Afel Pf. ܐܰܘܟ݂ܶܠ *Ettafal* Pf. ܐܶܬ݁ܬ݁ܰܘܟ݂ܰܠ—See under First-Yodh verbs (§ 63).

§ 63 First-Yodh verbs.

a) The conjugation in Pael and Ethpaal is entirely regular.

b) In accordance with § 6D, the initial Yodh is provided with a vowel /i/ where the regular verb would have no vowel, namely Pe Pf. except in the 1sg. and 3f.sg., and Ethpe: ܝܺܬ݂ܶܒ݂ /yiṯev/ 'he sat' (but ܝܶܬ݂ܒܰܬ݂ /yeṯbaṯ/ 'she sat'; Ethpe Ptc. ܡܶܬ݂ܝܠܶܕ 'being born.' Such an initial /yi-/ is often spelled ܐܝ-, e.g. ܐܝܢܶܩ /ʾineq/ 'to suck.'

c) In Pe. the commonest pattern is /*e-a*/: e.g. Pf. ܝܺܒܶܫ /yiveš/ 'to be dry'—Impf. ܢܺܐܒܰܫ (WS ܢܺܐܒܰܫ); ܐܺܝܠܶܕ 'to give birth'—ܢܺܐܠܰܕ; ܝܺܠܶܦ 'to learn'—ܢܺܐܠܰܦ. Forms such as ܝܺܩܰܪ 'to be heavy'—ܢܺܐܩܰܪ are not genuine exceptions, for the /a/ of ܝܺܩܰܪ is due to § 6B. Cf. verbs which are also Third-Yodh: Pf. ܐܺܝܡܳܐ 'to swear'—Impf. ܢܺܐܡܶܐ.

The vowel pattern /*e-e*/ is attested with certainty by only one verb: Pf. ܝܬ݂ܶܒ݂ /yiṯev/ 'to sit'—Impf. ܢܺܬ݁ܶܒ݂ /nettev/.

Note a common, but highly irregular verb ܝܗܒ: Pf. ܝܰܗ݇ܒ݂ /yav/ 'he gave' (< /*yhav/?), 2m.sg. ܝܰܗ݇ܒ݂ܬ݁ /yavt/ (but 1sg. ܝܶܗܒܶܬ݂ /yehbeṯ/; 3f.sg. ܝܶܗܒܰܬ݂ /yehbaṯ/), Impv. ܗܰܒ݂ /hav/. In the Impf. and Inf. this verb is represented by another root: ܢܶܬܶܠ, ܐܶܬܶܠ etc. (presumably from √ ܢܬܠ).[75]

The Impv. and Inf. are formed analogously to the Impf.: ܝܺܠܰܦ, ܢܺܐܠܰܦ, ܝܺܠܰܦ (Impv.)[76], ܡܺܐܠܰܦ; ܝܺܬ݂ܶܒ݂, ܢܺܬ݁ܶܒ݂, ܬ݂ܶܒ݂, ܠܡܶܬ݁ܰܒ݂. In other words, in the /*e-e*/ pattern, the initial Yodh is absent in the Impv.

[75] The alleged Impf. ܢܶܗܒ݂, attested twice (according to Brockelmann 1928:298), is doubtful: one occurs in a 12th cent. manuscript, and the other alongside a ptc., ܝܗܒ, hence easily a scribal error for ܢܶܬܶܠ. The Inf. ܠܡܶܗܰܒ݂ occurs rarely, usually replaced by ܠܡܶܬܰܠ.

Brockelmann (1962: § 175) holds that the striking final Lamadh of ܢܶܬܶܠ is due to the preposition Lamadh, which must often have followed the verb.

[76] E.g. Is 1.17; Mt 9.13.

d) In Afel and Ettafal, as in First-Alaf verbs, the initial Yodh appears as Waw: ܐܰܘܬܶܒ /ʾawtev/ 'to settle'; ܐܶܬܬܰܘܬܰܒ /ʾettawtav/ 'to be settled'; ܐܰܘܕܰܥ /ʾawdaʿ/ 'to make known.' Only two verbs show a Yodh instead: ܐܰܝܢܶܩ /ʾayneq/ 'to suckle'; ܐܰܝܠܶܠ 'to bemoan.'

e) The following is a synopsis in tabular form:

Peal

Pf. ܝܙܰܦ 'to borrow,' ܝܶܙܦܰܛ /yezpaṯ/, ܝܶܙܦܶܬ etc.

Impf. ܢܺܐܙܰܦ, ܢܺܐܙܦܽܘܢ etc. Impv. ܙܰܦ, ܙܰܦܝ etc.

ܢܺܬܶܒ, ܢܺܬܒܽܘܢ etc. ܬܶܒ, ܬܶܒܝ etc.

ܢܺܕܰܥ, ܢܺܕܥܽܘܢ etc. ܕܰܥ, ܕܰܥܝ etc.

Inf. ܠܡܺܐܙܰܦ, ܠܡܺܬܰܒ, ܠܡܺܕܰܥ

Ethpeel

Pf. ܐܶܬܝܙܶܦ, ܐܶܬܝܰܙܦܰܬ, ܐܶܬܝܰܙܦܶܬ etc. Impf. ܢܶܬܝܙܶܦ, ܢܶܬܝܰܙܦܽܘܢ etc.

Inf. ܠܡܶܬܝܙܳܦܽܘ

Afel

Pf. ܐܰܘܙܶܦ 'to lend,' Impf. ܢܰܘܙܶܦ, Impv. ܐܰܘܙܶܦ, Ptc. ܡܰܘܙܶܦ, Inf. ܠܡܰܘܙܳܦܽܘ

Ettafal

Pf. ܐܶܬܬܰܘܙܰܦ, Impf. ܢܶܬܬܰܘܙܰܦ, Ptc. ܡܶܬܬܰܘܙܰܦ, Inf. ܠܡܶܬܬܰܘܙܳܦܽܘ([77])

§ 64 Third-Yodh verbs (Paradigm II).([78])

This class comprises a very considerable number of verbs, and deviates from the regular verbs the most widely. Hence it calls for the maximum attention.

a) As in the case of the regular, triradical class which has two subgroups in Peal differentiated by the stem vowel in the Pf. (§ 56) —ܩܒܰܪ /qvar/ vs. ܩܪܶܒ /qrev/—Syriac shows a similar division among its Third-Yodh verbs in Peal: the more common type ܪܡܳܐ /rmaa/ 'to

[77] The expected Impv. of the type ܐܶܬܬܰܘܙܰܦ hardly occurs.

[78] In spite of the fact that the basic form traditionally quoted as representative of this class of verbs, namely Pe. Pf. 3m.sg., is spelled with Alaf as the third radical, it is best to call them "Third-Yodh" for a number of reasons, one such being that, although the great majority of original and genuine Third-Yodh verbs behave in Syriac exactly like original Third-Alaf verbs, there do still exist a small number of genuine Lamadh-Alaf verbs (§ 60).

The Ettafal is excluded from the paradigm on account of its extreme rarity.

throw' as against ܕܟܝ /dk̲i/ 'to be clean.' Other examples of the second type are ܚܕܝ /ḥd̲i/ 'to rejoice,' ܣܪܝ /sri/ 'to stink,' ܨܗܝ /ṣhi/ 'to be thirsty,' ܠܐܝ /li/ for /*lʾi/ (§ 6K) 'to be weary.'(79) Unlike with the regular verb, this division applies only to the Pf. Elsewhere in the Pe. paradigm there is a single type.

b) In the Pf. 2nd person, both sg. and pl., the suffix Taw is pronounced hard, even when it is preceded by a full vowel: e.g., not only in ܪܡܝܬ /rmayt/ (diphthong), but also in ܚܕܝܬ /ḥd̲it/ 'you (m.sg.) rejoiced,' which contrasts with ܚܕܝܬ /ḥd̲it̲/ 'I rejoiced.' This distinction applies to *all* patterns, not just Peal. Cf. § 6H. In the first Peal subgroup this 1sg. ending is spelled ܪܡܝܬ in ES, but ܪܡܝܬ in WS.

c) The pattern of all derived conjugations in the Pf. is similar to that of the ܕܟܝ type mentioned above: thus

	Peal	Pael	Afel
	'to be clean'	'to cleanse'	'to multiply' (√ ܣܓܐ)
3m.sg.	ܕܟܝ /dk̲i/	ܕܟܝ /dakki/	ܐܣܓܝ /ʾasgi/
f.sg.	ܕܟܝܬ /dek̲yat̲/	ܕܟܝܬ /dakyat̲/	ܐܣܓܝܬ /ʾasgyat̲/
2m.sg.	ܕܟܝܬ /dk̲it/	ܕܟܝܬ /dakkit/	ܐܣܓܝܬ /ʾasgit/
1c.	ܕܟܝܬ /dk̲it̲/	ܕܟܝܬ /dakkit̲/	ܐܣܓܝܬ /ʾasgit̲/
3m.pl.	ܕܟܝܘ /dk̲iw/	ܕܟܝܘ /dakkiw/	ܐܣܓܝܘ /ʾasgiw/

d) This is the only conjugation class in which the ending Waw for 3m.pl. *is* pronounced (ܪܡܘ /rmaw/; ܚܕܝܘ /ḥd̲iw/), not only in Pe, but in every pattern: e.g. Pa ܕܟܝܘ /dakkiw/ 'they cleansed.' Also in this class only are the Pf. 3m.pl. and 3f.pl. systematically distinguished: e.g. 3m.pl. Pe ܪܡܝܘ /rmiw/, Pa ܚܕܝܘ /ḥaddiw/ 'they gladdened' as against 3f.pl. Pe ܪܡܝ /rmay/, Pa ܚܕܝ /ḥaddi/.

e) The Impf. 2/3 m.pl. ending /-on/ appears in WS as /-un/: ES ܢܪܡܘܢ /nermon/, WS ܢܪܡܘܢ.

f) The original Yodh as third radical is often evident: for instance, in the Inf. in all derived conjugations Pa ܠܡܕܟܝܘ /lamd̲akkaayu/, Pe Inf. with a pronoun suffix, ܠܡܪܡܝܗ /lmermyaah/ 'to throw her', Pe Pf. 2m.sg. ܪܡܝܬ /rmayt/, Ptc. f.sg. Pe ܪܡܝܐ /raamyaa/, Af ܡܣܓܝܐ

79 Here belongs also ܐܫܬܝ /ʾešti/ 'to drink,' despite the secondary, initial Alaf, which occurs in the Pf. and Impv. only.

/masgyaa/ 'multiplying, ' f.pl. ܡܣܓܝ̈ܢ /masgyaan/, Pe Impv. f.sg. ܪܡܝ /rmaay/.

g) In the Ethpe Impv., WS has ܐܬܪܡܝ /ʔeṯrmay/, for which ES has ܐܬܪܡܝܝ /ʔeṯramy/, which is modelled on the regular verb.

h) As against the standard /-i/ ending of the Pe. Impv., a few verbs show the archaic ending /-ay/: ܝܡܝ /yimay/ 'to swear' alongside of ܝܡܝ /yimi/; ܐܫܬܝ /ʔeštay/ 'to drink.'

§ 65 Second-Waw or -Yodh verbs (Paradigm III).

The outstanding feature of this class of verbs is that in most forms one sees only two radicals with or without an undeletable vowel /i/ or /u/ in the middle. Verbs with such an /i/ are called Second-Yodh, and those with an /u/ Second-Waw.

a) The deviation from the regular type is observed in Peal, Afel, and Ettafal, whereas in Pael and Ethpaal the conjugation is regular, /y/ serving as middle radical: e.g. Pa ܩܝܡ /qayyem/ 'to establish'; Ethpa ܐܬܩܝܡ /ʔeṯqayyam/ 'to be established.'

b) ܡܝܬ /miṯ/ is the only Second-Yodh verb that shows a vowel letter between the two radicals in the Pf., all other verbs showing no such. The characteristic Waw or Yodh appears only in the Impf. and Impv.

	Second-Waw	Second-Yodh
Impf. 3m.sg.	ܢܩܘܡ /nqum/ 'he shall rise'	ܢܣܝܡ /nsim/ 'he shall put'
Impv. m.sg.	ܩܘܡ /qum/	ܣܝܡ /sim/

The above-mentioned ܡܝܬ is irregular: Impf. ܢܡܘܬ /nmuṯ/; Impv. ܡܘܬ /muṯ/.

c) The Ethpeel has been replaced by Ettafal, and there is only one paradigm, irrespective of whether a given verb is Second-Waw or Seocnd-Yodh: ܐܬܬܩܝܡ /ʔetqim/ 'it was constituted'; ܐܬܬܣܝܡ /ʔetsim/ 'he was put.'

§ 66 Geminate verbs (Paradigm IV)([80])

In the patterns other than Pael and Ethpaal, in which the conjugation is regular, only one of the two last, identical radicals is visible in most

[80] Cf. Boyd 1982.

of the forms as they are spelled.

a) In prefixed forms, i.e. Pe. Impf. and Inf., the whole of Af. and Ettaf., verbs of this class are conjugated like First-Nun verbs, this putative Nun getting assimilated to the first radical. Thus Pe Impf. ܢܒܘܙ /nebboz/ 'he shall plunder' as if from /*nenboz/, though the real root is √ ܒܙܙ. Likewise Pe Inf. ܠܡܒܙ /lmebbaz/ as if from /*lmenbaz/; Af Pf. ܐܥܠ /ʔaʿʿel/ 'he introduced' < √ ܥܠܠ 'to enter.'

b) Where two identical radicals have no vowel in between, a shorthand spelling is used, though phonetically there is a doubling, as in Pe Pf. 3f.sg. ܒܙܬ /bezzat/ 'she plundered,' Pe Ptc. act. f.sg. ܒܐܙܐ /baazzaa/ (= ܒܙܙܐ).

c) A Beghadhkephath as the identical last radical is pronounced hard in the Pe Ptc. f.sg., m./f. pl., and Pf. 3f.sg. and 1sg.: e.g. from ܦܟ /pak/ 'to shatter' we have therefore Ptc. ܦܟܐ /paakkaa/, ܦܟܝܢ /paakkin/, ܦܟܢ /paakkaan/, ܦܟܬ /pakkat/, and ܦܟܬ /pakket/.

d) In Pe, if one looks at the consonants only, the conjugation of many Second-Waw verbs and that of geminate verbs resemble each other very much, but a careful comparison of the two paradigms (III and IV) would reveal very many subtle differences in terms of the vowel length (e.g. ܩܡ /qaam/ vs. ܬܟ /tak/), the gemination or lack of it (e.g. ܢܩܘܡ /nqum/ vs. ܢܬܘܟ /nettok/) and a few more features.

e) In Pe Pf. there is only one pattern, with /a/. In the Impf. the stem vowel is /o/, /a/ or /e/, the last of which is represented by one verb only, ܢܦܕ /nepped/ 'he shall stray.' An example of the /a/ pattern is ܢܪܓ /nerrag/ 'he shall desire.'

f) In Ethpe the second and third radicals are kept apart: ܐܬܒܙܙ, not *ܐܬܒܙ, although the above-mentioned shorthand spelling is occasionally found as in Ptc. f.sg. ܡܬܦܣܐ 'chopped' for *ܡܬܦܣܣܐ.

§ 67 Some common anomalous verbs

ܐܫܟܚ /ʔeškaḥ/ Af 'to find, to be able to.'

ܐܬܐ Pe 'to come': Impv. sg.m. ܬܐ, f. ܬܝ /taay/, pl.m. ܬܘ /taw/, f. ܬܝܢ /taayeen/. Af. ܐܝܬܝ /ʔayti/ 'to bring.' Ettaf. ܐܬܬܝܬܝ /ʔettayti/ 'to be brought.'

ܐܙܠ Pe 'to go.' On the assimilation of /l/ as in Ptc. f.sg. ܐܙܠܐ

/ʾaazzaa/, see above, § 6M. Impf. ܢܐܙܠ /neezal/; Impv. ܙܠ /zel/ (with /e/!). On the assimilation of the same consonant in another verb of physical movement, ܣܠܩ /sleq/ 'to ascend,' see § 6M.

ܝܗܒ Pe 'to give.' Where the He would have been followed by the vowel /a/, the former is elided: 2m.sg. ܝܗܒܬ /yavt/, but 3f.sg. ܝܗܒܬ /yehbat/ and 1sg. ܝܗܒܬ /yehbet/. Impv. ܗܒ. The Impf. is ܢܬܠ /nettel/; likewise the Inf. ܠܡܬܠ /lmettal/ (very rarely ܠܡܗܒ /lmehhav/).

ܚܝܐ Pe 'to live.' The Pf. is regular: ܚܝܐ, ܚܝܬ, ܚܝܝܬ /ḥyayt/ etc., but Impf. ܢܚܐ /neḥḥee/, Inf. ܠܡܚܐ /lmeḥḥaa/, Af. ܐܚܝ /ʾaḥḥi/ 'to allow to stay in life,' all these as from a geminate root.

§ 68 Verbs with object suffix pronouns

Details need to be studied carefully from Paradigms V and VI. The following is a summary of the more important points. The forms of the object suffixes may be found in § 12.

a) The vowel deletion rule (§ 6A) is much in evidence: e.g. ܩܒܠܬܢܝ /qabbeltaan/ 'you (m.sg.) received me' but ܩܒܠܗ /qablaah/ 'he received her.'

b) The personal endings of the verb in the Perfect, to which object pronouns are attached, often differ from those of their free-standing equivalents.([81])

2m.sg. ending /-taa/ as in ܫܕܪܬܢܝ /šaddartaan/ 'you sent me'

2f.sg. ending /-ti/ as in ܫܕܪܬܝܢ /šaddartin/ 'you sent us'

3m.pl. ending /-u/ as in ܫܕܪܘܗ /šadruh/ 'they sent her'

3f.pl. ending /-aa/ as in ܫܕܪܟ /šadraak/ 'they sent you (m.sg.)'

1sg. with hard /t/ as against 3f.sg. with soft /t/ as in Af. ܐܦܩܬܗ /ʾappeqteeh/ 'I took him out' vs. ܐܦܩܬܗ /ʾappeqteeh/ 'she took him out'

the initial vowel /a/ of Pe. as in ܦܪܩܢܝ /parqan/ 'he saved me.'

c) The plural 'them' is expressed by means of a free-standing enclitic form: m. ܐܢܘܢ /ʾennon/ and f. ܐܢܝܢ /ʾenneen/. A participle requires, however, ܠܗܘܢ and ܠܗܝܢ respectively. E.g. ܫܕܪܬ ܐܢܘܢ /šadret ʾennon/ 'I sent them' vs. ܡܫܕܪ ܐܢܐ ܠܗܘܢ /mšaddar naa lhon/ 'I send them.'

[81] In general these deviating endings are more archaic.

d) When a verb form itself ends in /n/, this consonant is followed by /aa/ before the suffix with the exception of the 2f.sg. suffix ܟܝ /-eek̲/. This happens in Pf. 1pl., 2pl.; Impf. 2f.sg., and 3pl.; longer Impv. pl. with /n/. E.g., ܩܰܒܶܠܢܳܗ̇ /qabbelnaah/ 'we received her'; ܩܰܒܶܠܬܽܘܢܳܢ /qabbeltonaan/ 'you (m.pl.) received us'; ܬܩܰܒܠܺܝܢܳܢܝ /tqabbelinaan/ 'you (f.sg.) shall receive me'; ܐܰܪܺܝܡܽܘܢܳܗ̇ /ʔarimunaah/ 'Raise (m.pl.) her!.'

e) The 3m.sg. suffix is realised in a variety of ways. If a verb form ends in a consonant, the suffix itself is ܗ /-eeh/. If the former ends in a vowel, the suffix is uniformly spelled with a ܗ, which, however, is pronounced in various ways:

after /-aa/— ܗܝ /-aay/ as in ܩܰܒܶܠܬܳܗܝ /qabbeltaay/ 'you (m.sg.) accepted him'

after /-i/— ܝܗܝ /-iw/ as in ܫܰܕܰܪܬܺܝܗܝ /šaddartiw/ 'you (f.sg.) sent him'

after /-u/— ܘܗܝ /-uy/ as in ܫܰܕܪܽܘܗܝ /šadruy/ 'they sent him'

after /-ee/— ܝܗܝ /-eew/ as in ܢܰܚܶܝܗܝ /naḥḥeew/ 'we shall restore him to life.'

f) The Impf. forms ending in a consonantal radical, namely 3m./f.sg., 2m.sg., and 1sg./pl., insert an /-i/ before the 3sg. suffixes: e.g. ܐܰܣܩܺܝܗܝ /ʔasqiw/ 'I shall bring him up' (with the combination of the rule given above, [**d**]); ܬܰܦܩܺܝܗ̇ /tapqih/ 'you (m.sg.) [or: she] will bring her out.'

g) The Impv. m.sg., if ending in a consonantal radical, shows three allomorphs:

/-ay/ with a 1sg./pl. suffix as in ܣܺܝܡܰܝܢܝ /simayn/ 'Place me!'

/-aa/ with a 3m.sg. suffix as in ܣܺܝܡܳܝܗܝ /simaay/ 'Place him!' (with the rule [**e**] also at work)

/-ee/ with a 3 f.sg. suffix as in ܣܺܝܡܶܝܗ̇ /simeeh/ 'Place her!'

h) Third-Yodh verbs (Paradigm VI) retain in Peal the vowel /-aa/ of the 3m.sg., but without a merely graphic Alaf: e.g. ܒܥܳܐ /bʕaa/ 'he sought' vs. ܒܥܳܟ /bʕaak̲/ 'he sought you (m.sg.).' Likewise with the vowel endings of the root in the Impf. and Impv.: e.g. ܢܶܒܥܶܐ /nevʕee/ vs. ܢܶܒܥܶܝܢ /nevʕeen/ 'he will seek us'; ܒܥܺܝ /bʕi/ Impv. Pe m.sg. vs. ܒܥܺܝܢܝ /bʕin/ 'Seek me!'; Pa ܓܰܠܳܐ /gallaa/ 'Reveal!' vs. ܓܰܠܳܝܗܝ /gallaay/ 'Reveal him!' (with the rule [**e**] also at work).

i) The /-i/ of the Pf. 3m.sg. in Pa and Af and the /-aa/ of the Pe Inf. change to /-y/ except before the 2pl. suffixes, ܟܘܢ and ܟܝܢ: e.g. ܓܠܝ /galli/ 'he revealed,' but ܓܠܝܢܝ /galyan/ 'he revealed me' and ܓܠܝܟܘܢ /galli<u>k</u>on/ 'he revealed you (m.pl.)'; ܠܡܓܠܐ /lmeḡlaa/ 'to reveal' but ܠܡܓܠܟ /lmeḡlaa<u>k</u>/ 'to reveal you.'

j) Note the shift of the /-aw/ in Pf. 3m.pl. and the Impv. m.pl. to /-aʾu/, and the /-iw/ of Pa and Af Pf. 3.m.pl. and Impv. m.pl. to /-yu/, and the /-aay/ of the Impv. f.sg. to /-aaʾi/. E.g. ܪܡܐܘܗ /rmaʾuh/ 'they threw her' or 'Throw her!'; ܚܕܝܘܢܝ /ḥadyun/ 'they gladdened me' or 'Gladden me!'; ܪܡܐܝܢ /rmaaʾin/ 'Throw (f.sg.) us!'

k) The Inf. in the derived patterns, i.e. pattern other than Peal, takes an object suffix after having changed its ending /-u/ to /-u<u>t</u>/: e.g. ܠܡܓܠܝܘ /lamḡallaayu/, but ܠܡܓܠܝܘܬܗ /lamḡallaayu<u>t</u>eeh/ 'to reveal him.'

PART THREE

MORPHOSYNTAX AND SYNTAX

§ 69 Noun: Gender The feminine form of an adjective or a pronoun is sometimes used to refer to an abstract property, a manifestation of it, or a general thought, not an entity whose natural sex is female: e.g. ܐ̄ܚܪܺܬ݂ܳܐ 'something else,' ܗܳܕܶܐ 'this matter, this circumstance,' ܚܕܳܐ ܗ̄ܝ ܕܡܶܬ݂ܒܰܥܝܳܐ 'what is necessary is one,' ܛܳܒ݂ܬܳܐ 'the good.' However, the masculine form may also be so used indiscriminately: 2Sm 19.35 ܠܳܐ ܦܳܪܶܫ ܐ̄ܢܳܐ ܒܶܝܬ݂ ܛܳܒ݂ ܠܒܺܝܫ 'I cannot tell the good from the bad' vs. 1Kg 3.9 ܠܡܶܣܬܰܟܳܠܽܘ ܒܶܝܬ݂ ܛܳܒ݂ܬܳܐ ܠܒܺܝܫܬܳܐ 'to discern the good from the bad'; ܡܶܛܽܠ ܗܳܢܳܐ 'because of this.' In the plural, however, only the feminine is used: ܗܳܠܶܝܢ ܟܽܠ̈ܗܶܝܢ 'all these things'; ܗܳܠܶܝܢ ܬܰܪ̈ܬܰܝܗܶܝܢ 'these two matters.' A subject clause is considered feminine in Mt 19.23 ܥܰܛܺܝܠܳܐ ܗ̄ܝ ܠܥܰܬ݂ܺܝܪܳܐ ܕܢܶܥܽܘܠ ܠܡܰܠܟܽܘܬ݂ ܫܡܰܝܳܐ 'it is hard for a rich man to enter the kingdom of heaven' // ib. 24 ܕܰܦܫܺܝܩ ܗ̄ܘ ܠܓܰܡܠܳܐ ܠܡܶܥܰܠ ܒܚܪܽܘܪܳܐ ܕܡܚܰܛܳܐ 'it is easier for a camel to enter the hole of a needle.'

§ 70 Noun: Number Some nouns are used only in the plural (*pluralia tantum*), even when there is nothing plural about their meaning: e.g. ܡܰ̈ܝܳܐ 'water' (ܡܰ̈ܝܳܐ ܚܰ̈ܝܶܐ 'living [as against stagnant] water'); ܕܡܰ̈ܝܳܐ 'price'; ܚܺܐܪ̈ܽܘܬ݂ܳܐ 'freedom'; ܡܟ݂ܺܝܪ̈ܽܘܬ݂ܳܐ 'betrothal'; ܫܡܰ̈ܝܳܐ 'sky'; ܚܰ̈ܝܶܐ 'life'; ܐ̈ܰܦܶܐ 'face.'

There are nouns which refer to a plurarity of individuals, though singular in form: Mt 8.27 ܐ̄ܢܳܫܳܐ ܐܶܬ݂ܕܰܡܰܪܘ 'some people were amazed'; ib. 9.3 ܐ̄ܢܳܫܳܐ ܡܶܢ ܣܳܦ̈ܪܶܐ 'some of the scribes,' cf. ib.12.47 ܐܶܡܰܪ ܠܶܗ ܐ̄ܢܳܫ 'someone said to him' and ܟܽܠ̈ܢܳܫ 'everybody.'

§ 71 Noun: State The severely curtailed use of the absolute state (§ 18) is confined to the following cases([1]):

a) Distributive repetition: e.g. ܟܽܠ ܫܢܳܐ ܘܫܰܢܳܐ 'every year'; ܝܰܘܡ ܡܶܢ

[1] These are not, however, absolute rules: exceptions, namely the use of the emphatic state of the expected absolute, are not few.

ܝܘܡ 'from day to day'; ܥܕܳܢܺܝܢ ܥܕܳܢܺܝܢ /ʿeddaanin/ 'at times'; ܕܓܢܣ ܓܢܣ /dag̱nes .. / 'of all kinds'; Mt 20.9 ܢܣܒܘ ܕܝܢܪ ܕܝܢܪ 'they each got a dinar'; ib. 25.15 ܐܢܫ ܐܢܫ ܐܝܟ ܚܝܠܗ 'each according to his ability.'

b) After ܟܠ or cardinal numerals: e.g. ܒܟܠ ܚܦܝܛܘܬܗ 'with all zeal'; ܟܠ ܐܣܘ̈ܬܐ ܕܒܟܠ ܐܬܪ 'all physicians in every place'; ܚܕܐ ܢܦܫ ܘܚܕ ܪܥܝܢ 'one soul and one mind'; ܬܪܝܢ ܥܠܡܝܢ 'two worlds'; ܐܪܒܥܝܢ ܝܘܡܝܢ ܐܪܒܥܝܢ ܠܠܝܢ 'forty days and forty nights.' Likewise ܟܡܐ ܙܒܢܝܢ 'how many times?'

c) With negatives: e.g. ܠܝܬ ܡܘܬܪܐ 'there is no gain'; ܕܠܐ ܡܢܝܢ 'innumerable'; ܕܠܐ ܟܣܦ 'without money'; ܕܠܐ ܒܢܝܢ 'childless'; ܠܐ ܢܐܡܪ ܐܢܫ 'Let nobody say'; Mt 20.7 ܠܐ ܐܢܫ ܐܓܪܢ 'nobody has hired us.'

d) In certain idiomatic expressions introduced by a preposition: e.g. ܡܢ ܫܠܝ /men šel/ 'suddenly'; ܠܥܠܡ 'for ever'; ܒܪܓܠ 'on foot'; ܒܥܓܠ /baʿgal/ 'in haste.'

e) Adjectives used as predicate of a nominal clause: ܥܝܢܟ ܒܝܫܐ 'your eye is evil'; ܡܝܐ ܓܢܝܒܐ ܚܠܝܢ 'stolen water is sweet'; ܩܠܝܠ ܗܘܐ 'he was fast.' The st. emph. is sometimes used for no apparent reason: Mt 25.35-43 ... ܐܟܣܢܝܐ ܗܘܝܬ ... ܥܪܛܠܝܐ ܗܘܝܬ ... ܟܪܝܗ ܗܘܝܬ ... ܕܐܟܣܢܝܐ ܐܢܬ ... ܕܥܪܛܠܝܐ ܐܢܬ ... ܘܟܪܝܗܐ ܗܘܝܬ 'I was homeless ... I was naked ... I was sick ... that you were homeless ... that you were naked ... and I was sick.'

f) Some forms which look like those of the f.sg.cst. are in reality the residue of the archaic st. abs. used adverbially: ܪܒܬ /rabbaṯ/ 'exceedingly'; ܩܕܡܝܬ 'firstly'; ܐܚܪܝܬ 'in the end' as in Mt 4.2 ܐܚܪܝܬ ܕܝܢ ܟܦܢ 'in the end he became hungry'; Ez 23.29 ܢܫܒܩܘܢܟܝ ܥܪܛܠܝܐ ܘܥܪܝܬ 'they will abandon you bare and naked;' Ac 25.16 ܡܓܢ 'for nothing.'

§ 72 The loss of the originally determining force of the emphatic state of the noun is often compensated by the use of the demonstrative pronoun, especially of the ܗܘ series: Gn 37.15 ܓܒܪܐ ܗܘ (Heb.: הָאִישׁ); Ex 4.9 ܣܒ ܡܢ ܡܝܐ ܕܢܗܪܐ ... ܗܢܘܢ ܡܝܐ ܢܣܒ ܐܢܬ 'Take some water of the river ... you shall take that water (Heb.: הַמַּיִם).' This is especially common where the demonstrative so used is analogous in function to the anaphoric definite article. On the other hand, the addition of a form of the numeral "one" may have the effect of weakening the emphatic to that of the primitive, absolute state: Lk 14.28 ܓܒܪܐ ܚܕ (S omits ܚܕ: Gk ἄνθρωπός τις).

§ 73 Status constructus and periphrasis by means of -ܕ

a) Logical dependence between two nouns is sometimes synthetically expressed by putting the dependent noun in the status constructus as in ܪܒܝ ܟܗܢܐ /rabbay kaahnee/ 'chief priests' (lit. 'great ones among priests'); ܦܣܩ ܕܝܢܐ 'verdict' (lit. 'decision of judgement'). The standard syntax, however, favours periphrasis whereby two adjacent, logically dependent nouns are joined by means of the proclitic particle -ܕ: thus it is more common to say ܪܘܚܐ ܕܩܘܕܫܐ 'the spirt of holiness' (i.e. the Holy Spirit) rather than ܪܘܚ ܩܘܕܫܐ; ܡܠܟܐ ܕܒܒܠ 'the king of Babylon' vs. ܡܠܟ ܒܒܠ; Mt 11.12 ܡܠܟܘܬܐ ܕܫܡܝܐ vs. ib. 11.11 ܡܠܟܘܬ ܫܡܝܐ 'the kingdom of heaven.'

b) The synthetic structure tends to be confined to standing phrases verging on compound nouns as in the first two examples. Likewise ܒܪ ܚܐܪܐ /bar ḥeeree/ 'a son of the free (people),' i.e. free-born, noble man' (and many other combinations with ܒܪ or ܒܪܬ); ܒܝܬ ܟܢܘܫܬܐ 'synagogue' (and countless combinations with ܒܝܬ); even spelled as a single word as in ܫܬܐܣܬܐ 'foundation (of a building)' = ܫܬܬܐ 'ground' + ܐܣܬܐ 'wall.'

c) Note the use of the st. cst. of adjectives and passive participles as in: Ex 32.9 ܩܫܐ ܩܕܠܐ 'stiff-necked'; ܣܓܝ ܕܡܝܐ 'much of price,' i.e. 'costly, expensive,' likewise ܣܓܝܐܬ ܕܡܝܐ (used with a fem. noun); ܢܣܝܒ ܗܘܢܐ 'mind-taken,' i.e. 'mindless, senseless'; ܠܝܛ ܚܝܐ 'cursed of life,' i.e. 'leading an accursed life'; Mt 26.7 ܒܣܡܐ ܣܓܝ ܕܡܝܐ 'pricey perfume.' In most of these cases, though the adjective or participle agrees in gender and number with its grammatical antecedent, its logical antecedent is the noun immediately following. Thus in ܥܡܐ ܩܫܐ ܩܕܠܐ 'a stiff-necked people,' what is stiff is not the nation, but their neck.

d) Where both nouns in a relationship of dependence are logically determined, the dependent noun often takes, by way of anticipation, a pronoun—so-called proleptic—referring to the second noun: e.g.ܒܪܗ ܕܐܠܗܐ 'the son of God' (lit. 'his son, of God'). See below § 112.

e) The second term normally follows the first immediately; only inconsequential words can intervene, e.g. ... ܒܢ̈ܝ ܕܝܢ ܕܒܠܗܐ 'the sons of Bala, however, ...'; ... ܐܠܗܗ ܓܝܪ ܕܫܡܝܐ 'for the god of heaven ...'; ܒܢ̈ܝ ܐܢܘܢ ܕܙܕܝ̈ܩܐ 'they are sons of the righteous'; ܓܢܒܪ ܗܘܐ ܚܝܠܐ 'he was a warrior of might.'

f) The analytic structure makes for far more possibilities and lesser ambiguity of expression than would be the case with the synthetic structure: thus ܒܪܗ ܕܡܠܟܐ 'the son of the king' can be expanded, for instance, to ܒܪܐ ܗܘ ܚܟܝܡܐ ܕܗܕܐ ܡܠܟܬܐ ܪܒܬܐ 'that wise son of this great queen,' when synthetically one could use only one adjective and possibly only one demonstrative pronoun such as ܒܪ ܡܠܟܐ ܪܒܐ ܗܢܐ, which, besides, could mean either 'this great son of the king' or 'the son of this great king' (or possibly also 'this son of the great king'). See Mt 16.16 ܒܪܗ ܕܐܠܗܐ ܚܝܐ 'the son of the living God.'

§ 74 The non-enclitic forms of the **independent personal pronouns** (§ 9) are used with a finite verb, i.e. a verb form which is conjugated in respect of gender, number, and person, where the subject so marked is in contrast to another subject or is given some prominence. E.g. Jer 17.18 ܢܬܬܒܪܘܢ ܗܢܘܢ ܘܠܐ ܐܬܬܒܪ ܐܢܐ 'May *they* be crushed, and may *I* not be crushed!'; Dt 5.27 ܩܪܘܒ ܐܢܬ ... ܘܐܢܬ ܬܡܠܠ ܥܡܢ '*You* draw near ... and *you* shall speak to us' (i.e. we want you to represent us, we do not wish to speak to God ourselves); Mt 14.19 ܗܢܘܢ ܬܠܡܝܕܐ ܫܡܫܘ ܠܟܢܫܐ 'they the disciples (not Jesus Himself) served the crowd.'

A personal pronoun also occurs in introducing the main character to mark a new turn in a narrative: Mt 15.27 ܗܘ ܕܝܢ ܝܫܘܥ ܒܪ ܫܥܬܗ ܡܠܠ ܥܡܗܘܢ 'now Jesus spoke to them immediately.' This occurs often with a personal name as here.

§ 75 The third person forms of the **personal pronouns** can, in addition to persons spoken about, also refer to things, even inanimate, the choice of gender and number being determined by that of the noun of the object being referred to: ܚܙܘ ܩܪܝܬܐ ܘܥܡܪܘ ܒܗ 'they saw a village and lived in it.'

§ 76 Most **interrogative** words, when followed by the proclitic -ܕ, become generalising connectives:

ܡܰܢ "who?" — ܡܰܢ ܕ- 'whoever ...'
ܡܳܢܳܐ "what?" — ܡܳܢܳܐ ܕ- 'whatever, that which'(2)
ܐܰܝܟܳܐ "where?" — ܐܰܝܟܳܐ ܕ- 'wherever, where'
ܐܶܡܰܬܝ "when?" — ܐܶܡܰܬܝ ܕ- 'whenever, when'
ܐܰܝܢܳܐ "which?" — ܐܰܝܢܳܐ ܕ- 'whichever, one who'
ܟܡܳܐ "how much?" — ܟܡܳܐ ܕ- 'as much as'

To ܐܰܝܟܰܢܳܐ 'how?,' however, corresponds a shorter form: ܐܰܝܟ ܕ- /ʔa<u>k</u> d-/ as in ܐܰܝܟ ܕܣܳܒܰܪ ܐ̱ܢܳܐ 'as I think.'

§ 77 The ubiquitous, so-called proclitic **relative pronoun** -ܕ is indeclinable, and indicates that what follows it says something about the antecedent:

ܒܰܝܬܳܐ ܕܶܐܫܟܚܶܬ ܒܶܗ ܣܰܓܺܝ ܟܣܶܦܳܐ 'the house in which I found much money'
ܒܰܝܬܳܐ ܕܥܳܡܽܘܪ̈ܰܘܗ̄ܝ ܐܶܬܰܘ ܡܶܢ ܬܰܡܳܢ 'the house whose residents came from there'
ܢܒܺܝܳܐ ܕܫܰܕܪܶܬܶܗ ܠܘܳܬܟ݂ܽܘܢ 'the prophet whom I sent to you'
ܢܒܺܝܳܐ ܕܶܐܬܳܐ ܠܘܳܬܰܢ 'the prophet who came to us.'

Analogous to combinations mentioned under § 76 are the particle ܕ preceded by ܗܰܘ ܕ 'one who, he who'; ܗܳܝ ܕ 'she who; that which'; ܗܳܢܽܘܢ ܕ, ܗܳܢܶܝܢ ܕ, ܗܳܠܶܝܢ ܕ all meaning 'those who; those things which.' The two structures may be further combined as in ܗܰܘ ܡܰܢ ܕ, ܗܰܘ ܐܰܝܢܳܐ ܕ, and the addition of ܟܠ makes for greater generality: ܟܠ ܡܰܢ ܕ 'whosoever.'

A further variation is achieved when a noun is mentioned as antecedent: ܐܳܠܶܝܢ ܟܰܘܟ݁ܒ̈ܶܐ ܕ 'those stars which'; ܟܬܳܒ̈ܶܐ ... ܗܳܠܶܝܢ ܕ 'those documents ... which.'

The inanimate "that which" may be also expressed thorugh ܡܶܕܶܡ ܕ and ܗܰܘ ܕ-. This can be also expanded as to ܗܰܘ ܡܶܕܶܡ ܕ, and, ܡܶܕܶܡ being indeclinable, it can be also combined with a plural demonstrative as in ܗܳܠܶܝܢ ܡܶܕܶܡ ܕܫܰܦܺܝܪܺܝܢ 'those things which are beautiful.'

[2] Also 'when,' esp. referring to the future, even followed by a Perfect.

§ 78 Many **prepositions** function as logically related conjunctions when combined with the proclitic particle ܕ-.

ܩܕܡ 'before' (of time) — ܩܕܡ ܕ- (ܡܢ) 'before'
ܒܬܪ (ܡܢ) 'after' (of time) — ܒܬܪ ܕ- (ܡܢ) 'after'
ܡܛܠ 'because of' — ܡܛܠ ܕ- 'because'
ܐܝܟ 'like' (of similarity) — ܐܝܟ ܕ- 'just as'(3)

Note also ܥܕ- 'because'; ܥܠ ܕ- 'because'; ܡܢ ܕ- 'after.' The preposition ܥܕ 'until' is also used as a conjunction, however without ܕ- and meaning 'whilst,' 'before' (sometimes with the negative ܠܐ) as well as 'until.' As a preposition for "until" ܥܕܡܐ ܠ- /ʿdammaa l-/ is much more common: e.g. ܥܕܡܐ ܠܪܡܫܐ 'until evening.' As a conjunction for "until" one also uses ܥܕܡܐ ܕ-.

Some prepositions show a complementary distribution of allomorphs:

with a noun	with a suffix
ܡܛܠ ܡܛܪܐ 'because of rain'	ܡܛܠܬܗ 'because of it'
ܒܝܬ ܟܘܒܐ 'among the thorns'	ܒܝܢܬܗܘܢ or ܒܝܢܝܗܘܢ
ܒܝܢܬ ܚܛܐ 'among the wheats'	'amongst them'
ܡܢ ܒܝܢܝ ܙܕܝܩܐ 'from among the rightesous'	
ܐܝܟ ܡܠܟܐ 'like a king'	ܐܝܟܘܬܗ 'like him'

Moreover, with an adverb or a prepositional phrase we find ܐܝܟ ܕ-: ܐܝܟ ܕܒܫܡܝܐ 'as in heaven.'

§ 79 Impersonal passive A passive participle or an Eth-pattern is sometimes used impersonally where the use of the unmarked, third person masculine singular gives prominence to the fact that something is happening or happened, there being no actual actor matching the 3m.sg. noun being understood. Thus ܐܫܬܡܥ ܗܘܐ ܥܠܘܗܝ ܒܟܘܠܗ ܡܕܝܢܬܐ 'he became the talk of the whole town' (lit. 'there was heard on him ...'); Mt 7.2 ܒܟܝܠܬܐ ܕܟܝܠܝܢ ܐܢܬܘܢ ܡܬܟܝܠ ܠܟܘܢ 'with the measure with which you measure out it will be measured out to you.'

§ 80 Eth- conjugations with transitive force. Some verbs in an Eth-conjugation take a direct object: Mt 23.15 ܡܬܟܪܟܝܢ ܐܢܬܘܢ ܝܡܐ ܘܝܒܫܐ 'you go round the sea and the land'; 26.75 ܐܬܕܟܪ ... ܡܠܬܐ ܕܝܫܘܥ 'he

[3] This last, when followed by an Impf. or Inf., indicates a purpose or result.

remembered the word of Jesus'; Gn 42.7 ܐܶܫܬܰܘܕܰܥ ܐܶܢܽܘܢ 'he recognised them.'

§ 81 The **Perfect** indicates something that happened, has happened or had happened, thus essentially a past tense. Some Perfects may have the translation value of the Present, which is true especially of verbs which indicate states, permanent qualities, etc.: ܟܪܺܝܬ ܠܝ 'I am grieved'; ܪܶܓܬܶܢ /regtan/ 'I desire'; ܝܺܕܰܥܢ 'we have come to know, we know' (cf. *novimus*, οἴδαμεν). See also Mt 28.6 ܠܳܐ ܗܘܳܐ ܬܰܢܳܢ 'he is not here' (οὐκ ἔστιν ὧδε).

The Perfect is also used with ܡܳܐ ܕ with reference to an event or action which will have become reality in future: Mt 2.8 ܡܳܐ ܕܐܶܫܟܰܚܬܽܘܢܳܝܗ̱ܝ 'when you have found him.'

The Pf. is common in hypothetical conditional clauses: Mt 23.30 ܐܶܠܽܘ ܗܘܰܝܢ ܒܝܰܘܡܰܝ ܐܰܒܳܗܰܝܢ ܠܳܐ ܗܘܰܝܢ ܗ̄ܘܰܝܢ ܠܗܽܘܢ ܫܰܘܬܳܦܶܐ 'if we had been in the days of our fathers, we would not have been their partners.' In similar vein is the optative use of the tense as in Mc 16.3 ܡܰܢ ܕܶܝܢ ܓܰܠܶܠ 'who would roll (the stone away for us)?'; Dt 28.67 "In the morning you would say ܐܶܡܰܪܬܽܘܢ ܡܰܢ ܕܶܝܢ ܗܘܳܐ ܪܰܡܫܳܐ 'we wish it were evening' (lit. 'when would it be evening?')."

The Pf. is occasionally used to refer to an action which is performed by uttering the verb, so-called performative Perfect: e.g., 1Kg 15.19 ... ܗܳܐ ܫܶܕܪܶܬ ܠܳܟ 'Behold, I send you hereby ...'

§ 82 The **Imperfect** is very rarely used in independent clauses to indicate a future action or state. In such cases it often carries a modal nuance of *can*, *must*, *might*, *should*, *may*, etc.: e.g. Mt 22.13 ܬܰܡܳܢ ܢܶܗܘܶܐ ܒܶܟܝܳܐ 'there shall be weeping there'; Gn 42.37 ܠܬܪ̈ܶܝܢ ܒ̈ܢܰܝ ܬܶܩܛܽܘܠ 'you may kill my two sons.' Such an Impf. is also common in a negative command with ܠܐ as in ܠܳܐ ܬܶܥܽܘܠ 'Do not enter,' since the Imperative itself does not take ܠܐ.

The Imperfect is highly frequent in dependent clauses complementing another verb as in Mk 12.1 ܫܰܪܺܝ ܕܢܶܡܰܠܶܠ 'he began to speak'; Mt 8.18 ܦܰܩܶܕ ܕܢܺܐܙܠܽܘܢ ܠܥܶܒܪܳܐ 'he ordered them to go to the other side'(4); in purpose clauses introduced by ܕ as in Jn 14.2 ܐܳܙܶܠ ܐ̄ܢܳܐ ܕܐܰܛܝܶܒ ܠܟܽܘܢ ܐܰܬܪܳܐ 'I go to prepare a place for you'; in temporal clauses introduced by ܡܩܕܡ ܕ or ܥܕ ܠܐ as in Mt 26.34 ܡܩܕܡ ܕܢܩܪܐ ܬܪܢܓܠܐ 'before a cock crows'; ib. 1.18 ܥܕܠܐ ܢܬܩܪܒܘܢ 'before they came together'; Is 65.24 ܥܕܠܐ ܢܩܪܘܢ ܐܥܢܐ ܐܢܘܢ 'before they call, I shall answer them'; in conditional sentences as in ܐܢ ܢܐܡܪ ܢܚܣܪ 'if we speak, we shall be lacking'; in result clauses introduced by ܐܝܟ ܕ or ܐܝܟܢܐ ܕ: Mt 13.32 "it grew taller than all the other plants, becoming a tree ܐܝܟ ܕܬܐܬܐ ܦܪܚܬܐ ܕܫܡܝܐ ܬܩܢܐ ܒܣܘܟܘܗܝ 'so that a bird of the sky came and made a nest among its boughs'"; ib. 54 "he taught them in their synagogues ܐܝܟܢܐ ܕܢܬܕܡܪܘܢ 'as a result of which they marvelled'"; in final (purpose) clauses, introduced by ܕ, ܐܝܟ ܕ, or ܐܝܟܢܐ ܕ as in Jn 5.34 ܕܐܢ̱ܬܘܢ ܬܚܘܢ 'in order that you may be saved'; Mt 2.13 "Herod was about to seek the child out in order to destroy him (ܐܝܟ ܕܢܘܒܕܝܘܗܝ)"; Mt 5.44f. "they will persecute you so that you may become the children of your heavenly father (ܐܝܟܢܐ ܕܬܗܘܘܢ ܒܢܘܗܝ ܕܐܒܘܟܘܢ ܕܒܫܡܝܐ: ὅπως γένησθε ...)."

§ 83 The **Participle** may indicate what is happening at the moment of speaking (Actual Present) or what often or habitually happens (General Present): ܡܢܐ ܒܥܐ ܐܢ̱ܬ ... ܠܐܚܝ ܒܥܐ ܐ̱ܢܐ 'what are you looking for? .. I am looking for my brothers'; Jn 11.42 ܐܢܐ ܝܕܥ ܐ̱ܢܐ ܕܒܟܠܙܒܢ ܫܡܥ ܐܢ̱ܬ ܠܝ 'I know that you always hear me'; Mt 5.32 ܡܢ ܕܢܣܒ ܫܒܝܩܬܐ ܓܐܪ 'one who takes a divorcee commits adultery.' The Ptc. also expresses the idea of futurity, intention (Prospective Present) or immediacy and certainty of realisation like the Engl. syntagm *be going to* + Inf.: e.g. Gn 1.20 ܕܢܚܙܐ ܡܢܐ ܩܪܐ ܠܗܘܢ 'in order to see what he is going to call them'; ib. 15.2 ܗܘ ܝܪܬ ܠܝ 'he is going to inherit me'; ib. 18.17 ܡܕܡ ܕܥܒܕ ܐ̱ܢܐ 'that which I am going to, intend to do.'

The Ptc. is further used to indicate what has been going on for a while up to the moment of speaking: Lk 15.29 ܗܐ ܟܡܐ ܫܢܝܢ ܦܠܚ ܐ̱ܢܐ ܠܟ 'behold, for some years I have been rendering you service.'(5)

A special application of the use of the Ptc. for Actual Present is found in circumstantial clauses which describe what goes on simul-

4 Even when the subject of the main verb is identical with that of the subordinate clause: ܒܥܐ ܕܢܩܛܘܠ ܢܦܫܗ 'he wanted to kill himself.'

5 Fr. 'Voici tant d'années que je te sers'; Germ. 'Siehe, so viel Jahre diene ich dir.'

taneously with the main action: Gn 18.1 "the Lord appeared to him ... as he sat at the entrance of his tent" (ܘܗܘ ܝܬܒ ܒܬܪܥܐ ܕܡܫܟܢܗ); Nu 16.27 "Dathan and Abiram had come out, standing (ܗܘܘ ܩܝܡܝܢ) at the entrance of their tents." Also belong here participles after verbs of perception: Mt 15.31 ܚܙܝܢ ܚܪ̈ܫܐ ܕܡܡܠܠܝܢ 'seeing the dumb talking'; Ex 14.10 ܚܙܘ ܠܡܨܪ̈ܝܐ ܗܘܘ ܐܬܝܢ 'they saw the Egyptians coming'; Gn 21.9 ܚܙܬ ܣܪܐ ܠܒܪܗ ܕܗܓܪ ... ܡܓܚܟ 'Sarah saw the son of Hagar ... mocking.' Likewise the nominal clause, when embedded in a ܕ-clause, is indifferent to the time distinction: Gn 13.1 ܘܣܠܩ ܐܒܪܡ ܡܢ ܡܨܪܝܢ: ܗܘ ܘܐܢܬܬܗ ܘܟܠ ܕܐܝܬ ܠܗ 'and Abram went up from Egypt, he and his wife and all that he had' (instead of ܕܐܝܬ ܗܘܐ ܠܗ).

Further, the Ptc. is also found often in conditional sentences, in apodoses as well as in protases: ܘܐܢ ܐܦ ܠܢ ܫܦܪ ܡܫܬܘܝܢܢ ܥܡܟܘܢ 'and if it also pleases us, we shall agree with you.'

§ 84 The **passive participle** indicates a result of a past action: ܟܬܝܒ 'it is written' (= Germ. *ist geschrieben*, and not *wird geshrieben*). One often comes across what is passive in form only, but active in meaning: e.g., Lk 14.2 ܓܒܪܐ ܚܕ ܕܟܢܝܫ ܗܘܐ ܡܝ̈ܐ 'a man who has collected water,' i.d. dropsiac; Mk 14.13 ܓܒܪܐ ܕܫܩܝܠ ܡܐܢܐ ܕܡܝ̈ܐ 'a man carrying a water container' (i.e. having picked up ... and carrying).

Note especially the syntagm ܟܬܝܒ ܠ-, which has the same value as the Engl. (Present) Perfect *I have written*, expressing a result, and what follows the preposition represents the *subject* of the verb: ܣܓܝ̈ܐܢ ܐܢܝܢ ܐܝܠܝܢ ܕܥܒܝ̈ܕܢ ܠܢ 'many are things that we have done.' Also with a passive Ptc. in Pa. or Af.: ܐܝܟ ܦܘܩܕܢܐ ܘܡܘܠܦܢܐ ܕܡܩܒܠ ܗܘܐ ܠܗܘܢ ܡܢܗ ܕܐܕܝ 'in accordance with the commandment and instruction which they had received from Addai'; ܩܝܡܐ ܕܫܝܢܐ ܕܓܙܝܪ ܠܝ ܥܡ ܡܪܢ ܩܣܪ 'the peace treaty which I have concluded with our lord the Emperor.' The resultative force is apparent in intransitive verbs which, by definition, are not capable of having genuine passive forms: *Spic.* 43.7 ܡܗܠܟ ܠܝ ܒܡܘܠܦܢܐ 'I have walked in instruction.' In a case like the following, however, we have the usual passive participle: Mt 9.2 ܫܒܝܩܝܢ ܠܟ ܚܛܗܝ̈ܟ 'your sins have been forgiven you.'

§ 85 **Compound tense**: ܟܬܰܒ݂ ܗ̄ܘܳܐ. This syntagm, <Pf. + enclitic ܗ̄ܘܳܐ>, has exactly the same range of time reference as the simple Perfect: ܟܬܰܒ݂ܘ ܗ̄ܘܰܘ 'they wrote,' 'they have written,' 'they had written' or 'they will have written.'

§ 86 **Compound tense**: ܟܳܬܶܒ݂ ܗ̄ܘܳܐ. This highly frequent syntagm <Ptc. + enclitic ܗ̄ܘܳܐ> indicates an on-going, repeated or habitual action in the past: ܒܳܟܶܐ ܗ̄ܘܺܝܬ݂ 'I was weeping, kept weeping.'

This structure is also common in irreal or hypothetical conditional sentences: Jn 11.21 ܐܶܠܽܘ ܬ݁ܰܢܳܢ ܗ̄ܘܰܝܬ݁ ܠܳܐ ܡܳܐܶܬ݂ ܗ̄ܘܳܐ ܐܰܚܝ 'if you had been here, my brother would not have died'; ib. 14.28 ܐܶܠܽܘ ܪܳܚܡܺܝܢ ܗ̄ܘܰܝܬ݁ܽܘܢ ܠܺܝ ܚܳܕܶܝܢ ܗ̄ܘܰܝܬ݁ܽܘܢ 'if you loved me, you would be rejoicing'; Jdg 13.23 ܐܶܠܽܘ ܨܳܒܶܐ ܗ̄ܘܳܐ ܐܰܠܳܗܳܐ ܕ݁ܢܶܩܛܽܘܠܰܢ ܠܳܐ ܡܩܰܒ݁ܶܠ ܗ̄ܘܳܐ ܡܶܢܰܢ ܥܠܰܬ݂ܳܐ 'if God had wanted to kill us, he would not have accepted from us a burnt-offering.' Here also belongs a case such as Mt 18.6 ܦ݁ܩܰܚ ܗ̄ܘܳܐ ܠܶܗ ܕ݁ ... 'it would be more beneficial to him ...'

§ 87 **Compound tense**: ܗܘܳܐ ܟ݁ܳܬܶܒ݂. This syntagm, in which the verb ܗܘܐ is *not* enclitic, but fully pronounced, indicates a wish, advice or obligation of general applicability, but not a command for immediate execution, for which one uses the Imperative. An adjective may be found instead of a participle. E.g. ܗܘܰܝܬ݁ ܚܠܺܝܡ 'Be healthy!'; ܗܳܟܰܢܳܐ ܗܘܰܝܬ݁ ܥܳܒܶܕ݂ 'Act thus!'

§ 88 **Compound tense**: ܢܶܟ݂ܬ݁ܽܘܒ݂ ܗ̄ܘܳܐ. This syntagm is used in a past context, and in subordinate clauses, instead of the simple Impf.: ܡܶܢ ܩܕ݂ܳܡ ܕ݁ܢܺܐܙܠܽܘܢ ܗ̄ܘܰܘ ܠܬ݂ܰܡܳܢ 'before they went there.' Also in conditional or associated clauses: ܡܳܢ ܐܶܥܒ݁ܶܕ݂ ܗ̄ܘܺܝܬ݂ 'what ought I to have done?'

§ 89 **Compound tense**: ܢܶܗܘܶܐ ܟ݁ܳܬܶܒ݂ This syntagm occasionally replaces the simple Imperfect: ܐܰܫܠܛܶܗ ܕ݁ܢܶܗܘܶܐ ܥܳܒܶܕ݂ ܐܳܦ ܕ݁ܺܝܢܳܐ 'he gave him the authority to execute judgement as well'; ܢܶܫ̈ܶܐ ܠܰܓ݂ܡܰܪ ܠܳܐ ܢܶܗܘ̈ܝܳܢ ܥ̈ܳܐܠܳܢ ܠܕܰܝܪ̈ܰܝܗܽܘܢ 'women should never enter their monasteries.'

§ 90 **Noun expanded** A noun as the nucleus of a phrase may be expanded in various ways. Such an expanding constituent mostly follows the nucleus, but not infrequently precedes it.

§ 91 a) An **attributive adjective** mostly follows its nucleus noun: Mt

12.35 ܓܒܪܐ ܛܒܐ ܡܢ ܣܝܡܬܐ ܛܒܬܐ ܡܦܩ ܛܒܬܐ 'a good man produces good things from good treasures.' But it may precede: ܩܕܡܝܬܐ ܫܬܐܣܬܐ. 'the first foundation'; often with honorific, laudatory or condemnatory epithets as in ܛܘܒܢܐ ܡܪܝ، ܐܦܪܝܡ 'the blessed Mar Ephrem'; ܪܫܝܥܐ ܝܘܠܝܢܘܣ 'the wicked Julian.' Likewise with common quantifiers: ܐܚܪܢܐ ܡܬܠܐ 'another parable'; Mt 4.21 ܐܚܖ̈ܢܐ ܐܚ̈ܐ ܬܪܝܢ 'another two brothers'; 2Cor 11.4 ܐܚܪܢܐ ܝܫܘܥ 'a different kind of Jesus'; Jn 14.16 ܐܚܪܢܐ ܦܪܩܠܝܛܐ 'another comforter'; ܢܦܫ̈ܬܐ ܣܓܝ̈ܐܬܐ 'many souls' as against ܣܓܝ̈ܐܐ ܚܛܝ̈ܐ 'many sinners' and ܦܪ̈ܚܐ ܣܓܝ̈ܐܬܐ 'many birds.'

b) A **demonstrative pronoun** (§ 13) may either precede or follow: ܡܠܟܐ ܗܢܐ or ܗܢܐ ܡܠܟܐ 'this king.'

c) Likewise **cardinal numerals** (§ 44 a). The preceding numeral for "one," however, emphasises the notion of unity or oneness: ܚܕ ܒܣܪ 'one flesh' (of marital union); ܚܕܐ ܫܥܐ 'even one hour;' Mt 27.14 ܘܠܐ ܒܚܕܐ ܡܠܐ 'not even with one word.' Cf. ܓܒܪܐ ܚܕ 'a man,' where the numeral is equivalent to the indefinite article. In the case of other numerals, the preceding noun tends to be put in the st. emph., but with no functional difference: ܝܘ̈ܡܬܐ ܬܪܝܢ or ܬܪܝܢ ܝܘܡܝܢ 'two days,' cf. Mt 14.19 ܗܢܘܢ ܚܡܫܐ ܠܚܡܝܢ ܘܬܪܝܢ ܢܘܢܝܢ 'those five loaves and two fish,' the noun in the st. abs. even with a determiner, ܗܢܘܢ.

Where a noun is expanded by both the numeral "one" and an adjective, the numeral appears either immediately before or after the noun: ܚܕ ܒܪܐ ܝܚܝܕܝܐ 'the only beloved son' vs. ܥܓܠܬܐ ܚܕܐ ܚܕܬܐ 'a new wagon.'

Note also the position of the numeral for "one" in relation to an analytical noun phrase as in Mt 5.36 ܡܢܬܐ ܚܕܐ ܕܣܥܪܐ 'one hair.'

Likewise with numerals other than "one": ܗܠܝܢ ܬܪܥܣܪ ܬܠܡܝܕܘ̄ܗܝ، 'these twelve disciples of his'; ܗܠܝܢ ܫܒܥ ܢܩ̈ܘܬܐ ܕܥܢܐ 'these seven lambs.'

The same rule applies to a demonstrative pronoun as to the numeral for "one": ܥܡܐ ܗܢܐ ܪܒܐ 'this great nation' vs. ܗܠܝܢ ܬܕܡܪ̈ܬܐ ܪ̈ܘܪܒܬܐ 'these great wonders.'

Where a noun qualified by a numeral is considered logically determined, the latter may optionally take an anticipatory (pleonastic) suffix as in ܬܪ̈ܝܗܘܢ ܒ̈ܢܝ ܙܒܕܝ 'the two sons of Zebedee.'

d) The **quantifiers** ܣܓܝ /saggi/ 'many, much' and ܩܠܝܠ 'few, little' may either precede or follow the nucleus noun. ܩܠܝܠ, however, is indeclinable: e.g. ܗܠܝܢ ܡ̈ܠܐ ܩܠܝܠ 'these few words'; ܗܠܝܢ ܩܠܝܠ ܕܘܟܪ̈ܢܐ 'these few memories'; ܙܒ̈ܢܝܢ ܣܓܝ̈ܐܢ 'many times'; ܝܘ̈ܡܬܐ ܣܓܝ̈ܐܐ 'many days.'

Cf. also Mt 8.10 ܐܝܟ ܗܕܐ ܗܝܡܢܘܬܐ 'such a faith as this'; Gn 41.38 ܐܝܟ ܗܢܐ ܓܒܪܐ 'such a man like this,' but Mt 9.8 ܫܘܠܛܢܐ ܕܐܝܟ ܗܢܐ 'such an authority.'

ܡܕܡ also functions as a kind of quantifier: Mt 27.12 ܡܕܡ ܦܬܓܡܐ ܗܘ ܠܐ ܦܢܝ 'he, however, returned no word whatever'; ܡܕܡ ܝܘܬܪܢ 'some benefit.' It may also follow a noun: ܡܘܗܒܬܐ ܡܕܡ 'some gift.'

The ubiquitous ܟܠ /kul/ (or ܟܘܠ) may form close union with a noun: ܟܠ ܝܘܡ (also spelled ܟܠܝܘܡ) 'every day'; ܟܠ ܩܢܝ̈ܢܝ 'all possessions.' In such cases it usually takes a suffixal pronoun matching the noun in gender and number, whether proleptically (by anticipation) or resumptively: ܟܠܗ ܡܕܝܢܬܐ 'the entire city'; ܟܠܗ ܢܦܫܝ 'my entire soul'; ܟܠܗܘܢ ܚܛܗ̈ܐ 'all the sins'; ܗܠܝܢ ܟܠܗܝܢ ܨܒ̈ܘܬܐ 'all these things.' The syntagm <ܟܠ + NP in st. emph.> may also have the translation value 'every,' not 'the whole': Mt 3.10 ܟܠ ܐܝܠܢܐ 'every tree.'

The combination of a noun with a demonstrative pronoun and ܟܠ appears in a variety of patterns: Ex 18.18 ܟܠܗ ܥܡܐ ܗܢܐ 'all this people'; ib. 11.8 ܥܡܐ ܗܢܐ ܟܠܗ; Gn 33.8 ܗܕܐ ܟܠܗ ܡܫܪܝܬܐ 'all this encampment.'

e) A noun may be expanded by another, immediately following noun, in which case the preceding nucleus noun is in the **status constructus**: e.g. ܒܪ ܡܠܟܐ 'son of a king, prince' (§ 73). This synthetic structure is often replaced by an analytic one whereby two nouns or noun phrases are joined by a proclitic ܕ- as in ܗܝܡܢܘܬܐ ܕܒܪܟ 'the belief of your son.' The second, qualifying noun may be converted into a conjunctive pronoun as in ܗܝܡܢܘܬܗ 'his faith' or into an independent "possessive" pronoun as in ܗܝܡܢܘܬܐ ܕܝܠܗ.

At times the nucleus noun phrase to be qualified by the following

Dalath phrase is wanting: Mt 22.21 ܗܒܘ ܗܟܝܠ ܕܩܣܪ ܠܩܣܪ ܘܕܐܠܗܐ ܠܐܠܗܐ 'Give then that which is of Caesar to Ceaesar and that which is of God to God'; ib. 16.23 ܠܐ ܡܬܪܥܐ ܐܢܬ ܕܐܠܗܐ ܐܠܐ ܕܒܢܝ̈ܢܫܐ 'you are not thinking of things of God but of things of men.'

f) A noun phrase qualifying another noun phrase may be transformed into a suffix pronoun: ܣܦܪܐ ܕܢܒܝܐ 'the book of the prophet' → ܣܦܪܗ 'his book.' This synthetic structure can be transformed back into an analytic one by means of a ܕܝܠ- form when the qualifying constituent receives some emphasis: ܣܦܪܐ ܕܝܠܗ '*his* book.' Two alternative syntagms are: ܕܝܠܗ ܣܦܪܐ and ܣܦܪܗ ܕܝܠܗ, the latter with a proleptic pronoun.

g) When an adjective qualifies the first of the two nouns in analytical union mediated by the proclitic Dalat, it may either immediately follow the first noun or the second: Aphr I 29.12 ܥܒ̈ܕܐ ܛܒ̈ܐ ܕܗܝܡܢܘܬܐ 'the good works of faith' as against ܐܓܪܬܐ ܕܩܘܪܢܬܝܐ ܩܕܡܝܬܐ 'the First Epistle to the Corinthians.' Compare also Gn 44.2 ܐܣܩܘܦܐ ܕܝܠܝ ܕܣܐܡܐ 'my silver cup' with ib. 23.9 ܡܥܪܬܐ ܐܥܦܝܬܐ ܕܝܠܗ 'his double cave.'

h) A noun may be expanded by a ܕ-clause. Three patterns are to be distinguished here:

1) Such a clause may explain what is meant by the preceding noun —epexegetical: e.g. ܐܪܓܫ ܒܡܚܝܠܘܬܝ. ܕܠܐ ܡܫܟܚ ܐܢܐ ܠܡܣܝܒܪܘ ܐܘ̈ܠܨܢܐ 'he sensed my weakness that I am not able to cope with the pressures.'

2) The noun phrase serves as an "antecedent" which is referred back to by a pronominal element in the ܕ-clause—relative clause: ܒܝܬܐ ܕܒܗ ܥܡܪ ܐܢܐ 'a house in which I live'; Gn 35.15 ܐܬܪܐ ܗܘ ܕܡܠܠ ܥܡܗ ܬܡܢ ܐܠܗܐ 'that place where God had spoken with him.'

Such a pronominal reference, however, is usually absent when the antecedent is equivalent to the subject or direct object of the ܕ-clause: ܢܒܝܐ ܕܐܡܪ ܗܠܝܢ 'the prophet who said these things' or ܗܠܝܢ ܕܐܡܪ ܢܒܝܐ 'these things which the prophet said.' Thus Gn 9.3 ܟܠ ܪܚܫܐ ܕܚܝ 'every reptile that is alive,' but Nu 9.13 ܓܒܪܐ ܕܕܟܐ ܗܘ 'a man who is pure'; Dt 13.6 ܐܠܗܐ ܐܚܪ̈ܢܐ ܕܠܐ ܝܕܥܬܘܢ 'other gods whom you do not know.'

Where an embedded pronominal reference is lacking inside the relative clause, a preposition which would have been attached to such a pronominal element is occasionally found attached to the relative pronoun, whether simplex or compound: Mt 26.48 ܠܡܰܢ ܕܢܳܫܶܩ ܐ̱ܢܳܐ ܗܽܘܝܽܘ 'the one whom I shall kiss is him' instead of ܡܰܢ ܕܢܳܫܶܩ ܠܶܗ; Nu 22.6 ܠܡܰܢ ܕܡܒܰܪܶܟ ܐܢ̱ܬ ܡܒܰܪܰܟ ܗܽܘ ܘܠܡܰܢ ܕܠܳܐܶܛ ܐܢ̱ܬ ܠܺܝܛ ܗܽܘ 'he whom you bless is blessed, and he whom you curse is accursed.'

3) A prepositional phrase expanding a noun phrase is often introduced by the proclitic ܕ: Gn 3.2 ܐܺܝܠܳܢܶܐ ܕܒܓܰܢ̱ܬܳܐ 'the trees in the garden'; ib.44.15 ܓܰܒܪܳܐ ܕܐܰܝܟܘܳܬܝ 'a man like me.' But cf. Gn 3.6 ܠܒܰܥܠܳܗ ܥܰܡܳܗ 'to her husband (who was) with her.'

§ 92 Grammatical concord 1) In the majority of cases a satellite displays formal congruence with its nucleus in respect of gender and number: e.g., ܡܰܠܟܳܐ ܛܳܒܳܐ 'a good king' vs. ܡܰܠܟܳܬ݂ܳܐ ܛܳܒܳܬ݂ܳܐ 'good queens'; ܐܶܬ݂ܰܘ ܓܰܒܪ̈ܶܐ 'the men came' vs. ܐܶܬ݂ܝ̈ ܒܢ̈ܳܬ݂ܳܐ 'the daughters came'; ܒܰܝܬܳܐ ܗܰܘ 'that house' vs. ܟܢܽܘܫܬܳܐ ܗܳܝ 'that synagogue'; ܬܪܶܝܢ ܒܢ̈ܺܝܢ 'two sons' vs. ܬܰܪܬܶܝܢ ܒܢ̈ܳܢ 'two daughters.'

2) Some nouns, though singular in form, may refer to an entity consisting of more than one individual member—collective nouns—and concord with a plural verb: Ex 14.31 ܕܚܶܠܘ ܥܰܡܳܐ 'the people feared.'

3) As regards the state, however, a satellite adjective does not concord with its nucleus noun when the latter is in the construct state: e.g. ܒܰܪ ܡܰܠܟܳܐ ܛܳܒܳܐ 'the good son of the king.'

4) The quantifier ܩܰܠܺܝܠ 'few, little' often remains unchanged with a plural noun: Mt 15.34 ܩܰܠܺܝܠ ܢܽܘܢ̈ܶܐ ܙܥܽܘܪ̈ܶܐ 'a few small fish'; Mk 6.5 ܟܪ̈ܺܝܗܶܐ ܩܰܠܺܝܠ 'a few sick people'; Rev 3.4 ܩܰܠܺܝܠ ܫܡ̈ܳܗܶܐ 'a few names.' By contrast, ܣܰܓܺܝ 'many, much' may concord: Mt 13.17 ܣܰܓܺܝ̈ܐܶܐ ܢܒ̈ܺܝܶܐ 'many prophets,' but ܣܰܓܺܝ ܢܽܘܢ̈ܶܐ 'many fish' and ܣܰܓܺܝ ܨ̈ܒܽܘܳܬ݂ܳܐ 'many things.' Similarly ܐ̱ܚܪܺܝܢ 'another, other': Mt 12.45 ܫܒܰܥ ܪ̈ܽܘܚܶܐ ܐ̱ܚܪ̈ܢܝܳܢ 'seven other spirits,' but ib. 21.41 ܦܳܠ̈ܚܶܐ ܐ̱ܚܪ̈ܳܢܶܐ 'other workers' and ܡܳܪܳܐ ܐ̱ܚܪܺܝܢ 'another master.'

5) The verb ܗܘܳܐ, especially in the syntagm ܗܘܳܐ ܠ in the sense of "to possess," tends to be unchangeable, the 3m.sg. form serving for all persons and both genders: Mt 22.25 ܠܰܝܬ ܗܘܳܐ ܠܶܗ ܒܢ̈ܰܝܳܐ 'he had no sons' (instead of ܗܘܘ).

6) In the case of multiple constituents the first component may determine the choice: Mt 22.40 ܒܗܠܝܢ ܬܪܬܝܢ ܦܘܩܕܢܝܢ ܬܠܝܐ ܐܘܪܝܬܐ ܘܢܒܝܐ 'on these two commandments depend(s) the law and the prophets.'

§ 93 Negation

1) ܠܐ may be used as a prefix of a noun with a negative connotation: e.g. ܠܐ ܡܗܝܡܢܘܬܗܘܢ 'their disbelief'; ܠܐ ܡܬܚܒܠܢܘܬܐ 'incorruptibility, immortality.'

2) A rhetorical question is often cast in negative form. ܠܐ ܗܘܐ may be used, even without referring to the past: Mt 13.55 ܠܐ ܗܘܐ ܗܢܐ ܗܘ ܒܪܗ ܕܢܓܪܐ 'this is surely the son of the carpenter?,' which is immediatley followed by ܠܐ ܐܡܗ ܡܬܩܪܝܐ ܡܪܝܡ 'his mother is called Mary, isn't she?' A negating particle may not occupy the initial slot: ib. 56 ܘܐܚܘܬܗ ܟܠܗܝܢ ܠܐ ܗܐ ܠܘܬܢ ܐܝܬܝܗܝܢ 'and his sisters are all with us, aren't they?'

3) The non-existence of an entity is indicated by ܠܝܬ : Mt 12.43 ܠܝܬ ܒܗܘܢ ܡܝܐ 'there is no water in them'; Ac 4.12 ܠܝܬ ܒܐܢܫ ܐܚܪܢܐ ܦܘܪܩܢܐ 'there is no salvation in any other person.' This is followed by its fuller form, ܠܐ ܐܝܬ: ... ܠܐ ܓܝܪ ܐܝܬ ܫܡܐ ܐܚܪܢܐ 'for there is no other name ...' Non-existence in the past requires ܗܘܐ: Mt 13.6 ܠܝܬ ܗܘܐ ܠܗ ܥܩܪܐ 'it had no root.' ܠܝܬ may be used absolutely, i.e. no missing entity mentioned: Mt 13.13 ܡܢ ܕܠܝܬ ܠܗ 'he who has nothing.'

4) The verb is negated by ܠܐ: Mt 13.13 ܠܐ ܫܡܥܝܢ ܘܠܐ ܡܣܬܟܠܝܢ 'they do not listen and do not comprehend'; ib.14 ܠܐ ܬܣܬܟܠܘܢ 'you will not comprehend'; ib.16.11 ܐܝܟܢܐ ܠܐ ܐܣܬܟܠܬܘܢ 'how have you not comprehended?'

5) The force of the negation of the syntagm ܠܐ ܗܘܐ also affects only the immediately following constituent: Mt 15.11 ܠܐ ܗܘܐ ܡܕܡ ܕܥܐܠ ܠܦܘܡܐ ܡܣܐܒ ܠܒܪܢܫܐ 'it is not that which enters the mouth that defiles a man (but that which comes out of the mouth, that is what defiles a man)'; ib.16.11 ܠܐ ܗܘܐ ܥܠ ܠܚܡܐ ܐܡܪܬ ܠܟܘܢ 'it was not about the bread that I have said (that) to you.'

6) Where two coordinate nouns are negated, the negative is prefixed to each of them: Mt 6.20 ܠܐ ܣܐܣܐ ܘܠܐ ܐܟܠܐ ܠܐ ܡܚܒܠܝܢ 'neither moth nor rust damages'; Jer 49.31 ܠܐ ܬܪ̈ܥܐ ܘܠܐ ܣܘܟܪ̈ܐ ܠܗ 'it has neither doors nor bolts.'

7) In categorical negation affecting a noun the negative may stand detached from the noun: Gn 19.8 ܬܪ̈ܬܝܢ ܒ̈ܢܢ ܕܠܐ ܝܕܥ ܐܢܝܢ ܓܒܪ 'two daughters with whom no man had sex.'

8) Categorical negation is common with a noun, often, in st. abs. preceded by ܕܠܐ, e.g. Ps 118.1 ܐܝܠܝܢ ܕܕܠܐ ܡܘܡ ܐܢܘܢ ܒܐܘܪܚܐ 'those in whose way there is no blemish'; Mk 4.34 ܕܠܐ ܦܠܐܬܐ ܠܐ ܡܡܠܠ ܗܘܐ 'without parables he would not teach'; Ro 4.6 ܙܕܝܩܘܬܐ ܕܠܐ ܥܒ̈ܕܐ 'righteousness without works'; Phil 2.14 ܟܠܡܕܡ ܗܘܝܬܘܢ ܥܒܕܝܢ ܕܠܐ ܪܛܢܐ ܘܕܠܐ ܦܘܠܓܐ 'you ought to do everything wihtout disputing and without grumbling.' Here belongs ܠܐ ܐ̱ܢܫ 'nobody' as in Mk 3.27 ܠܐ ܐ̱ܢܫ ܡܫܟܚ ܕܢܥܘܠ ܠܒܝܬܗ ܕܚܣܝܢܐ 'nobody can enter the house of a strong man.' This kind of ܐܢܫ, however, does not have immediately to follow the negator: Mk 5.3 ܘܒܫܫܠܬܐ ܐ̱ܢܫ ܠܐ ܡܫܟܚ ܠܡܐܣܪܗ 'nobody could restrain him with a chain.'

9) To negate a clause constituent other than an adjective, a finite verb or a participle, ܠܐ ܗܘܐ or ܠܘ is often used(6): Mt 22.32 ܘܐܠܗܐ ܠܐ ܗܘܐ ܕܡ̈ܝܬܐ ܐܠܐ ܕܚ̈ܝܐ 'and the God is not that of the dead but of the living'; Mk 9.37 ܡܢ ܕܠܝ ܡܩܒܠ ܠܐ ܗܘܐ ܠܝ ܡܩܒܠ ܐܠܐ ܠܡܢ ܕܫܕܪܢܝ 'one who receives me does not receive me, but one who has sent me'; 1Cor 15.51 ܠܘ ܟܠܢ ܢܕܡܟ 'not all of us shall sleep.' The constituent negated by such a combination is usually focused. A mere ܠܐ, however, is also found: Mt 20.26 ܠܐ ܗܟܢܐ ܢܗܘܐ ܒܝܢܬܟܘܢ 'it should not be like that among you.' This is true where "neither ... nor" is meant: Mt 6.20 ܐܝܟܐ ܕܠܐ ܣܣܐ ܘܠܐ ܐܟܠܐ ܡܚܒܠܝܢ 'where niether moth nor rust causes damage,' cited above (**6**). In such a case the negator may be found also with the verb: Mt 12.32 ܠܐ ܢܫܬܒܩ ܠܗ ܠܐ ܒܗܢܐ ܥܠܡܐ ܘܠܐ ܒܥܠܡܐ ܕܥܬܝܕ 'he will not be forgiven, not in this world nor in the world to come.' Likewise where "nor" is meant: Mt 25:13 ܠܐ ܝܕܥܝܢ ܐܢܬܘܢ ܝܘܡܐ ܗܘ ܘܠܐ ܫܥܬܐ 'you do not know that day nor the hour.'

10) An adjective such as ܫܠܝܛ may be negated by a plain ܠܐ: Mt 20:15 ܠܐ ܫܠܝܛ ܠܝ ܕܡܕܡ ܕܨܒܐ ܐܢܐ ܐܥܒܕ ܒܕܝܠܝ 'Don't I have

6 Cf. Joosten 1992a.

authority to do with mine what I like?' See also Mt 19.10 ܠܐ ܦܩܚ ܠܡܣܒ ܐܢܬܬܐ 'it is no use marrying a woman.'

11) The focusing function is indicated by a pronoun component of ܠܘ [< ܠܐ ܗܘ] (see below, § 110): Jn 1.20 ܠܘ ܐܢܐ ܐܢܐ ܡܫܝܚܐ '*I* am not the messiah'; 1Pt 1.12 ܠܘ ܠܢܦܫܗܘܢ ܚܒܝܢ ܗܘܘ ܐܠܐ ܠܢ 'they were not seeking themselves, but us.'

§ 94 Passive

The noun or pronoun indicating the agent in a passive construction may be mediated by the preposition Lamadh: Mt 14.8 ܡܠܦܐ ܗܘܬ ܠܐܡܗ 'she had been instructed by her mother (ὑπὸ τῆς μητρὸς αὐτῆς),' but ܡܢ is by far the commonest: Mt 2.16 ܐܬܒܙܚ ܡܢ ܡܓܘܫܐ 'he was made a fool of by the magis'; Lk 2.18 ܐܬܡܠܠ ܠܗܘܢ ܡܢ ܪܥܘܬܐ 'was told them by the shepherds.'

§ 95 Apposition

1) Some nouns in apposition to another noun are virtually adjectival in function: Mt 14.13 ܐܬܪܐ ܚܘܪܒܐ 'desertlike place.' This is especially true of nouns of the pattern *Qattaal*, which indicate professional or habitual activities, and nomen agentis with the characteristic suffix /-aan/: Mt 14.26 ܚܙܘܐ ܕܓܠܐ 'deceptive spectre'; ib.16.4 ܫܪܒܬܐ ܒܝܫܬܐ ܓܝܪܬܐ 'an evil and adulterous generation'; Aphr. I 156.5 ܦܘܡܐ ܐܟܘܠܐ 'a voracious mouth'; ib. I 101.4 ܕܪܐ ܡܚܒܠܢܐ 'a corrupt (lit. corruptor) generation.'

2) Virtually otiose is ܓܒܪܐ in Mt 18.23 ܓܒܪܐ ܡܠܟܐ 'a king'([7]); Ge 13.8 ܓܒܪܐ ܐܚܐ ܚܢܢ 'we are brothers.'

3) Where an appositional phrase is prefixed with a preposition, the latter is not repeated: Gn 4.2 ܠܐܚܘܗܝ ܗܒܝܠ 'to his brother Abel'; 2Sm 20.21 ܥܠ ܡܠܟܐ ܕܘܝܕ 'on King David,' but exceptions do occur: e.g., Gn 23.7 ܠܥܡܐ ܕܐܪܥܐ ܠܒܢܝ ܚܝܬ 'to the local people, the sons of Heth.'

[7] The appositional character of this syntagm is confirmed by a comparison of Mt 20.1 "the kingdom of heaven is like ... ܓܒܪܐ ܡܪܐ ܒܝܬܐ ܕܢܦܩ ܒܨܦܪܐ 'a man, a landlord who went out in the morning ...' with ib. 21.33 "Hear another parable. ,,, ܓܒܪܐ ܚܕ ܐܝܬ ܗܘܐ ܡܪܐ ܒܝܬܐ ܘܢܨܒ ܟܪܡܐ 'there was a certain man, a landlord, and he planted a vineyard ...'

§ 96 Adjective expanded

a) The high degree or intensity of a quality indicated by an adjective is expressed by ܣܓܝ or ܠܚܕ: Mt 15.8 ܣܓܝ ܪܚܝܩ 'very far'; ib.19.25 ܬܡܗܝܢ ܗ̄ܘܘ ܠܚܕ 'were very surprised'; Gn 15.1 ܣܓܝ ܠܚܕ 'very much.' The position of ܠܚܕ varies: Gn 1.31 ܠܚܕ ܫܦܝܪ 'very good' (Heb: טוֹב מְאֹד) vs. Ex 9.3 ܡܘܬܢܐ ܕܒܝܫ ܠܚܕ 'a plague that was very severe.'

b) Some adjectives may be put in the status constructus and further qualified by the following noun: e.g. 1Sm 1.15 ܟܪܝܬ ܪܘܚܐ 'distressed of spirit'; Ex 32.9 ܥܡܐ ܩܫܐ ܩܕܠܐ 'a people stiff of neck'; Mt 13.46 ܝܩܝܪܬ ܕܕܡܝܐ 'costly.' Such an adjective may, however, be followed by a preposition which more explicitly specifies the logical relation between the adjective and the noun: Gn 12.11 ܫܦܝܪܬ ܒܚܙܘܐ 'pretty in appearance'; ܐܣܝܐ ܪܒܐ ܝܬܝܪ ܒܟܠ 'a great physician excelling in everything.' See also § 73 **c**.

c) The comparative degree of an adjective (and an adverb) is expressed not by any inflectional modification of the adjective itself, but by means of the preposition ܡܢ: Jdg 14.18 ܡܢܘ ܕܚܠܐ ܡܢ ܕܒܫܐ ܐܘ ܡܢܘ ܕܬܩܝܦ ܡܢ ܐܪܝܐ 'what is it that is sweeter than honey or who is it that is stronger than a lion?' Verbs which denote qualities may also show analogous structure: Gn 26.16 ܥܫܢܬ ܡܢܢ ܠܚܕ 'you are much mightier than we'; ib. 48.19 ܐܚܘܗܝ, ܙܥܘܪܐ ܢܪܒܐ ܡܢܗ 'his younger brother will be greater than he'; Lk 14.8 ܐܢܫ ܕܡܝܩܪ ܡܢܟ 'someone who is more distinguished than you.'

d) The adjective is often substantivised and used without a noun phrase which could serve as its head: Mt 5.45 ܕܡܕܢܚ ܫܡܫܗ ܥܠ ܛܒܐ ܘܥܠ ܒܝܫܐ ܗܘ 'he who makes his sun rise above the good and the evil'; 7.22 ܣܓܝܐܐ ܢܐܡܪܘܢ 'many will say.'

§ 97 Verb expanded

Most verbs are expanded and complemented by pronouns, nouns, noun phrases, verb forms—such as finite verb forms, infinitives, participles— ܕ-clauses, adverbs or their phrasal or clausal equivalents. The last category of complement, namely adverbials, may be considered non-essential: whilst *in the sky* in *A bird is flying in the sky* may be considered essential, *in the next room* in *Someone is snoring in the next room* can hardly be so considered.

Essential complements in the form of nouns or pronouns may be classified into direct and indirect objects. An object is direct when in the form of a noun it can be placed next to the verb without any formal marking: ܫܕܪܘ ܫܠܝܚܐ 'they sent an/the apostle.' A verb which is capable of such zero complementation may be called transitive. By contrast, an object is indirect when in the form of a noun it is necessarily mediated by some preposition or other: e.g. ܗܟܢܐ ܐܡܪܘ ܠܫܠܝܚܐ 'so they said to the apostle,' where the Lamad is not deletable. Likewise Is 41.6 ܓܒܪ ܠܚܒܪܗ ܡܥܕܪܝܢ 'they help each other.'

a) A direct object, however, may optionally be marked by the preposition Lamadh, leading to occasional syntactic ambiguity: ܫܕܪܘ ܫܠܝܚܐ given above may be replaced by ܫܕܪܘ ܠܫܠܝܚܐ. Thus at Josh 6.7 ܐܬܟܪܟܘ ܠܡܕܝܢܬܐ 'Go round the city!' the preposition Lamadh could be analysed as exponent of direct object only on the basis of an example such as Dt 2.3 ܡܬܟܪܟܝܢ ܐܢܬܘܢ ܠܛܘܪܐ ܗܢܐ 'you go round this mountain.'

b) A pronominal direct object is as a rule synthetically attached to the verb: ܫܕܪܘܗܝ 'they sent him' in contrast to ܗܟܢܐ ܐܡܪܘ ܠܗ 'so they said to him.' But cases such as Josh 15.19 ܝܗܒܬܢܝ /yavṯan/ 'you gave (it) to me' do occur where the pronominal suffix marks an indirect object.

c) A direct object "them" is always indicated analytically by ܐܢܘܢ m. or ܐܢܝܢ f.: ܩܒܠ ܐܢܘܢ 'he received them' or 'Receive them' (Impv.).

d) A pronominal direct object of a participle is always marked analytically with the use of the preposition Lamadh, even in the case of "them": ܡܫܕܪ ܐܢܐ ܠܗ̇ 'I am sending her'; ܡܢܘ ܡܩܒܠ ܠܗܘܢ 'Who is going to receive them?,' not ܐܢܘܢ.

e) The infinitive, by contrast, is apt to mark its pronominal object "them" either as a suffix pronoun or through ܐܢܘܢ / ܐܢܝܢ: ܠܡܥܒܕܗܝܢ 'to make them' or Gn 15.5 ܠܡܡܢܐ ܐܢܘܢ 'to count them.' Compare also ܠܡܕܟܝܘܬܝ 'to cleanse me' alongside ܠܡܕܟܝܘܬܢܝ with the same meaning.

f) In the following cases a pronominal direct object may be detached from its verb and suffixed to Lamadh:

i) Emphatic or contrastive fronting as in Gn 41.13 ܠܝ ܐܗܦܟܢܝ ܥܠ ܕܘܟܬܝ܆ ܘܠܗܘ ܙܩܦ *'me* he restored to my office, but *him* he hanged.' Such an object often precedes the verb: Lk 14.9 ܗܘ ܕܝܢ ܕܠܟ ܘܠܗ ܩܪܐ 'one who invited you and him.'

ii) With another co-ordinate object as in Gn 41.10 ܐܪܡܢ ܒܝܬ ܐܣܝܪܐ ... ܠܝ ܘܠܪܒ ܢܚܬܘܡܐ 'he threw us into the prison ... me and the chief baker.'

iii) With some particles as in Gn 38.10 ܐܡܝܬܗ ܐܦ ܠܗ 'he killed him also';1Sm 7.3 ܦܠܘܚܘܗܝ܆ ܠܗ ܠܒܠܚܘܕܘܗܝ 'Serve him alone'; Gn 39.9 ܠܐ ܚܣܟ ܡܢܝ ܡܕܡ ܐܠܐ ܐܢ ܠܟ 'he did not withhold from me anything but you.'

iv) Where both objects of a verb are pronominal: *Acta Thomae* 173. 7 ܚܘܝܗ ܠܗ ܡܢ ܪܘܚܩܐ ܠܬܐܘܡܐ 'he showed to him him, i.e. Thomas, from afar'; 2Sm 15.25 ܢܚܘܝܢܝ ܠܗ 'to show me it.'

g) The proleptic use of object pronouns (see § 112) is highly frequent: ܫܕܪܗ ܠܒܪܐ 'he sent him (, i.e.) the son' or, rarely without the preposition, ܫܕܪܗ ܒܪܐ. In sum, Syriac is capable of marking a noun phrase as direct object in a variety of ways with apparently no functional opposition between them:

ܩܒܠܘ ܫܠܝܚܐ 'they received an/the apostle'
ܩܒܠܘ ܠܫܠܝܚܐ
ܩܒܠܘܗܝ ܫܠܝܚܐ
ܩܒܠܘܗܝ ܠܫܠܝܚܐ

Moreover, the sequence of the two constituents can be reversed, resulting in four additional patterns, though the suffix pronoun would then be resumptive.

h) Some verbs may take two direct objects: Job 39.19 ܬܠܒܫ ܐܢܬ ܨܘܪܗ ܙܝܢܐ 'you clothe his neck with weapon'; Jer 35.2 ܐܫܩܐ ܐܢܘܢ ܚܡܪܐ 'let them drink wine'; Ps 80.5 ܐܘܟܠܬ ܐܢܘܢ ܠܚܡܐ ܒܕܡܥܬܐ 'you fed them bread with tears.'

§ 98 Verbs expanded other than by noun phrases or pronouns. Verbs may be further complemented by—

a) Infinitive: ܨܒܐ ܛܠܝܐ ܠܡܐܟܠ 'the boy wants to eat'; ܫܠܡ ܠܡܡܠܠܘ 'he finished speaking'; ܠܐ ܐܫܟܚ ܠܡܩܡ 'he could not stand';

Gn 8.21 ܠܐ ܐܘܣܦ ܬܘܒ ܠܡܠܛܗ̇ ܠܐܪܥܐ 'I shall not curse the earth any more'; Dt 4.10 ܢܐܠܦܘܢ ܠܡܕܚܠ ܡܢܝ 'they shall learn to fear me.'

b) Imperfect: Lk 18.13 ܠܐ ܨܒܐ ܗܘܐ ܐܦܠܐ ܥܝܢܘܗܝ ܢܪܝܡ ܠܫܡܝܐ 'he would not even raise his eyes to heaven'; Josh. Styl. 3.12 ܠܝ ܬܒܥܬ ܐܟܬܘܒ ܠܟ 'you demanded me to write to you'; Mt 7.4 ܫܒܘܩ ܐܦܩ ܓܠܐ 'Allow me to take out the mote.' Although the leading word is not strictly a verb, the following cases are analogous: Jer 9.12 ܡܢܘ ܓܒܪܐ ܕܢܚܟܡ ܢܣܬܟܠ ܗܕܐ 'who is the man that is wise enough to understand this?'; Hos 14.9 ܡܢܘ. ܕܢܚܟܡ ܢܣܬܟܠ ܗܠܝܢ 'who is the one who is wise enough to understand these things?'

c) ܕ + Impf., which is far commoner than bare Impf.: Gn 19.22 ܠܐ ܡܫܟܚ ܐܢܐ ܕܐܥܒܕ ܡܕܡ 'I cannot do anything'; Jdg 3.28 ܠܐ ܫܒܩܘ ܠܐܢܫ ܕܢܥܒܪ 'they did not allow anyone to cross over; Mt 26.9 ܡܫܟܚ ܗܘܐ ܕܢܙܕܒܢ ܗܢܐ ܒܣܓܝ 'it could have been sold for much'; Mt 16.5 ܛܥܘ ܕܢܣܒܘܢ ܥܡܗܘܢ ܠܚܡܐ 'they forgot to take bread with them'; Mt 16.3 ܐܬܘܬܐ ܕܙܒܢܐ ܗܢܐ ܠܐ ܝܕܥܝܢ ܐܢܬܘܢ ܕܬܦܪܫܘܢ 'the sings of this epoch you do not know how to interpret'; ib. 6.7 ܫܪܝ. ܕܢܫܕܪ ܐܢܘܢ ܬܪܝܢ ܬܪܝܢ 'he began to send them out two by two.'

d) Participle: Mt 19.14 ܫܒܘܩܘ ܠܛܠܝܐ ܢܐܬܘܢ ܠܘܬܝ 'Let the children come to me'; Ac 3.2 ܡܝܬܝܢ ܗܘܘ ܫܩܝܠܝܢ ܘܣܝܡܝܢ ܠܗ 'they were in the habit of bringing and placing him'; Mk 5.17 ܫܪܝܘ ܒܥܝܢ ܡܢܗ ܕܢܐܙܠ ܠܗ 'they began to beg him to go away'; Jn 5.19 ܠܐ ܡܫܟܚ ܒܪܐ ܠܡܥܒܕ ܡܕܡ 'the son can do nothing.'

e) Verbs of sense or intellectual perception, or verbal communication are complemented by—

i) the proclitic particle Dalath: ܫܡܥ ܕܐܬܐ ܝܫܘܥ 'he heard that Jesus had come.' The verb ܐܡܪ often gives the contents of a communication in the form of direct speech, and yet introduced by the proclitic: Lk 14.9 ܢܐܡܪ ܠܟ ܕܗܒ ܕܘܟܬܐ ܠܗܢܐ 'he might say to you, "Cede the place to this one".' Likewise with verbs of related meaning: Mt 2.4 ܡܫܐܠ ܗܘܐ ܠܗܘܢ ܕܐܝܟܐ ܡܬܝܠܕ ܡܫܝܚܐ 'he kept asking them, "Where is the messiah going to be born?"'

ii) Verbs of perception often take as direct object a noun denoting a person or a thing followed by a clause indicating what is observed or perceived about him or it: with a ܕ-clause — Gn 1.3 ܚܙܐ ܐܠܗܐ ܠܢܘܗܪܐ ܕܫܦܝܪ 'God saw the light that (it was) good'; Mt 25.24 ܝܕܥ ܗܘܝܬ ܠܟ ܕܩܫܝܐ ܐܢܬ ܓܒܪܐ 'I knew that you are a hard man'; with a ܟܕ-clause—Ex 2.11 ܚܙܐ ܠܓܒܪܐ ܡܨܪܝܐ ܟܕ ܡܚܐ ܠܓܒܪܐ ܥܒܪܝܐ 'he saw an Egyptian striking a Hebrew'; Mt 26.40 ܐܫܟܚ ܐܢܘܢ ܟܕ ܕܡܟܝܢ 'he found them asleep'; with no conjunction and with a ptc. instead of a finite verb—Gn 21.9 ܚܙܬ ܣܪܐ ܠܒܪܗ ܕܗܓܪ ... ܡܓܚܟ 'Sarah saw Hagar's son ... sporting'([8]); Jdg 3.25 ܚܙܘ ܠܡܪܗܘܢ ܕܪܡܐ ܥܠ ܐܪܥܐ ܡܝܬ 'they saw their master lying on the ground dead.'

f) Object complement. A structure similar to the one illustrated by Gn 21.9 and Jdg 3.25 cited in the immediately preceding paragraph is one whereby a constituent associated with a direct object constitutes with the latter a nominal clause: Gn 5.2 ܕܟܪܐ ܘܢܩܒܬܐ ܒܪܐ ܐܢܘܢ 'he created them male and female' (= they were m. and f.); Gn 30.6 ܩܪܬ ܫܡܗ ܕܢ 'she called his name Dan'; Is 3.4 ܐܩܝܡ ܛܠܝܐ ܪܘܫܢܝܗܘܢ 'I shall set the youth as their leaders.'

g) Asyndetic complementation. Besides examples quoted above where two verbs are simply juxtaposed without any formal marking of subordination, there are cases of tighter cohesion between the two verbs, so that hardly any other word intervenes between them: Gn 27.14 ܐܙܠ ܢܣܒ 'he went (and) took'; Ex 4.19 ܗܦܘܟ ܙܠ 'Go back'; Gn 25.34 ܩܡ ܐܙܠ 'he got up (and) went'; Mt 14.12 ܘܩܪܒܘ ܬܠܡܝܕܘܗܝ ܫܩܠܘ ܫܠܕܗ ܩܒܪܘ ܘܐܬܘ ܚܘܝܘ ܠܝܫܘܥ 'and his disciples approached, took his corpse, buried, and came, reported to Jesus'; Mt 24.45 ܩܕܡܬ ܐܡܪܬ 'I told beforehand'; Aphr. I 52.14 ܡܩܕܡ ܗܘܐ ܡܠܒ ܗܘܐ (Pa pass. Ptc.) 'was promised beforehand'([9]); Gn 45.13 ܣܪܗܒܘ ܐܚܬܘ ܠܐܒܝ 'Bring my father down quickly'([10]); Lk 14.5 ܕܠܐ ܢܓܕܝܘܗܝ 'it pulls up.' The two verbs mostly share same subject, and many of them indicate physical

[8] Cp. Gn 26.8 ܚܙܝܗܝ ܠܐܝܣܚܩ ܟܕ ܡܓܚܟ ܥܡ ܪܦܩܐ 'he saw Isaac laughing with Rebecca.'

[9] On the repetition of the enclitic, note also Lk 13.7 ܐܬܐ ܐܢܐ ܒܥܐ ܐܢܐ, but it need not be repeated as in ib. S ܐܬܐ ܒܥܐ ܐܢܐ 'I come looking for ...'

[10] Note the variety of syntagmas with the same verb: Gn 18.7 ܣܪܗܒ ܕܢܥܒܕܝܘܗܝ 'he cooked it quickly'; ib. 41.32 ܡܣܪܗܒ ܐܠܗܐ ܠܡܥܒܕܗ 'God hastens to do it.'

movement.

h) A verb may be complemented by a participle in particular which concords with the subject, indicating a contemporaneous and accompanying circumstance: Mt 16.1 ܘܩܪܒܘ ܦܪ̈ܝܫܐ ... ܡܢܣܝܢ ܠܗ 'the Pharisees came up ... testing him.'

i) Cognate objects. A verb may take an object noun derived from the same root as that of the verb. In most cases such an object is further expanded by an adjective or its equivalent, so that the real complement of the verb is such an adjective: Nu 11.33 ܘܡܚܐ ܡܪܝܐ ܒܥܡܐ ܡܚܘܬܐ ܕܛܒ ܪܒܐ 'and the Lord dealt the people a very great blow'; 1Sm 20.17 ܪܚܡܬܐ ܕܢܦܫܗ ܪܚܡܗ 'he loved him with self-love'; Mt 2.10 ܚܕܝܘ ܚܕܘܬܐ ܪܒܬܐ 'they rejoiced greatly.' From an example such as ܡܝܬ ܡܘܬܐ ܒܝܫܐ 'he died a terrible death' or ܐܒܕܬ ܐܒܕܢܗ ܐܚܪܝܐ 'it perished for the last time' where the verbs are hardly transitive, it is obvious that these are not direct objects in the usual sense, but rather adverbial complements.

j) Lamadh-less infinitive. An infinitive without the prefomative Lamadh is often added to a verb in order to reinforce the latter or indicate the tone of insistence: Gn 15.13 ܡܕܥ ܬܕܥ 'Do know'; Aphr. I 465.11 ܕܢܫܟܚ ܒܢܐ 'so that he can build (and not destroy).' Such an infinitive may follow the head verb (Dn 9.21 ܦܪܚ ܡܦܪܚ 'it did fly away') or be separated from the latter (Aphr. I 637.3 ܡܛܠܡܢܐ ܠܡܚܛܐ ܚܛܝܬ 'Why did you indeed sin?'). This kind of infinitive remains verbal in nature, capable of taking all kinds of complements, but where an adjective, numeral, relative clause and the like is to complement it, a straight nominal form is used instead: ܡܝܬ ܡܘܬܐ ܒܝܫܐ 'he died a terrible death' (quoted above); ܗܢܐ ܩܛܠܐ ܢܬܩܛܠ ܙܒܢܬܐ ܚܕܐ 'this one shall be killed once only.'

§ 99 Verbs expanded by adverbs or their equivalents. A verb may be modified by an adverb or its phrasal or clausal equivalent, the latter being an adverbial noun phrase, an infinitive, a prepositional phrase, a subordinate clause introduced by the subordinating conjunction ܕ or its various combinations with interrogatives such as ܐܡܬܝ ܕ 'when,' ܐܝܟܐ ܕ 'where,' ܐܝܟ ܕ 'as' (of manner, similarity) etc. (§ 76) or other conjunctions such as ܐܢ 'if,' ܟܐ 'where' and ܟܕ 'when.' These adverbials indicate a time, place, reason, manner, condition or such like. Some examples are: Gn 42.7 ܡܠܠ ܥܡܗܘܢ ܩܫܝܐܝܬ 'he spoke with them harshly'; Lk 2.49 ܒܝܬ ܐܒܝ ܘܠܐ ܠܝ ܕܐܗܘܐ 'it is proper that I should be in the house of my father'; Acts 5.21 ܢܦܩܘ ܥܡ ܨܦܪܐ 'they went out at daybreak'; Ex 23.17 ܬܠܬ ܙܒܢܝܢ ܒܫܢܬܐ ܢܬܚܙܐ ܟܠ ܕܘܟܪܢܟ ܩܕܡ ܡܪܝܐ 'three times per year every memory (!) should appear before the Lord'; Mt 2.2 ܘܐܬܝܢ ܠܡܣܓܕ ܠܗ 'we have come to worship him'; ib. 2.1 ܟܕ ܐܬܝܠܕ ܝܫܘܥ ܒܒܝܬ ܠܚܡ 'Jesus was born in Bethlehem'; ib. 2.8 ܟܕ ܐܫܟܚܬܘܢܝܗܝ ܬܘ ܚܘܐܘܢܝ 'when you have found him, come (and) tell me'; Jdg 4.8 ܐܢ ܐܙܠܐ ܐܢܬ ܥܡܝ ܐܙܠ ܐܢܐ 'should you go with me, I shall go.' Compare further Mt 28.7 ܙܠܝܢ ܒܥܓܠ 'Go quickly' with ib. 28.8 ܘܐܙܠ ܒܥܓܠ 'and they went quickly.'

§ 100 Prepositions modified by a prepositional phrase or adverb. When a preposition is complemented by a prepositional phrase or adverb instead of by a substantive, the proclitic Dalath is prefixed to the latter: e.g. Mt 10.37 ܡܢ ܕܪܚܡ ܐܒܐ ܐܘ ܐܡܐ ܝܬܝܪ ܡܢ ܕܠܝ 'he who loves (his) father or mother more than me'; Mt 26.55 ܐܝܟ ܕܥܠ ܓܝܣܐ ܢܦܩܬܘܢ 'you have come out as if against a bandit'; ib. 20.14 ܠܗܢܐ ܐܚܪܝܐ ܐܬܠ ܐܝܟ ܕܠܟ 'I shall give to this last one as to you'; ib. 21.46 ܐܝܟ ܕܠܢܒܝܐ ܐܚܝܕܝܢ ܗܘܘ ܠܗ 'they regarded him as a prophet.' Cf. also Mt 6.10 ܐܝܟܢܐ ܕܒܫܡܝܐ 'as in heaven'; Gn 4.13 ܪܒܐ ܗܝ ܚܘܒܬܝ ܡܢ ܕܠܡܫܬܒܩܘ 'my sin is greater than to be forgiven.'

§ 101 Clause structure. Two types of clause may be recognised: verbal and nominal. A *verbal clause* contains as one of its core constituents a finite verb (Pf., Impf., Impv.) which may include within itself its grammatical subject as in ܟܬܒܬ ܟܬܒܐ 'I wrote a book' or the subject may be positioned outside of the clause nucleus either before or after the verb as in ܫܠܝܚܐ ܫܕܪ ܐܝܙܓܕܐ 'the apostle sent an envoy' or ܟܬܒܘ ܫܠܝܚܐ ܟܬܒܐ 'the apostles wrote a book.' The position of the participle in this scheme of classification is ambiguous. All other well-formed clauses may be regarded *nominal*.

§ 102 The Syriac **nominal clause** displays a rich variety of patterns and structures capable of expressing rather subtle nuances of predication.[11] Leaving aside clauses with ܐܝܬ to be dealt with later, the Syriac nominal clause may be formally classified according to the number of its core constituents, mostly three but occasionally two or four. In addition, one can identify three structural meanings which may be assigned to each of those patterns: descriptive, identificatory, and contrastive.

§ 103 Examples of **bipartite** nominal clauses are: Lk 22.26S ܐܢ̄ܬܘܢ ܠܐ ܗܟܢܐ 'you are not like that'; Gn 9.12 ܗܕܐ ܐܬܐ ܕܩܝܡܐ 'this is the sign of the covenant' (cf. ib. 17 ܗܕܐ ܗ̄ܝ ܐܬܐ ܕܩܝܡܐ); Mt 5.12 ܐܓܪܟܘܢ ܣܓܝ ܒܫܡܝܐ 'your reward is plentiful in heaven'; 9.37 ܚܨܕܐ ܣܓܝ ܘܦܥܠܐ ܙܥܘܪܝܢ 'the harvest is abundant and labourers are few'; Gn 27.22 ܩܠܐ ܕܝܥܩܘܒ ܘܓܫܫܬ ܐܝܕܝܐ ܕܥܣܘ 'the voice is that of Jacob and the feel of the hands is that of Esau'; 33.13 ܛܠܝܐ ܛܠܝܢ 'the children are young'; Ru 1.16 ܥܡܟܝ ܥܡܝ ܐܠܗܟܝ ܐܠܗܝ 'your people is my people, your god is my god.'

§ 104 The standard **tripartite** nominal clause contains an enclitic personal pronoun (§ 10), which brings the immediately preceding clause constituent into focus. The enclitic is normally that of the third person concording with the subject: e.g. Jn 8.39 ܐܒܘܢ ܕܝܠܢ ܐܒܪܗܡ ܗ̄ܘ 'our father is Abraham'; Mt 16.16 ܐܢ̄ܬ ܗ̄ܘ ܡܫܝܚܐ 'you are the Christ.' The enclitic, however, may be assimilated in form to the preceding constituent when it is a personal pronoun: Mt 24.5 ܐܢܐ ܐܢ̄ܐ ܡܫܝܚܐ 'I am the Christ.'

The sequence of ܗܘ followed by its enclitic form is spelled as one word in the form of ܗܘܝܘ: e.g. Mt 16.20 ܗܘܝܘ ܡܫܝܚܐ 'he is the Christ.' By contrast the combination of the feminine ܗܝ is ܗܝ ܗ̄ܝ, pronounced /hiyi/.

Where the constituent immediately preceding the enclitic consists of more than one word, there occurs a discontinuous constituent, with the second and subsequent words following the enclitic: Gn 18.27 ܘܐܢܐ ܥܦܪܐ ܐܢ̄ܐ ܘܩܛܡܐ 'and I am dust and ashes'; Jn 8.53 ܠܡܐ ܐܢ̄ܬ

[11] For details, see Muraoka 1987 (1996) §§ 102-108 and the literature cited there.

ܪܒ ܐܢܬ ܡܢ ܐܒܘܢ 'why are you greater than our father?'; Jonah 1.8 ܡܢ ܐܝܢܐ ܐܢܬ ܥܡܐ 'Which people do you belong to?'; Gn 4.9 ܢܛܘܪܗ ܐܢܐ ܠܡ ܕܐܚܝ 'Am I then the keeper of my brother?'; Dt 31.2 ܒܪ ܡܐܐ ܐܢܐ ܘܥܣܪܝܢ ܫܢܝܢ ܝܘܡܢܐ 'today I am hundred and twenty years old.'

§ **105** Schematically presented and leaving prosodic aspects out of consideration, 'David is my master' may be rendered in Syriac by four tripartite structures:

a) ܡܪܝ[12] ܗܘ ܕܘܝܕ P - s - S[13]

b) ܕܘܝܕ ܗܘ ܡܪܝ P - s - S

c) ܕܘܝܕ ܡܪܝ ܗܘ S - P - s

d) ܡܪܝ ܕܘܝܕ ܗܘ P - S - s

The last pattern is not very widely attested to: e.g. ܒܠ ܦܓܪ̈ܝܢ ܢܠܒܠܗ ܐܢܬ ܗܘ 'you are master of our bodies'; ܩܕܝܫ ܐܢܬ ܗܘ 'you are holy'; ܐܪܙܗ ܕܐܠܗܐ ܡܫܝܚܐ ܗܘ 'Christ is a mystery of God'([14]); Mt 12.8S ܡܪܗ ܕܫܒܬܐ ܒܪܗ ܗܘ ܕܐܢܫܐ 'the son of man is lord of the sabbath'; *Odes of Solomon* 5.2 ܣܒܪܝ ܐܢܬ ܗܘ 'you are my hope'; Jn 9.9S ܗܢܘ ܗܘ 'this is him.'

§ **106** A pronominal subject of bipartite nominal clauses may be deleted in a relative clause, a clause complementing verbs of knowledge or perception etc., or a circumstantial clause. Such deletion is extremely rare with the first and second persons. Examples are:

Acta Thomae 194.15 ܕܪܚܝܩܝܢ ܡܢܗ '(things) which are far from it'; Lk 21.21 ܐܝܠܝܢ ܕܒܝܗܘܕ ܐܢܘܢ .. ܐܝܠܝܢ ܕܒܓܘܗ ܐܢܘܢ .. ܕܒܩܘܪ̈ܝܐ 'those who are in Judaea ... and those who are in it ... and those who are in villages'; Mt 15.31 .. ܚܙܘ ܚܪ̈ܫܐ ܕܡܡܠܠܝܢ ܘܦܟܝ̈ܓܐ ܕܡܬܚܠܡܝܢ '... saw the dumb speaking and the maimed recovering'; *Acta Thomae*

[12] Pronounce: (a) /maaru daawi<u>d</u>/, (b) /daawi<u>d</u>u maar/, /daawi<u>d</u> maaru/ and /maar daawi<u>d</u>u/ respectively.

[13] The lower case "s" signifies, in accordance with Jespersen (1937: 91-93), "small subject." S = subject; P = predicate; E = enclitic pronoun.

[14] References: *Euphemia*, p. 13; Bedjan, *J. Sarugensis*, I, pp. 222; Ephrem, *L'Évangile concordant*, p. 2.

200.4 ܠܗ ܐܩܝܡ ܟܕ ܚܝ 'to raise him up alive.'

The enclitic is normally retained in causal clauses: Ex 5.8 ܡܛܠ ܕܒܛܝܠܐ ܐܢܘܢ 'because they are idle.'

Where there are two or more coordinate predicatives, the identical enclitic subject need not be repeated: Ac 1.11 ܡܢܐ ܩܝܡܝܢ ܐܢܬܘܢ ܘܚܝܪܝܢ ܒܫܡܝܐ 'why are you standing and looking at the sky?' but ib. 2.33 ܚܙܝܢ ܐܢܬܘܢ ܘܫܡܥܝܢ ܐܢܬܘܢ 'you see and hear' (ὑμεῖς καὶ βλέπετε καὶ ἀκούετε).

§ 107 Structural meaning Where "David is my master" is, or can be construed as, a reply to the question "What is David?", the nominal clause may be said to be descriptive in meaning. If it is, or can be construed as, a reply to the question "Who (or: Which) among you (or: them) is David?", its structural meaning is that of identification. Finally, "David is my master" may be in contrast, whether explicitly or implicitly, with, say, "John is my servant."

Of the four patterns mentioned above (§ 105), **a** and **d** are usually descriptive, **b** identificatory, and *c* contrastive. For example—

a) **Descriptive**: ܡܪܟ ܗܘ ܗܢܐ 'Is this your master?'; Aphr. I 116.9f ܣܓܝܐܝܢ ܐܢܘܢ ܥܒܘܕܘܗܝ 'its makers are many.' For examples of (**d**), see above, § 105 end.

Where the subject is a personal pronoun, the bipartite construction <X + pron.> is the norm: Mt 8.26 ܠܡܢܐ ܕܚܘܠܬܢܝܢ ܐܢܬܘܢ 'why are you fearful?'

b) **Identificatory**: Mt 27.11 ܐܢܬ ܗܘ ܡܠܟܐ ܕܝܗܘܕܝܐ 'are *you* the king of the Jews?'; Lk 7.19 ܐܢܬ ܗܘ ܕܐܬܐ 'are *you* the one who is to come?'; Jn 4.29 ܗܘܝܘ ܡܫܝܚܐ (= * ܗܘ ܗܘ) '*he* is the messiah.'

The enclitic ܗܘ may be replaced by one matching with the preceding personal pronoun: Mt 24.5 ܐܢܐ ܐܢܐ ܡܫܝܚܐ '*I* am the messiah.' With the second person, ܐܢܬ ܗܘ, for instance, seems to be preferred to ܐܢܬ ܐܢܬ, perhaps for the sake of euphony: note Mt 14.28 ܐܢ ܐܢܬ ܗܘ as against ib. 27 ܐܢܐ ܐܢܐ 'it's me.'

This structure is highly frequent with interrogatives as predicates: ܡܢܘ 'who is it that ... ?'; ܐܝܟܘ /ʾaykaw/ 'where is it that ... ?'

c) **Contrastive**: Mt 20.15 ܥܝܢܟ ܒܝܫܐ ܘܐܢܐ ܛܒ ܐܢܐ 'your eye is evil, but I am good'; Jn 8.23 ܐܢܬܘܢ ܡܢ ܕܠܬܚܬ ܐܢܬܘܢ ܘܐܢܐ ܡܢ ܕܠܥܠ ܐܢܐ 'you are one of those who are below, but I am one of those who are above.' The same structural meaning can be expressed in a bipartite form with the subject preceding: Jn 15.5S ܐܢܐ ܓܘܦܢܐ ܘܐܢܬܘܢ ܫܒܝܛܐ 'I am the vine and you are the branches.'

§ 108 There are found on occasion *quadripartite* nominal clauses as an extension of the pattern P—E—S or S—E—P used apparently in order to avoid clumsiness or misunderstanding: Dt 7.9 ܡܪܝܐ ܐܠܗܟ ܗܘܝܘ ܐܠܗܐ 'the Lord your God is the God'; Mt 13.39S ܙܪܘܥܗܘܢ ܗܘܝܘ ܒܝܫܐ 'their sower is the evil one.'

§ 109 Existence, location and ܐܝܬ.(15) That some object exists ("existential" clause) or is to be found at a specific location ("locative") is normally expressed with the mediation of the particle ܐܝܬ, though the latter may be absent as in Mt 1.23S ܐܠܗܐ ܥܡܢ 'God is with us'; Gn 41.12 ܘܬܡܢ ܥܡܢ ܛܠܝܐ ܥܒܪܝܐ 'and there was there with us a Hebrew lad.' Compare Lk 1.66S ܐܝܕܗ ܕܡܪܝܐ ܥܡܗ 'the hand of the Lord (was) with him' with ib. P ܐܝܕܗ ܕܡܪܝܐ ܐܝܬ ܗܘܬ ܥܡܗ.

With very few exceptions the unsuffixed ܐܝܬ has a logically indeterminate object whose existence or non-existence (the latter with ܠܝܬ /layt/) is indicated. Conversely, when the subject is determinate, the particle is, if used, suffixed with the matching pronoun: e.g., Jn 4.37 ܒܗܕܐ ܐܝܬܝܗ ܡܠܬܐ ܕܫܪܪܐ 'herein is the word of truth.'

Both sequences, NP - ܐܝܬ and ܐܝܬ - NP, are attested with little difference between them.(16)

In addition to the "existential" and "locative" uses, ܐܝܬ is also used as a substitute for a pronominal enclitic of tripartite nominal clauses: e.g. Mt 12.8 ܡܪܗ ܕܫܒܬܐ ܐܝܬܘܗܝ ܒܪܗ ܕܐܢܫܐ 'the son of man is the lord of sabbath'; Lk 19.46 ܒܝܬܝ ܒܝܬ ܨܠܘܬܐ ܐܝܬܘܗܝ 'my house is the house of prayer'; Mt 13.38 ܘܚܩܠܐ ܐܝܬܘܗܝ ܥܠܡܐ 'and the field is the world.'

15 See Muraoka 1977.

16 See Joosten 1996: 100.

When some object is said to have existed in the past, the enclitic ܗܘܳܐ follows ܐܝܬ: thus ܒܢܰܗܪܳܐ ܐܺܝܬ ܗܘܰܘ ܢܽܘܢܶܐ 'there were fishes in the river'; ܬܡܳܢ ܐܺܝܬ ܗܘܳܬ ܡܕܺܝܢܬܳܐ ܫܰܦܺܝܪܬܳܐ 'there was there a beautiful city.'

Applied to the past, ܐܺܝܬ ܗܘܳܐ is occasionally treated as indeclinable: Lk 1.7 ܠܰܝܬ ܗܘܳܐ ܠܗܽܘܢ ܕܽܘܟܬܳܐ 'they had no place,' instead of ܗܘܳܬ.

§ 110 Focusing function of the enclitic ܗܘ. In many of the examples cited above the enclitic ܗܘ, sometimes made to match formally the preceding component, serves to indicate focus on the immediately preceding clause constituent. Similar function may be identified where the preceding constituent is other than a pronoun or noun phrase: *Mart.* 1:227 paen ܠܚܰܕ ܗܽܘ ܐܰܠܳܗܳܐ ܦܳܠܚܺܝܢܰܢ 'it is the only one God that we worship'; *Spic.* 1.15 ܐܶܢ ܠܡܶܐܠܰܦ ܗܽܘ ܪܳܓܶܒܬ 'if it is learning that you desire'; Jdg 7.2 ܐܺܝܕܝ ܗܽܘ ܙܰܟܝܳܬܰܢܝ (ܐܺܝܕܳܐ is fem.) 'it is my hand that won me victory'; Aphr. I 140.27 ܢܽܘܪܳܐ ܗܘ ܡܠܰܚܟܳܐ ܗܘܳܬ ܠܗܽܘܢ 'it was fire that was licking them'; Mt 12.33 ܡܶܢ ܦܺܐܪܰܘܗ̱ܝ ܗܘ ܓܶܝܪ ܡܶܬܝܕܰܥ ܐܺܝܠܳܢܳܐ 'for it is by its fruits that the tree can be assessed.' See also above, § 93.11.

§ 111 Antecedentless relative clauses. A relative clause may lack an explicit antecedent, amounting to 'that which; one who, he who' and the like: e.g. ܕܫܰܠܺܝܛ ܓܶܝܪ ܒܟܽܠ ܚܰܕ ܗܽܘ 'he who controls all is one'; Mt 5.44 ܥܒܶܕܘ ܕܫܰܦܺܝܪ 'Do what is good'; 8.10 ܘܶܐܡܰܪ ܠܕܳܐܬܶܝܢ ܥܰܡܶܗ 'and he said to those who were coming with him.'

This type of relative clause of anonymous reference, however, commonly takes a dummy antecedent such as a demonstrative pronoun, an interrogative pronoun or ܡܶܕܶܡ: e.g. Is 56.4 ܢܶܓܒܽܘܢ ܡܶܕܶܡ ܕܨܳܒܶܐ ܐ̱ܢܳܐ 'they choose what I desire'; Josh 10.11 ܣܰܓܺܝܐܺܝܢ ܗܘܰܘ ܕܡܺܝܬܘ ܒܟܺܐܦܶܐ ܕܒܰܪܕܳܐ ܡܶܢ ܗܳܢܽܘܢ ܕܩܰܛܠܘ ܒܢܰܝ ܐܺܝܣܪܳܝܶܠ ܒܚܰܪܒܳܐ 'more were those who died with hailstones than those who the Israelites slew with the sword'; Mt 5.6 ܛܽܘܒܰܝܗܽܘܢ ܠܰܐܝܠܶܝܢ ܕܟܰܦܢܺܝܢ ܘܨܗܶܝܢ ܠܟܺܐܢܽܘܬܳܐ 'Blessed are those who hunger and thirst for righteousness'; Mt 10.40 ܡܰܢ ܕܠܝ ܡܩܰܒܶܠ ܠܡܰܢ ܕܫܰܠܚܰܢܝ ܡܩܰܒܶܠ 'he who receives me receives him who has sent me'; Mt 10.13 ܘܗܰܘ ܕܐܺܝܬ ܠܶܗ ܢܶܬܬܽܘܣܰܦ ܢܶܬܝܰܗܒ 'that which he has will also be taken away from him.' These deictics may be multiplied: ܗ̇ܘ ܡܰܢ ܕ, ܗ̇ܘ ܡܶܕܶܡ ܕ, ܗ̇ܢܳܐ ܡܶܕܶܡ ܕ, ܗ̇ܢܘܢ ܐ̱ܝܠܶܝܢ ܕ, ܗ̇ܠܶܝܢ ܐ̱ܝܠܶܝܢ ܕ, ܐ̱ܝܢܳܐ ܕ, ܗ̇ܠܶܝܢ ܡܶܕܶܡ ܕ. Similar are combinations such as ܟܠ ܡܰܢ ܕ, ܟܠ ܐ̱ܝܢܳܐ ܕ, ܟܠ ܐ̱ܝܠܶܝܢ ܕ.

§ 112 Prolepsis. When a person or a thing is considered contextually definite, Syriac is fond of referring to such an entity in advance with the concording pronoun first, and later specifying it by using the noun phrase itself. This taking-in-advance, *prolepsis* (πρόληψις), may occur in various syntactic relations.

a) Simple prepositional adverbial adjuncts

ܡܰܠܶܦ ܗ̱ܘܳܐ ܒܶܗ ܒܣܦܺܝܢ݇ܬܳܐ 'he was teaching in the boat'

ܒܶܗ ܒܠܺܠܝܳܐ 'on that same night'

b) Indirect objects

ܐܶܡܪܰܬ ܠܶܗ ܠܡܰܠܟܳܐ 'she said to the king'

c) Direct objects

ܩܰܒܠܶܗ ܠܡܶܠܬܳܐ or ܩܰܒܠܶܗ ܡܶܠܬܳܐ 'he accepted the word'

ܩܰܒܶܠ ܐܶܢܶܝܢ ܠܡ̈ܶܠܶܐ or ܩܒܠ ܐܢܝܢ ܡ̈ܠܐ 'he accepted the words'

ܡܩܰܒܶܠ ܐ̱ܢܳܐ ܠܗܶܝܢ ܠܡ̈ܶܠܶܐ 'I accept the words'

d) ܕ-mediated analytical substitute for construct phrases

ܡ̈ܶܠܰܘܗ̱ܝ ܕܡܳܪܝܳܐ 'the words of the Lord'

e) ܕ-mediated prepositional adjuncts

ܥܰܡܗܶܝܢ ܕܒ̈ܢܳܬܶܗ 'together with his daughters'

f) With ܟܠ 'all, every'

ܟܽܠܗܘܢ ܥܰܡ̈ܡܶܐ 'all the nations'

g) With numerals

ܬܪ̈ܰܬܰܝܗܶܝܢ ܡܕ̈ܺܝܢܳܬܳܐ 'the two cities'

h) With possessive pronouns ܕܺܝܠ-

ܕܺܝܠܗܽܘܢ ܕܬܪ̈ܶܥܣܰܪ ܫܠܺܝ̈ܚܺܝܢ ܫ̈ܡܳܗܶܐ 'the names of the twelve apostles' (Mt 10.2); ܡܫܰܡ̈ܫܳܢܶܐ ܕܺܝܠܶܗ ܕܡܶܠܬܳܐ 'the ministers of the word' (Lk 1.2)

i) Third person independent pronouns

ܐܶܡܰܪ ܗܽܘ ܐܶܪܡܝܳܐ 'Jeremiah said'

ܗܝ ܗܕܐ ܠܡܥܒܕ 'to do this'

ܠܐ ܗܐ ܐܦ ܡܟܣܐ ܗܝ ܗܕܐ ܥܒܕܝܢ 'Surely the tax-collectors also do that?' (Mt 5.46)

j) With ܐܝܬ

ܐܝܬܘܗܝ ܗܘܐ ܕܝܢ ܚܙܘܗ ܐܝܟ ܒܪܩܐ 'now his appearance was like a lightning' (Mt 28.3)

A proleptic pronoun may be separated by an intervening word or words from the noun phrase to which it refers: Mt 13.56S ܡܢ ܐܝܡܟܐ ܠܗ ܗܠܝܢ ܟܠܗܝܢ ܠܗܢܐ 'whence did this one get all this?'; Ac 8.10 ܗܢܘ ܚܝܠܗ ܪܒܐ ܕܐܠܗܐ 'this is the great power of God.'

§ 113 Compound sentence. A topicalised clause constituent is placed at the beginning of a clause and is subsequently referred back by means of a concording pronoun: Ps 125.2 ܐܘܪܫܠܡ ܛܘܪܐ ܚܕܪܝܢ ܠܗ 'Jerusalem is surrounded by mountains'; Aphr I 33.9 ܗܒܝܠ ܓܝܪ ܡܛܠ ܗܝܡܢܘܬܗ ܐܬܩܒܠ ܩܘܪܒܢܗ 'for in the case of Abel his offering was accepted because of his faith'; Mt 17.27 ܢܘܢܐ ܩܕܡܝܐ ܕܣܠܩ ܦܬܘܚ ܦܘܡܗ 'the first fish that comes up—open its mouth!'

EXERCISES

(**1**) Transliterate the following piece into the Latin alphabet, ignoring silent letters. [§§ 2-3, 6]

ܒܪܺܫܺܝܬ ܒܪܳܐ ܐܰܠܳܗܳܐ ܝܳܬ ܫܡܰܝܳܐ ܘܝܳܬ ܐܰܪܥܳܐ. ܘܰܐܪܥܳܐ ܗܘܳܬ ܬܘܗ
ܘܒܘܗ ܘܚܶܫܘܽܟܳܐ ܥܰܠ ܐܰܦܰܝ̈ ܬܗܘܳܡܳܐ ܘܪܘܚܶܗ ܕܰܐܠܳܗܳܐ ܡܪܰܚܦܳܐ ܥܰܠ
ܐܰܦܰܝ̈ ܡܰܝ̈ܳܐ. ܘܶܐܡܰܪ ܐܰܠܳܗܳܐ: ܢܶܗܘܶܐ ܢܘܽܗܪܳܐ: ܘܰܗܘܳܐ ܢܘܽܗܪܳܐ.
ܘܰܚܙܳܐ ܐܰܠܳܗܳܐ ܠܢܘܽܗܪܳܐ ܕܫܰܦܺܝܪ ܘܰܦܪܰܫ ܐܰܠܳܗܳܐ ܒܶܝܬ ܢܘܽܗܪܳܐ
ܠܚܶܫܘܽܟܳܐ. ܘܩܪܳܐ ܐܰܠܳܗܳܐ ܠܢܘܽܗܪܳܐ ܐܺܝܡܳܡܳܐ ܘܰܠܚܶܫܘܽܟܳܐ ܩܪܳܐ
ܠܺܠܝܳܐ ܘܰܗܘܳܐ ܪܰܡܫܳܐ ܘܰܗܘܳܐ ܨܰܦܪܳܐ ܝܰܘܡܳܐ ܚܰܕ. ܘܶܐܡܰܪ ܐܰܠܳܗܳܐ
ܢܶܗܘܶܐ ܪܩܺܝܥܳܐ ܒܰܡܨܰܥܬ ܡܰܝ̈ܳܐ ܘܢܶܗܘܶܐ ܦܳܪܶܫ ܒܶܝܬ ܡܰܝ̈ܳܐ ܠܡܰܝ̈ܳܐ.
ܘܰܥܒܰܕ ܐܰܠܳܗܳܐ ܪܩܺܝܥܳܐ ܘܰܦܪܰܫ ܒܶܝܬ ܡܰܝ̈ܳܐ ܕܰܠܬܰܚܬ ܡܶܢ ܪܩܺܝܥܳܐ
ܘܒܶܝܬ ܡܰܝ̈ܳܐ ܕܰܠܥܶܠ ܡܶܢ ܪܩܺܝܥܳܐ. ܘܰܗܘܳܐ ܗܳܟܰܢܳܐ. ܘܩܪܳܐ ܐܰܠܳܗܳܐ
ܠܪܩܺܝܥܳܐ ܫܡܰܝܳܐ ܘܰܗܘܳܐ ܪܰܡܫܳܐ ܘܰܗܘܳܐ ܨܰܦܪܳܐ ܝܰܘܡܳܐ ܕܬܰܪܶܝܢ.
ܘܶܐܡܰܪ ܐܰܠܳܗܳܐ: ܢܶܬܟܰܢܫܽܘܢ ܡܰܝ̈ܳܐ ܕܰܠܬܚܶܝܬ ܫܡܰܝܳܐ ܠܰܐܬܪܳܐ ܚܰܕ.
ܘܬܶܬܚܙܶܐ ܝܰܒܺܫܬܳܐ ܘܰܗܘܳܐ ܗܳܟܰܢܳܐ. ܘܩܪܳܐ ܐܰܠܳܗܳܐ ܠܝܰܒܺܫܬܳܐ
ܐܰܪܥܳܐ ܘܰܠܟܶܢܫܳܐ ܕܡܰܝ̈ܳܐ ܩܪܳܐ ܝܰܡܡ̈ܶܐ ܘܰܚܙܳܐ ܐܰܠܳܗܳܐ ܕܫܰܦܺܝܪ.

(**2**) Rewrite the following in the Estrangela script. Silent letters have been added within the brackets.

we(ʾ)mar ʾalaahaa(ʾ): tappeq ʾarʿaa(ʾ) te<u>d</u>(ʾ)aa(ʾ) ʿesbaa(ʾ) dmezdraʿ zarʿaa(ʾ) lgenseeh w(ʾ)ilaanaa(ʾ) dfee(ʾ)ree(ʾ) dʿaave<u>d</u> pee(ʾ)ree(ʾ) lgenseeh: dneṣbṯeeh beeh ʿal ʾarʿaa(ʾ): wahwaa(ʾ) haa<u>k</u>annaa(ʾ).
wa(ʾ)pqaṯ ʾarʿaa(ʾ) te<u>d</u>(ʾ)aa(ʾ) ʿesbaa(ʾ) dmezdraʿ zarʿaa(ʾ) lgenseeh: wi(ʾ)laanaa(ʾ) dʿaave<u>d</u> pee(ʾ)ree(ʾ) dneṣbṯeeh beeh lgenseeh: waḥzaa(ʾ) ʾalaahaa(ʾ) dšappir.

wahwaa(ʾ) ramšaa(ʾ) wahwaa(ʾ) ṣafraa(ʾ) yawmaa(ʾ) da<u>t</u>laa<u>t</u>aa(ʾ).
we(ʾ)mar ʾalaahaa(ʾ): nehwon nahhiree(ʾ) barqiʿaa(ʾ) dašmayyaa: lmefraš bee<u>t</u> ʾimaamaa(ʾ) lleelyaa(ʾ): wnehwon laa(ʾ)<u>t</u>waa<u>t</u>aa(ʾ): walzavnee(ʾ) walyawmaa<u>t</u>aa(ʾ) wlašnayyaa(ʾ). manhrin barqiʿaa(ʾ) dašmayyaa lmanhaaru ʿal ʾarʿaa(ʾ): wahwaa(ʾ) haa<u>k</u>annaa(ʾ).
waʿva<u>d</u> ʾalaahaa(ʾ) treen nahhiree(ʾ) rawrvee(ʾ): nahhiraa(ʾ) rabbaa(ʾ) lšulṭaanaa(ʾ) di(ʾ)maamaa(ʾ): wnahhiraa(ʾ) zʿoraa(ʾ) lšulṭaanaa(ʾ) dleelyaa(ʾ): w<u>k</u>awkvee(ʾ).
wya(h)v ʾennon ʾalaahaa(ʾ) barqiʿaa(ʾ) dašmayyaa(ʾ) lmanhaaru ʿal ʾarʿaa(ʾ).

(**3**) By using all the independent personal pronouns, write out short sentences in Syriac: "I [both m. and f.] am beautiful [ܫܦܝܪ and ܫܦܝܪܐ]," "You are beautiful," etc. Make sure that you use the enclitic forms of the pronouns. [§§ 9, 10, 17].

(**4**) Decline fully the adjective ܩܕܝܫ "sacred; saint" and the noun ܡܠܬܐ "word" (pl. ܡ̈ܠܐ). [§ 17, 27]

(**5**) Attach all the suffixed personal pronouns to ܡܪܐ "master" (sg.), ܡܠܬܐ "word" (sg.), ܐܠܗ̈ܐ "gods" (pl.) and ܒ̈ܢܬܐ "daughters" (pl.), and the preposition ܥܠ "on." [§§ 40, 41, 42, 46]

(**6**) Conjugate the following verbs fully in the pattern indicated:
ܟܦܪ "to deny" (Pe: §§ 54, 57; § 55, Type 1); ܦܬܚ "to open" (Pe: § 55, Type 3); ܕܡܟ "to sleep" (Pe: § 55, Type 2; 56); ܟܕܒ "to tell a lie" (Pa: § 57); ܟܪܙ "to proclaim" (Af); ܟܪܟ "to go round" (Ethpe); ܫܒܚ "to be praised" (Ethpa); ܢܣܒ "to take" (Pe: § 61; § 55, Type 3); ܣܠܩ "to bring/take up" (Af: § 61); ܐܒܕ "to perish" (Pe: § 62; § 55, Type 2); ܐܟܠ "to feed" (Af: § 62); ܝܬܒ "to sit" (Pe: § 63; § 55, Type 6); ܝܠܦ "to learn" (Pe: § 63); ܝܕܥ "to make known" (Af: § 63); ܒܢܐ "to build" (Pe: § 64); ܚܕܝ "to be glad" (Pe: § 64); ܫܢܝ "to depart" (Pa: § 64); ܪܦܝ "to let go of" (Af: § 64); ܕܘܢ "to judge" (Pe: § 65); ܩܘܡ "to

move" (Af: § 65); ܢܘܚ "to have rest" (Ettaf: § 65); ܒܙܙ "to rob" (Pe: § 66); ܥܠܠ "to introduce" (Af: § 66).

(**7**) Analyse and translate the following verb forms with suffixed personal pronouns. [§ 68]

(1) ܩܛܠܘܢܝ; (2) ܩܛܠܬܗ; (3) ܩܛܠܢܗܝ; (4) ܩܛܠܬܘܗ; (5) ܩܛܠܝܗ; (6) ܢܩܛܠܘܢܟܘܢ; (7) ܩܒܪܢ; (8) ܠܡܩܒܪܘܬܟܝ; (9) ܐܩܒܪܬܢ; (10) ܩܒܪܘܗ; (11) ܩܒܪܬܝܗܝ; (12) ܢܩܒܪܝܗܝ; (13) ܟܬܒܟ; (14) ܟܬܒܝܗ; (15) ܟܬܒܢܗ; (16) ܬܟܬܒܝܗܝ; (17) ܟܬܒܘܟ; (18) ܐܫܟܚܢܝ; (19) ܐܫܟܚܬܗ; (20) ܐܦܩܘܢ; (21) ܐܦܝܩܢ; (22) ܐܦܩܢ; (23) ܐܦܩܬܗ; (24) ܐܩܝܡܗܝ; (25) ܬܩܝܡܟ; (26) ܠܡܦܩܘܬܟܝ; (27) ܢܩܝܡܝܗ; (28) ܡܢܝܗ; (29) ܕܢܝܗ; (30) ܪܒܬܡܢ; (31) ܚܙܢ; (32) ܚܙܬܟ; (33) ܚܙܝܬܗ; (34) ܐܫܩܝܬܟ; (35) ܠܡܫܩܝܘܬܟܝ; (36) ܐܫܩܝܗܝ; (37) ܐܫܩܢ; (38) ܢܫܩܝܢ; (39) ܚܙܐܘܗ; (40) ܚܙܝܢܗܝ.

KEY TO EXERCISES (pp. 90-92)

(1) breešiṯ braa ʾalaahaa yaaṯ šmayyaa wyaaṯ ʾarʿaa. warʿaa hwaaṯ toh wvoh wḥeššoḵaa ʿal ʾappay thomaa. wruḥeeh dalaahaa mraḥfaa ʿal ʾappay mayyaa. wemar ʾalaahaa: nehwee nuhraa: wahwaa nuhraa. waḥzaa ʾalaahaa lnuhraa dšappir wafraš ʾalaahaa beeṯ nuhraa lḥeššoḵaa. waqraa ʾalaahaa lnuhraa ʾimaamaa walḥeššoḵaa qraa leelyaa wahwaa ramšaa wahwaa ṣafraa yawmaa ḥaḏ. wemar ʾalaahaa nehwee rqiʿaa bmeṣʿaṯ mayyaa wnehwee paareš([1]) beeṯ mayyaa lmayyaa. waʿvaḏ ʾalaahaa rqiʿaa wafraš beeṯ mayyaa dalṯaḥt men rqiʿaa wveeṯ mayyaa dalʿel men rqiʿaa wahwaa haaḵannaa. waqraa ʾalaahaa larqiʿaa šmayyaa wahwaa ramšaa wahwaa ṣafraa yawmaa daṯreen. wemar ʾalaahaa: neṯkanšun mayyaa dalṯaḥt men šmayyaa laṯraa ḥaḏ wṯeṯḥzee yabbištaa wahwaa haaḵannaa. waqraa ʾalaahaa lyabbištaa ʾarʿaa walḵenšaa dmayyaa qraa yammee waḥzaa ʾalaahaa dšappir.

(2)

ܘܐܡܪ ܐܠܗܐ: ܬܦܩ ܐܪܥܐ ܬܕܐܐ ܥܣܒܐ ܕܡܙܕܪܥ ܙܪܥܐ
ܠܓܢܣܗ؛ ܘܐܝܠܢܐ ܕܦܐܪܐ ܥܒܕ ܦܐܪܐ ܠܓܢܣܗ؛ ܕܙܪܥܗ ܒܗ
ܥܠ ܐܪܥܐ؛ ܘܗܘܐ ܗܟܢܐ.
ܘܐܦܩܬ ܐܪܥܐ ܬܕܐܐ ܥܣܒܐ ܕܡܙܕܪܥ ܙܪܥܐ ܠܓܢܣܗ؛
ܘܐܝܠܢܐ ܕܥܒܕ ܦܐܪܐ ܕܙܪܥܗ ܒܗ ܠܓܢܣܗ؛ ܘܚܙܐ ܐܠܗܐ
ܕܫܦܝܪ.
ܘܗܘܐ ܪܡܫܐ ܘܗܘܐ ܨܦܪܐ ܝܘܡܐ ܕܬܠܬܐ.
ܘܐܡܪ ܐܠܗܐ: ܢܗܘܘܢ ܢܗܝܪܐ ܒܪܩܝܥܐ ܕܫܡܝܐ؛ ܠܡܦܪܫܘ ܒܝܬ
ܐܝܡܡܐ ܠܠܠܝܐ؛ ܘܢܗܘܘܢ ܠܐܬܘܬܐ ܘܠܙܒܢܐ؛ ܘܠܝܘܡܬܐ؛
ܘܠܫܢܝܐ.
ܘܢܗܘܘܢ ܡܢܗܪܝܢ ܒܪܩܝܥܐ ܕܫܡܝܐ ܠܡܢܗܪܘ ܥܠ ܐܪܥܐ؛ ܘܗܘܐ
ܗܟܢܐ.
ܘܥܒܕ ܐܠܗܐ ܬܪܝܢ ܢܗܝܪܝܢ ܪܘܪܒܐ؛ ܢܗܝܪܐ ܪܒܐ ܠܫܘܠܛܢܐ
ܕܐܝܡܡܐ؛ ܘܢܗܝܪܐ ܙܥܘܪܐ ܠܫܘܠܛܢܐ ܕܠܠܝܐ؛ ܘܟܘܟܒܐ.
ܘܝܗܒ ܐܢܘܢ ܐܠܗܐ ܒܪܩܝܥܐ ܕܫܡܝܐ ܠܡܢܗܪܘ ܥܠ ܐܪܥܐ.

---

[1] In a case like this one may also pronounce **/faareš/** under the influence of the last vowel of the immediately preceding verb, with which it forms a semantic and phonetic unit.

(**3**) "I" (m.) ܫܦܝܪ ܐܢܐ; ܫܦܝܪܢܐ

"you" (m.s.) ܫܦܝܪ ܐܢ̄ܬ; ܫܦܝܪܬ

"you" (f.s.) ܫܦܝܪܐ ܐܢ̄ܬܝ; ܫܦܝܪܬܝ

"he" ܫܦܝܪ ܗ̄ܘ; ܫܦܝܪܘ /šappiru/

"she" ܫܦܝܪܐ ܗ̄ܝ /šappiraay/

"we" (m.) ܫܦܝܪܝܢ ܚ̄ܢܢ; ܫܦܝܪܝܢܢ /šappirinnan/

"we" (f.) ܫܦܝܪܢ ܚ̄ܢܢ; ܫܦܝܪܢܢ /šappiraanan/

"you" (m.pl.) ܫܦܝܪܝܢ ܐܢ̄ܬܘܢ; ܫܦܝܪܝܢܬܘܢ

"you" (f.pl.) ܫܦܝܪܢ ܐܢ̄ܬܝܢ; ܫܦܝܪܢܬܝܢ

"they" (m.) ܫܦܝܪܝܢ ܐܢܘܢ

"they" (f.) ܫܦܝܪܢ ܐܢܝܢ

(**4**)

	sg.			pl.		
	st. abs.	cst.	emph.	abs.	cst.	emph.
m.	ܩܕܝܫ	ܩܕܝܫ	ܩܕܝܫܐ	ܩܕܝܫܝܢ	ܩܕܝܫ̈ܝ	ܩܕܝܫ̈ܐ
f.	ܩܕܝܫܐ	ܩܕܝܫܬ	ܩܕܝܫܬܐ	ܩܕܝܫܢ	ܩܕܝܫ̈ܬ	ܩܕܝܫ̈ܬܐ
	ܓܠܐ	ܓܠܝܬ	ܓܠܝܬܐ	ܓܠܝܢ	ܓ̈ܠܝ	ܓ̈ܠܝܐ

(**5**)

"my"	ܡܪܝ	ܓ̈ܠܝܬܝ	ܐܒܗ̈ܝ	ܟ̈ܠܒܬܝ	ܟܠܒܝ
"your" (m.s.)	ܡܪܟ	ܓ̈ܠܝܬܟ	ܐܒܗ̈ܝܟ	ܟ̈ܠܒܬܟ	ܟܠܒܟ
"your" (f.s.)	ܡܪܟܝ	ܓ̈ܠܝܬܟܝ	ܐܒܗ̈ܝܟܝ	ܟ̈ܠܒܬܟܝ	ܟܠܒܟܝ
"his"	ܡܪܗ	ܓ̈ܠܝܬܗ	ܐܒܗ̈ܘܗ̄ܝ	ܟ̈ܠܒܬܗ	ܟܠܒܗ̄ܝ
"her"	ܡܪܗ	ܓ̈ܠܝܬܗ	ܐܒܗ̈ܝܗ	ܟ̈ܠܒܬܗ	ܟܠܒܗ
"our"	ܡܪܢ	ܓ̈ܠܝܬܢ	ܐܒܗ̈ܝܢ	ܟ̈ܠܒܬܢ	ܟܠܒܢ
"your" (m.pl.)	ܡܪܟܘܢ	ܓ̈ܠܝܬܟܘܢ	ܐܒܗ̈ܝܟܘܢ	ܟ̈ܠܒܬܟܘܢ	ܟܠܒܟܘܢ
"your" (f.pl.)	ܡܪܟܝܢ	ܓ̈ܠܝܬܟܝܢ	ܐܒܗ̈ܝܟܝܢ	ܟ̈ܠܒܬܟܝܢ	ܟܠܒܟܝܢ
"their" (m.pl.)	ܡܪܗܘܢ	ܓ̈ܠܝܬܗܘܢ	ܐܒܗ̈ܝܗܘܢ	ܟ̈ܠܒܬܗܘܢ	ܟܠܒܗܘܢ
"their" (f.pl.)	ܡܪܗܝܢ	ܓ̈ܠܝܬܗܝܢ	ܐܒܗ̈ܝܗܝܢ	ܟ̈ܠܒܬܗܝܢ	ܟܠܒܗܝܢ

(**6**) [Where more than one alternative form exists in the Pf. and Impv., only the shorter variant has been given.]

	ܚܦܪ	ܦܠܚ	ܕܡܟ	ܚܫܒ	ܐܒܕ
Pf. 3ms	ܚܦܪ	ܦܠܚ	ܕܡܟ	ܚܫܒ	ܐܒܕ
f	ܚܦܪܬ	ܦܠܚܬ	ܕܡܟܬ	ܚܫܒܬ	ܐܒܕܬ
2ms	ܚܦܪܬ	ܦܠܚܬ	ܕܡܟܬ	ܚܫܒܬ	ܐܒܕܬ
f	ܚܦܪܬܝ	ܦܠܚܬܝ	ܕܡܟܬܝ	ܚܫܒܬܝ	ܐܒܕܬܝ
1	ܚܦܪܬ	ܦܠܚܬ	ܕܡܟܬ	ܚܫܒܬ	ܐܒܕܬ
3mpl	ܚܦܪܘ	ܦܠܚܘ	ܕܡܟܘ	ܚܫܒܘ	ܐܒܕܘ
f	ܚܦܪ	ܦܠܚ	ܕܡܟ	ܚܫܒ	ܐܒܕ
2mpl	ܚܦܪܬܘܢ	ܦܠܚܬܘܢ	ܕܡܟܬܘܢ	ܚܫܒܬܘܢ	ܐܒܕܬܘܢ
f	ܚܦܪܬܝܢ	ܦܠܚܬܝܢ	ܕܡܟܬܝܢ	ܚܫܒܬܝܢ	ܐܒܕܬܝܢ
1	ܚܦܪܢ	ܦܠܚܢ	ܕܡܟܢ	ܚܫܒܢ	ܐܒܕܢ
Impf. 3ms	ܢܚܦܘܪ	ܢܦܠܘܚ	ܢܕܡܟ	ܢܚܫܒ	ܢܒܕ
f	ܬܚܦܘܪ	ܬܦܠܘܚ	ܬܕܡܟ	ܬܚܫܒ	ܬܒܕ
2ms	ܬܚܦܘܪ	ܬܦܠܘܚ	ܬܕܡܟ	ܬܚܫܒ	ܬܒܕ
f	ܬܚܦܪܝܢ	ܬܦܠܚܝܢ	ܬܕܡܟܝܢ	ܬܚܫܒܝܢ	ܬܒܕܝܢ
1	ܐܚܦܘܪ	ܐܦܠܘܚ	ܐܕܡܟ	ܐܚܫܒ	ܐܒܕ
3mpl	ܢܚܦܪܘܢ	ܢܦܠܚܘܢ	ܢܕܡܟܘܢ	ܢܚܫܒܘܢ	ܢܒܕܘܢ
f	ܢܚܦܪܢ	ܢܦܠܚܢ	ܢܕܡܟܢ	ܬܚܫܒܢ	ܢܒܕܢ
2mpl	ܬܚܦܪܘܢ	ܬܦܠܚܘܢ	ܬܕܡܟܘܢ	ܬܚܫܒܘܢ	ܬܒܕܘܢ
f	ܬܚܦܪܢ	ܬܦܠܚܢ	ܬܕܡܟܢ	ܬܚܫܒܢ	ܬܒܕܢ
1	ܢܚܦܘܪ	ܢܦܠܘܚ	ܢܕܡܟ	ܢܚܫܒ	ܢܒܕ
Impv. ms	ܚܦܘܪ	ܦܠܘܚ	ܕܡܟ	ܚܫܒ	ܐܒܕ
f	ܚܦܘܪܝ	ܦܠܘܚܝ	ܕܡܟܝ	ܚܫܒܝ	ܐܒܕܝ
mpl	ܚܦܘܪܘ	ܦܠܘܚܘ	ܕܡܟܘ	ܚܫܒܘ	ܐܒܕܘ
f	ܚܦܘܪܝ	ܦܠܘܚܝ	ܕܡܟܝ	ܚܫܒܝ	ܐܒܕܝ
Ptc. act. ms	ܚܦܪ	ܦܠܚ	ܕܡܟ	ܡܚܫܒ	ܡܒܕ
f	ܚܦܪܐ	ܦܠܚܐ	ܕܡܟܐ	ܡܚܫܒܐ	ܡܒܕܐ
mpl	ܚܦܪܝܢ	ܦܠܚܝܢ	ܕܡܟܝܢ	ܡܚܫܒܝܢ	ܡܒܕܝܢ
f	ܚܦܪܢ	ܦܠܚܢ	ܕܡܟܢ	ܡܚܫܒܢ	ܡܒܕܢ
pass. ms	ܚܦܝܪ	ܦܠܝܚ		ܡܚܫܒ	ܡܒܕ
f	ܚܦܝܪܐ	ܦܠܝܚܐ		ܡܚܫܒܐ	ܡܒܕܐ
mpl	ܚܦܝܪܝܢ	ܦܠܝܚܝܢ		ܡܚܫܒܝܢ	ܡܒܕܝܢ
f	ܚܦܝܪܢ	ܦܠܝܚܢ		ܡܚܫܒܢ	ܡܒܕܢ
Inf.	ܠܡܚܦܪ	ܠܡܦܠܚ	ܠܡܕܡܟ	ܠܡܚܫܒܘ	ܠܡܒܕܘ

ܐܟܠ	ܐܡܪ	ܣܠܩ	ܢܚܬ	ܥܒܕ	ܚܕܝ
ܐܟܠ	ܐܡܪ	ܣܠܩ	ܢܚܬ	ܐܫܬܥܒܕ	ܐܬܚܕܝ
ܐܟܠܬ	ܐܡܪܬ	ܣܠܩܬ	ܢܚܬܬ	ܐܫܬܥܒܕܬ	ܐܬܚܕܝܬ
ܐܟܠܬ	ܐܡܪܬ	ܣܠܩܬ	ܢܚܬܬ	ܐܫܬܥܒܕܬ	ܐܬܚܕܝܬ
ܐܟܠܬܝ	ܐܡܪܬܝ	ܣܠܩܬܝ	ܢܚܬܬܝ	ܐܫܬܥܒܕܬܝ	ܐܬܚܕܝܬܝ
ܐܟܠܬ	ܐܡܪܬ	ܣܠܩܬ	ܢܚܬܬ	ܐܫܬܥܒܕܬ	ܐܬܚܕܝܬ
ܐܟܠܘ	ܐܡܪܘ	ܣܠܩܘ	ܢܚܬܘ	ܐܫܬܥܒܕܘ	ܐܬܚܕܝܘ
ܐܟܠ	ܐܡܪ	ܣܠܩ	ܢܚܬ	ܐܫܬܥܒܕ	ܐܬܚܕܝ
ܐܟܠܬܘܢ	ܐܡܪܬܘܢ	ܣܠܩܬܘܢ	ܢܚܬܬܘܢ	ܐܫܬܥܒܕܬܘܢ	ܐܬܚܕܝܬܘܢ
ܐܟܠܬܝܢ	ܐܡܪܬܝܢ	ܣܠܩܬܝܢ	ܢܚܬܬܝܢ	ܐܫܬܥܒܕܬܝܢ	ܐܬܚܕܝܬܝܢ
ܐܟܠܢ	ܐܡܪܢ	ܣܠܩܢ	ܢܚܬܢ	ܐܫܬܥܒܕܢ	ܐܬܚܕܝܢ
ܢܐܟܘܠ	ܢܐܡܪ	ܢܣܩ	ܢܚܘܬ	ܢܫܬܥܒܕ	ܢܬܚܕܐ
ܬܐܟܘܠ	ܬܐܡܪ	ܬܣܩ	ܬܚܘܬ	ܬܫܬܥܒܕ	ܬܬܚܕܐ
ܬܐܟܘܠ	ܬܐܡܪ	ܬܣܩ	ܬܚܘܬ	ܬܫܬܥܒܕ	ܬܬܚܕܐ
ܬܐܟܠܝܢ	ܬܐܡܪܝܢ	ܬܣܩܝܢ	ܬܚܬܝܢ	ܬܫܬܥܒܕܝܢ	ܬܬܚܕܝܢ
ܐܟܘܠ	ܐܡܪ	ܐܣܩ	ܐܚܘܬ	ܐܫܬܥܒܕ	ܐܬܚܕܐ
ܢܐܟܠܘܢ	ܢܐܡܪܘܢ	ܢܣܩܘܢ	ܢܚܬܘܢ	ܢܫܬܥܒܕܘܢ	ܢܬܚܕܘܢ
ܢܐܟܠܢ	ܢܐܡܪܢ	ܢܣܩܢ	ܢܚܬܢ	ܢܫܬܥܒܕܢ	ܢܬܚܕܝܢ
ܬܐܟܠܘܢ	ܬܐܡܪܘܢ	ܬܣܩܘܢ	ܬܚܬܘܢ	ܬܫܬܥܒܕܘܢ	ܬܬܚܕܘܢ
ܬܐܟܠܢ	ܬܐܡܪܢ	ܬܣܩܢ	ܬܚܬܢ	ܬܫܬܥܒܕܢ	ܬܬܚܕܝܢ
ܢܐܟܘܠ	ܢܐܡܪ	ܢܣܩ	ܢܚܘܬ	ܢܫܬܥܒܕ	ܢܬܚܕܐ
ܐܟܘܠ	ܐܡܪ	ܣܩ	ܚܘܬ	ܐܫܬܥܒܕ	ܐܬܚܕܝ
ܐܟܘܠܝ	ܐܡܪܝ	ܣܩܝ	ܚܘܬܝ	ܐܫܬܥܒܕܝ	ܐܬܚܕܝ
ܐܟܘܠܘ	ܐܡܪܘ	ܣܩܘ	ܚܘܬܘ	ܐܫܬܥܒܕܘ	ܐܬܚܕܘ
ܐܟܘܠܝ	ܐܡܪܝ	ܣܩܝ	ܚܘܬܝ	ܐܫܬܥܒܕܝ	ܐܬܚܕܝ
ܐܟܠ	ܐܡܪ	ܣܠܩ	ܢܚܬ	ܡܫܬܥܒܕ	ܡܬܚܕܐ
ܐܟܠܐ	ܐܡܪܐ	ܣܠܩܐ	ܢܚܬܐ	ܡܫܬܥܒܕܐ	ܡܬܚܕܝܐ
ܐܟܠܝܢ	ܐܡܪܝܢ	ܣܠܩܝܢ	ܢܚܬܝܢ	ܡܫܬܥܒܕܝܢ	ܡܬܚܕܝܢ
ܐܟܠܢ	ܐܡܪܢ	ܣܠܩܢ	ܢܚܬܢ	ܡܫܬܥܒܕܢ	ܡܬܚܕܝܢ
ܐܟܝܠ			ܢܚܝܬ		
ܐܟܝܠܐ			ܢܚܝܬܐ		
ܐܟܝܠܝܢ			ܢܚܝܬܝܢ		
ܐܟܝܠܢ			ܢܚܝܬܢ		
ܠܡܐܟܠ	ܠܡܐܡܪ	ܠܡܣܩ	ܠܡܚܬ	ܠܡܫܬܥܒܕܘ	ܠܡܬܚܕܝܘ

	ܝܬܒ	ܝܠܦ	ܝܪܒ	ܒܢܐ	ܚܙܐ
Pf. 3ms	ܝܺܬܶܒ	ܝܺܠܶܦ	ܝܺܪܶܒ	ܒܢܳܐ	ܚܙܳܐ
f	ܝܺܬܒܰܬ	ܝܺܠܦܰܬ	ܝܺܪܒܰܬ	ܒܶܢܳܬ	ܚܶܙܳܬ
2ms	ܝܺܬܰܒܬ	ܝܺܠܰܦܬ	ܝܺܪܰܒܬ	ܒܢܰܝܬ	ܚܙܰܝܬ
f	ܝܺܬܰܒܬܝ	ܝܺܠܰܦܬܝ	ܝܺܪܰܒܬܝ	ܒܢܰܝܬܝ	ܚܙܰܝܬܝ
1	ܝܺܬܒܶܬ	ܝܺܠܦܶܬ	ܝܺܪܒܶܬ	ܒܢܺܝܬ	ܚܙܺܝܬ
3mpl	ܝܺܬܒܘ	ܝܺܠܦܘ	ܝܺܪܒܘ	ܒܢܰܘ	ܚܙܰܘ
f	ܝܺܬܶܒ	ܝܺܠܶܦ	ܝܺܪܶܒ	ܒܢܰܝ	ܚܙܰܝ
2mpl	ܝܺܬܰܒܬܽܘܢ	ܝܺܠܰܦܬܽܘܢ	ܝܺܪܰܒܬܽܘܢ	ܒܢܰܝܬܽܘܢ	ܚܙܰܝܬܽܘܢ
f	ܝܺܬܰܒܬܶܝܢ	ܝܺܠܰܦܬܶܝܢ	ܝܺܪܰܒܬܶܝܢ	ܒܢܰܝܬܶܝܢ	ܚܙܰܝܬܶܝܢ
1	ܝܺܬܰܒܢ	ܝܺܠܰܦܢ	ܝܺܪܰܒܢ	ܒܢܰܝܢ	ܚܙܰܝܢ
Impf. 3ms	ܢܺܬܶܒ	ܢܺܐܠܰܦ	ܢܺܪܰܒ	ܢܶܒܢܶܐ	ܢܶܚܙܶܐ
f	ܬܺܬܶܒ	ܬܺܐܠܰܦ	ܬܺܪܰܒ	ܬܶܒܢܶܐ	ܬܶܚܙܶܐ
2ms	ܬܺܬܶܒ	ܬܺܐܠܰܦ	ܬܺܪܰܒ	ܬܶܒܢܶܐ	ܬܶܚܙܶܐ
f	ܬܺܬܒܺܝܢ	ܬܺܐܠܦܺܝܢ	ܬܺܪܒܺܝܢ	ܬܶܒܢܶܝܢ	ܬܶܚܙܶܝܢ
1	ܐܺܬܶܒ	ܐܺܠܰܦ	ܐܺܪܰܒ	ܐܶܒܢܶܐ	ܐܶܚܙܶܐ
3mpl	ܢܺܬܒܽܘܢ	ܢܺܐܠܦܽܘܢ	ܢܺܪܒܽܘܢ	ܢܶܒܢܽܘܢ	ܢܶܚܙܽܘܢ
f	ܢܺܬܒܳܢ	ܢܺܐܠܦܳܢ	ܢܺܪܒܳܢ	ܢܶܒܢܝܳܢ	ܢܶܚܙܝܳܢ
2mpl	ܬܺܬܒܽܘܢ	ܬܺܐܠܦܽܘܢ	ܬܺܪܒܽܘܢ	ܬܶܒܢܽܘܢ	ܬܶܚܙܽܘܢ
f	ܬܺܬܒܳܢ	ܬܺܐܠܦܳܢ	ܬܺܪܒܳܢ	ܬܶܒܢܝܳܢ	ܬܶܚܙܝܳܢ
1	ܢܺܬܶܒ	ܢܺܐܠܰܦ	ܢܺܪܰܒ	ܢܶܒܢܶܐ	ܢܶܚܙܶܐ
Impv. ms	ܬܶܒ	ܝܺܠܰܦ	ܪܰܒ	ܒܢܺܝ	ܚܙܺܝ
f	ܬܶܒܝ	ܝܺܠܰܦܝ	ܪܰܒܝ	ܒܢܳܝ	ܚܙܳܝ
mpl	ܬܶܒܘ	ܝܺܠܰܦܘ	ܪܰܒܘ	ܒܢܰܘ	ܚܙܰܘ
f	ܬܶܒܶܝܢ	ܝܺܠܰܦܶܝܢ	ܪܰܒܶܝܢ	ܒܢܳܝܶܝܢ	ܚܙܳܝܶܝܢ
Ptc. act. ms	ܝܳܬܶܒ	ܝܳܠܶܦ	ܝܳܪܶܒ	ܒܳܢܶܐ	ܚܳܙܶܐ
f	ܝܳܬܒܳܐ	ܝܳܠܦܳܐ	ܝܳܪܒܳܐ	ܒܳܢܝܳܐ	ܚܳܙܝܳܐ
mpl	ܝܳܬܒܺܝܢ	ܝܳܠܦܺܝܢ	ܝܳܪܒܺܝܢ	ܒܳܢܶܝܢ	ܚܳܙܶܝܢ
f	ܝܳܬܒܳܢ	ܝܳܠܦܳܢ	ܝܳܪܒܳܢ	ܒܳܢܝܳܢ	ܚܳܙܝܳܢ
pass. ms		ܝܺܠܺܝܦ	ܝܺܪܺܝܒ	ܒܢܶܐ	
f		ܝܺܠܺܝܦܳܐ	ܝܺܪܺܝܒܳܐ	ܒܢܶܝܳܐ	
mpl		ܝܺܠܺܝܦܺܝܢ	ܝܺܪܺܝܒܺܝܢ	ܒܢܶܝܢ	
f		ܝܺܠܺܝܦܳܢ	ܝܺܪܺܝܒܳܢ	ܒܢܶܝܳܢ	
Inf.	ܠܡܺܬܰܒ	ܠܡܺܐܠܰܦ	ܠܡܺܪܰܒ	ܠܡܶܒܢܳܐ	ܠܡܶܚܙܳܐ

ܝܬܒ	ܐܬܐ	ܪܦܐ	ܥܠܐ
ܐܘܬܒ	ܐܝܬܝ	ܐܪܦܝ	ܐܥܠܝ
ܐܘܬܒܬ	ܐܝܬܝܬ	ܐܪܦܝܬ	ܐܥܠܝܬ
ܐܘܬܒܬ	ܐܝܬܝܬ	ܐܪܦܝܬ	ܐܥܠܝܬ
ܐܘܬܒܬܝ	ܐܝܬܝܬܝ	ܐܪܦܝܬܝ	ܐܥܠܝܬܝ
ܐܘܬܒܬ	ܐܝܬܝܬ	ܐܪܦܝܬ	ܐܥܠܝܬ
ܐܘܬܒܘ	ܐܝܬܝܘ	ܐܪܦܝܘ	ܐܥܠܝܘ
ܐܘܬܒ	ܐܝ̈ܬܝ	ܐܪ̈ܦܝ	ܐܥ̈ܠܝ
ܐܘܬܒܬܘܢ	ܐܝܬܝܬܘܢ	ܐܪܦܝܬܘܢ	ܐܥܠܝܬܘܢ
ܐܘܬܒܬܝܢ	ܐܝܬܝܬܝܢ	ܐܪܦܝܬܝܢ	ܐܥܠܝܬܝܢ
ܐܘܬܒܢ	ܐܝܬܝܢ	ܐܪܦܝܢ	ܐܥܠܝܢ
ܢܘܬܒ	ܢܝܬܐ	ܢܪܦܐ	ܢܥܠܐ
ܬܘܬܒ	ܬܝܬܐ	ܬܪܦܐ	ܬܥܠܐ
ܬܘܬܒ	ܬܝܬܐ	ܬܪܦܐ	ܬܥܠܐ
ܬܘܬܒܝܢ	ܬܝܬܝܢ	ܬܪܦܝܢ	ܬܥܠܝܢ
ܐܘܬܒ	ܐܝܬܐ	ܐܪܦܐ	ܐܥܠܐ
ܢܘܬܒܘܢ	ܢܝܬܘܢ	ܢܪܦܘܢ	ܢܥܠܘܢ
ܢܘܬ̈ܒܢ	ܢܝ̈ܬܝܢ	ܢܪ̈ܦܝܢ	ܢܥ̈ܠܝܢ
ܬܘܬܒܘܢ	ܬܝܬܘܢ	ܬܪܦܘܢ	ܬܥܠܘܢ
ܬܘܬ̈ܒܢ	ܬܝ̈ܬܝܢ	ܬܪ̈ܦܝܢ	ܬܥ̈ܠܝܢ
ܢܘܬܒ	ܢܝܬܐ	ܢܪܦܐ	ܢܥܠܐ
ܐܘܬܒ	ܐܝܬܐ	ܐܪܦܐ	ܐܥܠܐ
ܐܘܬܒܝ	ܐܝܬܝ	ܐܪܦܝ	ܐܥܠܝ
ܐܘܬܒܘ	ܐܝܬܘ	ܐܪܦܘ	ܐܥܠܘ
ܐܘܬܒܝ	ܐܝ̈ܬܝ	ܐܪ̈ܦܝ	ܐܥ̈ܠܝ
ܡܘܬܒ	ܡܝܬܐ	ܡܪܦܐ	ܡܥܠܐ
ܡܘܬܒܐ	ܡܝܬܝܐ	ܡܪܦܝܐ	ܡܥܠܝܐ
ܡܘܬܒܝܢ	ܡܝܬܝܢ	ܡܪܦܝܢ	ܡܥܠܝܢ
ܡܘܬܒܢ	ܡܝ̈ܬܝܢ	ܡܪ̈ܦܝܢ	ܡܥ̈ܠܝܢ
ܡܘܬܒ	ܡܝܬܝ	ܡܪܦܝ	
ܡܘܬܒܐ	ܡܝܬܝܐ	ܡܪܦܝܐ	
ܡܘܬܒܝܢ	ܡܝܬܝܢ	ܡܪܦܝܢ	
ܡܘܬܒܢ	ܡܝ̈ܬܝܢ	ܡܪ̈ܦܝܢ	
ܠܡܘܬܒܘ	ܠܡܝܬܝܘ	ܠܡܪܦܝܘ	ܠܡܥܠܝܘ

	ܢܘܚ	ܚܙܐ	ܥܠܠ
Pf. 3ms	ܐܬܬܢܝܚ	ܚܙܐ	ܐܥܠ
f	ܐܬܬܢܝܚܬ	ܚܙܬ	ܐܥܠܬ
2ms	ܐܬܬܢܝܚܬ	ܚܙܝܬ	ܐܥܠܬ
f	ܐܬܬܢܝܚܬܝ	ܚܙܝܬܝ	ܐܥܠܬܝ
1	ܐܬܬܢܝܚܬ	ܚܙܝܬ	ܐܥܠܬ
3mpl	ܐܬܬܢܝܚܘ	ܚܙܘ	ܐܥܠܘ
f	ܐܬܬܢܝܚ	ܚܙܝ	ܐܥܠ
2mpl	ܐܬܬܢܝܚܬܘܢ	ܚܙܝܬܘܢ	ܐܥܠܬܘܢ
f	ܐܬܬܢܝܚܬܝܢ	ܚܙܝܬܝܢ	ܐܥܠܬܝܢ
1	ܐܬܬܢܝܚܢ	ܚܙܝܢ	ܐܥܠܢ
Impf. 3ms	ܢܬܬܢܝܚ	ܢܚܙܐ	ܢܥܠ
f	ܬܬܬܢܝܚ	ܬܚܙܐ	ܬܥܠ
2ms	ܬܬܬܢܝܚ	ܬܚܙܐ	ܬܥܠ
f	ܬܬܬܢܝܚܝܢ	ܬܚܙܝܢ	ܬܥܠܝܢ
1	ܐܬܬܢܝܚ	ܐܚܙܐ	ܐܥܠ
3mpl	ܢܬܬܢܝܚܘܢ	ܢܚܙܘܢ	ܢܥܠܘܢ
f	ܢܬܬܢܝܚܢ	ܢܚܙܝܢ	ܢܥܠܢ
2mpl	ܬܬܬܢܝܚܘܢ	ܬܚܙܘܢ	ܬܥܠܘܢ
f	ܬܬܬܢܝܚܢ	ܬܚܙܝܢ	ܬܥܠܢ
1	ܢܬܬܢܝܚ	ܢܚܙܐ	ܢܥܠ
Impv. ms	ܐܬܬܢܝܚ	ܚܙܝ	ܐܥܠ
f	ܐܬܬܢܝܚܝ	ܚܙܝ	ܐܥܠܝ
mpl	ܐܬܬܢܝܚܘ	ܚܙܝܘ	ܐܥܠܘ
f	ܐܬܬܢܝܚܝ	ܚܙܝܝ	ܐܥܠܝ
Ptc. act. ms	ܡܬܬܢܝܚ	ܚܙܐ	ܡܥܠ
f	ܡܬܬܢܝܚܐ	ܚܙܝܐ	ܡܥܠܐ
mpl	ܡܬܬܢܝܚܝܢ	ܚܙܝܢ	ܡܥܠܝܢ
f	ܡܬܬܢܝܚܢ	ܚܙܝܢ	ܡܥܠܢ
pass. ms		ܚܙܝ	ܡܥܠ
f		ܚܙܝܐ	ܡܥܠܐ
mpl		ܚܙܝܝܢ	ܡܥܠܝܢ
f		ܚܙܝܢ	ܡܥܠܢ
Inf.	ܠܡܬܬܢܚܘ	ܠܡܚܙܐ	ܠܡܥܠܘ

(7) [1] 'they (m.) sent you (m.s.)'; [2] 'I sent him'; [3] 'we sent him'; [4] 'she sent him'; [5] 'Send her!' (Impv. m.s.); [6] 'they (m.) shall send you (m.pl.)'; [7] 'he sent me'; [8] 'to send us'; [9] 'you (m.s.) shall send me'; [10] 'they (m.) sent her'; [11] 'you (f.s.) sent him'; [12] 'we (or: he) will send him'; [13] 'he made us'; [14] 'Make her!' (Impv. m.s.); [15] 'we made her'; [16] 'you (m.s.) (or: she) will make him'; [17] 'they made us'; [18] 'he found you (m.s.)' or 'I shall find you'; [19] 'I (or: you [m.s.]) found her'; [20] 'Bring me out!' (Impv. m.pl.); [21] 'Bring me out' (Impv. m.s.); [22] 'he brought me out'; [23] 'she brought her out'; [24] 'I shall raise him'; [25] 'she (or: you [m.s.]) shall raise him'; [26] 'to raise us'; [27] 'they (f) shall raise him'; [28] 'Rob her!' (Impv. m.s.); [29] 'Judge her!' (Impv. f.s.); [30] 'you (fpl) judged us'; [31] 'he saw me'; [32] 'she saw you (m.pl.)'; [33] 'I saw him'; [34] 'I multiplied you (m.pl.)'; [35] 'to multiply us'; [36] 'I shall multiply him'; [37] 'Multiply us!' (Impv. m.s.); [38] 'he will multiply us'; [39] 'they (m.) saw her'; [40] they (f.) saw him.'

PARADIGMS

[Typical forms only are given. For uncommon forms, refer to the appropriate paragraphs in the Morphology section. A degree of artificiality is unavoidable. Thus the verb root chosen for Paradigm I, namely √ ܟܬܒ, is not attested in Pael, Ethpaal, and Ettafal. The quššaya and rukkakha dot has been omitted from Beghadhkephath letters when the latter appear as the first letter of a verb form. The seyame has also been omitted from some fem. pl. forms for the sake of clearer presentation.]

I. Regular Triliteral Verbs (§§ 55-57)

		Peal		Ethpeel	
Pf.	sg. 3m	ܟܬܒ	*k̲t̲av*	ܐܬܟܬܒ	*ʾet̲k̲t̲ev*
	f	ܟܬܒܬ	*ket̲vat̲*	ܐܬܟܬܒܬ	*ʾet̲kat̲vat̲*
	2m	ܟܬܒܬ	*k̲t̲avt*	ܐܬܟܬܒܬ	*ʾet̲k̲t̲evt*
	f	ܟܬܒܬܝ	*k̲t̲avt*	ܐܬܟܬܒܬܝ	*ʾet̲k̲t̲evt*
	1	ܟܬܒܬ	*ket̲vet̲*	ܐܬܟܬܒܬ	*ʾet̲kat̲vet̲*
	pl. 3m	ܟܬܒܘ	*k̲t̲av*	ܐܬܟܬܒܘ	*ʾet̲k̲t̲ev*
	f	ܟܬܒ	*k̲t̲av*	ܐܬܟܬܒ	*ʾet̲k̲t̲ev*
	2m	ܟܬܒܬܘܢ	*k̲t̲avton*	ܐܬܟܬܒܬܘܢ	*ʾet̲k̲t̲evton*
	f	ܟܬܒܬܝܢ	*k̲t̲avteen*	ܐܬܟܬܒܬܝܢ	*ʾet̲k̲t̲evteen*
	1	ܟܬܒܢ	*k̲t̲avn*	ܐܬܟܬܒܢ	*ʾet̲k̲t̲evn*
Impf.	sg. 3m	ܢܟܬܘܒ	*nek̲tov*	ܢܬܟܬܒ	*net̲k̲t̲ev*
	f	ܬܟܬܘܒ	*tek̲tov*	ܬܬܟܬܒ	*tet̲k̲t̲ev*
	2m	ܬܟܬܘܒ	*tek̲tov*	ܬܬܟܬܒ	*tet̲k̲t̲ev*
	f	ܬܟܬܒܝܢ	*tek̲tvin*	ܬܬܟܬܒܝܢ	*tet̲kat̲bin*
	1	ܐܟܬܘܒ	*ʾek̲tov*	ܐܬܟܬܒ	*ʾet̲k̲t̲ev*
	pl. 3m	ܢܟܬܒܘܢ	*nek̲tvun*	ܢܬܟܬܒܘܢ	*net̲kat̲bun*
	f	ܢܟܬܒܢ	*nek̲tvaan*	ܢܬܟܬܒܢ	*net̲kat̲baan*
	2m	ܬܟܬܒܘܢ	*tek̲tvun*	ܬܬܟܬܒܘܢ	*tet̲kat̲bun*
	f	ܬܟܬܒܢ	*tek̲tvaan*	ܬܬܟܬܒܢ	*tet̲kat̲baan*
	1	ܢܟܬܘܒ	*nek̲tov*	ܢܬܟܬܒ	*net̲k̲t̲ev*
Impv.	sg.m	ܟܬܘܒ	*k̲t̲ov*	ܐܬܟܬܒ	*ʾet̲kat̲b*
	f	ܟܬܘܒܝ	*k̲t̲ov*	ܐܬܟܬܒܝ	*ʾet̲kat̲b*
	pl. m	ܟܬܘܒܘ	*k̲t̲ov*	ܐܬܟܬܒܘ	*ʾet̲kat̲b*
	f	ܟܬܘܒܝ	*k̲t̲ov*	ܐܬܟܬܒܝ	*ʾet̲kat̲b*
		ܟܬܘܒܝܢ	*k̲t̲oveen*	ܐܬܟܬܒܝܢ	*ʾet̲kat̲been*
Ptc.	act.m	ܟܬܒ	*kaat̲ev*	ܡܬܟܬܒ	*met̲k̲t̲ev*
	f	ܟܬܒܐ	*kaat̲vaa*	ܡܬܟܬܒܐ	*met̲kat̲baa*
	pass.m	ܟܬܝܒ	*k̲t̲iv*		
	f	ܟܬܝܒܐ	*k̲t̲ivaa*		
Inf.		ܠܡܟܬܒ	*lmek̲tav*	ܠܡܬܟܬܒܘ	*lmet̲k̲t̲aavu*

I. **Regular Triliteral Verbs** (§§ 55-57) (cont.)

		Pael		Ethpaal	
Pf.	sg. 3m	ܟܰܬܶܒ	*kattev*	ܐܶܬ݂ܟܰܬܰܒ	*ʾeṯkattav*
	f	ܟܰܬܒܰܬ	*katvaṯ*	ܐܶܬ݂ܟܰܬܒܰܬ	*ʾeṯkatvaṯ*
	2m	ܟܰܬܶܒܬ	*kattevt*	ܐܶܬ݂ܟܰܬܰܒܬ	*ʾeṯkattavt*
	f	ܟܰܬܶܒܬܝ	*kattevt*	ܐܶܬ݂ܟܰܬܰܒܬܝ	*ʾeṯkattavt*
	1	ܟܰܬܒܶܬ	*katveṯ*	ܐܶܬ݂ܟܰܬܒܶܬ	*ʾeṯkatveṯ*
	pl. 3m	ܟܰܬܶܒܘ	*kattev*	ܐܶܬ݂ܟܰܬܰܒܘ	*ʾeṯkattav*
	f	ܟܰܬܶܒ	*kattev*	ܐܶܬ݂ܟܰܬܰܒ	*ʾeṯkattav*
	2m	ܟܰܬܶܒܬܘܢ	*kattevton*	ܐܶܬ݂ܟܰܬܰܒܬܘܢ	*ʾeṯkattavton*
	f	ܟܰܬܶܒܬܶܝܢ	*kattevteen*	ܐܶܬ݂ܟܰܬܰܒܬܶܝܢ	*ʾeṯkattavteen*
	1	ܟܰܬܶܒܢ	*kattevn*	ܐܶܬ݂ܟܰܬܰܒܢ	*ʾeṯkattavn*
Impf.	sg. 3m	ܢܟܰܬܶܒ	*nk̲attev*	ܢܶܬ݂ܟܰܬܰܒ	*neṯkattav*
	f	ܬܟܰܬܶܒ	*tk̲attev*	ܬܶܬ݂ܟܰܬܰܒ	*teṯkattav*
	2m	ܬܟܰܬܶܒ	*tk̲attev*	ܬܶܬ݂ܟܰܬܰܒ	*teṯkattav*
	f	ܬܟܰܬܒܝܢ	*tk̲atvin*	ܬܶܬ݂ܟܰܬܒܝܢ	*teṯkatvin*
	1	ܐܶܟܰܬܶܒ	*ʾekkattev*	ܐܶܬ݂ܟܰܬܰܒ	*ʾeṯkattav*
	pl. 3m	ܢܟܰܬܒܘܢ	*nk̲atvun*	ܢܶܬ݂ܟܰܬܒܘܢ	*neṯkatvun*
	f	ܢܟܰܬܒ̈ܳܢ	*nk̲atvaan*	ܢܶܬ݂ܟܰܬܒ̈ܳܢ	*neṯkatvaan*
	2m	ܬܟܰܬܒܘܢ	*tk̲atvun*	ܬܶܬ݂ܟܰܬܒܘܢ	*teṯkatvun*
	f	ܬܟܰܬܒ̈ܳܢ	*tk̲atvaan*	ܬܶܬ݂ܟܰܬܒ̈ܳܢ	*teṯkatvaan*
	1	ܢܟܰܬܶܒ	*nk̲attev*	ܢܶܬ݂ܟܰܬܰܒ	*neṯkattav*
Impv.	sg.m	ܟܰܬܶܒ	*kattev*	ܐܶܬ݂ܟܰܬܰܒ	*ʾeṯkattav*
	f	ܟܰܬܶܒܝ	*kattev*	ܐܶܬ݂ܟܰܬܰܒܝ	*ʾeṯkattav*
	pl. m	ܟܰܬܶܒܘ	*kattev*	ܐܶܬ݂ܟܰܬܰܒܘ	*ʾeṯkattav*
	f	ܟܰܬܶܒ̈ܝ	*kattev*	ܐܶܬ݂ܟܰܬܰܒ̈ܝ	*ʾeṯkattav*
		ܟܰܬܶܒ̈ܶܝܢ	*katteveen*	ܐܶܬ݂ܟܰܬܰܒ̈ܶܝܢ	*ʾeṯkattaveen*
Ptc.	act.m	ܡܟܰܬܶܒ	*mk̲attev*	ܡܶܬ݂ܟܰܬܰܒ	*meṯkattav*
	f	ܡܟܰܬܒܳܐ	*mk̲atvaa*	ܡܶܬ݂ܟܰܬܒܳܐ	*meṯkatvaa*
	pass.m	ܡܟܰܬܰܒ	*mk̲attav*		
	f	ܡܟܰܬܒܳܐ	*mk̲atvaa*		
Inf.		ܠܰܡܟܰܬܳܒܘ	*lamk̲attaavu*	ܠܡܶܬ݂ܟܰܬܳܒܘ	*lmeṯkattaavu*

I. Regular Triliteral Verbs (§§ 55-57) (cont.)

	Afel		Ettafal	
Pf.sg. 3m	ܐܟܬܒ	ʾa*k*tev	ܐܬܬܟܬܒ	ʾetta*k*tav
f	ܐܟܬܒܬ	ʾa*k*tva*t*	ܐܬܬܟܬܒܬ	ʾetta*k*tva*t*
2m	ܐܟܬܒܬ	ʾa*k*tevt	ܐܬܬܟܬܒܬ	ʾetta*k*tavt
f	ܐܟܬܒܬܝ	ʾa*k*tevt	ܐܬܬܟܬܒܬܝ	ʾetta*k*tavt
1	ܐܟܬܒܬ	ʾa*k*tve*t*	ܐܬܬܟܬܒܬ	ʾetta*k*tve*t*
pl. 3m	ܐܟܬܒܘ	ʾa*k*tev	ܐܬܬܟܬܒܘ	ʾetta*k*tav
f	ܐܟܬܒ	ʾa*k*tev	ܐܬܬܟܬܒ	ʾetta*k*tav
2m	ܐܟܬܒܬܘܢ	ʾa*k*tevton	ܐܬܬܟܬܒܬܘܢ	ʾetta*k*tavton
f	ܐܟܬܒܬܝܢ	ʾa*k*tevteen	ܐܬܬܟܬܒܬܝܢ	ʾetta*k*tavteen
1	ܐܟܬܒܢ	ʾa*k*tevn	ܐܬܬܟܬܒܢ	ʾetta*k*tavn
Impf. sg. 3m	ܢܟܬܒ	na*k*tev	ܢܬܬܟܬܒ	netta*k*tav
f	ܬܟܬܒ	ta*k*tev	ܬܬܬܟܬܒ	tetta*k*tav
2m	ܬܟܬܒ	ta*k*tev	ܬܬܬܟܬܒ	tetta*k*tav
f	ܬܟܬܒܝܢ	ta*k*tvin	ܬܬܬܟܬܒܝܢ	tetta*k*tvin
1	ܐܟܬܒ	ʾa*k*tev	ܐܬܬܟܬܒ	ʾetta*k*tav
pl. 3m	ܢܟܬܒܘܢ	na*k*tvun	ܢܬܬܟܬܒܘܢ	netta*k*tvun
f	ܢܟܬܒܢ	na*k*tvaan	ܢܬܬܟܬܒܢ	netta*k*tvaan
2m	ܬܟܬܒܘܢ	ta*k*tvun	ܬܬܬܟܬܒܘܢ	tetta*k*tvun
f	ܬܟܬܒܢ	ta*k*tvaan	ܬܬܬܟܬܒܢ	tetta*k*tvaan
1	ܢܟܬܒ	na*k*tev	ܢܬܬܟܬܒ	netta*k*tav
Impv. sg.m	ܐܟܬܒ	ʾa*k*tev	ܐܬܬܟܬܒ	ʾetta*k*tav
f	ܐܟܬܒܝ	ʾa*k*tev	ܐܬܬܟܬܒܝ	ʾetta*k*tav
pl. m	ܐܟܬܒܘ	ʾa*k*tev	ܐܬܬܟܬܒܘ	ʾetta*k*tav
f	ܐܟܬܒܝ	ʾa*k*tev	ܐܬܬܟܬܒܝ	ʾetta*k*tav
	ܐܟܬܒܝܢ	ʾa*k*teveen	ܐܬܬܟܬܒܝܢ	ʾetta*k*taveen
Ptc. act. m	ܡܟܬܒ	ma*k*tev	ܡܬܬܟܬܒ	metta*k*tav
f	ܡܟܬܒܐ	ma*k*tvaa	ܡܬܬܟܬܒܐ	metta*k*tvaa
pass. m	ܡܟܬܒ	ma*k*tav		
f	ܡܟܬܒܐ	ma*k*tvaa		
Inf.	ܠܡܟܬܒܘ	lma*k*taavu	ܠܡܬܟܬܒܘ	lme*t*kattaavu

II. Third-Yodh Verbs (§ 64)

	Peal				Ethpeel	
Pf. sg. 3m	ܒܟܐ	bkaa	ܕܟܝ	dki	ܐܬܒܟܝ	ʾetbki
f	ܒܟܬ	bkaat	ܕܟܝܬ	dekyat	ܐܬܒܟܝܬ	ʾetbakyat
2m	ܒܟܝܬ	bkayt	ܕܟܝܬ	dkit	ܐܬܒܟܝܬ	ʾetbkit
f	ܒܟܝܬܝ	bkayt	ܕܟܝܬܝ	dkit	ܐܬܒܟܝܬܝ	ʾetbkit
1	ܒܟܝܬ	bkeet	ܕܟܝܬ	dkit	ܐܬܒܟܝܬ	ʾetbkit
pl. 3m	ܒܟܘ	bkaw	ܕܟܝܘ	dkiw	ܐܬܒܟܝܘ	ʾetbkiw
f	ܒܟܝ	bkay	ܕܟܝ	dki	ܐܬܒܟܝ	ʾetbki
2m	ܒܟܝܬܘܢ	bkayton	ܕܟܝܬܘܢ	dkiton	ܐܬܒܟܝܬܘܢ	ʾetbkiton
f	ܒܟܝܬܝܢ	bkayteen	ܕܟܝܬܝܢ	dkiteen	ܐܬܒܟܝܬܝܢ	ʾetbkiteen
1	ܒܟܝܢ	bkayn	ܕܟܝܢ	dkin	ܐܬܒܟܝܢ	ʾetbkin
Impf. sg. 3m	ܢܒܟܐ	nevkee			ܢܬܒܟܐ	netbkee
f	ܬܒܟܐ	tevkee			ܬܬܒܟܐ	tetbkee
2m	ܬܒܟܐ	tevkee			ܬܬܒܟܐ	tetbkee
f	ܬܒܟܝܢ	tevkeen			ܬܬܒܟܝܢ	tetbkeen
1	ܐܒܟܐ	ʾevkee			ܐܬܒܟܐ	ʾetbkee
pl. 3m	ܢܒܟܘܢ	nevkon			ܢܬܒܟܘܢ	netbkon
f	ܢܒܟܝܢ	nevkyaan			ܢܬܒܟܝܢ	netbakyaan
2m	ܬܒܟܘܢ	tevkoon			ܬܬܒܟܘܢ	tetbkon
f	ܬܒܟܝܢ	tevkyaan			ܬܬܒܟܝܢ	tetbakyaan
1	ܢܒܟܐ	nevkee			ܢܬܒܟܐ	netbkee
Impv. sg.m	ܒܟܝ	bki			ܐܬܒܟܝ	ʾetbkay
f	ܒܟܝ	bkaay			ܐܬܒܟܝ	ʾetbkaay
pl. m	ܒܟܘ	bkaw			ܐܬܒܟܘ	ʾetbkaw
f	ܒܟܝܝܢ	bkaayeen			ܐܬܒܟܝܝܢ	ʾetbkaayeen
Ptc. act.sg.m.	ܒܟܐ	baakee			ܡܬܒܟܐ	metbkee
f	ܒܟܝܐ	baakyaa			ܡܬܒܟܝܐ	metbakyaa
pl.m	ܒܟܝܢ	baakeen			ܡܬܒܟܝܢ	metbkeen
f	ܒܟܝܢ	baakyaan			ܡܬܒܟܝܢ	metbakyaan
pass.sg.m	ܒܟܐ	bkee				
f	ܒܟܝܐ	bakyaa				
pl.m	ܒܟܝܢ	bkeen				
f	ܒܟܝܢ	bakyaan				
Inf.	ܠܡܒܟܐ	lmevkaa			ܠܡܬܒܟܝܘ	lmetbkaayu

[Hardly any Third-Yodh verb occurs in Ettafal. ܒܟܐ 'wept'; ܕܟܝ 'was clean.']

II. Third-Yodh verbs (§ 64) (cont.)

	Pael		Ethpaal		Afel	
Pf. sg. 3m	ܒܟܝ	*bakki*	ܐܬܒܟܝ	*ʾeṯbakki*	ܐܒܟܝ	*ʾavki*
f	ܒܟܝܬ	*bakyaṯ*	ܐܬܒܟܝܬ	*ʾeṯbakyat*	ܐܒܟܝܬ	*ʾavkyaṯ*
2m	ܒܟܝܬ	*bakkit*	ܐܬܒܟܝܬ	*ʾeṯbakkit*	ܐܒܟܝܬ	*ʾavkit*
f	ܒܟܝܬܝ	*bakkit*	ܐܬܒܟܝܬܝ	*ʾeṯbakkit*	ܐܒܟܝܬܝ	*ʾavkit*
1	ܒܟܝܬ	*bakkiṯ*	ܐܬܒܟܝܬ	*ʾeṯbakkiṯ*	ܐܒܟܝܬ	*ʾavkiṯ*
pl. 3m	ܒܟܝܘ	*bakkiw*	ܐܬܒܟܝܘ	*ʾeṯbakkiw*	ܐܒܟܝܘ	*ʾavkiw*
f	ܒܟܝ	*bakki*	ܐܬܒܟܝ	*ʾeṯbakki*	ܐܒܟܝ	*ʾavki*
2m	ܒܟܝܬܘܢ	*bakkiton*	ܐܬܒܟܝܬܘܢ	*ʾeṯbakkiton*	ܐܒܟܝܬܘܢ	*ʾavkiton*
f	ܒܟܝܬܝܢ	*bakkiteen*	ܐܬܒܟܝܬܝܢ	*ʾeṯbakkiteen*	ܐܒܟܝܬܝܢ	*ʾavkiteen*
1	ܒܟܝܢ	*bakkin*	ܐܬܒܟܝܢ	*ʾeṯbakkin*	ܐܒܟܝܢ	*ʾavkin*
Impf. sg. 3m	ܢܒܟܐ	*nvakkee*	ܢܬܒܟܐ	*neṯbakkee*	ܢܒܟܐ	*navkee*
f	ܬܒܟܐ	*tvakkee*	ܬܬܒܟܐ	*teṯbakkee*	ܬܒܟܐ	*tavkee*
2m	ܬܒܟܐ	*tvakkee*	ܬܬܒܟܐ	*teṯbakkee*	ܬܒܟܐ	*tavkee*
f	ܬܒܟܝܢ	*tvakkeen*	ܬܬܒܟܝܢ	*teṯbakkeen*	ܬܒܟܝܢ	*tavkeen*
1	ܐܒܟܐ	*ʾebbakkee*	ܐܬܒܟܐ	*ʾeṯbakkee*	ܐܒܟܐ	*ʾavkee*
pl. 3m	ܢܒܟܘܢ	*nvakkon*	ܢܬܒܟܘܢ	*neṯbakkon*	ܢܒܟܘܢ	*navkon*
f	ܢܒܟܝܢ	*nvakyaan*	ܢܬܒܟܝܢ	*neṯbakyaan*	ܢܒܟܝܢ	*navkyaan*
2m	ܬܒܟܘܢ	*tvakkon*	ܬܬܒܟܘܢ	*teṯbakkon*	ܬܒܟܘܢ	*tavkon*
f	ܬܒܟܝܢ	*tvakyaan*	ܬܬܒܟܝܢ	*teṯbakyaan*	ܬܒܟܝܢ	*tavkyaan*
1	ܢܒܟܐ	*nvakkee*	ܢܬܒܟܐ	*neṯbakkee*	ܢܒܟܐ	*navkee*
Impv. sg. m	ܒܟܐ	*bakkaa*	ܐܬܒܟܐ	*ʾeṯbakkaa*	ܐܒܟܐ	*ʾavkaa*
f	ܒܟܝ	*bakkaay*	ܐܬܒܟܝ	*ʾeṯbakkaay*	ܐܒܟܝ	*ʾavkaay*
pl. m	ܒܟܘ	*bakkaw*	ܐܬܒܟܘ	*ʾeṯbakkaw*	ܐܒܟܘ	*ʾavkaw*
f	ܒܟܝܝܢ	*bakkaayeen*	ܐܬܒܟܝܝܢ	*ʾeṯbakkaayeen*	ܐܒܟܝܝܢ	*ʾavkaayeen*
Ptc.act.sg.m	ܡܒܟܐ	*mvakkee*	ܡܬܒܟܐ	*meṯbakkee*	ܡܒܟܐ	*mavkee*
f	ܡܒܟܝܐ	*mvakyaa*	ܡܬܒܟܝܐ	*meṯbakyaa*	ܡܒܟܝܐ	*mavkyaa*
pl.m	ܡܒܟܝܢ	*mvakkeen*	ܡܬܒܟܝܢ	*meṯbakkeen*	ܡܒܟܝܢ	*mavkeen*
f	ܡܒܟܝܢ	*mvakyaan*	ܡܬܒܟܝܢ	*meṯbakyaan*	ܡܒܟܝܢ	*mavkyaan*
pass.sg.m	ܡܒܟܝ	*mvakkay*			ܡܒܟܝ	*mavkay*
f	ܡܒܟܝܐ	*mvakyaa*			ܡܒܟܝܐ	*mavkyaa*
pl.m	ܡܒܟܝܢ	*mvakkeen*			ܡܒܟܝܢ	*mavkeen*
f	ܡܒܟܝܢ	*mvakyaan*			ܡܒܟܝܢ	*mavkyaan*
Inf.	ܠܡܒܟܝܘ	*lamvakkaayu*	ܠܡܬܒܟܝܘ	*lmeṯbakkaayu*	ܠܡܒܟܝܘ	*lmavkaayu*

III. Second-Waw/Yodh Verbs (§ 65)

Peal

Pf. sg. 3m	ܩܳܡ	*qaam*	ܡܺܝܬ	*mit̲*
f	ܩܳܡܰܬ	*qaamat̲*	ܡܺܝܬܰܬ	*mit̲at̲*
2m	ܩܳܡܬ	*qaamt*	ܡܺܝܬܬ	*mit*
f	ܩܳܡܬܝ	*qaamt*	ܡܺܝܬܬܝ	*mit*
1	ܩܳܡܶܬ	*qaamet̲*	ܡܺܝܬܶܬ	*mit̲et̲*
pl. 3m	ܩܳܡܘ	*qaam*	ܡܺܝܬܘ	*mit̲*
f	ܩܳܡ	*qaam*	ܡܺܝܬ	*mit̲*
2m	ܩܳܡܬܽܘܢ	*qaamton*	ܡܺܝܬܬܽܘܢ	*mitton*
f	ܩܳܡܬܶܝܢ	*qaamteen*	ܡܺܝܬܬܶܝܢ	*mitteen*
1	ܩܳܡܢ	*qaamn*	ܡܺܝܬܢ	*mit̲n*
Impf. sg.3m	ܢܩܽܘܡ	*nqum*	ܢܣܺܝܡ	*nsim*
f	ܬܩܽܘܡ	*tqum*	ܬܣܺܝܡ	*tsim*
2m	ܬܩܽܘܡ	*tqum*	ܬܣܺܝܡ	*tsim*
f	ܬܩܽܘܡܺܝܢ	*tqumin*	ܬܣܺܝܡܺܝܢ	*tsimin*
1	ܐܩܽܘܡ	*ʾaqum*	ܐܣܺܝܡ	*ʾasim*
pl. 3m	ܢܩܽܘܡܽܘܢ	*nqumun*	ܢܣܺܝܡܽܘܢ	*nsimun*
f	ܢܩܽܘܡܳܢ	*nqumaan*	ܢܣܺܝܡܳܢ	*nsimaan*
2m	ܬܩܽܘܡܽܘܢ	*tqumun*	ܬܣܺܝܡܽܘܢ	*tsimun*
f	ܬܩܽܘܡܳܢ	*tqumaan*	ܬܣܺܝܡܳܢ	*tsimaan*
1	ܢܩܽܘܡ	*nqum*	ܢܣܺܝܡ	*nsim*
Impv. sg. m	ܩܽܘܡ	*qum*	ܣܺܝܡ	*sim*
f	ܩܽܘܡܝ	*qum*	ܣܺܝܡܝ	*sim*
pl. m	ܩܽܘܡܘ	*qum*	ܣܺܝܡܘ	*sim*
f	ܩܽܘܡܶܝܢ	*qumeen*	ܣܺܝܡܶܝܢ	*simeen*
Ptc. act.sg.m	ܩܳܐܶܡ	*qaaʾem*	ܣܳܐܶܡ	*saaʾem*
f	ܩܳܝܡܳܐ	*qaaymaa*	ܣܳܝܡܳܐ	*saaymaa*
pl. m	ܩܳܝܡܺܝܢ	*qaaymin*	ܣܳܝܡܺܝܢ	*saaymin*
f	ܩܳܝܡܳܢ	*qaaymaan*	ܣܳܝܡܳܢ	*saaymaan*
pass.sg. m			ܣܺܝܡ	*sim*
f			ܣܺܝܡܳܐ	*simaa*
pl. m			ܣܺܝܡܺܝܢ	*simin*
f			ܣܺܝܡܳܢ	*simaan*
Inf.	ܠܡܶܩܳܡ	*lamqaam*	ܠܡܶܣܳܡ	*lamsaam*

III. Second-Waw/Yodh Verbs (§ 65)

	Afel		Ethpeel (=Ettafal)	
Pf. sg. 3m	ܐܦܝܫ	*ʾafiš*	ܐܬܬܦܝܫ	*ʾetfiš*
f	ܐܦܝܫܬ	*ʾafišaṯ*	ܐܬܬܦܝܫܬ	*ʾetfišaṯ*
2m	ܐܦܝܫܬ	*ʾafišt*	ܐܬܬܦܝܫܬ	*ʾetfišt*
f	ܐܦܝܫܬܝ	*ʾafišt*	ܐܬܬܦܝܫܬܝ	*ʾetfišt*
1	ܐܦܝܫܬ	*ʾafišeṯ*	ܐܬܬܦܝܫܬ	*ʾetfišeṯ*
pl. 3m	ܐܦܝܫܘ	*ʾafiš*	ܐܬܬܦܝܫܘ	*ʾetfiš*
f	ܐܦܝܫ	*ʾafiš*	ܐܬܬܦܝܫ	*ʾetfiš*
2m	ܐܦܝܫܬܘܢ	*ʾafišton*	ܐܬܬܦܝܫܬܘܢ	*ʾetfišton*
f	ܐܦܝܫܬܝܢ	*ʾafišteen*	ܐܬܬܦܝܫܬܝܢ	*ʾetfišteen*
1	ܐܦܝܫܢ	*ʾafišn*	ܐܬܬܦܝܫܢ	*ʾetfišn*
Impf. sg.3m	ܢܦܝܫ	*nfiš*	ܢܬܬܦܝܫ	*netfiš*
f	ܬܦܝܫ	*tfiš*	ܬܬܬܦܝܫ	*tetfiš*
2m	ܬܦܝܫ	*tfiš*	ܬܬܬܦܝܫ	*tetfiš*
f	ܬܦܝܫܝܢ	*tfišin*	ܬܬܬܦܝܫܝܢ	*tetfišin*
1	ܐܦܝܫ	*ʾafiš*	ܐܬܬܦܝܫ	*ʾetfiš*
pl. 3m	ܢܦܝܫܘܢ	*nfišun*	ܢܬܬܦܝܫܘܢ	*netfišun*
f	ܢܦܝܫܢ	*nfišaan*	ܢܬܬܦܝܫܢ	*netfišaan*
2m	ܬܦܝܫܘܢ	*tfišun*	ܬܬܬܦܝܫܘܢ	*tetfišun*
f	ܬܦܝܫܢ	*tfišaan*	ܬܬܬܦܝܫܢ	*tetfišaan*
1	ܢܦܝܫ	*nfiš*	ܢܬܬܦܝܫ	*netfiš*
Impv. sg. m	ܐܦܝܫ	*ʾafiš*	ܐܬܬܦܝܫ	*ʾetfiš*
f	ܐܦܝܫܝ	*ʾafiš*	ܐܬܬܦܝܫܝ	*ʾetfiš*
pl. m	ܐܦܝܫܘ	*ʾafiš*	ܐܬܬܦܝܫܘ	*ʾetfiš*
f	ܐܦܝܫܝܢ	*ʾafišeen*	ܐܬܬܦܝܫܝܢ	*ʾetfišeen*
Ptc. act.sg.m	ܡܦܝܫ	*mfiš*	ܡܬܬܦܝܫ	*metfiš*
f	ܡܦܝܫܐ	*mfišaa*	ܡܬܬܦܝܫܐ	*metfišaa*
pl. m	ܡܦܝܫܝܢ	*mfišin*	ܡܬܬܦܝܫܝܢ	*metfišin*
f	ܡܦܝܫܢ	*mfišaan*	ܡܬܬܦܝܫܢ	*metfišaan*
pass.sg. m	ܡܦܫ	*mfaaš*		
f	ܡܦܫܐ	*mfaašaa*		
pl. m	ܡܦܫܝܢ	*mfaašin*		
f	ܡܦܫܢ	*mfašaan*		
Inf.	ܠܡܦܫܘ	*lamfaašu*	ܠܡܬܬܦܫܘ	*lmetfaašu*

[√ܦܘܫ : Pe 'to remain,' Af 'to desist from; to miss, lose']

IV. Geminate Verbs (§ 66)

	Peal		Afel	
Pf. sg. 3m	ܬܟ	*tak̲*	ܐܬܟ	*ʾattek̲*
f	ܬܟܟܬ	*tekkat̲*	ܐܬܟܬ	*ʾatk̲at̲*
2m	ܬܟܬ	*tak̲t*	ܐܬܟܬ	*ʾattek̲t*
f	ܬܟܬܝ	*tak̲t*	ܐܬܟܬܝ	*ʾattek̲t*
1	ܬܟܟܬ	*tekket̲*	ܐܬܟܬ	*ʾatk̲et̲*
pl. 3m	ܬܟܘ	*tak̲*	ܐܬܟܘ	*ʾattek̲*
f	ܬܟ	*tak̲*	ܐܬܟ	*ʾattek̲*
2m	ܬܟܬܘܢ	*tak̲ton*	ܐܬܟܬܘܢ	*ʾattek̲ton*
f	ܬܟܬܝܢ	*tak̲teen*	ܐܬܟܬܝܢ	*ʾattek̲teen*
1	ܬܟܢ	*tak̲n*	ܐܬܟܢ	*ʾattek̲n*
Impf. sg. 3m	ܢܬܘܟ	*nettok̲*	ܢܬܟ	*nattek̲*
f	ܬܬܘܟ	*tettok̲*	ܬܬܟ	*tattek̲*
2m	ܬܬܘܟ	*tettok̲*	ܬܬܟ	*tattek̲*
f	ܬܬܟܝܢ	*tetk̲in*	ܬܬܟܝܢ	*tatk̲in*
1	ܐܬܘܟ	*ʾettok̲*	ܐܬܟ	*ʾattek̲*
pl. 3m	ܢܬܟܘܢ	*netk̲un*	ܢܬܟܘܢ	*natk̲un*
f	ܢܬܟܢ	*netk̲aan*	ܢܬܟܢ	*natk̲aan*
2m	ܬܬܟܘܢ	*tetk̲un*	ܬܬܟܘܢ	*tatk̲un*
f	ܬܬܟܢ	*tetk̲aan*	ܬܬܟܢ	*tatk̲aan*
1	ܢܬܘܟ	*nettok̲*	ܢܬܟ	*nattek̲*
Impv. sg. m	ܬܘܟ	*tok̲*	ܐܬܟ	*ʾattek̲*
f	ܬܘܟܝ	*tok̲*	ܐܬܟܝ	*ʾattek̲*
pl. m	ܬܘܟܘ	*tok̲*	ܐܬܟܘ	*ʾattek̲*
f	ܬܘܟܝܢ	*tok̲een*	ܐܬܟܝܢ	*ʾattek̲een*
Ptc. act.sg.m	ܬܐܟ	*taaʾek̲*	ܡܬܟ	*mattek̲*
f	ܬܟܟܐ	*taakkaa*	ܡܬܟܐ	*matk̲aa*
pl. m	ܬܟܟܝܢ	*taakkin*	ܡܬܟܝܢ	*matk̲in*
f	ܬܟܢ	*taakaan*	ܡܬܟܢ	*matk̲aan*
pass.sg.m	ܬܟܝܟ	*tk̲ik̲*	ܡܬܟ	*mattak̲*
f	ܬܟܝܟܐ	*tk̲ik̲aa*	ܡܬܟܐ	*matk̲aa*
pl.m	ܬܟܝܟܝܢ	*tk̲ik̲in*	ܡܬܟܝܢ	*matk̲in*
f	ܬܟܝܟܢ	*tk̲ik̲aan*	ܡܬܟܢ	*matk̲aan*
Inf.	ܠܡܬܟ	*lmettak̲*	ܠܡܬܟܘ	*lmattaak̲u*

[√ ܬܟܟ : Pe. 'to oppress,' Af. 'to do harm.']

V. Regular Verbs with

Pf. Peal	sg. 1	sg. 2m	sg. 2f
sg. 3m	ܩܛܠܢܝ ***qaṭlan***	ܩܛܠܟ ***qaṭlaak***	ܩܛܠܟܝ ***qaṭleek***
f	ܩܛܠܬܢܝ ***qṭaltan***	ܩܛܠܬܟ ***qṭaltaak***	ܩܛܠܬܟܝ ***qṭalteek***
2m	ܩܛܠܬܢܝ ***qṭaltaan***	--------	--------
f	ܩܛܠܬܝܢܝ ***qṭaltin***	--------	--------
1	--------	ܩܛܠܬܟ ***qṭaltaak***	ܩܛܠܬܟܝ ***qṭalteek***
pl. 3m	ܩܛܠܘܢܝ ***qaṭlun***	ܩܛܠܘܟ ***qaṭluk***	ܩܛܠܘܟܝ ***qaṭluk***
f	ܩܛܠ̈ܢܝ ***qaṭlaan***	ܩܛܠ̈ܟ ***qaṭlaak***	ܩܛܠ̈ܟܝ ***qaṭleek***
2m	ܩܛܠܬܘܢܢܝ ***qṭaltonaan***	--------	....
f	ܩܛܠܬܝܢܢܝ ***qṭalteenaan***	--------	--------
1	--------	ܩܛܠܢܟ ***qṭalnaak***	ܩܛܠܢܟܝ ***qṭalneek***
Impf. Pe. sg. 3m	ܢܩܛܠܢܝ ***neqṭlan***	ܢܩܛܠܟ ***neqṭlaak***	ܢܩܛܠܟܝ ***neqṭleek***
2m	ܬܩܛܠܢܝ ***teqṭlan***	--------	....
	ܬܩܛܘܠܝܢܝ ***teqṭolayn***		
f	ܬܩܛܠܝܢܢܝ ***teqṭlinaan***	--------	--------
pl. 3m	ܢܩܛܠܘܢܢܝ ***neqṭlunaan***	ܢܩܛܠܘܢܟ ***neqṭlunaak***	ܢܩܛܠܘܢܟܝ ***neqṭluneek***
f	ܢܩܛܠ̈ܢܢܝ ***neqṭlaanaan***	ܢܩܛܠ̈ܢܟ ***neqṭlaanaak***	ܢܩܛܠ̈ܢܟܝ ***neqṭlaaneek***

Object Suffixes (§ 68) (cont.)

sg. 3m	sg. 3f	pl. 1	pl. 2m
ܩܛܠܗ	ܩܛܠܗ̇	ܩܛܠܢ	ܩܛܠܟܘܢ
qaṭleeh	*qaṭlaah*	*qaṭlan*	*qṭal<u>k</u>on*
ܩܛܠܬܗ	ܩܛܠܬܗ̇	ܩܛܠܬܢ	ܩܛܠܬܟܘܢ
qṭal<u>t</u>eeh	*qṭal<u>t</u>aah*	*qṭal<u>t</u>an*	*qeṭla<u>tk</u>on*
ܩܛܠܬܝܗܝ	ܩܛܠܬܗ̇	ܩܛܠܬܢ	--------
qṭaltaay	*qṭaltaah*	*qṭaltaan*	
ܩܛܠܬܝܘܗܝ	ܩܛܠܬܝܗ̇	ܩܛܠܬܝܢ	--------
qṭaltiw	*qṭaltih*	*qṭaltin*	
ܩܛܠܬܗ	ܩܛܠܬܗ̇	--------	ܩܛܠܬܟܘܢ
qṭalteeh	*qṭaltaah*		*qṭalt<u>k</u>on*
ܩܛܠܘܗܝ	ܩܛܠܘܗ̇	ܩܛܠܘܢ	ܩܛܠܘܟܘܢ
qaṭluy	*qaṭluh*	*qaṭlun*	*qaṭlu<u>k</u>on*
ܩܛ̈ܠܘܗܝ	ܩܛ̈ܠܗ̇	ܩܛ̈ܠܢ	ܩܛܠܟܘܢ
qaṭlaay	*qaṭlaah*	*qaṭlaan*	*qṭal<u>k</u>on*
ܩܛܠܬܘܢܝܗܝ	ܩܛܠܬܘܢܗ̇	ܩܛܠܬܘܢܢ	--------
qṭaltonaay	*qṭaltonaah*	*qṭaltonaan*	
ܩܛܠܬܝܢܝܗܝ	ܩܛܠܬܝܢܗ̇	ܩܛܠܬܝܢܢ	--------
qṭalteenaay	*qṭalteenaah*	*qṭalteenaan*	
ܩܛܠܢܝܗܝ	ܩܛܠܢܗ̇	--------	ܩܛܠܢܟܘܢ
qṭalnaay	*qṭalnaah*		*qṭalnaa<u>k</u>on*
ܢܩܛܠܗ / ܢܩܛܠܝܘܗܝ	ܢܩܛܠܝܗ̇	ܢܩܛܠܢ	ܢܩܛܘܠܟܘܢ
neqṭleeh / *neqṭliw*	*neqṭlih*	*neqṭlan*	*neqṭol<u>k</u>on*
ܬܩܛܠܝܘܗܝ / ܬܩܛܠܗ	ܬܩܛܠܝܗ̇	ܬܩܛܠܢ	--------
teqṭliw / *teqṭleeh*	*teqṭlih*	*teqṭlan*	
ܬܩܛܘܠܝܗܝ	ܬܩܛܘܠܝܗ̇	ܬܩܛܘܠܝܢ	
teqṭolaay	*teqṭoleeh*	*teqṭolayn*	
ܬܩܛܠܝܢܗ / ܬܩܛܠܝܢܝܗܝ	ܬܩܛܠܝܢܗ̇	ܬܩܛܠܝܢܢ	--------
teqṭlineeh / *teqṭlinaay*	*teqṭlinaah*	*teqṭlinaan*	
ܢܩܛܠܘܢܗ / ܢܩܛܠܘܢܝܗܝ	ܢܩܛܠܘܢܗ̇	ܢܩܛܠܘܢܢ	ܢܩܛܠܘܢܟܘܢ
neqṭluneeh / *neqṭlunaay*	*neqṭlunaah*	*neqṭlunaan*	*neqṭlunaa<u>k</u>on*
ܢܩܛ̈ܠܢܗ / ܢܩܛ̈ܠܢܝܗܝ	ܢܩܛ̈ܠܢܗ̇	ܢܩܛ̈ܠܢܢ	ܢܩܛ̈ܠܢܟܘܢ
neqṭlaaneeh / *neqṭlaanaay*	*neqṭlaanaah*	*neqṭlaanaan*	*neqṭlaanaa<u>k</u>on*

N.B. Note the contrast: *qṭal<u>t</u>eeh* 'she killed him' and *qṭalteeh* 'I killed him.'

V. Regular Verbs with

		sg. 1	sg. 2m	sg. 2f
Impv. Pe	sg.m	ܩܛܘܠܝܢܝ *qṭolayn*	--------	--------
	f	ܩܛܘܠܝܢܝ *qṭolin*	--------	--------
	pl. m	ܩܛܘܠܘܢܝ *quṭlun*	--------	....
		ܩܛܘܠܘܢܢܝ *quṭlunaan*	--------	--------
	f	ܩܛܘܠܢܝ *qṭolaan*	--------	--------
		ܩܛܘܠܝܢܢܝ *qṭoleenaan*	--------	--------
Inf. Pe		ܠܡܩܛܠܢܝ *lmeqṭlan*	ܠܡܩܛܠܟ *lmeqṭlaaḵ*	ܠܡܩܛܠܟܝ *lmeqṭleeḵ*
Pa		ܠܡܩܛܠܘܬܢܝ *lamqaṭṭaaluṯan*	ܠܡܩܛܠܘܬܟ *lamqaṭṭaaluṯa aḵ*	ܠܡܩܛܠܘܬܟܝ *lamqaṭṭaaluṯeeḵ*

VI. Third-Yodh Verbs with

		sg. 1	sg. 2m	sg. 2f
Pf. sg. 3m	Pe	ܓܠܢܝ *glaan*	ܓܠܟ *glaaḵ*	ܓܠܟܝ *glaaḵ*
	Pa	ܓܠܝܢܝ *galyan*	ܓܠܝܟ *galyaaḵ*	ܓܠܝܟܝ *galyeeḵ*
3f	Pe	ܓܠܬܢܝ *glaaṯan*	ܓܠܬܟ *glaaṯa aḵ*	ܓܠܬܟܝ *glaaṯeeḵ*
	Pa	ܓܠܝܬܢܝ *galyaṯan*	ܓܠܝܬܟ *galyaṯa aḵ*	ܓܠܝܬܟܝ *galyaṯeeḵ*
2m	Pe	ܓܠܝܬܢܝ *glaytaan*	--------	--------
	Pa	ܓܠܝܬܢܝ *gallitaan*	--------	--------

Object Suffixes (§ 68) (cont.)

sg. 3m	sg. 3f	pl. 1	pl. 2m
ܩܛܠܝܗܝ	ܩܛܠܝܗ	ܩܛܠܝܢ	--------
qṭolaay	*qṭoleeh*	*qṭolayn*	
ܩܛܠܝܘܗܝ	ܩܛܠܝܗ	ܩܛܠܝܢ	--------
qṭoliw	*qṭolih*	*qṭolin*	
ܩܛܠܘܗܝ	ܩܛܠܘܗ	ܩܛܠܘܢ	--------
quṭluw	*quṭluwh*	*quṭlun*	
ܩܛܠܘܢܝܗܝ	ܩܛܠܘܢܗ	ܩܛܠܘܢܢ	--------
quṭlunaay	*quṭlunaah*	*quṭluwnaan*	
ܩܛܠܝܗܝ	ܩܛܠܗ	ܩܛܠܢ	--------
qṭolaay	*qṭolaah*	*qṭolaan*	
ܩܛܠܝܢܝܗܝ	ܩܛܠܝܢܗ	ܩܛܠܝܢܢ	--------
qṭoleenaay	*qṭoleenaah*	*qṭoleenaan*	
ܠܡܩܛܠܗ	ܠܡܩܛܠܗ	ܠܡܩܛܠܢ	ܠܡܩܛܠܟܘܢ
lmeqṭleeh	*lmeqṭlaah*	*lmeqṭlan*	*lmeqṭalk̲on*
ܠܡܩܛܠܘܬܗ	ܠܡܩܛܠܘܬܗ	ܠܡܩܛܠܘܬܢ	ܠܡܩܛܠܘܬܟܘܢ
lamqaṭṭaaluṯeeh	*lamqaṭṭaaluṯaah*	*lamqaṭṭaaluṯan*	*lamqaṭṭaluṯk̲on*

Object Suffixes (§ 68) (cont.)

sg. 3m	sg 3f	pl. 1	pl. 2m
ܓܠܝܗܝ	ܓܠܗ	ܓܠܢ	ܓܠܟܘܢ
glaay	*glaah*	*glaan*	*glaak̲on*
ܓܠܝܗ	ܓܠܝܗ	ܓܠܝܢ	ܓܠܝܟܘܢ
galyeeh	*galyaah*	*galyan*	*gallik̲on*
ܓܠܬܗ	ܓܠܬܗ	ܓܠܬܢ	ܓܠܬܟܘܢ
glaaṯeeh	*glaaṯaah*	*glaaṯan*	*glaaṯk̲on*
ܓܠܝܬܗ	ܓܠܝܬܗ	ܓܠܝܬܢ	ܓܠܝܬܟܘܢ
galyaṯeeh	*galyaṯaah*	*galyaṯan*	*galyaṯk̲on*
ܓܠܝܬܝܗܝ	ܓܠܝܬܗ	ܓܠܝܬܢ	——
glaytaay	*glaytaah*	*glaytaan*	
ܓܠܝܬܝܗܝ	ܓܠܝܬܗ	ܓܠܝܬܢ	——
gallitaay	*gallitaah*	*gallitaan*	

VI. Third-Yodh Verbs with

		sg. 1	sg. 2m	sg. 2f
Pf. 2f	Pe	ܓܠܝܬܝܢ	--------	--------
		glaytin		
	Pa	ܓܠܝܬܝܢ	--------	--------
		gallitin		
1	Pe	--------	ܓܠܝܬܟ	ܓܠܝܬܟܝ
			gleet̲a ak̲	***gleet̲eek̲***
	Pa	--------	ܓܠܝܬܟ	ܓܠܝܬܟܝ
			gallit̲a ak̲	***gallit̲eek̲***
pl. 3m	Pe	ܓܠܐܘܢ	ܓܠܐܘܟ	ܓܠܐܘܟܝ
		glaʾun	***glaʾuk̲***	***glaʾuk̲***
	Pa	ܓܠܝܘܢ	ܓܠܝܘܟ	ܓܠܝܘܟܝ
		galyun	***galyuk̲***	***galyuk̲***
3f	Pe	ܓܠܝܢ	ܓܠܝܟ	ܓܠܝܟܝ
		glayaan	***glayaak̲***	***glayeek̲***
	Pa	ܓܠܝܢ	ܓܠܝܟ	ܓܠܝܟܝ
		galyaan	***galyaak̲***	***galyeek̲***
2m	Pe	ܓܠܝܬܘܢܢ	--------	--------
		glaytonaan		
	Pa	ܓܠܝܬܘܢܢ	--------	--------
		gallitonaan		
1	Pe	--------	ܓܠܝܢܟ	ܓܠܝܢܟܝ
			glaynaak̲	***glayneek̲***
	Pa	--------	ܓܠܝܢܟ	ܓܠܝܢܟܝ
			gallinaak̲	***gallineek̲***
Impf. sg. 3m	Pe	ܢܓܠܝܢ	ܢܓܠܝܟ	ܢܓܠܝܟܝ
		neḡleen	***neḡleek̲***	***neḡleek̲***

Object Suffixes (§ 68) (cont.)

sg. 3m	sg 3f	pl. 1	pl. 2m
ܓܠܝܬܝܘܗܝ	ܓܠܝܬܝܗ	ܓܠܝܬܢ	——
glaytiw	*glaytih*	*glaytin*	
ܓ݁ܠܝܬܝܘܗܝ	ܓ݁ܠܝܬܝܗ	ܓ݁ܠܝܬܢ	——
gallitiwy	*gallitih*	*gallitin*	
ܓܠܝܬܶܗ	ܓܠܝܬܳܗ	——	ܓܠܝܬܟܘܢ
gleet̲eeh	*gleet̲aah*		*gleet̲k̲on*
ܓ݁ܠܝܬܶܗ	ܓ݁ܠܝܬܳܗ	——	ܓ݁ܠܝܬܟܘܢ
gallit̲eeh	*gallit̲aah*		*gallit̲k̲on*
ܓܠܐܘܗܝ	ܓܠܐܘܗ	ܓܠܐܘܢ	ܓܠܐܘܟܘܢ
gla'uy	*gla'uh*	*gla'un*	*gla'uk̲on*
ܓ݁ܠܝܘܗܝ	ܓ݁ܠܝܘܗ	ܓ݁ܠܝܘܢ	ܓ݁ܠܝܘܟܘܢ
galyuw	*galyuwh*	*galyuwn*	*galyuwk̲on*
ܓܠܝ̈ܗܝ	ܓܠܝ̈ܗ	ܓܠܝ̈ܢ	?
glayaay	*glayaah*	*glayaan*	
ܓ݁ܠܝ̈ܗܝ	ܓ݁ܠܝ̈ܗ	ܓ݁ܠܝ̈ܢ	?
galyaay	*galyaah*	*galyaan*	
ܓܠܝܬܘܢܝܗܝ	ܓܠܝܬܘܢܗ	ܓܠܝܬܘܢܢ	——
glaytonaay	*glaytonaah*	*glaytonaan*	
ܓ݁ܠܝܬܘܢܝܗܝ	ܓ݁ܠܝܬܘܢܗ	ܓ݁ܠܝܬܘܢܢ	——
gallitonaay	*gallitonaah*	*gallitonaan*	
ܓܠܝܢܝܗܝ	ܓܠܝܢܗ	——	ܓܠܝܢܟܘܢ
glaynaay	*glaynaah*		*glaynaak̲on*
ܓ݁ܠܝܢܝܗܝ	ܓ݁ܠܝܢܗ	——	ܓ݁ܠܝܢܟܘܢ
gallinaay	*gallinaah*		*gallinaak̲on*
ܢܓܠܝܘܗܝ	ܢܓܠܝܗ	ܢܓܠܝܢ	ܢܓܠܝܟܘܢ
neḡleew	*neḡleeh*	*neḡleen*	*neḡleek̲on*

VI. Third-Yodh Verbs with

		sg. 1	sg. 2m	sg. 2f
Impv. sg.m.	Pe	ܓܠܝܼܢ *glin*	--------	--------
	Pa	ܓܲܠܵܢ *gallaan*	--------	--------
f	Pe	ܓܠܵܐܝܼܢ *glaa'in*	--------	------
pl. m	Pe	ܓܠܵܐܘܼܢ *gla'un*	--------	------
f	Pe	ܓܠܵܝܹܝܢܵܢ *glaayeenaan*	--------	-------
Inf.	Pe	ܠܡܸܓܠܝܲܢ *lmeḡlyan*	ܠܡܸܓܠܝܵܟ݂ *lmeḡlyaa<u>k</u>*	ܠܡܸܓܠܝܹܟ݂ *lmeḡlyee<u>k</u>*
	Pa	ܠܲܡܓܲܠܵܝܘܼܬ݂ܲܢ *lamḡallaayu<u>t</u>an*	ܠܲܡܓܲܠܵܝܘܼܬ݂ܵܟ݂ *lamḡallaayu<u>t</u>a a<u>k</u>*	ܠܲܡܓܲܠܵܝܘܼܬ݂ܹܟ݂ *lamḡallaayu<u>t</u>ee<u>k</u>*

Object Suffixes (§ 68) (cont.)

sg. 3m	sg 3f	pl. 1	pl. 2m
ܓܠܝܘܗܝ	ܓܠܝܗ	ܓܠܝܢ	--------
gliw	*glih*	*glin*	
ܓܠܝܗܝ	ܓܠܝܗ	ܓܠܢ	--------
gallay	*gallaah*	*gallaan*	
ܓܠܐܝܘܗܝ	ܓܠܐܝܗ	ܓܠܐܝܢ	--------
glaaʾiw	*glaaʾih*	*glaaʾin*	
ܓܠܐܘܗܝ	ܓܠܐܘܗ	ܓܠܐܘܢ	--------
glaʾuy	*glaʾuh*	*glaʾun*	
ܓܠܝܢܝܗܝ	ܓܠܝܢܗ	ܓܠܝܢܢ	--------
glaayeenaay	*glaayeenaah*	*glaayeenaan*	
ܠܡܓܠܝܗ	ܠܡܓܠܝܗ	ܠܡܓܠܝܢ	ܠܡܓܠܟܘܢ
lmeḡlyeeh	*lmeḡlyaah*	*lmeḡlyan*	*lmeḡlaaḵon*
ܠܡܓܠܝܘܬܗ	ܠܡܓܠܝܘܬܗ	ܠܡܓܠܝܘܬܢ	ܠܡܓܠܝܘܬܟܘܢ
lamḡallaayuṯeeh	*lamḡalaayuṯaah*	*lamḡallaayuṯan*	*lamḡallaayuṯḵon*

N.B. 1. Some forms are extremely rare or not attested at all. Hence their absence from t above paradigm.

2. For a discussion of details, see Nöldeke, § 194-98. A fuller paradigm is given Mingana 1905.

SUBJECT INDEX

References are to paragraphs
¶ = see

SELECT BIBLIOGRAPHY

by

S. P. Brock

1. Histories of Syriac Literature
2. Grammars
3. Dictionaries
4. Grammatical and Lexical Studies
5. Instrumenta Studiorum
   (a) Bibliographies
   (b) Concordances
6. Specific Topics
7. General Studies and Collected Volumes
8. Syriac Texts (Select)
   (a) Bible
   (b) Syriac Authors: Main Editions
   (c) Collections of Texts
   (d) Translations into Syriac

Abbreviations of titles of journals, series etc.

1. HISTORIES OF SYRIAC LITERATURE

A. Abouna: Ådāb al-lugha al-ārāmīya. Beirut, 1970.

M. Albert: Langue et littérature syriaques. In A. Guillaumont and others, Christianismes orientaux. Introduction à l'étude des langues et des littératures (Paris, 1993), pp. 299-372.

J.S. Assemani: Bibliotheca Orientalis, I-III. Rome, 1719-28; repr. Hildesheim 1975.

I.E. Barsaum: Al-luʾluʾ al-manṯūr fī taʾrīkh al-ʿulūm wal-ādāb al suryānīya. Aleppo, [2]1956; repr. Baghdad, 1976. Syriac translation by Philoxenos Y. Daulabani. Qamishli, 1967.

A. Baumstark: Geschichte der syrischen Literatur. Bonn, 1922; repr. Berlin, 1968.

- : "Die syrische Literatur." In his Die christlichen Literaturen des Orients I (Leipzig, 1911), pp. 39-106.

A. Baumstark, A. Rücker: "Die syrische Literatur." In Semitistik (Handbuch der Orientalistik III; Leiden, 1954), pp. 168-207.

P. Bettiolo: "Lineamenti di Patrologia Siriaca." In A.Quacquarelli (ed.), Complementi interdisciplinari di Patrologia (Rome, 1989), pp. 503-603.

M. Breydy: Geschichte der syro-arabischen Literatur der Maroniten vom VII. bis XVI. Jahrhundert. Opladen, 1985.

J.-B. Chabot: Littérature syriaque. Paris, 1934.

R. Duval: La littérature syriaque. Paris, ^{3}1907.

de Lacy O'Leary: The Syriac Fathers. London, 1909.

R. Macuch: Geschichte der spät- und neusyrischen Literatur. Berlin, 1976.

I. Ortiz de Urbina: Patrologia Syriaca. Rome, ^{2}1965.

P. Sarmas: Tashᶜītā d-seprāyūtā atōrāytā, I-III. Tehran, 1963-70.

W. Wright: A Short History of Syriac Literature. London, 1894.

2. GRAMMARS (* denotes a grammar for pedagogical use)

T. Arayathinal: Aramaic Grammar, I-II. Mannanam, 1957-59.

C. Brockelmann: Syrische Grammatik mit Paradigmen, Literatur, Chrestomathie und Glossar. Leipzig, ^{10}1965.

L. Costaz: Grammaire syriaque. Beirut, 1964.

P.Y. Daulabani: Ktābā d-shetʾestā ʿal qānōne d-leʿzā sūryāyā*. 1961; repr. Glane, 1982.

R. Duval: Traité de grammaire syriaque. Paris, 1881; repr. Amsterdam 1969.

A. Frey: Petite grammaire syriaque*. Fribourg/Göttingen, 1984.

Gabriel of St Joseph: Syro-Chaldaic (Aramaic) Grammar. Mannanam, 1922; ^{7}1984.

J. Healey: First Studies in Syriac*. Birmingham, 1980.

G. Kiraz: The Syriac Primer: Reading, Writing, Vocabulary*. Sheffield, 1988.

A. Mingana: Clef de la langue araméenne ou grammaire complète et pratique des deux dialectes syriaques occidental et oriental. Mosul, 1905.

T. Muraoka: Classical Syriac for Hebraists*. Wiesbaden, 1987.

E. Nestle: Brevis Linguae Syriacae Grammatica. Leipzig, 1881. ET Berlin, 1889.

T. Nöldeke: Kurzgefasste syrische Grammatik. Repr. with Anhang, ed. A. Schall. Darmstadt, 1966. (ET by J.A. Crichton, Compendious Syriac Grammar. London, 1904).

A. Nouro: Suloko/Sulōqō*, Book 1. Glane, 1989.

L. Palacios: Grammatica Syriaca*. Rome, 1954.

T.H. Robinson: Paradigms and Exercises in Syriac Grammar*. Oxford, ^{4}1968.

K.G. Tsereteli: Sirijskij Yazik. Moscow, 1979.

A. Ungnad: Syrische Grammatik*. München, ^{2}1932.

3. DICTIONARIES

S. Atto: Nederlands Suryoyo Woordenboek/Leksiqōn Suryōyō Holandōyō. Enschede, 1986.

- : Sfar melle: Suryōyō-Turkōyō/Suryanice-Türkçe Sözlük. Enschede, 1989.
T. Audo: Dictionnaire de la langue chaldéenne, I-II. Mosul, 1897; repr. (as one vol.) Glane, 1985. [Syriac-Syriac].
Bar ʿAli: Syrisch-arabische Glossen. Erster Band..Bar Alis Lexicon von Alaf bis Mim, ed. G.Hoffmann. Kiel, 1884. The Syriac Arabic Glosses of Ishoʿ bar ʿAli, Part II, ed. R.J.H. Gottheil. Rome, 1908-28.
Bar Bahlul: Lexicon Syriacum auctore Hassano Bar Bahlule, ed. R. Duval, I-III. Paris, 1901.
C. Brockelmann: Lexicon Syriacum. Halle, ^{2}1928; repr. Hildesheim, 1982.
A. Bulut: Woordenboek Nederlands-Suryoyo, Suryoyo-Nederlands. Enschede, c.1994.
G. Cardahi: Al-Lobab, seu Dictionarium Syro-Arabicum, I-II. Beirut, 1887-91.
L. Costaz: Dictionnaire syriaque-français/Syriac-English Dictionary/ Qāmūs suryānī ʿarabī. Beirut, 1963.
T.C. Falla: A Key to the Peshitta Gospels, I (ʾAlaph-Dalath). Leiden, 1991.
M.H. Goshen-Gottstein: A Syriac-English Glossary with Etymological Notes. Wiesbaden,1970. [Based on C. Brockelmann's Chrestomathie].
I. Hanna: Mini-Wörterbuch Deutsch Assyrisch/Ktōbō d-hašḥōtō Suryōyō-Germanōyō. Augsburg, 1984.
K. Jacob and A. Elkhoury: Mhadyono: Leksiqon Suryoyo wa Swōdōyō /The Guide: The First Literary Colloquial Syriac Dictionary. Stockholm, 1985.
W. Jennings (rev.U.Gantillon): Lexicon to the Syriac New Testament (Peshitta). Oxford, 1926.
G. Kiraz: Lexical Tools to the Syriac New Testament. Sheffield 1994.
R. Köbert: Vocabularium Syriacum. Rome, 1956. [Addenda in Orientalia 39 (1970), pp. 315-19].
I. Löw: Aramaische Pflanzennamen. Leipzig, 1881.
J. E. Manna: Vocabulaire chaldéen-arabe. 2nd ed. (with Supplement by R. Bidawid) Beirut, 1975.
J. P. Margoliouth: Supplement to the Thesaurus Syriacus of R. Payne Smith. Oxford, 1927.
J. Payne Smith (Mrs Margoliouth): A Compendious Syriac Dictionary. Oxford, 1903.
R. Payne Smith: Thesaurus Syriacus, I-II. Oxford, 1879-1901.

4. GRAMMATICAL AND LEXICAL STUDIES

M. Albert: La langue syriaque: remarques stylistiques. PdO 13 (1986) 225-48.
I. Avinery: Syntax de la Peshitta sur le pentateuque. Ph. D. diss. Jerusalem, 1973.
- : Pronominal objects in the Peshitta version [in Hebrew]. Leshonenu 38 (1973/4) 220-24, III.
- : The position of the demonstrative pronoun in Syriac. JNES 34 (1975) 123-27.

- : Notes on ordinals versus cardinals in Syriac. Israel Oriental Studies 5 (1975) 45-46.

- : Problèmes de variation dans la traduction syriaque du Pentateuque. Semitica 25 (1975) 105-9.

- : The position of declined *kl* in Syriac. Afroasiatic Linguistics 3 (1976) 108-9.

- : La conception de 'plus determiné' en ancien syriaque. Le Muséon 90 (1977) 421-26.

- : On the nominal clause in the Peshitta. JSS 22 (1977) 48-49.

- : The position of declined *kl* in Syriac. JAOS 104 (1984) 333.

E. Beck: Die konditionale Periode in der Sprache Ephräms des Syrers. OC 64 (1980) 1-31.

- : Die Vergleichpartikel ܐܝܟ in der Sprache Ephräms. In Studien aus Arabistik und Semitistik. A. Spitaler überreicht zum siebzigsten Geburtstag (Wiesbaden 1980), pp. 15-41.

- : Grammatisch-syntaktische Studien zur Sprache Ephraems des Syrers. OC 68 (1984) 1-26; 69 (1985) 1-32.

S.F. Bennett: Objective pronominal suffixes in Aramaic. Ph.D. diss. Yale, 1984.

K. Beyer: Der reichsaramäische Einschlag in der ältesten syrischen Literatur. ZDMG 116 (1966) 242-54.

H. Birkeland: The Syriac phonematic vowel systems. In Festskrift til Professor Olaf Broch (Oslo 1947), pp. 13-39.

J. Blau: The origin of the open and closed *e* in Proto-Syriac. Bulletin of the School of Oriental and African Studies 32 (1969) 1-9.

J. L. Boyd III: The development of the West Semitic Qal perfect of the double ʿayin verb with particular reference to its transmission in Syriac. Journal of Northwest Semitic Languages 10 (1982) 11-23.

M.M. Bravmann: Syriac*dalma*, "lest", "perhaps", and some related Arabic pronomina. JSS 15 (1970) 189-204.

- : The infinitive in the function of the 'psychological predicate' in Syriac. Le Muséon 89 (1971) 219-23.

S.P. Brock: Greek words in the Syriac Gospels (vet and pe). Le Muséon 80 (1967) 389-426.

- : Some observations on the use of Classical Syriac in the late twentieth century. JSS 34 (1989) 363-75.

- : Diachronic aspects of Syriac word formation: an aid for dating anonymous texts. V Symposium Syriacum (OCA 236: 1990), pp. 321-30.

- : Greek words in Syriac: some general features. Scripta Classica Israelica 15 (1996) 251-62.

W. Fischer: Zur Chronologie morphophonematischer Gesetzmässig-keiten im Aramäischen, in id. (ed.), Festgabe für Hans Wehr zum 60. Geburtstag am 5.

Juli 1969 überreicht von seinen Schülern (Wiesbaden, 1969), pp. 175-91.

G. Goldenberg: Tautological infinitive. Israel Oriental Stuides 1 (1971) 36-85, esp. 47-59.

- : On Syriac sentence structure. In M. Sokoloff (ed.), Arameans, Aramaic and the Aramaic Literary Tradition (Ramat Gan, 1983), pp. 97-140.

- : On some niceties of Syriac syntax. V Symposium Syriacum (OCA 236: 1990), pp. 335-44.

- : On predicative adjectives and Syriac syntax. BO 48 (1991) 716-26.

- : Bible translation and Syriac idiom. In P.B. Dirksen and A. van der Kooij, The Peshitta as a Translation (Leiden, 1995), pp. 25-39.

J. Greppin: Syriac loan-words in Classical Armenian. In Festschrift for G. Krotkoff (Baltimore, 1994).

A. Guillaumont: La phrase dite "nominale" en syriaque. Comptes rendus du groupe linguistique d'études chamito-sémitiques 5 (1948/51) 31-33.

- : Détermination et indétermination du nom en syriaque. Ibid. 91-94.

E. Hartwig: Untersuchungen zur Syntax des Afraates. I. Die Relativ-partikel und der Relativsatz. Leipzig, 1893.

T. Harviainen: On the loss of the Greek /h/ and the so-called aspirated Rhō. Studia Orientalia 45 (1976) 1-88.

E. Jenni: Alsyrische Inschriften. Theologische Zeitschrift 21 (1965) 371-85.

J. Joosten: The use of some particles in the Old Testament Peshitta. Textus 14 (1988) 175-83.

- : The predicative adjective in the status emphaticus in Syriac. BO 46 (1989) 18-24.

- : The function of the so-called Dativus Ethicus in Classical Syriac. Orientalia 58 (1989) 473-92.

- : West Aramaic elements in the Old Syriac and Peshitta Gospels. Journal of Biblical Literature 110 (1991) 271-89.

- : The negation of the non-verbal clause in early Syriac. JAOS 112 (1992) 584-88.

- : Two West Aramaic elements in the Old Syriac and Peshitta Gospels. Biblische Notizen 61 (1992) 17-21.

- : On the ante-position of the attributive adjective in Classical Syriac and Biblical Hebrew. Zeitschrift für Althebraistik 6 (1993) 188-92.

- : West Aramaic elements in the Syriac Gospels: Methodological considerations. VI Symposium Syriacum 1992. OCA 247 (Rome, 1994), pp. 101-109.

- : The Syriac Language of the Peshitta and Old Syriac Versions of Matthew (Studies in Semitic Languages and Linguistics 22). Leiden, 1996.

G. Khan: Object markers and agreement pronouns in Semitic languages. Bulletin of the School of Oriental and African Studies 47 (1984) 468-500.

- : Studies in Semitic Syntax. Oxford, 1988.

G. A. Kiraz: Introduction to Syriac Spirantization. Glane, 1995.

I. Löw: Aramäische Fischnamen. In C. Bezold (ed.), Orientalische Studien Th. Nöldeke ... gewidmet, I (Giessen, 1906), pp. 549-70.

- : Aramäische Lurchnamen. In Z. Günzburg, I. Markon (eds), Zikkaron le-Avraham Elijahu [Harkavy-Festschrift] (Berlin, 1908), pp. 37-62; Florilegium ... M. de Vogué (Paris, 1909), pp. 391-406; and Zeit- schrift für Assyriologie 26 (1912) 126-47.

J.P.P. Martin: Jacques d'Edesse et les voyelles syriennes. JAs VI.13 (1869) 447-82.

- : Tradition karkaphienne, ou la Massore chez les Syriens. JAs VI.14 (1869) 245-379.

- : Syriens orientaux et occidentaux. Essai sur les deux principaux dialectes araméens. JAs VI.19 (1872) 305-483.

- : Histoire de la ponctuation ou de la massore chez les Syriens. JAs VII.5 (1875) 81-208.

- : De la métrique chez les Syriens. Leipzig, 1879.

M. Maroth: Der politische Wortschatz altgriechischer Herkunft im Syrischen. In E.C. Welskopf (ed.), Das Fortleben altgriechischer sozialer Typenbegriffe in den Sprachen der Welt, II (Berlin, 1982), pp. 485-507.

A. Merx: Historia artis grammaticae apud Syros. Leipzig, 1889.

Sh. Morag: The Vocalization Systems of Arabic, Hebrew, and Aramaic. 's-Gravenhage, 1962, pp. 45-59

T. Muraoka: Remarks on the syntax of some types of noun modifier in Syriac. JNES 31 (1972) 192-94.

- : On the nominal clause in the Old Syriac Gospels. JSS 20 (1975) 28-37.

- : On the Syriac particle *ʾiṯ*. BO 34 (1977) 21-22.

- : Response to G. Goldenberg, "Bible translations and Syriac idiom." In P.B. Dirksen and A. van der Kooij, The Peshitta as a Translation (Leiden, 1995), pp. 41-46.

- : On the Classical Syriac particles for "between" (forthcoming).

F. Rundgren: Das altsyrische Verbalsystem. Sprakvetenskapliga Sällskapets i Uppsala Förhandligar 1958/60, pp. 51-75.

A. Schall: Studien über griechische Fremdwörter im Syrischen. Darmstadt, 1960.

J. Schleiffer: Berichtigungen und Ergänzungen zum Supplement des Thesaurus Syriacus. Orientalia 8 (1939) 25-58.

F. Schulthess: Homonyme Wurzeln im Syrischen. Berlin, 1900.

J.B. Segal: The Diacritical Point and the Accents in Syriac. London, 1953.

- : Quššaya and Rukkaka: a historical introduction. JSS 34 (1989) 483-91.

U. Seidel: Methodische Probleme der syrischen (ostaramäischen) Lexikologie. Hallesche Beiträge zur Orientwissenschaft 7 (1985) 23-46.

- : Mögliglichkeiten der syrischen (aramäischen) Lexikologie für die Sozial- und Wirtschaftsgeschichtsschreibung des Vorderen Orients. Hallesche Beiträge zur

Orientwissenschaft 10 (1986) 53-77.

- : Studien zum Vokabular der Landwirtschaft im Syrischen, I-II. Altorientalische Forschungen 15 (1988) 133-73; 16 (1989) 89-139.

N. Sims-Williams: Syro-Sogdica: Syriac elements in Sogdian. In A Green Leaf: Papers in Honour of Prof. J. P. Asmussen (Leiden, 1988), pp. 145-56.

L. Van Rompay: Some remarks on the language of Syriac incantation texts. In V Symposium Syriacum (OCA 236: 1990), pp. 369-81.

- : Some reflections on the use of post-predicative hwā in Classical Syriac. In K. Jongeling et al. (eds), Studies in Hebrew and Aramaic Syntax [Fschr. J. Hoftijzer] (Leiden, 1991), pp. 210-19.

- : Some preliminary remarks on the origin of Classical Syriac as a standard language: the Syriac version of Eusebius of Caesarea's Ecclesiastical History. In G. Goldenberg and S. Raz (eds), Semitic and Cushitic Studies (Wiesbaden, 1994), pp. 70-89.

E. Wardini: Neologisms in Modern Literary Syriac. Some Preliminary Results. Oslo 1995.

T. Weiss: Zur ostsyrischen Laut- und Akzentlehre. Stuttgart, 1933.

J.W. Wesselius: The spelling of the third person masculine singular suffixed pronoun in Syriac. BO 39 (1982) 251-54.

5. INSTRUMENTA STUDIORUM

(a) BIBLIOGRAPHIES

Kh. Alwan: Bibliographie générale raisonnée de Jacques de Saroug (+521). PdO 13 (1986) 313-83.

S.P. Brock: Syriac Studies 1960-1970. A classified bibliography. PdO 4 (1973) 393-465.

- : Syriac Studies 1971-1980. A classified bibliography. PdO 10 (1981/2) 291-412.

- : Syriac Studies 1981-1985. A classified bibliography. PdO 14 (1987) 289-360.

- : Syriac Studies 1986-1990. A classified bibliography. PdO 17 (1992) 211-301.

_ : Syriac Studies 1960-1990. A Classified Bibliography. Bibliothèque de l'Université Saint Esprit. Kaslik (forthcoming).

- : Syriac inscriptions: a preliminary check list of European publications. AION 38 (1968) 255-71. Repr. in S.P. Brock, Studies in Syriac Christianity, ch. 1. Aldershot, 1992.

J.T. Clemons: Un supplément américain au "Syriac Catalogue" de C.Moss. L'Orient Syrien 8 (1963) 469-84.

J.F. Coakley: The Archbishop of Canterbury's Assyrian Mission Press: a bibliography. JSS 30 (1985) 35-73.

K. Den Biesen: Bibliography of Ephrem the Syrian. CSCO Subsidia (forthcoming).

A. Desreumaux: Pour une bibliographie sur l'épigraphie syriaque. AION 40 (1980)

704-8.

A. Desreumaux and F. Briquel-Chatonnet: Répertoire des bibliothèques et des catalogues de manuscrits syriaques. Paris, 1991.

P.B. Dirksen: An Annotated Bibliography of the Peshitta of the Old Testament. Leiden, 1989.

J.-M. Fiey: Esquisse d'une bibliographie de Bar Hebraeus (+1286). PdO 13 (1986) 279-312.

C. Moss: Catalogue of Syriac Printed Books and Related Literature in the British Museum. London, 1962.

E. Nestle: Litteratura Syriaca, in his Brevis Linguae Syriacae Grammatica [see Section 2], pp. 1-66 [of separate pagination].

P. Peeters: Bibliotheca Hagiographica Orientalis. Brussels, 1910.

Peshitta Institute: List of Old Testament Peshitta Manuscripts (Preliminary issue). Leiden, 1961.

J. Raymond: Essai de Bibliographie Maronite. Kaslik, 1980.

M.P. Roncaglia: Essai de bibliographie sur S. Ephrem le Syrien. PdO 4 (1973) 343-70.

Kh. Samir: Compléments de bibliographie ephrémienne. PdO 4 (1973) 371-91.

J.-M. Sauget: Bibliographie des liturgies orientales (1900-1960). Rome, 1962.

P. Yousif: A Classified Bibliography on the East Syrian Liturgy. Rome, 1990.

(b) CONCORDANCES

[Anon.]: The Concordance to the Peshitta Version of the Aramaic New Testament. New Knoxville, 1983. [Wordlist only].

D. Barthélemy and O. Rickenbacher: Konkordanz zum hebräischen Sirach mit syrisch-hebräischem Index. Göttingen, 1973.

G. Kiraz: A Computer-Generated Concordance to the Syriac New Testament, I-VI. Leiden, 1993.

N. Sprenger: Konkordanz zum syrischen Psalter. GOFS 10 (1976).

W. Strothmann, K. Johannes, M. Zumpe: Konkordanz zur syrischen Bibel. Der Pentateuch, I-IV. GOFS 26 (1986); Die Propheten, I-IV. GOFS 25 (1985).

W. Strothmann: Konkordanz des syrischen Koheletbuches nach der Peschitta und der Syrohexapla. GOFS 4 (1973).

- : Wörterverzeichnis der apokryphen-deuterokanonischen Schriften des Alten Testaments in der Peshitta. GOFS 27 (1988).

M.M. Winter: A Concordance to the Peshitta Version of Ben Sira. Leiden, 1976.

6. SPECIFIC TOPICS

L. Bernhard: Die Chronologie der Syrer (Sb.Österr.Ak.Wiss. 264; Wien, 1969).

- : Die Chronologie der syrischen Handschriften. Wiesbaden, 1971.

S.P. Brock: An introduction to Syriac studies. In J.H. Eaton (ed.), Horizons in Semitic Studies (Birmingham/Sheffield, 1980), pp. 1- 33.

- : Syriac historical writing: a survey of the main sources. Journal of the Iraqi Academy (Syriac Corporation) 5 (1979/80) 296-326; repr. in S.P. Brock, Studies in Syriac Christianity. Aldershot, 1992.

- : The published verse homilies of Isaac of Antioch, Jacob of Serugh and Narsai. Index of incipits. JSS 32 (1987) 279-313.

- : A brief guide to the main editions and translations of the works of St Ephrem. The Harp: A Review of Syriac and Oriental Studies (Kottayam) 3 (1990), pp. 7-29.

- : Syriac dispute poems: the various types. In G.J. Reinink and H.J.L. Vanstiphout (eds), Dispute Poems and Dialogues in the Ancient and Medieval Near East (OLA 42: 1991), pp. 109-19.

- : The Syriac Commentary tradition. In C. Burnett (ed.), Glosses and Commentaries on Aristotelian Logical Texts (Warburg Institute Surveys and Texts 23: 1993), pp. 3-18.

- : The development of Syriac studies. In K.J. Cathcart (ed.), The Edward Hincks Bicentenary Lectures (Dublin, 1994), pp. 94-113.

- : Syriac studies in the last three decades. In VI Symposium Syriacum (OCA 247: 1994), pp. 13-29.

R. Contini: Gli inizi della linguistica siriaca nell'Europa rinascimentale. Rivista degli Studi Orientali 68 (1994) 15-30.

R. Degen: Ein Corpus Medicorum Syriacorum. Medizin-historisches Journal 7 (1972) 114-22.

- : Galen im Syrischen. In V. Nutton (ed.), Galen: Problems and Prospects (London, 1981), pp. 131-66.

A.de Halleux: Philoxène de Mabbog: sa vie, ses écrits, sa théologie (Louvain, 1963).

J.-M. Fiey: Assyrie chrétienne, I-III. Beirut, 1965-68.

- : Chrétiens syriaques sous les Mongols (CSCO Subsidia 44, 1975).

- : Nisibe, métropole syriaque orientale (CSCO Subsidia 54, 1977).

- : Communautés chrétiennes en Iran et Iraq des origines à 1552. London, 1979.

- : Chrétiens syriaques sous les Abbasides (CSCO Subsidia 59, 1980).

- : Pour un Oriens Christianus Novus. Répertoire des diocèses orientaux et occidentaux. Beirut/Stuttgart, 1993.

W. Hage: Die syrisch-jakobitische Kirche in frühislamischer Zeit. Wiesbaden, 1966.

W.H.P. Hatch: An Album of Dated Syriac Manuscripts. Boston, 1946.

G. Hölscher: Syrische Verskunst. Leipzig, 1932.

E. Honigmann: Evêques et évêchés monophysites d'Asie antérieure au VIe siècle (CSCO Subsidia 2, 1951).

- : Le couvent de Barsauma et le Patriarcat jacobite d'Antioche et de Syrie (CSCO Subsidia 7, 1954).

P. Kawerau: Die jakobitische Kirche im Zeitalter der syrischen Renaissance. Berlin, 1960.

J. Leroy: Les manuscrits syriaques à peintures, I-II. Paris, 1964.

B.M. Metzger: Early Versions of the New Testament, ch.1. Oxford, 1972.

R. Murray: Symbols of Church and Kingdom. A Study in Early Syriac Tradition. Cambridge, 1975.

P. Nagel: Grundzüge syrischer Geschichtsschreibung. Berliner Byzanti-nische Arbeiten 55 (1990) 245-59.

E. Riad: Studies in the Syriac Preface (Studia Semitica Upsaliensia 11, 1988).

F. Rosenthal: Das Syrische. In his Die aramaistische Forschung seit Theodor Nöldeke's Veröffentlichungen. Leiden, 1939 [repr. 1964]. pp. 179-211.

J.B. Segal: Edessa, "the Blessed City". Oxford, 1970.

W. Selb: Orientalisches Kirchenrecht. Band 1, Die Geschichte des Kir-chenrechts der Nestorianer: von den Anfängen bis zur Mongolenzeit (Sb.Österr.Ak.Wiss., ph.-hist.Kl. 388: 1981). Band 2, Die Geschichte des Kirchenrechts der Westsyrer: von Anfängen bis zur Mongolenzeit (Sb.Österr.Ak.Wiss., ph. hist.Kl. 543: 1989).

W. Strothmann: Die Anfänge der syrischen Studien in Europa (GOFS 1, 1971).

A. Vööbus: Studies in the History of the Gospel Text in Syriac, I-II (CSCO Subsidia 3, 79; 1951, 1987).

- : A History of Asceticism in the Syrian Orient, I-III (CSCO Subsidia 14, 17, 81; 1958, 1969, 1988).

- : History of the School of Nisibis (CSCO Subsidia 26, 1965).

- : Syrische Kanonessammlungen. IA-B, Westsyrische Original-urkunden (CSCO Subsidia 35, 38; 1970).

- : Handschriftliche Überlieferung der Memre-Dichtung des Jaʿqob von Serug, I-IV (CSCO Subsidia 39-40, 60-61; 1973, 1980).

7. GENERAL STUDIES AND COLLECTIVE VOLUMES

[I]-VI Symposium Syriacum. OCA 197 (1974); 205 (1978); 221 (1983); 229 (1987); 236 (1990); 247 (1994).

S. Abouzayd (ed.): Festschrift for Dr Sebastian P. Brock (Aram Periodical 5; 1993 [1996]).

S.P. Brock: Syriac Perspectives on Late Antiquity. London, 1984.

- : Studies in Syriac Christianity. Aldershot, 1992.

R.G. Coquin, E. Lucchesi (eds): Mélanges A. Guillaumont (Geneva, 1988).

A. Dietrich (ed.): Synkretismus im syrisch-persichen Kulturgebiet (Abh. Akad. Wiss. Göttingen 96, 1975).

P.B. Dirksen and M.J. Mulder (eds): The Peshitta: its Early Text and History.

Leiden, 1988.
P.B. Dirksen and A. van der Kooij (eds): The Peshitta as a Translation. Leiden, 1995.
H.J.W. Drijvers: East of Antioch. London, 1984.
- : History and Religion in Late Antique Syria. Aldershot, 1994.
R. Fischer (ed.): A Tribute to Arthur Vööbus. Chicago, 1977.
N. Garsoian, T. Mathews, R.W. Thomson (eds): East of Byzantium: Syria and Armenia in the Formative Period. Washington, 1982.
Göttinger Arbeitkreis für syrische Kirchengeschichte (ed.): Paul de Lagarde und die syrische Kirchengeschichte. Göttingen, 1968.
F. Graffin (ed.): Mémorial Mgr. G. Khouri-Sarkis. Louvain, 1969.
C. Laga, J.A. Munitiz, L. Van Rompay (eds): After Chalcedon. [Festschrift for A. Van Roey] (OLA 18, 1985).
M. Tamcke, W. Schwaigert, E. Schlarb (eds): Syrisches Christentum weltweit: Festschrift W. Hage. Münster, 1995.
G. Wiessner (ed.): Erkenntnisse und Meinungen I-II (GOFS 3, 17; 1973, 1978).

8. SYRIAC TEXTS (SELECT)

(a) BIBLE

Current standard editions (in chronological order).
OT and NT: Ktābe qaddishe. United Bible Societies, 1979 [reprint of S. Lee, 1832, with Apocrypha added]; 1988 [Lee's New Testament now replaced by British and Foreign Bible Society's edition]. The Urmia Bible (OT) in the East Syrian script reprinted by the Trinitarian Bible Society, London (1958), and the Mosul Bible (OT and NT), also in the East Syrian script (, 1887-91, 1951).

OT Peshitta

A.M. Ceriani: Translatio Syra Pescitto Veteris Testamenti ex codice Ambrosiano sec. fere VI photolithographice edita. Milan, 1876-83.
Vetus Testamentum Syriace (Peshitta Institute, Leiden); I.1 Gen., Exod.(1977); I.2 and II.1b Lev., Num., Deut., Josh.(1991); II.1a Job (1982); II.2 Judg., Sam.(1978); II.3 Pss.(1980); II.4 Kings (1976); II.5 Prov., Wis., Qoh., Cant.(1979); III.1 Isaiah (1987); III.3 Ezek. (1985); III.4 XII Proph., Dan. (1980); IV.3 Apoc.Bar., IV Ezra (1973); IV.6 Odes, Apocr. Pss., Pss. of Solomon, Tob., 1(3) Ezra (1972).

OT Syro-Hexapla

W. Baars: New Syro-Hexaplaric Texts. Leiden, 1968.
A.M. Ceriani: Codex Syro-Hexaplaris Ambrosianus photolithographice editus (Monumenta Sacra et Profana 7, 1874).
P. de Lagarde: Bibliotheca Syriaca ... quae ad philologiam sacram pertinent. Göttingen,

1892.
A. Vööbus: The Pentateuch in the Version of the Syro-Hexapla (CSCO Subsidia 45, 1975).

Apocrypha

P. de Lagarde: Libri Veteris Testamenti Apocryphi Syriace. Leipzig, 1861.

NT Old Syriac

F.C. Burkitt: Evangelion da-Mepharreshe I-II. Cambridge, 1904.
A.S. Lewis: The Old Syriac Gospels. London, 1910.

NT Peshitta

P.E. Pusey and G.H. Gwilliam: Tetraevangelium Syriacum. Oxford, 1901.
The New Testament in Syriac [British and Foreign Bible Society edition]. London, 1920 and reprints.
The Aramaic New Testament. New Knoxville, 1983.

NT Harklean

B. Aland and A. Juckel: Das Neue Testament in syrischer Überlieferung. I, Die grossen katholischen Briefe; II.1-2, Die Paulinischen Briefe. Münster, 1986, 1991, 1995. [Peshitta and Harklean].

G. Kiraz: Comparative Edition of the Syriac Gospels, I-IV. Leiden, 1996. [Old Syriac, Peshitta and Harklean].

A. Vööbus: The Apocalypse in the Harklean Version (CSCO Subsidia 56, 1978).

J. White: Sacrorum Evangeliorum versio Syriaca Philoxeniana. Oxford, 1778.
- : Actuum Apostolorum et Epistularum ... versio Syriaca Philoxeniana. Oxford, 1799-1803.

(b) SYRIAC AUTHORS: MAIN EDITIONS

Before fourth century

ANON: Odes of Solomon, ed.+ ET J.H. Charlesworth (Oxford, 1973). Ed.+ GT M. Lattke, (Fribourg/Göttingen, 1979-80).
- : Acts of Thomas, ed.+ ET W. Wright (London, 1871).
BARDAISAN: Book of the Laws of the Countries, ed.+ ET H.J.W. Drijvers (Assen, 1965).

Fourth century

ANON: Liber Graduum, ed.+ LT M. Kmosko (PS I.3; 1927)
APHRAHAT: Demonstrations, ed. W. Wright (London, 1869). Ed.+ LT J. Parisot (PS I.1-2; 1894, 1907).
EPHREM (d. 373): Hymni (madrāshe), ed.+ GT E. Beck (CSCO Syr. 73-74 (1955) = H. de Fide; 76-77 (1957) = H. c. Haereses; 78-79 (1957) = H. de Paradiso, c.

Julianum; 82-83 (1959) = H. de Nativitate, Epiphania; 84-85 (1969) = H. de Ecclesia; 92-93, 102-3 (1961, 1963) = Carmina Nisibena; 94-95 (1962) = H. de Virginitate; 106-7 (1964) = H. de Ieiunio; 108-9 (1964) = H. de Azymis, Crucifixione, Resurrectione; 140-41 (1972) = H. de Abraham Qidunaya, Juliano Saba; 159-60 (1975) = Nachträge).

- : Sermones (memre), ed.+ GT E. Beck (CSCO Syr.88-89 (1961) = de Fide; 130-31 (1969) = Sermones I; 134-35 (1970) = Serm. II; 138-39 (1972) + Serm. III; 148-49 (1973) = Serm. IV; 181-82 (1979) = S. in Hebdomadam Sanctam). On Joseph, ed. P. Bedjan (Paris/Leipzig, 1891).

- : Sermo de Domino Nostro [in artistic prose], ed.+ GT E. Beck (CSCO Syr.116-17, 1966).

- : Letter to Publius [in artistic prose], ed.+ ET S.P. Brock, Le Muséon 89 (1976) 261-305.

- : Prose Refutations, I-II, ed.+ ET C. Mitchell (London, 1912, 1921).

- : Commentary on Gen. Exod., ed.+ LT R.-M. Tonneau (CSCO Syr. 71-72, 1955).

- : Commentary on the Diatessaron, ed.+ LT L. Leloir (Dublin, 1963; Louvain, 1990).

Fifth century

ANON: Life of Abraham Qidunaya, ed.+ LT T. Lamy, Sancti Ephraem Hymni et Sermones IV (Malines, 1902), cols 1-84.

- : Life of Alexis, ed.+ FT A. Amiaud (Paris, 1889).

- : Life of Rabbula, ed. J.J. Overbeck, S. Ephraemi Syri, Rabulae ... opera selecta (Oxford, 1865), pp. 159-209.

- : Life of Simeon the Stylite, ed. S.E. Assemani, ASM II, pp. 227 412; and P. Bedjan AMS 4, pp. 507-605.

- : Martyrdom of Simeon bar Ṣabbaᶜe, ed.+ LT M. Kmosko (PS I.2; 1907).

- : Teaching of Addai, ed.+ ET G. Phillips (London, 1876). Ed.+ ET G. Howard (Chico, 1981).

- : 'Julian Romance', ed. J.G.E. Hoffmann (Leiden, 1880).

BALAI: ed. J.J. Overbeck, S. Ephraemi Syri ... opera selecta (Oxford, 1865), pp. 251-336.

CYRILLONA: ed. G. Bickell, ZDMG 27 (1873) 566-98.

ISAAC of ANTIOCH: ed.+ LT G. Bickell [37 memre, madrāshe] (I II, Giessen, 1873-77). Ed. P. Bedjan [66 memre] (Paris/Leipzig, 1903).

JOHN the SOLITARY (JOHN of APAMEA): Dialogue on the Soul, ed. S. Dedering (Leipzig, 1936).

- : Three Letters, ed. L.G. Rignell (Lund, 1941).

- : Three Discourses, ed. L.G. Rignell (Lund, 1960).

- : Dialogues and Letters, ed. W. Strothmann (Patristische Texte und Studien 11, 1972).

- : Commentary on Qohelet, ed. W. Strothmann (GOFS 30, 1988).

NARSAI (E): Memre (verse homilies), ed. A. Mingana (I-II, Mosul, 1905). Ed. Patriarchal Press (I-II, San Francisco, 1970).

- : Select memre: On Three Doctors, ed.+ FT F. Martin (JAs IX.14-15, 1899-1900); On Joseph, ed. P. Bedjan (Paris, 1902), and in Liber Superiorum ... auctore Thoma Margensi (Paris/Leipzig, 1901), 519-629; On Creation, ed.+ FT P. Gignoux (PO 34, 1968); On the dominical Feasts, ed.+ ET F.G. McLeod (PO 40, 1979); On Parables, ed.+ FT E.P. Siman (Paris, 1984); Six biblical memre, ed.+ ET J. Frishman (Leiden, 1992).

Sixth century

AḤUDEMMEH: On Composition of Man, ed.+ FT F. Nau (PO 3, 1905).

ANON (Ps. Zacharias; W): Ecclesiastical History, I, ed.+ LT E.W. Brooks (CSCO Syr. 38, 41 [III 5]; 1919, 1924); II, ed. E.W. Brooks (CSCO 39, 42 [III 6]; 1921, 1924). [I includes Joseph and Aseneth, Acts of Silvester, Seven Sleepers of Ephesus].

ANON: Homilies on Epiphany, ed.+ FT A. Desreumaux (PO 38, 1977); On High Priest, On Sinful Woman, ed.+ FT F.Graffin (PO 41, 1984).

BARḤADBESHABBA ʿARBAYA (E): Ecclesiastical History, ed.+ FT F. Nau (Part I, PO 23, 1932; Part II, PO 9, 1913).

BARḤADBESHABBA of ḤALWAN (E): Cause of the Foundation of the Schools, ed. + FT A. Scher (PO 4, 1907).

CYRUS of EDESSA (E): Cause of the Liturgical Feasts, ed.+ ET W. Macomber (CSCO Syr.155-56, 1974).

ELIJAH (W): Life of John of Tella, ed.+ LT E.W. Brooks (CSCO 7 8 [III 25], 1907).

JACOB of SERUGH (W; d. 521): Memre (verse homilies), ed. P. Bedjan (I-V, Paris/Leipzig, 1905-10), and in S. Martyrii qui et Sahdona quae supersunt omnia (Paris/Leipzig, 1902), 603-835.

- : Select memre: On Hosea, ed.+ GT W. Strothmann (GOFS 5, 1973); On Apostle Thomas, ed.+ GT W. Strothmann (GOFS 12, 1976); Against the Jews, ed.+ FT M. Albert (PO 38, 1976); On Creation, ed.+ FT Kh. Alwan (CSCO Syr. 214-15, 1989); On Ephrem, ed.+ ET J. Amar (PO 47, 1995).

- : Turgame (prose homilies), ed. + FT F. Rilliet (PO 43, 1986).

- : Letters, ed. G. Olinder (CSCO Syr. 57 [II 45], 1937).

JOHN of EPHESUS (W): Ecclesiastical History, Part III, ed.+ LT E.W. Brooks (CSCO Syr. 54-55 [III 3], 1935-6).

- : Lives of Eastern Saints, I-III, ed.+ ET E.W. Brooks (PO 17-19, 1923-24).

PETER of KALLINIKOS (W): Anti-Tritheist Dossier, ed.+ET R.Y. Ebied, A.van Roey, L.R. Wickham (OLA 10, 1981).

- : Discourses against Damian, I, II, ed.+ ET R.Y. Ebied, A.van Roey, L.R. Wickham

(Turnhout, 1994, 1996).

PHILOXENUS (W; d. 523): Tractatus tres de Trinitate et Incarnatione, ed.+ LT A. Vaschalde (CSCO Syr. 9-10 [II 27], 1907).

- : Dissertationes decem de uno e sancta Trinitate incorporato et passo, ed.+ LT/FT M. Brière, F. Graffin (PO 15, 38-39, 41; 1920, 1977, 1979, 1982).

- : Ascetic Discourses, ed.+ ET E.A.W. Budge (2 vols, London, 1894).

- : Three Letters of Philoxenus, ed. + ET A. Vaschalde (Rome, 1902).

- : Letter to Patricius, ed.+ FT R. Lavenant (PO 30, 1963).

- : Letter to the Monks of Senun, ed.+ FT A. de Halleux (CSCO Syr.98-99, 1963).

- : Comm. on Prologue of John, ed.+ FT A. de Halleux (CSCO Syr. 165-66, 1977).

- : Comm. on Matthew and Luke (fragments), ed.+ ET. J.W. Watt (CSCO Syr. 171-72, 1978).

SIMEON of BETH ARSHAM (W): On the Himyarite Martyrs, ed.+ ET I. Shahid, The Martyrs of Najran (Bruxelles, 1971).

STEPHEN bar SUDAILE (W): Book of the Holy Hierotheos, ed.+ ET F.S. Marsh (London, 1927).

Seventh century

ABRAHAM (E): Life of Rabban Bar ᶜIdta, ed.+ ET E.A.W. Budge (London, 1902).

ᶜANANISHOᶜ (E; ed.): Paradise of the Fathers, ed.+ ET E.A.W. Budge (2 vols, London, 1894). Ed. P. Bedjan, AMS 7.

ANON: Memra on Alexander the Great, ed.+ GT G.J. Reinink (CSCO 195-96, 1983).

ANON (Ps. Methodius): Apocalypse, ed.+ GT G.J. Reinink (CSCO Syr. 220-21, 1993).

ANON (W): Life of Aḥudemmeh, ed.+ FT F. Nau (PO 3, 1905).

BABAI the GREAT (E; d. 628): Liber de Unione, ed.+ LT A. Vaschalde (CSCO Syr. 34-35 [II 61], 1915).

- : Comm. on Evagrius, Centuries, ed.+ GT W. Frankenberg (Abh.Kon. Ges.Wiss. Göttingen, ph.-hist.Kl., NF 13, 2; 1912).

- : Martyrdom of George Mihrangushnasp, ed. P. Bedjan, in Histoire de Jabalaha ... (Paris/Leipzig, 1895), 416-571.

DADISHOᶜ (E): On Stillness, ed.+ ET A. Mingana (in WS 7, 1934).

- : Comm. on Asceticon of Abba Isaiah, ed.+ FT R. Draguet (CSCO Syr. 144-45, 1972).

DENHA (W): Life of Marutha, ed.+ FT F. Nau (PO 3, 1905).

GREGORY of CYPRUS (E): De theoria sancta, ed.+ LT I. Hausherr (Rome, 1937).

ISAAC of NINIVEH (E): Part I, ed. P. Bedjan (Paris/Leipzig, 1909); - : Part II, ch. IV-XLI, ed.+ ET S.P. Brock (CSCO Syr. 224-25, 1995).

ISHOᶜYAHB III (E): Letters, ed.+ LT R. Duval (CSCO Syr. 11-12 [II 64], 1904-5).

- : Life of Ishoᶜsabran, ed. J.-B. Chabot (Paris, 1897).

JACOB of EDESSA (W; d. 708): Grammar (fragments), ed. A.Merx, Historia artis grammaticae apud Syros (Leipzig, 1889), pp. 74*-84*.

- : Hexaemeron, ed.+ LT I.-B. Chabot, A. Vaschalde (CSCO 44, 48 [II 56]; 1928, 1932). Ed. J. Çiçek (Glane, 1985).

JOHN of the SEDRE (W): ed. J. Martikainen (GOFS 34, 1991).

SAHDONA (MARTYRIUS) (E): Book of Perfection, ed. P. Bedjan (Paris/Leipzig, 1902). Ed.+ FT A. de Halleux (CSCO Syr. 86-87, 90-91, 110-113; 1960, 1961, 1965).

SHEMᶜON d-ṬAYBUTEH (E): ed. A. Mingana (in WS 7, 1934).

Eighth century

ANON.(Ps. Dionysius) (W): Zuqnin Chronicle, I, ed.+LT/FT I.-B. Chabot (CSCO Syr.43, 66 [III 1]; 1927, 1949); II, ed. I.-B. Chabot (CSCO Syr. 53 [III 2], 1933). [I includes 'Chronicle of Joshua the Stylite', also ed. separately + ET W. Wright (Cambridge 1882)].

ANON (E): Commentary on Gen.-Exod. 9:32, ed.+ FT L.Van Rompay (CSCO Syr. 205-6, 1986).

ELIJAH (W): Letter to Leo of Harran, ed.+ LT A.Van Roey (CSCO Syr. 201-2, 1985).

GEORGE, bishop of the ARABS (W; d. 724): Verse homily on Severus, ed.+ ET K.E. McVey (CSCO Syr. 216-17, 1993).

- : Comm. on Liturgy, ed. R.H. Connolly and H.W. Codrington (London, 1913).

JOHN of DARA (W): Comm. on Liturgy, ed.+ FT J. Sader (CSCO 132-33, 1970).

JOHN SABA (JOHN of DALYATHA; E): Letters, ed.+ FT R. Beulay (PO 39, 1978).

JOSEPH ḤAZZAYA (the SEER; E): ed. A. Mingana (in WS 7, 1934).

- : Letter on the Three Stages, ed.+ FT P. Harb, F. Graffin (PO 45, 1992).

SERGIUS the STYLITE (W): Disputation against a Jew, ed.+ ET A.P. Hayman (CSCO Syr. 152-53, 1973).

THEODORE bar KONI (E): Scholia on OT and NT, I, ed.+ FT A. Scher, R. Hespel, R. Draguet (CSCO Syr. 19 [II 65],187; 1910, 1981); II, ed.+ FT A. Scher, R. Hespel, R. Draguet (CSCO Syr. 26 [II 66], 188; 1912, 1982. I-II, ed.+ FT R. Hespel (CSCO Syr.193-94, 197-98; 1983-84).

Ninth century

ANON (Ps. George of Arbela; E): Comm. on Liturgy, I-II, ed.+ LT R.H. Connolly (CSCO Syr. 25, 28 [II 91], 29, 32 [II 92]; 1911-15).

ANON (E): Comm. on Gen.1-18, ed.+ ET A. Levene (London, 1951).

ANTON of TAGRIT (W): Rhetoric, Book 5, ed.+ ET J.W. Watt (CSCO Syr. 203-4, 1986).

DAVID bar PAULOS (W): Letters, ed. P.Y. Daulabani (Mardin, 1953).

GABRIEL of BOSRA (E): Rechtssammlung, ed.+ GT H. Kaufhold (Berlin, 1976).

ISHOᶜ bar NUN (E): Select Questions on Pentateuch, ed. + ET E.G. Clarke (Leiden, 1962).

ISHOᶜDAD of MERV (E): Comm. on OT, ed.+ FT J.-M. Vosté, C.Van den Eynde (CSCO Syr. 67, 75 [Gen.], 1950, 1955; 80, 81 [Ex.-Deut.], 1958; 96-97 [Book of Sessions], 1963; 128-29 [Is., XII Proph.], 1969; 146-47 [Jer., Ez., Dan.], 1972; 185-86 [Pss.], 1981).

- : Comm. on NT, ed.+ ET M.D. Gibson (3 vols, Cambridge, 1911- 16).

ISHOᶜDNAḤ (E): Liber Castitatis, ed.+ FT J.-B. Chabot (Paris/Rome, 1891).

JOB of EDESSA (E): Book of Treasures, ed.+ ET A. Mingana (Cambridge, 1935).

MOSHE bar KEPHA (d. 903; W): Comm. on John, ed.+ GT L. Schlimme (4 vols, GOFS 18, 1978, 1981).

- : Comm. on Romans, ed.+ GT J. Reller (GOFS 35, 1994).

- : Comm. on Liturgy, ed.+ ET R.H. Connolly and H.W. Codrington (London, 1913).

- : On Myron, ed.+ GT W. Strothmann (GOFS 7, 1973).

NONNUS of NISIBIS (W): Apology, ed.+ LT A. Van Roey (Louvain, 1948).

THOMAS of MARGA (E): Liber Superiorum, ed. P. Bedjan (Paris/Leipzig, 1901). Ed.+ ET E.A.W. Budge (London, 1893).

TIMOTHY I (E): Letters, ed.+ LT O. Braun (CSCO Syr. 30-31 [II 67], 1914-15).

Tenth/Eleventh century

ᶜABDISHOᶜ bar BAHRIZ (E): Legal texts, ed.+ GT W. Selb (Sb.Österr. Ak.Wiss. 268, 1970).

ELIJAH bar SHINAYA (E): Opus Chronologicum, ed.+ LT E.W. Brooks, I.-B. Chabot (CSCO Syr. 21-24 [III 7-8], 1909-10).

- : Grammar, ed.+ ET R.J.H. Gottheil (Berlin, 1887).

- : Book of the Interpreter, ed. P. de Lagarde, Praetermissorum Libri Duo (Göttingen, 1879), pp. 1-89.

ELIJAH of TIRHAN (E): Grammar, ed.+ GT F. Baethgen (Leipzig, 1880).

ISHO`YAHB IV (E): Questions on the Eucharist, ed. C. Van Unnik (Amsterdam, 1937; repr. 1970).

Twelfth century

DIONYSIUS bar ṢALIBI (d. 1171; W): Comm. on Qohelet, ed.+ GT W. Strothmann (GOFS 31, 1988).

- : Comm. on Gospels [Mt-Lk], I, ed.+ LT I. Sedlaček, I.-B. Chabot (CSCO Syr. 15-16, 33, 40 [II 98]; 1906, 1915, 1922); II, ed.+ LT A. Vaschalde CSCO Syr. 47, 49, 60-61 [II 99]; 1931, 1933, 1939, 1940); Comm. on John, ed. R .Lejoly (Dison, 1975).

- : Comm. on Acts and Apocalypse, ed.+ LT I.Sedlaček (CSCO Syr. 18, 20 [II

101]; 1909-10).
- : Comm. on Liturgy, ed.+ LT H. Labourt (CSCO Syr. 13-14 [II 93], 1903).
- : Comm. on Evagrius, Centuries, ed. J. Çiçek (Glane, 1991).
- : Against the Armenians, ed.+ ET A. Mingana (WS 4, 1931).
- : Against the Melkites, ed.+ ET A. Mingana (WS 1, 1927).
- : Against the Jews, ed. J. de Zwaan (Leiden, 1906).
MICHAEL the GREAT (d. 1199; W): Chronicle, ed.+ FT J.-B.Chabot (Paris, 1899-1924; repr. Bruxelles 1963).

Thirteenth century

ANON (W): Chronicle to AD 1234, I, ed.+ LT I.-B. Chabot (CSCO Syr. 36, 56 [III 14], 1920, 1937); II, ed.+ FT I-B. Chabot, A. Abouna, J.-M. Fiey (CSCO 37 [II 15], 154; 1916, 1974).
BARHEBRAEUS (GREGORY ABUʾL FARAJ; d. 1286; W): Comm. on OT [Awṣar rāze], Gen.-Sam., ed.+ ET M. Sprengling, W.O. Graham (Chicago, 1931).
- : Comm. on the Gospels [Awṣar rāze], ed.+ ET W.E.W. Carr (London, 1925).
- : Candelabra of the Sanctuary [Mnārat qudshe]. I-II, ed.+ FT J. Bakoš (PO 22, 24; 1930, 1933); III, ed.+ FT F. Graffin (PO 27, 1957); IV, ed.+ FT J. Khoury (PO 31, 1964); V, ed.+ FT A. Torbey (PO 30, 1962); VI, ed.+ GT P.R. Kohlhaas (Münster, 1959); VII, ed.+ FT M. Albert (PO 30, 1962); VIII, ed.+ FT J. Bakoš (Leiden, 1948); IX, ed.+ FT P-H. Poirier (PO 43, 1985); XI-XII, ed.+ FT N. Sed (PO 41, 40; 1983, 1981).
- : Ethikon [Itiqon], ed. P. Bedjan (Paris/Leipzig, 1898). Ed. J. Çiçek (Glane, 1985). Memra I, ed.+ FT H.G.B. Teule (CSCO Syr. 218-19, 1993).
- : Book of the Dove, ed. P. Bedjan, in Ethicon, seu Moralia Gregorii Barhebraei (Paris/Leipzig, 1898), pp. 521-99. Ed. J. ◊ içek (Glane, 1983).
- : Nomocanon [Hudaye], ed. P.Bedjan (Paris/Leipzig, 1898). Ed. J. Çiçek (Glane, 1986).
- : Swād Sōfiyā, ed.+ FT H.F. Janssens (Liège/Paris, 1937).
- : Ecclesiastical History, I-III, ed.+ LT J.B. Abbeloos and T. Lamy (Paris/Louvain, 1872-77).
- : Secular History (Chronicle), ed. P. Bedjan (Paris/Leipzig, 1890). Ed.+ ET E.A.W. Budge (2 vols, London, 1932). Ed. J. Çiçek (Glane, 1987).
- : Poems, ed. A. Scebabi (Rome, 1887). Ed. P.Y. Daulabani (Jerusalem, 1929; repr. Glane, 1981).
- : Poem on Wisdom, ed. P.N. Darauni (Rome, 1880).
- : Laughable Stories [tunnāye mgaḥḥkāne], ed.+ ET E.A.W. Budge (London ,1897). Ed. J. ◊ içek (Glane, 1983).
- : Grammar [Ktābā d-Ṣemḥe], ed.+ GT A. Moberg (Leipzig/Lund, 1907-22).
- : Small Grammar (in verse), ed. J.P.P. Martin (Paris, 1872).

- : Ktāba d-sullāqā hawnānāyā, ed.+ FT F. Nau (Paris, 1899-1900).

ELIJAH of QARTMIN: Verse Life of Philoxenus, ed.+ FT A. de Halleux (CSCO Syr. 100-101, 1963).

JACOB bar SHAKKO (d. 1241; W): Book of Dialogues, I, ed. A. Merx, Historia artis grammaticae apud Syros (Leipzig, 1889), pp. 1*-48*.

JOHN bar MAʿDANI (d. 1263; W): Poems, ed. P.Y. Daulabani (Jerusalem, 1929; repr. Hengelo 1980).

JOHN of MOSUL (E): Verse comm. on Bar Sira, ed. W. Strothmann (GOFS 19, 1979).

SOLOMON of BOSRA (E): Book of the Bee, ed.+ ET E.A.W. Budge (Oxford, 1886).

Fourteenth century

ʿABDISHOʿ (d. 1318; E): Catalogue of Authors, ed. J. Habbi (Baghdad, 1986). [Also in J.S. Assemani, Bibliotheca Orientalis III.i, 1-362, with LT].

- : Paradise of Eden, ed. G. Cardahi (Beirut, 1889). Ed.J. de Qelayta (Mosul, 1928; repr. Chicago, 1988). Selection, ed.+ LT H. Gismondi (Beirut, 1888).

- : Pearl, ed.+ LT A. Mai, in Scriptorum Veterum Nova Collectio 10, 2 (Rome, 1838), pp. 317-66.

ANON (E): Life of Yahballaha III and Rabban Ṣauma, ed. P. Bedjan (Paris/Leipzig, 1895).

DIOSCORUS of GAZARTA (W): Verse Life of Barhebraeus, ed. J. Çiçek (Glane, 1985).

TIMOTHY II (d. 1353; E): Comm. on Baptismal Liturgy, ed.+ ET P.B. Kadicheeni (Bangalore, 1980).

Fifteenth century

MASʿUD of ṬUR ʿABDIN (W): The Spiritual Ship, ed.+ LT B.L. Van Helmond (Louvain, 1942).

SARGIS bar WAHLE (E): Verse Life of Rabban Hormizd, ed. E.A.W. Budge (Berlin, 1894).

Sixteenth to nineteenth centuries

[see Cardahi 1875, and Çiçek 1981, 1987, in Section 8(c)].

Twentieth century

GHATTAS MAQDASI ELYAS: Bugōne (Aleppo, 1994).

PAULOS BIDARY (d-Bet Dara; d. 1974): Selected poems, ed. A. Abouna (Baghdad, 1977).

PAULOS GABRIEL (d.1971) and GHATTAS MAQDASI ELYAS: Myatrutō [translation of Bernardin de Saint Paul, Paul et Verginie] (Beirut, 1955).

PHILOXENOS Y.DAWLABANI (d. 1969): Teʾodora [translation from Arabic of play by Paulos Behnam, 1956] (Glane, 1977; 1983).

Anonymous works of uncertain date

- : Story of Ahiqar, ed.+ ET F.C. Conybeare, J.R. Harris, A.S. Lewis (Cambridge, 1913).
- : Cave of Treasures, ed.+ FT Su-Min Ri (CSCO Syr. 207-8, 1987).
- : Causa Causarum, ed.+ GT K. Kayser (2 vols, Leipzig, 1889; Strassburg, 1893).

(c) COLLECTIONS OF TEXTS

L. Abramowski, A.E. Goodman: A Nestorian Collection of Christological Texts, I-II. Cambridge, 1972.
S.E. Assemani: Acta Sanctorum Martyrum Orientalium et Occidentalium, I-II. Rome, 1748; repr. Farnborough, 1970.
A. Baumstark: Aristoteles bei den Syrern. Leipzig, 1900.
P. Bedjan: Acta Martyrum et Sanctorum, I-VII. Paris/Leipzig, 1890-97; repr. Hildesheim, 1968. [Indice agiografico by I. Guidi, Rendiconti della Reale Academia dei Lincei, Cl. di Scienze morali, V, 28 (1919), pp. 207-29].
- : Histoire de Mar Jabalaha, de trois autres patriarches, d'un prêtre et de deux laïques, nestoriens. Paris/Leipzig, 1895.
S.P. Brock: Sughyātā mgabbyātā. Glane, 1982.
- : Malpānūtā d-abāhātā. suryāye d-ʿal ṣlōtā. Glane, 1988.
- : Luqqāṭā d-memre d-ʿal ktābay qudshā. Glane, 1993.
C.E.G. Bruns, C.E. Sachau: Syrisch-römisches Rechtsbuch aus dem fünften Jahrhundert. Leipzig, 1880.
F.C. Burkitt: Euphemia and the Goth. London, 1913.
G. Cardahi: Liber Thesauri de Arte Poetica Syrorum. Rome, 1875.
J.-B. Chabot (ed.): Synodicon Orientale. Paris, 1902.
- : Documenta ad origines monophysitarum illustrandas (CSCO 17, 52 [III 37]; 1908, 1933).
J.Y. Çiçek: Memre d-ʿal sayfā [verse, 18th-20th cent.]. Glane, 1981.
- : Martyānūtā d-abāhātā d-ʿidtā. Glane, 1985.
- : Tenḥātā d-Ṭur ʿAbdin [verse, 11th-19th cent.]. Glane, 1987.
W. Cureton: Spicilegium Syriacum. London, 1855.
- : Ancient Syriac Documents. London, 1864; repr. Amsterdam, 1967.
P. de Lagarde: Reliquiae Iuris Ecclesiasticae Antiquissimae Syriace. Leipzig, 1856.
- : Analecta Syriaca. Leipzig, 1858; repr. Osnabrück, 1967.
M.D. Gibson, A. S.Lewis: Studia Sinaitica, I-XII. London, 1894-1907.
- : Horae Semiticae, I-XI. London, 1903-16.
I. Guidi, E.W. Brooks, J.-B. Chabot: Chronica Minora, I-III (CSCO Syr. 1-6 [III 4], 1903-7.
G. Hoffmann: Opuscula Nestoriana Syriace. Kiel, 1880.

H. Kaufhold: Syrische Texte zum islamischen Recht (Abh.Bayer. Ak. Wiss. ph.-hist.Kl. NF 74, 1971).
D. Jenks: Ktabona d-Partute. Urmi, 1898.
J.P. Land: Anecdota Syriaca, I-IV. Leiden, 1862-75.
J.P.P. Martin: Patres Antenicaeni. In J.B. Pitra, Analecta Sacra 4 (Paris, 1983; repr. Farnborough, 1966).
E. Manna: Morceaux choisis de littérature araméenne, I-II. Mosul, 1901-2; repr. Baghdad, 1977.
A. Mingana: Sources Syriaques, I. Mosul, 1908.
J.J. Overbeck: Sancti Ephraemi Syri, Rabulae Episcopi Edesseni, Balaei aliorumque opera selecta. Oxford, 1865.
A. Raes and others: Anaphorae Syriacae, I, 1-3; II, 1-3; III, 1. Rome, 1939-81.
I.E. Rahmani: Studia Syriaca, I-V. Charfet, 1904-9.
E. Sachau: Inedita Syriaca. Halle, 1870; repr. Hildesheim, 1968.
- : Syrische Rechtsbücher, I-III. Berlin, 1907-14.
A. Van Roey, P. Allen: Monophysite Texts of the Sixth Century (OLA 56, 1994).
A. Vööbus: The Synodicon in the West Syrian Tradition, I-II (CSCO Syr. 161-62, 1975).
P. Zingerle: Monumenta Syriaca ex Romanis Codicibus Collecta, I-II. Oeniponti, 1869-78.

(d) TRANSLATIONS INTO SYRIAC

AESOP: Fables, ed.+ FT B. Lefèvre (Paris, 1941).
AMMONIUS: Letters, ed.+ LT M. Kmosko (PO 1O, 1914).
ANON: Didascalia, ed.+ ET A. Vööbus (CSCO 175-76, 179-80, 1979).
ANON: Testamentum Domini, ed.+ LT I.E. Rahmani (Mainz, 1899).
ANON: Kalilah and Dimnah, ed.+ GT F. Schulthess (2 vols, Berlin, 1911) [from Middle Persian]. Ed. W. Wright (Oxford, 1884) [from Arabic].
ANON (Ps. Callisthenes): History of Alexander the Great, ed. E.A.W. Budge (Cambridge, 1889; repr. Amsterdam, 1976).
ARISTIDES: Apology, ed.+ ET J.R. Harris (Cambridge, 1891).
ARISTOTLE: see Section 6, under S.P. Brock (1993).
ATHANASIUS: Athanasiana Syriaca I-IV, ed.+ ET R.W. Thomson (CSCO Syr. 114-15, 118-19, 142-43, 167-68; 1965, 1967, 1972, 1977).
- : Festal Letters, ed.+ ET W. Cureton (2 vols, London, 1848, 1854).
- : Life of Anthony, ed. + FT R. Draguet (CSCO Syr. 183-84, 1980).
BASIL: Hexaemeron, ed.+ ET R.W. Thomson (CSCO Syr. 22-23, 1995).
CLEMENT of ROME: Letters, ed. R.L. Bensly (Cambridge, 1899).
CLEMENT (Ps.): Recognitions, ed. P. de Lagarde (Leipzig, 1861).
CYRIL of ALEXANDRIA: Comm. on Luke, ed.+ LT I.-B. Chabot, R.-M. Tonneau

(CSCO Syr. 27 [IV 1], 70; 1912, 1953).
- : Letters, ed.+ ET R.Y. Ebied, L.R. Wickham (CSCO Syr. 157-58, 1975).
DIONYSIUS the AREOPAGITE (Ps): Ecclesiastical Hierarchy, On Myron, ed.+ GT W. Strothmann (2 vols, GOFS 15, 1977).
DIONYSIUS THRAX: Grammar, ed.+ GT A. Merx, Historia artis grammaticae apud Syros (Leipzig, 1889), pp. 50*-72*.
EPIPHANIUS: Weights and Measures, ed.+ ET J.E. Dean (Chicago, 1935).
EUSEBIUS: Ecclesiastical History, ed. P. Bedjan (Paris/Leipzig, 1897). Ed. W. Wright, N. McLean (Cambridge, 1898).
- : Martyrs of Palestine, ed.+ ET W. Cureton (London, 1861).
- : Theophania, ed.+ ET S. Lee (2 vols London, 1842, 1843).
EVAGRIUS: Antirrheticus, Gnosticus, Letters, ed.+ Greek retroversion W. Frankenberg (Berlin, 1912).
- : Evagriana Syriaca, ed.+ FT J. Muyldermans (Louvain, 1952).
- : Kephalaia Gnostica, ed.+ FT A. Guillaumont (PO 28, 1958).
GALEN: see Section 6, under R. Degen.
GREGORY of NAZIANZUS: Iambics, ed. P.J. Bollig, H. Gismondi (Beirut, 1895-96).
HIPPOCRATES: Aphorisms, ed. H. Pognon (Leipzig, 1903).
IGNATIUS: Letters, ed.+ ET W. Cureton (London, 1849). Ed. W. Wright, in J.B. Lightfoot, The Apostolic Fathers II, iii (London, 1899), pp. 73-124.
ISAIAH, Abba: Asceticon, ed.+ FT R. Draguet (CSCO Syr. 120-24, 1968).
JOHN PHILOPONUS: Diaitetes, ed.+ LT A. Šanda (Beirut, 1930).
- : Opuscula Monophysitica, ed.+ LT A. Šanda (Beirut, 1930).
JOHN RUFUS: Plerophoria, ed.+ FT F. Nau (PO 8, 1911).
- : Life of Peter the Iberian, ed.+ GT R. Raabe (Leipzig, 1895).
JOSEPHUS: War, Book VI, ed.P. Bedjan, in Homiliae Selectae Mar Jacobi Sarugensis, I (Paris/Leipzig, 1905), pp. 770-837.
MACARIUS: ed.+ GT W. Strothmann (2 vols, GOFS 21, 1981).
MARCIANUS: ed. + LT A. van Roey (Louvain, 1968).
NESTORIUS: Liber Heracleidis, ed. P. Bedjan (Paris/Leipzig, 1910).
NICHOLAS of DAMASCUS: On the Philosophy of Aristotle, ed.+ ET H.J. Drossaart Lulofs (Leiden, 1969).
NILUS: ed.+ IT P. Bettiolo (Louvain, 1983).
NONNUS, Ps.: Mythological Scholia, ed.+ ET S.P. Brock (Cambridge, 1971).
PALLADIUS: Lausiac History, ed.+ FT R. Draguet (CSCO Syr. 169- 70, 173-74; 1978).
PHYSIOLOGUS: ed.+ GT K. Ahrens (Kiel, 1892).
SECUNDUS the SILENT PHILOSOPHER: ed.+ ET B.P. Perry (New York, 1964).
SEVERUS: Liber contra impium Grammaticum, ed.+ LT I. Lebon (CSCO Syr. 45-46 [IV 5], 50-21 [IV 6], 58-59 [IV 4]; 1929, 1933, 1938).

- : Discourses ad Nephalium, Correspondence with Sergius, ed.+ LT I. Lebon (CSCO Syr. 64-65 [IV 7], 1949).
- : Polemic against Julian of Halicarnassus, ed.+ FT R. Hespel (CSCO 104-5, 124-27, 136-37; 1964, 1968-69, 1971).
- : Select Letters, ed.+ ET E.W. Brooks (4 vols, London, 1902-4).
- : A Collection of Letters, I-II, ed.+ ET E.W. Brooks (PO 12, 14; 1916, 1920).
- : Hymns, I-II, ed.+ ET E.W. Brooks (PO 6-7, 1910-11).
- : Philalethes, ed.+ FT R. Hespel (CSCO 68-69, 1952).
- : 125 Cathedral Homilies, ed.+ LT/FT M. Brière and others (PO 4, 8, 12, 16, 20, 22-23, 25-26, 29, 35-38; 1906-77).

THEODORE of MOPSUESTIA: Fragmenta Syriaca, ed.+ LT E. Sachau (Leipzig, 1869).
- : Comm. on Pss., ed.+ FT L. Van Rompay (CSCO Syr. 189-90, 1981).
- : Comm. on Qohelet, ed. W. Strothmann (GOFS 28, 1988).
- : Comm. on John, ed.+ LT I-M. Vosté (CSCO Syr. 62-63 [IV 3], 1940).
- : Catechetical Homilies, ed.+ ET A. Mingana (WS 5-6, 1932-33). Ed.+ FT R.-M. Tonneau (Studi e Testi 145, 1949).

TITUS of BOSTRA: Against the Manichaeans, ed. P. de Lagarde (Berlin, 1859; repr. Osnabrück, 1967).

ZACHARIAS SCHOLASTICUS: Life of Severus, ed.+ FT M. Kugener (PO 2, 1904).

ABBREVIATIONS

AION: Annali del'Istituto Orientale, Napoli

AMS: P. Bedjan, Acta Martyrum et Sanctorum [see Section 8(c)]

ASM: S.E. Assemani, Acta Sanctorum et Martyrum [see Section 8(c)]

BO: Bibliotheca Orientalis

CSCO: Corpus Scriptorum Christianorum Orientalium

CSCO: Syr. CSCO Scriptores Syri

E: East Syrian

ET: English translation

FT: French translation

GOFS: Göttinger Orientforschungen, Reihe Syriaca

GT: German translation

IT: Italian translation

JAs: Journal Asiatique

JAOS: Journal of the American Oriental Society

JNES: Journal of Near Eastern Studies

JSS: Journal of Semitic Studies

LT: Latin translation

OC: Oriens Christianus
OCA: Orientalia Christiana Analecta
OLA: Orientalia Lovaniensia Analecta
PO: Patrologia Orientalis
PdO: Parole de l'Orient
PS: Patrologia Syriaca
W: West Syrian
WS: Woodbrooke Studies
ZDMG: Zeitschrift der Deutschen Morgenländischen Gesellschaft.

CHRESTOMATHY

1. An inscription of Serrîn (73 C.E.)[1]

ܒܝܪܚ[2] ܬܫܪܝ[3] ܩܕܡ ܫܢܬ 385[4]
ܒܠܝܬ ܐܢܐ[5] ܡܥܢܘ ܡܫܝܫܐ
ܒܕܪ[6] ܕܐܢܚ ܒܪ ܡܥܢܘ ܒܪ ܒܪܗ ܕܫܪܕܘܢܐ
ܢܦܫܐ ܗܕܐ ܠܢܦܫܝ ܘܠܒܢܝ ܒܪ ܫܢܝܢ 90
ܡܢ ܕܢܥܒܕ ܢܬܒܥܘܢܗ ܐܠܗܐ ܟܠܗܘܢ ܘܒܥܡܪܐ[7]
ܘܚܝܐ ܢܗܘܐ ܠܗ ܡܢ ܕܢܐܬܐ[8] ܘܗܢܐ ܒܥܒܕܐ ܢܣܟܠ
ܘܗܠܝܢ ܓܪܡܐ[9] [- - - -] ܘܩܦܪܐ[10] ܠܐ ܢܗܘܐ
ܠܗ ܘܒܢܝܐ ܕܢܪܕܦܘܢ ܒܥܦܪܐ ܟܠ ܒܢܘܗܝ ܠܐ
ܢܬܟܣܘܢ ܠܗ]

(**1**) See Drijvers 1972: 2f. Note that the Impf. prefix /y-/ had not yet changed to /n-/: ܢܥܒܕ (5), ܢܬܒܥܘܢܗ (5), ܢܗܘܐ (6,7), ܢܐܬܐ (6), ܢܣܟܠ (6), ܢܪܕܦܘܢ (8), ܢܬܟܣܘܢ (9). (**2**) In the actual inscription there is no diacritical point used to distinguish Dalath from Resh. (**3**) The names of the months of the Syriac calendar are: ܬܫܪܝ ܩܕܝܡ or ܬܫܪܝܢ ܩܕܝܡ (Oct), ܬܫܪܝ[ܢ] ܐܚܪܝ (Nov), ܟܢܘܢ ܩܕܝܡ (ܩܕܡܝ) (Dec), ܟܢܘܢ ܐܚܪܝ (Jan), ܫܒܛ (Feb), ܐܕܪ (March), ܢܝܣܢ (Apr), ܐܝܪ (May), ܚܙܝܪܢ (June), ܬܡܘܙ (July), ܐܒ (Aug), ܐܝܠܘܠ (Sept). (**4**) Various symbols are used for "units," "hundreds," and "twenties." (**5**) The use of the independent personal pronoun is typical of boasting or self-assertive inscriptions of this kind: § 74. (**6**) Apparently some sort of priestly dignitary. (**7**) Note the defective spelling without a Waw for ܥܘܡܪܐ /ʿumraa/. (**8**) Note the phonetic spelling for the standard (and etymological-historical) ܢܐܬܐ. (**9**) For ܓܪܡܝܐ 'bones' for the standard pl. form ܓܪ̈ܡܬܐ. (**10**) Most likely = ܩܒܪܐ 'tomb.'

2. The great flood of November 201 C.E.: from the archives of Edessa[1]

ܒܫܢܬ ܫܬܡܐܐ ܘܬܠܬܥܣܪ̈ܐ ܒܡܠܟܘܬܗ ܕܣܘܝܪܘܣ ܘܒܡܠܟܘܬܗ
ܕܐܒܓܪ ܡܠܟܐ ܒܪ ܡܥܢܘ ܡܠܟܐ. ܒܐܝܪܚ[2] ܬܫܪܝܢ ܐܚܪܝ,[3] ܣܓܝ
ܗܘܐ[4] ܡܒܘܥܐ ܕܡ̈ܝܐ ܕܢܦܩ ܡܢ ܐܦܕܢܐ ܪܒܐ. ܕܐܒܓܪ ܡܠܟܐ
ܪܒܐ. ܘܣܓܝ ܘܣܠܩ ܐܝܟ ܒܥܕܢܗ ܡܕܡܟܐ. ܘܡܠܐ ܗܘܐ ܘܫܦܥ
ܠܟܘܠ ܓܢ̈ܝܢ.[5] ܘܫܪܝ,[6] ܗܘܐ ܕܪ̈ܬܐ ܘܐܣܛ̈ܘܐ ܘܒ̈ܬܐ ܕܡܠܟܘܬܐ
ܕܢܬܡܠܘܢ[7] ܡ̈ܝܐ. ܘܟܕ ܚܙܐ ܡܪܢ ܐܒܓܪ ܡܠܟܐ. ܣܠܩ ܗܘܐ ܠܗ[8]
ܠܬܘܟܢܐ ܕܦܠܛܪܐ ܕܠܥܠ ܡܢ ܐܦܕܢܐ ܕܝܠܗ.[9] ܐܝܟܐ ܕܡܬܒܢܝܢ[10]
ܘܡܥܡܪܝܢ. ܒ̈ܬܝ, ܒܪ̈ܝܐ[11] ܕܝܠܗ̇ ܕܡܠܟܘܬܐ. ܘܟܕ ܢ̈ܦܫܬܐ ܡܬܚܫܒܝܢ
ܗܘܘ: ܕܡܝܐ[12] ܢܣܓܘܢ ܠܗܘܢ[13] ܠܓ̈ܢܐ ܡܬܪ̈ܐ ܕܐܬܬܘܣܦܘ ܗܘܘ.
ܓܕܫ ܘܗܘܐ ܡܛܪܐ ܪܒܐ ܘܡܥܝܢܐ ܒܠܠܝܐ. ܘܐܬܐ ܕܡܝ ܕܠܐ
ܒܙܒܢܗ ܘܕܠܐ ܒܚܫܚܬܗ.[14] ܘܐܬܘ ܡ̈ܝܐ ܢܘܟܪ̈ܝܐ. ܘܐܫܟܚܘ ܐܢܘܢ[15]
ܠܦܠܛܪܝܐ ܟܕ ܐܚܝܕܝܢ[16] ܒܬܪ̈ܥܐ ܘܬܪ̈ܥܐ[17] ܕܡܪܝܡܝܢ ܗܘܘ
ܘܡܬܟܣܝܐ ܕܬܪ̈ܥܐ ܕܡܫܪ̈ܪܝܢ[18] ܗܘܘ. ܘܕܠܐ[19] ܐܫܬܟܚܘ ܠܗܘܢ[20]
ܡܦܩܢܐ ܠܡ̈ܝܐ. ܗܘܐ ܠܗ[21] ܝܡܐ ܪܒܐ ܠܒܪ ܡܢ ܫܘܪܝܗ̇ ܕܡܕܝܢܬܐ.
ܘܫܪܝܘ ܗܘܘ ܡ̈ܝܐ ܢܦܩܝܢ[22] ܡܢ ܒܝܬ ܟ̈ܘܝܬܐ ܕܫܘܪܐ ܠܡܕܝܢܬܐ.
ܘܐܒܓܪ ܡܠܟܐ ܟܕ ܩܐܡ ܗܘܐ ܒܦܘܪܓܘܣܐ ܪܒܐ ܕܡܬܩܪܐ[23]
ܕܦܪ̈ܣܝܐ. ܚܙܐ ܗܘܐ ܒܠܡܦܐܕܐ[24] ܕܢܘܪܐ ܠܡ̈ܝܐ.[25] ܘܦܩܕ ܗܘܐ.
ܘܐܫܬܩܠܘ ܗܘܘ ܬܪ̈ܥܐ ܘܦܠܛܪ̈ܝܐ ܬܚ̈ܬܝܢܐ ܕܫܘܪܐ ܡܥܪܒܝܐ[26]
ܕܡܕܝܢܬܐ ܡܢ ܐܝܟܐ ܕܢܦܩ ܢܗܪܐ.[26a] ܘܒܗ̇ ܒܫܥܬܐ.[27] ܬܪ̈ܥܘܗܝ,[28]
ܗܘܘ ܡ̈ܝܐ ܠܫܘܪܐ ܡܥܪܒܝܐ ܕܡܕܝܢܬܐ. ܘܥܠܘ ܠܓܘ ܡܕܝܢܬܐ.
ܘܟܘܪܬ ܠܐܦܕܢܐ ܪܒܐ ܘܫܦܝܐ ܕܡܪܢ ܡܠܟܐ. ܘܫܩܠܘ ܗܘܘ ܟܠ
ܡܕܡ ܕܐܫܬܟܚ ܗܘܐ ܩܕܡܝܗܘܢ. ܒܢ̈ܝܢܐ ܪ̈ܓܝܓܐ ܘܦܐ̈ܝܐ
ܕܡܕܝܢܬܐ. ܟܠ ܡܕܡ ܕܩܪܝܒ ܗܘܐ ܠܢܗܪܐ ܡܢ ܬܝܡܢܗ ܘܠܓܪܒܝܗ.[29]
ܘܚܪܒ ܗܘܐ ܬܘܒ ܗܝܟܠܐ ܕܥܕܬܐ ܕܟܪ̈ܣܛܝܢܐ. ܘܡܝܬܘ ܗܘܘ
ܒܗܢܐ ܚܒܠܐ. ܝܬܝܪ ܡܢ ܬܪ̈ܝܢ ܐ̈ܠܦܝܢ ܕܒܢ̈ܝܢܫܐ.[30] ܦ̈ܓܪܐ ܕܝܢ
ܡܢܗܘܢ. ܟܕ ܕܡܟܝܢ[31] ܗܘܘ ܒܠܠܝܐ. ܒܠܗ ܒܠܚܘܕܝܗܘܢ ܚܙ̈ܐ ܡܢ
ܥܠܡܐ[32] ܘܐܬܦܨܝܘ ܗܘܘ. ܟܕ ܡܠܝܐ ܗܘܬ ܡܕܝܢܬܐ ܟܠܗ̇ ܕܩܠ̈ܠܬܐ.
ܘܟܕ ܚܙܐ ܐܒܓܪ ܡܠܟܐ ܚܘܪܒܢܐ ܗܢܐ ܕܗܘܐ ܗܘܐ.[33] ܦܩܕ
ܗܘܐ. ܕܟܠܗܘܢ ܐ̈ܘܡܢܐ ܕܡܕܝܢܬܐ ܢܦܩܘܢ ܗܘܘ[34] ܢ̈ܫܘܬܗܘܢ
ܡܢ ܠܘܬ ܢܗܪܐ. ܘܐܢܫ ܠܘܬ ܢܗܪܐ. ܠܐ ܢܒܢܐ ܠܗ[35] ܫܘܩܬܐ.
ܘܒܣܬܘܐ ܕܫܢ̈ܝܐ ܘܬܪ̈ܬܝܢ.[36] ܐܬܬܣܝܡ[37] ܫ̈ܘܩܬܐ ܕܒܢܝܐ

ܢܗܘܐ ܦܬܝܗ ܕܢܗܪܐ.[38] ܘܐܘܣܦܘ ܗܘܘ ܥܠ ܡ̈ܫܘܚܬܗ ܦ̈ܕܒܥܬܐ،
ܐܦ ܠܒܪ ܬ̈ܚܘܡܐ ܗܠܟܝܢ ܗܘܘ ܘܡܫܬܦܝܢ. ܐܠܐ[39] ܐܦ ܗ̇ܘ[40]
ܦܬܝܗ ܕܢܗܪܐ ܙܥܘܪ ܗܘܐ. ܕܬ̈ܚܘܡܐ ܕܪ̈ܓܠܬܐ[41] ܚܡ̈ܫܝܢ ܘܫ̈ܒܥ
ܒܡܫܠ ܗܘܐ ܒܒܠܡܫܘܬܗܘܢ ܕܡܢ ܟܠ ܓ̈ܒܝܢ. ܘܦܩܕ ܗܘܐ ܐܒܓܪ
ܡ̈ܠܟܐ. ܕܟܠܗܘܢ ܗ̇ܢܘܢ[42] ܕܝܬܒܝܢ ܒܐܣܛܘܐ ܘܦܠܚܝܢ ܠܘܩܒܠ

(**1**) Hallier 1892: 145-47 (Syr. text), 84-88 (Germ. tr.); Guidi 1903: text, pp. 1-3, Lat. tr. pp. 3-4. (**2**) ܝܪܚ, st. cst. of ܝܪܚܐ 'month.' (**3**) On the native names of the months, see Text 1, n. 3. (**4**) A compound preterite typical of historical narrative: see § 85. (**5**) On the use of the st. abs. in conjunction with ܟܠ, see § 71 b. (**6**) An error for pl. ܥܒܪܘ. (**7**) On the complementation of the verb ܫܪܝ 'to begin,' see § 98 c. (**8**) On the centripetal preposition Lamadh, see Joüon - Muraoka, § 133 *d.* (**9**) On the proclitic of ܕܝܠܐ, see § 91 h, 3. (**10**) On ܐܝܟܐ ܕ /ʾaykaa d-/, see § 76. (**11**) /ʿaavday ʿvaadaa/ 'those who do (Pe. ptc. m.pl. cst.) the work.' On the proleptic ܕܝܠܗ, see § 112 h. (**12**) The proclitic is similar to that which introduces direct speech: § 98 e, i. (**13**) On the proleptic Lamadh, see § 112 a. (**14**) 'not on its (expected, usual) day nor in its (expected, usual) month.' (**15**) Proleptic: § 112 c. (**16**) On the proclitic Dalath with ܐܝܟܢ, see § 98 e, ii. (**17**) /rawrvee/, an irregular pl. formation through reduplication from /rab/ 'great.' (**18**) /mšarrin waw/ 'were secured,' Pa. pass. ptc. (**19**) The Dalath introduces a causal clause. (**20**) Proleptic: § 112 b. (**21**) Centripetal Lamadh: see above, n. 8. (**22**) On the syntax of verb complementation here, see § 98 d. (**23**) '(the tower) of the Persians,' the name of a tower. (**24**) A variant spelling for ܠܒܘܪܐ. (**25**) The Lamadh is a direct object marker. (**26**) According to Segal 1970: 24, an error for ܡܕ̈ܢܚܝܐ 'eastern.' (**26a**) On the position of the preposition ܡܢ, see § 91 h, 2. (**27**) 'at that moment': prolepsis (§ 112 a). (**28**) /tarʿuy/, Pe. 3m.pl. + 3m.s. (proleptically referring to the following ܠܫܘܪܐ). (**29**) 'on its southern and northern side': the fem. suffix refers to ܡܕܝܢܬܐ. (**30**) /bnaynaašaa/ 'persons,' pl. of /barnaašaa/. (**31**) /damkin/, pl. of /dmek/ 'asleep.' (**32**) /men šelyaa/ 'suddenly, unexpectedly.' (**33**) /hwaa waa/: see § 85. (**34**) On this compound tense, see § 88. (**35**) 'for himself,' dativus commodi. (**36**) Nomina agentis Peal /maašoḥee wyaadoʿee/, 'measurers and knowers,' i.e. 'surveyors and experts.' (**37**) Ethpe, Pf. 3 f.pl. {**38**) 'as far as the breadth of the river would extend' (?). (**39**) Translate: 'yet, nonetheless.' (**40**) Proleptic pronoun: § 112 i. (**41**) /reglaataa/, pl. of /rgeltaa/ 'rivulet, tributary.' On the position of the numeral, see § 91 c. (**42**) On the syntagm ܟܠܗܘܢ ܗ̇ܢܘܢ, see § 111.

ܢܗܪܐ. ܕܡܢ ܬܫܪܝ ܩܕܡ[43] ܘܒܪܡܫܐ[44] ܠܠܝܐ. ܠܐ ܗܘܘ ܒܛܠܝܢ[45]
ܦܠܚܘܬܗܘܢ. ܐܠܐ ܠܓܪ̈ܝܐ ܕܢܛ̈ܪܝܢ ܡܕܝܢܬܐ. ܡܛ̈ܪܐ ܐܢܫܐ ܡܢܗܘܢ
ܗܘܘ ܒܛܠܝܢ ܒܥܘܪܐ. ܠܒܪ ܡܢ ܕܘܟܬܐ ܕܥܠܝܢ ܒܗ̇ ܡ̈ܝܐ ܠܡܕܝܢܬܐ
ܟܠܗ ܙܒܢܐ ܕܫܗܪܐ.[46] ܘܡܝܐ ܕܐܬܓܪܒܘ[47] ܒܠܠܝܐ ܘܫܡܥܘ ܘܠܐ
ܕܡ̈ܝܐ ܢܛܘ̈ܪܐ ܕܫܪܝܘ ܕܢܥܠܘܢ[48] ܠܡܕܝܢܬܐ.[49] ܘܟܠ ܡ̇ܢ[50] ܕܫܡ̇ܥ[51]
ܠܐ ܘܡܗܡܐ[52] ܘܠܐ ܢܦܩ. ܗܐ ܡ̈ܝܐ[53] ܬܒܥܝܢ ܡܢܗ ܒܡܫܝܐ[54]
ܕܥܠ ܦܘܩܕܢܗ ܕܡܠܟܐ, ܘܐܬܬܣܝܡ ܗܘܐ ܗܢܐ ܦܘܩܕܢܐ ܡܢ.
ܗܢܐ ܙܒܢܐ ܕܗ̣ܘܐ ܒܗ ܡܚܒܠܐ.[55] ܒܪܡܫܐ ܠܦܠܓܘܬ ܠ̈ܠܝܐ. ܗܘ
ܕܝܢ ܐܒܓܪ ܡܠܟܐ. ܦܩܕ ܗܘܐ ܘܐܬܒܥܝ ܠܗ ܒܢܝܢܐ ܠܡܥܡܪܐ
ܕܡܠܟܘܬܗ. ܒܝܬ ܫܘܩܐ ܒܝܬ ܬܒܪܐ.[56] ܘܬܡܢ ܚ̇ܙܐ ܗܘܐ[57] ܟܠܗ
ܙܒܢܐ ܕܫܗܪܐ. ܘܡܫܩܠܐ ܗܘܬ ܗܘܐ ܠܗ ܠܐܦܕܢܐ ܚܕܬܐ ܕܐܬܒܢܝ
ܗܘܐ ܠܗ ܒܟܠ ܦܪܣ ܡܟܘܡܬܐ. ܘܐܦ ܗ̣ܢܘܢ[58] ܚܐܪ̈ܐ ܕܝܠܗ̇. ܒܢܘ
ܠܗܘܢ ܒ̈ܢܝܢܐ ܠܡܥܡܪܗܘܢ ܒܡܥܡܪܘܬܐ ܕܗ̇ܘܐ ܒܗ̇ ܡܠܟܐ ܒܡܘܬܒܐ
ܪܡܐ ܕܡܬܩܪܐ ܒ[ܝܬ] ܣܗܪ̈ܝܐ.[59] ܘܡܛܠ ܕܢܦܩܬ ܗܘܐ[60] ܫܥܬܗ̇
ܕܡܕܝܢܬܐ ܡܕܒܪܐ.[61] ܦܩܕ ܗܘܐ ܐܒܓܪ ܡܠܟܐ. ܘܐܫܬܒܩ ܢܛܘ̈ܪܬܐ

(**43**) /tešrin qdem/ 'former Tishri': see also n. 3 above. The preceding conjunction Dalath is redundant, for the object clause of ܦܩܕ ܗܘܐ has already been introduced by the same proclitic in ... ܕܟܠܗܘܢ. (**44**) The conjunction Waw is often idiomatically added in an expression for "from *x* until *y*." (**45**) On this compound tense, see § 87. (**46**) The preceding ܓܪ̈ܝܐ referred to by the suffix pronoun is the subject of this compound sentence: § 113. (**47**) Despite the preterital tense, the reference is to a future event: § 81. (**48**) On the syntax, see § 98 c. (**49**) Several words appear to be missing at this point. (**50**) The dot above is diacritical, distinguishing the word /man/ from its homograph /men/ with a diacritical dot below: see § 4 a. (**51**) The dot over the Mem distinguishes the form, Pe ptc. /šaamaᶜ/, from its homograph, ܫܡܥ /šmaᶜ/, Pf. (**52**) /mahmee/, Af. ptc. (**53**) ' (shouting,) Look, water (is) here!' (**54**) 'they shall accuse him of negligence.' (**55**) 'in which this (disaster) fell.' (**56**) 'at Beth Tvara,' a locality in Edessa. The preposition ܒ is missing by haplography. (**57**) The dot above the letter ᶜE indicates a ptc., hence the compound tense mentioned in § 86. (**58**) /hennon/, 'they,' proleptic (§ 112 i), with a diacritic dot (§ 4 a). (**59**) /beeṯ saḥraayee/, the name of a street in Edessa. (**60**) On the syntax, see § 88. (**61**) On the position of the adjective qualifying ܡܝܐ, see § 91 g.

ܕܬܫܒܚܬܐ ܡܢ ܟܘ̈ܪܐ ܕܡܕܝܢܬܐ. ܘܡܢ ܐܝܠܝܢ[62] ܕܒܟܦܪ̈ܝܢ ܒܩܘܪ̈ܝܐ[63]
ܘܡܐܟܘ̈ܠܣܐ ܘܐܬܟܬܒܬ ܒܟܬܒܬܐ ܡܢܝܘܗܝ ܫܒܥ ܙ̈ܒܢܝܢ. ܒܐܝܕܐ
ܕܒܝܬ ܡܕܝܢܬܐ ܒܐܪܟܘܢܬܐ ܘܐܬܟܠܠܬ ܒܫ̈ܠܝܢܘܬܗ.[64]

(**62**) On ܐܝܠܝܢ ܕ-, see § 111. (**63**) /quryee/, an irregular pl. of ܩܪܝܬܐ /qriṯaa/ 'village.' (**64**) The document concludes with the names of two secretaries of the town hall of Edessa and two of its archivists.

3. A deed of sale on parchment from Dura Europos (243 C.E.)[1]

I[2]

ܒܐܝܪ ܕ31 ܙܒ[3] ܡ(ܪܩܝܐ) ܐ(ܘܪܠܝܐ) ܡܬܪܥܬܐ
ܒܪܬ ܫܒܕܢ ܙܒ ܠܬܝܪܘ ܒܪ ܒܪܒܥܫܐ
ܐܡܬܐ ܡܬܩܪܝܢ ܒ(ܕܝܢܪ̈ܐ) 700 ܒܪܬ ܫܢܝܢ 28

II

1 ܒܫܢܬ ܫܬ ܕܐܘܛܩܪܛܘܪ[4] ܩܣܪ ܡܪܩܘܣ
ܐܢܛܘܢܝܘܣ ܓܪܕܝܢܘܣ ܐܘܣܒܝܘܣ[5] ܐܘܛܘܟܣ[6]
2 ܣܒܣܛܘܣ[7] ܒܗܦܛܝܐ[8] ܕܐܢܝܘܣ ܐܪܝܘܣ[9]
ܘܕܛܪܝܒܘܢܘܣ[10] ܦܦܘܣ ܒܝܪܚ ܐܝܪ ܫܢܬ

(**1**) As presented and studied by J.A. Goldstein (1966). Like Text no. 1 this one makes no use of the diacritical mark, either, to distinguish Dalath from Resh. (**2**) The first two lines, in a different hand from the main body of the text (up to line 20 middle), summarise the contents of the deed in abbreviated style: the names and the noun ܕܝܢܪܐ are abbreviated, what stands enclosed within the brackets representing a spelling-out of what is understood. (**3**) Possibly a defectively spelled verbal noun /zubbaan/ 'sale.' (**4**) A partly defective spelling for ܐܘܛܘܩܪܛܘܪ (αὐτοκράτωρ) 'emperor.' (**5**) A Greek equivalent (Εὐσέβειος) of Lat. *Pius*. (**6**) A Greek equivalent (Εὔτυχος) of Lat. *Felix*. (**7**) A Greek equivalent (Σενεστής) of Lat. *Augustus*. (**8**) Note the defective spelling for ܗܘܦܛܝܐ. (**9**) An error for ܐܪܝܢܘܣ *Arrianus* ? (**10**) 'tribune, tribunius.'

3 ܚܡܫܡܐܐ ܘܚܡܫܝܢ ܘܐܪܒܥ ܒܡܢܝܢܐ ܩܕܡܝܐ
ܘܒܫܢܬ ܬܠܬܝܢ ܘܚܕܐ ܕܫܘܪܝܗ[11]
4 ܕܐܢܛܘܢܝܢܐ ܐܕܣܐ[12] ܢܨܝܚܬܐ ܩܘܠܘܢܝܐ[13]
ܡܛܪܦܘܠܝܣ[14] ܐܘܪܠܝܐ ܐܠܟܣܢܕܪܝܐ ܒܟܘܡܪܘܬܐ[15]
5 ܕܡܪܩܘܣ ܐܘܪܠܝܘܣ ܐܢܛܝܘܟܘܣ ܗܦܩܘܣ[16]
ܪܗܘܡܘܣ[17] ܒܪ ܒܠܫܘ ܘܒܐܣܛܪܛܓܘܬܐ[18] ܕܡܪܩܘܣ
6 ܐܘܪܠܝܘܣ ܐܒܓܪ ܗܦܩܘܣ ܪܗܘܡܘܣ ܒܪ ܡܥܢܘ
ܒܪ ܐܓܐ ܘܕܐܒܓܪ ܒܪ ܫܡܫܝ ܒܪ ܒܪ - ܥ - -
7 ܕܬܪܬܝܢ ܘܒܠܝܢ ܒܝܘܡ ܬܫܥܐ ܡܘܕܝܢܐ[19]
ܡܪܩܐ ܐܘܪܠܝܐ ܡܬܪܒܬܐ ܒܪܬ
8 ܫܡܫܒܪܝ ܒܪ ܐܒܓܪ ܕܢܬܐ ܐܕܣܝܬܐ ܠܠܘܣ
ܐܘܪܠܝܣ ܬܝܪܘ ܒܪ ܒܪ ܒܒܫܡܝܢ
9 ܚܪܝܢܐ[20] ܕܩܒܠܬ ܒܗܢ ܕܝܢܪܐ ܫܒܥܡܐܐ[21] ܘܙܒܢܬ
ܠܗ ܐܡܬܣܝܢ[22] ܐܡܬܐ ܕܝܠܗ
10 ܙܒܢܐ ܬܗܘܐ ܒܪܬ ܫܢܝܢ ܥܣܪܝܢ[23] ܘܬܡܢܐ
ܡܬܪ ܐܘ ܫܡܝܪ[24] ܡܢ ܫܒܝܐ[25] ܗܢ
11 ܕܡܢ ܝܘܡܢܐ ܘܠܥܠܡܐ ܬܗܘܐ ܐܢܬ[26] ܬܪܘ
ܙܒܢܐ ܘܢܬܦܩ[27] ܫܠܝܛ ܒܐܡܬܐ ܗܕܐ
12 ܕܙܒܢܬ ܠܟ ܠܡܙܒܢܐ ܘܠܡܘܗܒܗ ܘܠܡܥܒܕ ܒܗ
ܟܠ ܕܬܨܒܐ ܘܐܢ ܐܢܫ ܢܕܘܢ ܐܘ
13 ܢܬܗܓܐ[28] ܒܗ ܬܚܘܬ ܙܒܢܐ ܐܘ ܒܗ ܢܬܩܘܗܝ
ܟܠ ܫܥܝܢ[29] ܐܡܬܐ ܗܕܐ ܕܙܒܢܬ ܠܗ
14 ܐܘܩܡ ܐܢܐ ܡܬܪܒܬܐ ܡܙܒܢܢܝܬܐ[30] ܘܝܪܬܝ
ܘܐܕܘܢ ܘܐܡܪܩ[31] ܘܐܕܟܐ ܘܐܦܣܩܗ
15 ܒܓܕܗ[32] ܕܬܢܘ ܙܒܢܐ ܘܠܐ ܐܫܬܠܛ ܠܡܦܣܩܝ
ܒܟܠ ܫܛܪܐ ܗܢܐ ܘܙܒܢܬܗ[33]
16 ܠܟ ܐܡܬܐ ܗܕܐ [- -]ܐܡ[- - - - -] ܢܡܘܣ
ܕܡܟܐ ܘܡܙܒܢܐ ܠܚܪܝܐ ܫܬܐ ܫܠܡܝܢ[34]
17 ܘܗܟܢܐ ܗܘܬ ܬܢܘܝ[35] ܒܢܝܬܗܘܢ ܕܐܢ[36]

ܬܡܪܩ ܠܗ[37] ܐܡܬܐ ܗܕܐ ܡܢ ܝܘܡܢܐ
18 ܘܠܗܠ[38] ܡܢ ܟܕܗ ܕܬܪܩ ܙܒܘܢܐ ܘܐܬܬܒܬܒܘ
ܠܒܝܬܐ ܗܕܐ ܫܛܪܐ ܬܪܝܢ
19 ܚܕ[39] ܦܚܡܗ ܐܚܝܕ ܠܕܟܪܘܢ[40] ܢܚܠ ܒܐܪܟܝܘܢ[41]
ܕܐܦܘܠܝܢܐ ܐܕܣܐ ܠܚܣܝܬܐ

(**11**) 'its (fem.) freedom' with a proleptic pronoun suffix: § 112. (**12**) The city of Edessa. (**13**) For ܩܘܠܘܢܝܐ 'colony' (κολωνία). (**14**) = ܡܝܛܪܦܘܠܝܣ metropolis (μητρόπολις). (**15**) Defectively spelled for ܦܘܡܪܩܘܬܐ. (**16**) 'Horseman, eques' (ἱππεύς). (**17**) Crude representation of Lat. *Romanus.* (**18**) 'Commander.' (**19**) 'I declare': /mawdyaanaa/, Af Ptc. f.sg. + enclitic 1sg. pronoun (§ 10). (**20**) 'Harranaean,' hailing from Harran. (**21**) = ܫܒܥܐܐ, a spelling testifying to the weakening of the guttural. (**22**) Correct form for ܡܛܠܣ, earlier at I, with an aphaeresis of the initial Alaf (§ 6J). (**23**) The spelling with ܫ for the standard ܣ is strikingly archaic (as in Heb. עֶשְׂרִים). See also ܬܪܬܥܫܪܐ (21) and ܥܫܪ (24 et passim). (**24**) 'more or less; give or take.' (**25**) 'Prisoners': /švayyaa/, Pe pass. ptc. m.pl. emph. from ܫܒܐ 'to take prisoner,' or /šabbaayee/ 'captors' (m.pl.emph.), or /ševyaa/ 'captives' (m.sg.emph. collectively used). (**26**) Juridic "emphasis" on the parties involved. (**27**) 'your heirs' (/yaartayk/, Pe. ptc. used as a noun). The singular verb is in concord with the principal constituent of the multiple subject. (**28**) 'he enters into a legal dispute, contends,' /neṯhaggee/, Ethpa. (**29**) Defectively spelled for ܚܘܫܒܢ /ḥušbaan/: 'on account of.' (**30**) 'vendor,' /mzabnaaniṯaa/, Pa. nomen agentis, f.sg. (§ 20). (**31**) Defectively spelled for ܐܡܪܩ 'I shall cleanse.' Further examples are ܬܡܪܩ (17), ܢܚܠ (19), ܐܒܓܪ (22). (**32**) 'in his possession,' /bḡaddeeh/, with a proleptic pronoun (§ 112). (**33**) 'I sold her,' /zabbentaah/ with a proleptic pronoun suffix (§ 112). (**34**) If the meaning is "until six months will have elapsed," one has here a mixture of two constructions, viz. prep. ܥܕܡܐ ܠ and conj. ܥܕܡܐ ܕ. (**35**) This type of fem. nouns (§ 28) is always attested in the sg. abs. form. Cf. Mt 27.64 ܛܘܥܝܝ ܐܚܪܝܬܐ 'the recent error' (with a st. emph. adjective). (**36**) The particle Dalath is comparable to that which introduces direct speech. (**37**) Centripetal Lamadh: cf. Joüon-Muraoka, § 133 *d*. (**38**) 'and beyond,' thus 'from this day onward.' (**39**) 'one, a copy of it,' in contrast to ܐܚܪܢܐ 'the other' (20). (**40**) For the standard spelling ܕܘܟܪܢ, but cf. BA דִּכְרוֹנָה and Christian Palestinian Aramaic ܕܟܪܘܢ alongside ܕܘܟܪܘܢ. (**41**) 'archives' (ἀρχεῖον).

20 ܘܐܚܪܢܐ[42] ܦܨܝܓܗ ܢܗܘܐ ܠܘܬܗ[43] ܕܬܪܝܘ
ܙܒܘܢܐ ܡܒܘܕܢܐ[44] ܐܘܪܠܝܣ ܚܦܣܝ
21 ܒܪ ܫܡܫܓܪܡ ܐܕܣܝܢܐ ܡܢ ܦܘܠܝܣ[45]
ܕܬܪܬܒܫܪܐ ܕܟܬܒܬ ܚܠܦ ܐܘܪܠܝܐ
22 ܡܬܪܒܬܐ ܐܢܬܬܝ, ܒܪܫܡܐ ܕܣܦܪܐ ܠܐ
ܚܟܡܐ[46] ܕܙܒܢܬ ܐܡܬܐ ܗܕܐ ܕܝܠܗ
23 ܘܩܒܠܬ ܕܡܝܗ[47] ܐܝܟ ܕܟܬܝܒ ܡܢ ܠܥܠ
24 ܡܪܩܘܣ ܐܘܪܠܝܣ ܒܪ ܒܠܥܐ ܫܗܕ[48]
25 ܡܪܩܘܣ ܐܘܪܠܝܣ ܒܪ ܦ[- -] ܫܗܕ
26 ܒܪܫܡܐ ܕܡܒܩܪܐ[49] ܠܫܛܪܝܢ
27 Αὐρ(ήλιος) Μάννος ὁ ἐπὶ τοῦ ἱεροῦ καὶ
28 τοῦ πολειτικοῦ μ(α)ρ(τυρῶ)[50]
29 ܡܪܩܘܣ ܐܘܪܠܝܘܣ ܒܠܥܘ ܒܪ
30 ܡܩܝܡܘ ܣܦܪܐ ܟܬܒܬ ܫܛܪܐ ܗܢܐ
31 Seal

Verso

1 ܐܘܪܠܝܐ ܡܬܪܒܬܐ ܒܪܬ ܫܡܫܝ ܡܙܒܢܢܝܬܐ ܥܠ ܢܦܫܗ ܫܗܕܐ
2 ܐܘܪܠܝܣ ܚܦܣܝ ܒܪ ܫܡܫܓܪܡ ܚܬܡܬ ܥܠ ܫܛܪܐ ܗܢܐ
3 ܐܘܪܠܝܣ ܐܒܓܪ ܣܛܪܛܓܐ[51] ܫܗܕ ʺΑβγαρος
4 ܐܒܓܪ ܒܪ ܒܪܣܡܝܐ ܫܗܕ
5 ܐܘܪܠܝܐ ܡܬܪܒܬܐ ܒܪܬ ܫܡܫܝ ܡܙܒܢܢܝܬܐ ܥܠ ܢܦܫܗ ܫܗܕܐ

(**42**) 'the other, (also) a copy of it.' (**43**) On the proleptic pronoun with a preposition followed by ܕ, see § 112 e. (**44**) Masc. sg., cf. above, line 7. (**45**) 'tribe' (φυλή). (**46**) 'she is not versed in the art of signing a document.' Either ܚܟܡܐ (Pe ptc.f.) or = ܚܟܝܡܬܐ (adj.). (**47**) /dmayyeeh/ 'her price,' plurale tantum (§ 70). (**48**) Archaic spelling for ܣܗܕ (probably Pe ptc.). All the witnesses have put their own signature. (**49**) 'inspector,' Pa ptc. (**50**) "I Aurelius Mannus in charge of the sacred and civic archives bear witness." (**51**) 'strategos' (στρατηγός).

4. Abraham's temptation (Genesis 22:1-19)[1]

(1) ܘܗܘܐ ܡܢ ܒܬܪ ܦܬܓ̈ܡܐ ܗܠܝܢ. ܐܠܗܐ ܢܣܝ ܠܐܒܪܗܡ
ܘܐܡܪ ܠܗ. ܐܒܪܗܡ. ܘܐܡܪ ܗܐ ܐܢܐ. (2) ܘܐܡܪ ܠܗ. ܕܒܪ
ܠܒܪܟ[2] ܠܝܚܝܕܝܟ[3] ܕܪܚܡܬ ܐܢܬ ܠܐܝܣܚܩ. ܘܙܠ ܠܟ[4] ܠܐܪܥܐ
ܕܐܡܘܪܝܐ ܘܐܣܩܝܗܝ[5] ܬܡܢ ܠܥܠܬܐ ܥܠ ܚܕ ܡܢ ܛܘܪ̈ܐ ܕܐܡܪ
ܠܟ܀ (3) ܘܩܕܡ ܐܒܪܗܡ ܒܨܦܪܐ. ܘܐܪܟܒ ܥܠ ܚܡܪܗ. ܘܕܒܪ
ܠܬܪ̈ܝܢ ܛܠܝ̈ܘܗܝ ܥܡܗ. ܘܠܐܝܣܚܩ ܒܪܗ. ܘܨܠܚ ܩܝ̈ܣܐ ܠܥܠܬܐ.
ܘܩܡ ܐܙܠ[6] ܠܐܬܪܐ ܕܐܡܪ ܠܗ ܐܠܗܐ. (4) ܘܠܝܘܡܐ[7] ܬܠܝܬܝܐ.
ܐܪܝܡ[8] ܐܒܪܗܡ ܥܝ̈ܢܘܗܝ ܘܚܙܝܗܝ[9] ܠܐܬܪܐ ܗܘ ܡܢ ܪܘܚܩܐ. (5)
ܘܐܡܪ ܠܥܠܝ̈ܡܘܗܝ ܦܘܫܘ ܠܟܘܢ[10] ܗܪܟܐ ܠܘܬ ܚܡܪܐ. ܘܐܢܐ
ܘܛܠܝܐ ܢܐܙܠ ܥܕܡܐ ܠܗܪܟܐ ܘܢܣܓܘܕ܆ ܘܢܗܦܘܟ ܠܘܬܟܘܢ. (6)
ܘܢܣܒ ܐܒܪܗܡ ܩܝ̈ܣܐ ܠܥܠܬܐ. ܘܣܡ ܥܠ ܐܝܣܚܩ ܒܪܗ. ܘܢܣܒ
ܒܐܝܕܗ ܢܘܪܐ ܘܣܟܝܢܐ ܘܐܙܠܘ ܬܪܝܗܘܢ ܐܝܟ ܚܕܐ. (7) ܘܐܡܪ
ܐܝܣܚܩ ܠܐܒܪܗܡ ܐܒܘܗܝ. ܘܐܡܪ. ܐܒܐ.[11] ܘܐܡܪ ܗܐ ܐܢܐ
ܒܪܝ. ܘܐܡܪ ܠܗ. ܗܐ ܢܘܪܐ ܘܩܝ̈ܣܐ. ܐܝܟܘ[12] ܐܡܪܐ ܠܥܠܬܐ. (8)
ܘܐܡܪ ܐܒܪܗܡ. ܐܠܗܐ ܢܚܙܐ ܠܗ ܐܡܪܐ ܠܥܠܬܐ ܒܪܝ. ܘܐܙܠܘ
ܬܪܝܗܘܢ ܐܟܚܕܐ.[13] (9) ܘܐܬܘ ܠܐܬܪܐ ܕܐܡܪ ܠܗ ܐܠܗܐ. ܘܒܢܐ
ܬܡܢ ܐܒܪܗܡ ܡܕܒܚܐ. ܘܣܕܪ ܩܝ̈ܣܐ. ܘܟܦܬܗ ܠܐܝܣܚܩ ܒܪܗ.
ܘܣܡܗ ܥܠ ܡܕܒܚܐ ܠܥܠ ܡܢ ܩܝ̈ܣܐ. (10) ܘܐܘܫܛ[14] ܐܝܕܗ

(**1**) *The Old Testament in Syriac according to the Peshiṭta Version* etc., Part I, fasc. I (Leiden, 1977). Some diacritics added. (**2**) The Lamadh marks a direct object: § 97a. (**3**) The Alaf is secondary: § 6D. (**4**) A centripetal Lamadh: see Joüon-Muraoka § 133 *d*, but see also Joosten 1989. (**5**) 'Lift him up': Af Impv. + suf. < √ ܣܠܩ. (**6**) Asyndetic: § 98 g. (**7**) "On the arrival of the third day (of the journey)" as against ... ܒܬܠܝܬܝܐ "in the course of the third day." Cf. Mt 26.61 "I can demolish God's temple and rebuild it in three days (ܠܬܠܬܐ ܝܘ̈ܡܝܢ)." (**8**) "Lifted": Af 3m.sg. < √ ܪܘܡ. (**9**) "and he saw it" with a proleptic pronoun (§ 112 c). (**10**) On the centripetal Lamadh, see n. 4 above. (**11**) The st. emph. form of kinship terms is used as vocative. (**12**) ܐܝܟܐ /ʔaykaa/ 'where?' + enclitic ܗܘ. (**13**) A variant, more common spelling of ܐܝܟ ܚܕܐ 'together' (vs. 6). (**14**) 'Stretched out': Af. Pf. 3m.sg. < √ ܦܫܛ.

ܐܒܪܗܡ. ܘܢܣܒ ܣܟܝܢܐ ܠܡܟܣܗ[15] ܠܒܪܗ. (11) ܘܩܪܐ ܠܗ
ܡܠܐܟܗ[16] ܕܐܠܗܐ ܡܢ ܫܡܝܐ ܘܐܡܪ ܐܒܪܗܡ ܐܒܪܗܡ. ܘܐܡܪ
ܗܐ ܐܢܐ. (12) ܘܐܡܪ ܠܐ ܬܘܫܛ ܐܝܕܝܟ ܥܠ ܛܠܝܐ. ܘܠܐ
ܬܥܒܕ ܠܗ ܡܕܡ. ܡܛܠ ܕܗܫܐ ܐܘܕܥܬ[17] ܕܕܚܠܗ ܐܢ̄ܬ ܕܐܠܗܐ.
ܕܠܐ ܚܣܟܬ ܠܒܪܟ ܠܝܚܝܕܟ ܡܢܝ. (13) ܘܐܪܝܡ ܐܒܪܗܡ
ܥܝܢ̈ܘܗܝ، ܘܚܙܐ. ܘܗܐ ܕܟܪܐ ܚܕ ܐܚܝܕ ܒܣܘܟܬܐ ܒܩܪ̈ܢܬܗ. ܘܐܙܠ
ܐܒܪܗܡ ܘܢܣܒܗ ܠܕܟܪܐ. ܘܐܣܩܗ ܠܥܠܬܐ ܚܠܦ ܒܪܗ. (14)
ܘܩܪܐ ܐܒܪܗܡ ܫܡܗ ܕܐܬܪܐ ܗܘ ܡܪܝܐ ܚܙܐ. ܕܐܬܐܡܪ
ܝܘܡܢܐ ܒܛܘܪܐ ܗܢܐ ܡܪܝܐ ܚܙܐ ⁘ (15) ܘܩܪܐ ܡܠܐܟܗ
ܕܐܠܗܐ ܠܐܒܪܗܡ ܕܬܪ̈ܬܝܢ ܙܒ̈ܢܝܢ[18] ܡܢ ܫܡܝܐ. (16) ܘܐܡܪ. ܒ
ܡܝܡܬ ܐܡܪ ܡܪܝܐ. ܚܠܦ[19] ܕܥܒܕܬ ܦܬܓܡܐ ܗܢܐ. ܘܠܐ ܚܣܟܬ
ܠܒܪܟ ܠܝܚܝܕܟ ܡܢܝ. (17) ܡܒܪܟܘ ܐܒܪܟܟ.[20] ܘܡܣܓܐܘ
ܐܣܓܐ ܙܪܥܟ. ܐܝܟ ܟܘܟ̈ܒܝ ܫܡܝܐ. ܘܐܝܟ ܚܠܐ ܕܥܠ ܣܦܬܗ
ܕܝܡܐ ܘܢܐܪܬ ܙܪܥܟ ܐܪ̈ܥܬܐ ܕܒܥܠܕܒܒ̈ܘܗܝ، (18) ܘܢܬܒܪܟܘܢ
ܒܙܪܥܟ ܟܠܗܘܢ[21] ܥܡ̈ܡܐ ܕܐܪܥܐ. ܚܠܦ ܕܫܡܥܬ ܒܩܠܝ. (19)
ܘܗܦܟ ܐܒܪܗܡ ܠܘܬ ܥܠܝܡ̈ܘܗܝ، ܘܩܡܘ ܘܐܙܠܘ ܐܟܚܕܐ
ܠܒܐܪܫܒܥ. ܘܝܬܒ ܐܒܪܗܡ ܒܒܐܪܫܒܥ.

(**15**) 'To slaughter him': Pe Inf. + proleptic 3m.sg. suf. < √ ܢܟܣ. (**16**) 'His angel' with a proleptic pronoun (§ 112 d). (**17**) 'You have made known': Af. Pf. < √ ܝܕܥ. The Hebrew here says "I have come to know." (**18**) 'For a second time': the noun ܙܒ̈ܬܐ /zvattaa/, when used as a fem. noun as here, means 'time' (of frequency), but m. ܙܒܢܐ /zavnaa/, 'time' (as against 'space'). (**19**) ܚܠܦ ܕ 'because,' cf. Gk ἀνθ' ὧν. (**20**) A Lamadh-less infinitive, reflecting the underlying, emphatic Hebrew syntagm <Inf. absolute + finite verb>: § 98j. (**21**) 'All of them' with a proleptic pronoun (§ 98 j).

TRANSLITERATION—

(1) wahwaa men baaṯar peṯḡaamee haalleen ʾalaahaa nassi lavraahaam wemar leeh. ʾavraahaam. wemar: haa ʾenaa. (2) wemar leeh. dvar lavraak̠ liḥid̠aak̠ draaḥem ʾat lisḥaaq. wzel laak̠ larʿaa daamoraayee wasseqaay tammaan laʿlaaṯaa ʿal ḥad̠ men ṭuree deemar laak̠. (3) wqaddem ʾavraahaam bṣafraa. warmi ʿal ḥmaareeh wad̠var laṯreen ʿlaymaw ʿammeeh wlisḥaaq breeh. wṣallaḥ qaysee laʿlaaṯaa. wqaam ʾezal laṯraa demar leeh alaahaa. (4) walyawmaa tliṯaayaa ʾarim ʾavraahaam ʿaynaw waḥzaay laṯraa haw men ruḥqaa. (5) wemar laʿlaymaw. puš lk̠on haarkaa lwaaṯ ḥmaaraa wenaa wṭalyaa neezal ʿd̠ammaa

lhaarkaa nesgod̲ wnehpok̲ lwaat̲kon. (6) wansav ʾavraahaam qaysee laʿlaat̲aa wsaam ʿal ʾisḥaaq breeh. wansav bid̲eeh nuraa wsakkinaa wezal trayhon ʾak̲ ḥd̲aa. (7) wemar ʾisḥaaq lavraahaam ʾavuy wemar. ʾavaa. wemar haa ʾenaa beer. wemar leeh. haa nuraa wqaysee. aykaw ʾemraa laʿlaat̲aa. (8) wemar ʾavraahaam. ʾalaahaa neḥzee leeh ʾemraa laʿlaat̲aa, beer. wezal trayhon ʾak̲ḥd̲aa. (9) wet̲aw lat̲raa demar leeh ʾalaahaa. wavnaa tammaan ʾavraahaam mad̲bḥaa wasd̲ar qaysee wfak̲reeh lisḥaaq breeh wsaameeh ʿal mad̲bḥaa lʿel men qaysee. (10) wawšeṭ ʾid̲eeh ʾavraahaam wansav sakkinaa lmekseeh lavreeh. (11) waqraa leeh malak̲eeh dalaahaa men šmayyaa wemar ʾavraahaam ʾavraahaam. wemar. haa ʾenaa. (12) wemar laa tawšeṭ ʾid̲aak̲ ʿal ṭalyaa. wlaa teʿbed̲ leeh meddem. meṭṭul dhaašaa ʾawdaʿt dd̲aaḥleeh ʾat dalaahaa dlaa ḥsak̲t lavraak̲ lisḥaaq men. (13) warim ʾavraahaam ʿaynaw waḥzaa. whaa dek̲raa ḥad̲ ʾaḥid̲ bsawkt̲aa bqarnaat̲eeh. wezal ʾavraahaam wnasbeeh ld̲ek̲raa wasqeeh laʿlaat̲aa ḥlaaf breeh. (14) waqraa ʾavraahaam šmeeh dat̲raa haw maaryaa neḥzee det̲emar yawmaanaa bṭuraa haanaa maaryaa neḥzee. (15) waqraa malak̲eeh dalaahaa lavraahaam dt̲arteen zavnin men šmayyaa. (16) wemar bi yimit̲ ʾaamar maaryaa. ḥlaaf daʿvat pet̲g̲aamaa haanaa wlaa ḥsak̲t lavraak̲ liḥid̲aak̲ men. (17) mvarraak̲u ʾebbark̲aak̲ wmasgaayu ʾasgee zarʿaak̲ ʾak̲ kawkvay šmayyaa wak̲ ḥaalaa dʿal seft̲eeh dyammaa wneerat̲ zarʿaak̲ ʾarʿaat̲aa davʿeldvaavaw. (18) wnet̲bark̲un bzarʿaak̲ kulhon ʿammee darʿaa ḥlaaf dašmaʿt bqaal. (19) wahfak̲ ʾavraahaam lwaat̲ ʿlaymaw wqaam wezal ʾak̲ḥd̲aa lveeršvaʿ wit̲ev ʾavraahaam bveeršvaʿ.

5. The raising of Lazarus (John 11:1-57)[1]

(1) ܘܗܘܐ ܕܟܪܝܗ[2] ܠܥܙܪ ܡܢ ܒܝܬ ܥܢܝܐ ܐܚܘܗ ܕܡܪܝܡ
ܘܕܡܪܬܐ. (2) ܡܪܝܡ ܕܝܢ ܗܕܐ ܐܝܬܝܗ[3] ܕܐܫܝܓܬ ܪ̈ܓܠܐ ܕܝܫܘܥ.
ܐܚܘܗ ܗܘܐ ܕܗܕܐ ܗܘ[4] ܠܥܙܪ ܕܟܪܝܗ ܗܘܐ. (3) ܫܠܚ ܕܝܢ ܠܗ[5]

---

(1) From Lewis: 1910: ܪܡܘ - ܪܡܒ. To facilitate smooth reading, some punctuation marks including the seyame have been added. (2) A relative clause without its antecedent: 'one who (was) sick': § 111. (3) On the function of a suffixed ܐܝܬ in a nominal clause, see § 109. (4) On a 3rd pers. pronoun preceding a subject noun, esp. a personal name, see § 112 i. (5) 'they sent a message to him': the verb is 3f.pl. The pronoun of ܠܗ is proleptic.

ܬܪ̈ܬܝܗܝܢ[6] ܐܚܘ̈ܬܗ ܠܝܫܘܥ ܡܪܢ. ܗܐ ܟܪܝܗ ܗܘ[7] ܕܪܚܡ ܐܢܬ.
(4) ܟܕ ܫܡܥ ܝܫܘܥ ܐܡܪ. ܗܢܐ ܟܘܪܗܢܐ ܠܐ ܗܘܐ[7a] ܠܡܘܬܐ
ܐܠܐ ܚܠܦ ܬܫܒܘܚܬܗ ܕܐܠܗܐ ܕܢܫܬܒܚ ܒܗ ܒܪܗ. (5) ܗܘ ܕܝܢ
ܝܫܘܥ ܡܚܒ ܗܘܐ[8] ܠܗܠܝܢ ܬܠܬܝܗܘܢ ܐܚܐ ܠܡܪܝܡ[9] ܠܡܪܬܐ
ܠܠܥܙܪ. (6) ܘܡܢ[10] ܕܫܡܥ ܕܟܪܝܗ ܠܥܙܪ ܗܘ، ܥܠ ܕܒܕܘܟܬܗ ܬܪ̈ܝܢ
ܝܘܡ̈ܝܢ. (7) ܘܐܡܪ ܠܬܠܡܝ̈ܕܘܗܝ، ܬܘ[11] ܢܐܙܠ ܠܝܗܘܕ. (8) ܐܡܪ̈ܝܢ
ܠܗ ܬܠܡܝ̈ܕܘܗܝ، ܪܒܢ. ܗܐ ܝܗܘ̈ܕܝܐ ܒܥܝܢ ܗܘܘ ܠܡܪܓܡܟ
ܘܬܘܒ ܐܙܠ ܐܢܬ ܠܬܡܢ. (9) ܐܡܪ ܠܗܘܢ ܝܫܘܥ ܠܐ ܬܪ̈ܬܥܣܪܐ
ܫܥܝܢ ܐܝܬ ܒܝܘܡܐ. ܡܢ ܕܒܐܝܡܡܐ ܡܗܠܟ ܠܐ ܡܬܬܩܠ[12] ܡܛܠ
ܕܚܙܐ ܢܘܗܪܗ ܕܥܠܡܐ ܗܢܐ. (10) ܡܢ ܕܒܠܠܝܐ ܕܝܢ ܡܗܠܟ
ܡܬܬܩܠ ܡܛܠ ܕܢܘܗܪܐ ܠܝܬ ܒܗ. (11) ܘܟܕ ܐܡܪ ܗܠܝܢ ܐܡܪ
ܠܗܘܢ. ܠܥܙܪ ܪܚܡܢ ܫܟܒ ܐܠܐ ܐܙܠ ܐܢܐ ܕܐܥܝܪܝܘܗܝ.[13] (12)
ܐܡܪܝܢ ܠܗ. ܡܪܢ ܐܢ ܕܡܟ[14] ܗܘ ܚܝܐ. (13) ܗܘ ܕܝܢ ܝܫܘܥ ܥܠ
ܕܡܝܬ ܗܘ ܠܗ[15] ܠܥܙܪ ܐܡܪ ܗܘܐ ܠܗܘܢ ܘܗܢܘܢ ܣܒܪܝܢ ܗܘܘ
ܕܥܠ ܫܢܬܐ ܗܘ[16] ܐܡܪ. (14) ܬܘܒ ܐܡܪ ܠܗܘܢ ܝܫܘܥ
ܦܫܝܩܐܝܬ.[17] ܠܥܙܪ ܡܝܬ ܠܗ. (15) ܘܚܕܐ[18] ܡܛܠܬܟܘܢ[19]
ܕܬܗܝܡܢܘܢ ܕܠܐ ܗܘܝܬ ܬܡܢ ܐܠܐ ܗܠܟܘ ܢܐܙܠ ܠܘܬܗ. (16)
ܐܡܪ ܠܗܘܢ ܬܐܘܡܐ ܠܚܒܪ̈ܘܗܝ ܬܠܡܝ̈ܕܐ. ܬܘ ܐܦ ܐܚܢܢ ܢܐܙܠ
ܢܡܘܬ ܥܡܗ. (17) ܘܟܕ ܐܬܐ ܝܫܘܥ ܠܒܝܬ ܥܢܝܐ ܐܫܟܚ
ܕܩܒܪܘܗܝ، ܠܠܥܙܪ ܡܢ ܩܕܡܘܗܝ، ܐܪܒܥܐ ܝܘܡ̈ܝܢ. (18) ܘܗܘܬ ܕܝܢ
ܒܝܬ ܥܢܝܐ ܩܪܝܒܐ ܡܢ ܐܘܪܫܠܡ ܐܣܛܕ̈ܘܬܐ[20] ܚܡܫܬܥܣܪ ܕܗܘ̈ܝܢ
ܡܝ̈ܠܐ[21] ܬܪ̈ܝܢ. (19) ܘܣܓܝ̈ܐܐ ܡܢ ܝܗܘ̈ܕܝܐ ܢܦܩܘ ܠܒܝܬ ܥܢܝܐ
ܕܢܒܝܐܘܢ[22] ܠܒܗܝܢ ܕܡܪܬܐ ܘܕܡܪܝܡ. (20) ܘܟܕ ܫܡܥܬ ܡܪܬܐ
ܕܝܫܘܥ ܐܬܐ ܢܦܩܬ ܠܐܘܪܥܗ ܘܡܪܝܡ ܦܫܬ ܒܒܝܬܐ. (21)
ܘܐܡܪܐ ܠܗ ܡܪܬܐ ܠܝܫܘܥ. ܐܠܘ ܠܟܐ[23] ܗܘܝܬ ܠܐ ܡܐܬ
ܗܘܐ ܐܚܝ.[24] (22) ܐܠܐ ܐܦ ܗܫܐ ܝܕܥܐ[25] ܕܡܕܡ ܕܫܐܠܬ
ܠܐܠܗܐ ܝܗܒ ܠܟܝ. (23) ܐܡܪ ܠܗ ܝܫܘܥ. ܢܩܘܡ ܐܚܘܟܝ. (24)
ܐܡܪܬ ܠܗ ܡܪܬܐ. ܝܕܥܐ ܐܢܐ ܕܒܩܝܡܬܐ ܒܝܘܡܐ ܐܚܪܝܐ.
(25) ܐܡܪ ܠܗ̇ ܝܫܘܥ. ܐܢܐ ܐܢܐ[26] ܚܝܘܬܐ ܘܡܢ ܕܡܗܝܡܢ ܒܝ
ܐܦ ܡܐܬ ܚܝܐ.[27] (26) ܘܡܢ ܕܚܝ ܘܡܗܝܡܢ ܒܝ ܠܥܠܡ ܠܐ ܡܐܬ.
ܡܗܝܡܢܬܝ[28] ܗܠܝܢ.[29] (27) ܐܡܪܐ ܠܗ ܡܪܬܐ. ܐܝܢ ܡܪܝ،
ܡܗܝܡܢܐ ܐܢܐ ܕܐܢܬ ܗܘ[30] ܡܫܝܚܐ ܒܪܗ ܕܐܠܗܐ ܕܐܬܐ.

ܠܡܐܬܐ ܠܚܠܡܐ. (28) ܘܟܕ ܐܡܪܬ ܗܠܝܢ ܐܙܠܬ ܫܬܝܩܐܝܬ[31]
ܘܩܪܬ ܠܡܪܝܡ. ܘܐܡܪܐ ܠܗ. ܪܒܢ ܐܬܐ ܘܩܪܐ ܠܟܝ. (29) ܘܟܕ
ܫܡܥܬ ܡܪܝܡ ܫܘܪܬ[32] ܘܚܦܝܛܐܝܬ[33] ܐܙܠܬ ܠܘܬܗ. (30) ܘܗܘ
ܝܫܘܥ ܠܐ ܥܕܡܐ ܠܗܫܐ ܥܠ ܗܘܐ[34] ܠܩܪܝܬܐ ܐܠܐ ܒܗ[35] ܗܘܐ
ܒܕܘܟܬܐ ܕܐܪܥܬܗ ܗܘܬ ܡܪܬܐ. (31) ܐܦ ܗܢܘܢ ܕܡܠܝܢ ܗܘܘ
ܒܠܒܗ ܕܡܪܝܡ ܟܕ ܚܙܘ ܕܗܒܘܬ ܬܘܗܬ ܢܦܩܬ[36] ܐܙܠܘ ܠܗܘܢ
ܒܬܪܗ. ܣܒܪܝܢ ܗܘܘ ܕܠܩܒܪܐ ܐܙܠܐ ܠܡܒܟܐ. (32) ܘܗܝ[37] ܡܪܝܡ
ܟܕ ܡܛܬ ܠܘܬܗ[38] ܕܝܫܘܥ ܢܦܠܬ ܥܠ ܪ̈ܓܠܘܗܝ. ܘܐܡܪܐ ܠܗ ܐܠܘ
ܬܢܢ ܗܘܝܬ ܡܪܝ. ܠܐ ܡܐܬ ܗܘܐ ܐܚܝ. (33) ܘܗܘ ܝܫܘܥ ܟܕ ܚܙܗ

(**6**) On the determining force of the pronoun with a numeral, see § 91 c end. (**7**) Probably a demonstrative pron. /haw/, 'he who,' rather than the enclitic subject of /krih/. (**7a**) Cp. § 81 init. and 93.9. (**8**) A compound tense, <ptc. + enclitic ܗܘ̄ܐ> (§ 86). The verb, /maḥḥev/, is an Af ptc.act. of √ ܚܒܒ. (**9**) The preposition marks a direct object, and not a substitute for ܕ. So are the following two cases of it, though the way the multiple objects are arranged is unusual. (**10**) /men d-/ 'when, after.' (**11**) /taw/, Impv. Pe pl. m. of ܐܬܐ 'to come': § 67. (**12**) /metqel/ < /mettqel/ < /meṯtqel/, Ethpe Ptc. of √ ܬܩܠ, with the assimilation of /t/: § 6M. (**13**) A mere orthographic variant of the standard ܐܚܝܢܗ̄ܝ ? The verb is Af Impf. 1sg. + "him" (√ ܚܝ). (**14**) Prob. a verbal adjective /dmek/ 'asleep,' thus /dmeku/. (**15**) A centripetal Lamadh. See Text 4, n. 4. (**16**) Enclitic for focusing: /šentaw ᵓemar/ 'it was about sleep that he was speaking.' (**17**) 'plainly,' with an adverbial ending (§ 47). (**18**) ܚܕܝܢܐ = ܚܕܝܐ ܐܢܐ /ḥaadeenaa/ 'I am glad' (simplified spelling: § 10). (**19**) ܠܘܬ + 2m.pl. suf. (§ 46). (**20**) ܐܣܛܕ̈ܝܐ 'stadia' (στάδια). (**21**) ܡ̈ܝܠܐ: 'two miles' (μίλιον). (**22**) ܡܠܐ ܠܒܐ = 'to comfort.' (**23**) Usually 'hither,' but here loosely 'here.' See vs. 32. (**24**) On the syntax of irreal conditional sentences, see § 86. (**25**) = ܝܕܥܐ ܐܢܐ (§ 10). Likewise later in the verse: ܫܐܠܬ = ܫܐܠ ܐܢܬ. (**26**) On the repeated pronoun, see § 104; on the ligature, see § 10. (**27**) Pe Impf. 3m.sg. of ܚܝܐ 'to live' (§ 67). (**28**) = ܡܫܝܚܐ ܐܢܬ (§ 10). (**29**) For the standard ܗܠܝܢ. Cf. אֵלֵּין :see Fassberg 1990:120f. (**30**) On the syntactic function of the enclitic, see § 107 b. (**31**) 'silently,' with an adverbial morpheme: § 47. (**32**) 'she jumped up,' Pe from ܫܘܪ.: the Waw is a radical. (**33**) 'eagerly': for the root, cf. Heb. חָפֵץ 'to be desirous.' (**34**) A compound tense: § 85. ܥܠ 'he entered' < √ ܥܠܠ. So ܗܘ̄ܬ ܐܪܥܬܗ later in the verse. (**35**) Prolepsis, the suffix pointing forward to ܕܘܟܬܐ: § 112 a. (**36**) Asyndetic: § 98 g. (**37**) See n. 4 above. (**38**) On the prolepsis with a preposition, see § 112 e.

ܕܒܟܝܐ ܘܚܙܐ ܠܝܗܘ̈ܕܝܐ ܗܢܘܢ ܕܥܡܗ ܕܒܟ̈ܝܢ. ܪܬܚ[39] ܒܢܦܫܗ[40] ܘܐܬܒܝܢ[41] ܒܪܘܚܗ. (34) ܘܐܡܪ ܐܝܟܐ ܣܡܬܘܢܝܗܝ، ܐܡܪܝܢ ܠܗ. ܡܪܢ ܬܐ ܚܙܝ. (35) ܘܐܬܝܢ ܗܘ، ܕܡ̈ܥܘܗܝ، ܕܝܫܘܥ. (36) ܘܟܕ ܚܙܘ ܝܗܘ̈ܕܝܐ ܐܡܪܝܢ ܗܘܘ. ܚܙܘ ܟܡܐ ܪܚܡ ܗܘܐ ܠܗ. (37) ܘܐܢܫ ܡܢܗܘܢ ܕܐܡܪܝܢ ܗܘܘ[42] ܕܗܢܐ ܕܦܬܚ ܥܝ̈ܢܘܗܝ، ܕܗܘ ܕܣܡܝܐ ܗܘܐ ܡܢ ܟܪܣܐ ܕܐܡܗ.[43] ܠܐ ܟܒܪ[44] ܡܫܟܚ ܗܘܐ ܕܢܥܒܕ ܗܢܐ[45] ܕܠܐ ܢܡܘܬ.

(38) ܝܫܘܥ ܕܝܢ ܟܕ ܡܬܥܙܙ ܗܘܐ ܒܪ̈ܥܝܢܘܗܝ، ܘܠܗ[46] ܐܬܐ ܠܒܝܬ ܡܩܒܪܐ ܘܗܘ ܒܝܬ ܡܩܒܪܐ ܢܩܝܪܐ[47] ܗܘܐ. ܐܝܟ ܡܥܪܬܐ ܘܡܟܣܝ[48] ܬܪܥܗ ܒܟܐܦܐ. (39) ܐܡܪ ܝܫܘܥ ܫܩܘܠܘ ܟܐܦܐ ܗܕܐ. ܐܡܪܐ ܠܗ ܡܪܬܐ. ܡܪܝ، ܡܢܐ ܫܩܠܝܢ ܠܗ ܠܟܐܦܐ ܕܗܐ ܣܪܝ،[49] ܠܗ. ܡܛܠ ܕܐܪ̈ܒܥܐ ܠܗ ܝܘܡ̈ܝܢ. (40) ܐܡܪ ܠܗ. ܐܡܪܬ ܠܟܝ ܕܐܢ ܬܗܝܡܢܝܢ ܬܚܙܝܢ ܫܘܒܚܗ ܕܐܠܗܐ. (41) ܗܝܕܝܢ ܐܢܫܐ ܗܢܘܢ ܕܩܝܡܝܢ ܩܪܒܘ ܫܩܠܘܗ ܠܟܐܦܐ. ܗܘ ܕܝܢ ܫܩܠ ܥܝ̈ܢܘܗܝ، ܠܫܡܝܐ ܘܐܡܪ. ܐܒܐ ܡܘܕܢܐ ܠܟ ܕܫܡܥܬܢܝ. (42) ܘܐܢܐ ܝܕܥܢܐ ܕܒܟܠܙܒܢ ܫܡܥ ܐܢܬ ܠܝ ܐܠܐ ܡܛܠ ܟܢܫܐ ܗܢܐ ܕܐܢܫܐ ܐܡܪܢܐ ܗܠܝܢ ܕܢܗܝܡܢܘܢ ܕܐܢܬ ܫܕܪܬܢܝ. (43) ܘܟܕ ܗܠܝܢ ܐܡܪ ܩܥܐ ܒܩܠܐ ܪܡܐ ܘܐܡܪ. ܠܥܙܪ ܦܘܩ ܠܒܪ. (44) ܘܒܗ[50] ܒܫܥܬܐ ܢܦܩ ܗܘ ܡܝܬܐ ܟܕ ܡܟܪܟܢ[51] ܐܝ̈ܕܘܗܝ، ܘܪ̈ܓܠܘܗܝ، ܒܦܣܩܝ̈ܬܐ.[52] ܘܡܟܪܟܢ ܐܦ̈ܘܗܝ، ܒܣܘܕܪܐ.[53] ܗܝܕܝܢ ܐܡܪ ܡܪܢ. ܫܪܘܗܝ،[54] ܘܫܒܩܘܗ ܐܙܠ.[55] (45) ܘܣ̈ܓܝܐܐ[56] ܡܢ ܝܗܘ̈ܕܝܐ ܕܐܬܘ ܠܘܬ ܝܫܘܥ ܡܛܠ ܡܪܝܡ. ܡܢ ܗ̇ܝ، ܫܥܬܐ ܗܝܡܢܘ ܒܝܫܘܥ. (46) ܘܐܢܫ ܗܘܘ ܡܢܗܘܢ ܕܠܐ ܗܝܡܢܘ ܐܙܠܘ ܠܗܘܢ ܠܘܬ ܦܪ̈ܝܫܐ ܘܐܫܬܥܝܘ ܠܗܘܢ ܡܕܡ ܕܥܒܕ ܝܫܘܥ.

(47) ܗܝܕܝܢ ܪ̈ܒܝ ܟܗ̈ܢܐ ܘܦܪ̈ܝܫܐ ܐܬܟܢܫܘ ܘܥܒܕܘ ܐܦܪܣܢܐ[57] ܘܐܡܪܝܢ ܗܘܘ. ܡܢܐ ܢܥܒܕ ܕܗܢܐ ܓܒܪܐ ܐܬܘ̈ܬܐ ܣܓܝ̈ܐܬܐ ܥܒܕ. (48) ܘܐܢ ܫܒܩܝܢ ܐܢܚܢܢ ܠܗ ܗܟܢܐ ܟܠܗܘܢ ܐܢ̈ܫܐ ܡܗܝܡܢܝܢ ܒܗ ܘܐܬܝܢ ܪ̈ܗܘܡܝܐ ܫܩܠܝܢ ܡܕܝܢܬܢ ܘܥܡܢ. (49) ܚܕ ܡܢܗܘܢ ܕܝܢ ܩܝܦܐ ܫܡܗ ܗܘܐ ܪܒ ܟܗܢܐ ܕܟܠܗܘܢ ܕܗ̇ܝ، ܫܢܬܐ ܐܡܪ ܠܗܘܢ. ܗܘ ܡܦܩܐ. ܐܢܬܘܢ ܠܐ ܝܕܥܝܢ ܐܢܬܘܢ ܡܕܡ. (50) ܘܠܐ ܡܬܪܥܝܢ ܐܢܬܘܢ ܕܦܩܚ ܠܢ ܕܚܕ ܓܒܪܐ[58] ܢܡܘܬ ܥܠ ܐܦ̈ ܥܡܐ ܟܠܗ.[59] ܘܠܐ ܟܠܗ ܥܡܐ ܢܐܒܕ. (51) ܗܕܐ ܕܝܢ ܡܠܬܐ

ܠܐ ܡܢ ܨܒܘܬ ܪܥܝܢܗ[60] ܐܡܪܗ ܐܠܐ ܡܛܠ ܕܪܒ ܟܗܢܐ ܗܘܐ
ܐܬܢܒܝ ܡܛܠ ܕܝܫܘܥ ܥܬܝܕ ܗܘܐ ܠܡܡܬ ܚܠܦ ܥܡܐ. (52)
ܘܠܐ ܚܠܦ ܥܡܐ ܒܠܚܘܕ ܐܠܐ ܕܐܦ ܒ̈ܢܝܐ ܕܐܠܗܐ ܕܡܒܕܪܝܢ
ܢܟܢܫ ܠܚܕܐ. (53) ܡܢ ܗܘ ܕܝܢ ܝܘܡܐ ܐܬܪܥܝܘ ܗܘܘ
ܠܡܩܛܠܗ. (54) ܝܫܘܥ ܕܝܢ ܠܐ ܡܗܠܟ ܗܘܐ ܒܦܪܗܣܝܐ[61]
ܠܒܝܢ ܝܗܘ̈ܕܝܐ ܐܠܐ ܐܙܠ ܠܗ ܠܐܬܪܐ ܕܩܪܝܒ ܠܡܕܒܪܐ
ܕܡܬܩܪܐ ܐܦܪܝܡ ܘܬܡܢ ܡܬܗܦܟ ܗܘܐ ܥܡ ܬܠܡ̈ܝܕܘܗܝ܀
(55) ܘܗܘܐ ܗܘܐ ܩܪܝܒ ܦܨܚܐ ܕܝܗܘ̈ܕܝܐ ܘܣܠܩܘ ܣܓܝ̈ܐܐ
ܡܢ ܩܘܪܐ[62] ܠܐܘܪܫܠܡ ܕܢܕܟܘܢ ܢܦܫܗܘܢ. (56) ܘܒܥܝܢ ܗܘܘ ܠܗ
ܠܝܫܘܥ ܘܐܡܪܝܢ ܚܕ ܠܚܕ[63] ܒܗܝܟܠܐ. ܣܒܪܝܢ ܐܢܬܘܢ ܕܟܒܪ ܠܐ
ܐܬܐ ܠܥܐܕܐ. (57) ܘܪ̈ܒܝ ܟܗ̈ܢܐ ܘܦܪ̈ܝܫܐ ܦܩܕܘ ܕܡܢ ܕܚܙܐ ܠܗ
ܢܐܬܐ ܢܘܕܥ ܠܗܘܢ ܕܢܐܚܕܘܢܝܗܝ.

(**39**) ܪܬܚ Pe Pf., 'he was deeply moved.' (**40**) Literally: 'in his soul,' inwardly, emotionally, and not 'in himself.' (**41**) 'he was deeply touched, agitated,' Ethpa from √ܙܘܥ. (**42**) Lit. 'there are some of them who were saying,' i.e. 'some of them were saying.' (**43**) 'This is the one who opened the eyes of one who had been blind ...,' an identificatory nominal clause (§ 107 b) followed by an antecedentless relative clause (§ 111). (**44**) 'indeed' with a touch of irony or sarcasm. (**45**) Emphatically extraposed; logically it belongs to the following clause. (**46**) 'in private.' Cf. Heb. בֵּינוֹ וּלְבֵין עַצְמוֹ. (**47**) 'a hewn-out cave.' (**48**) 'covered,' Pa pass. Ptc. (**49**) 'it stinks.' (**50**) 'on that very moment, instantly': on the periphrasis, see § 112a. (**51**) 'bandaged, bound up,' Pa Ptc. f.pl. (**52**) 'with bandages' < ܦܣܩܝܬܐ. (**53**) 'a head-cloth' (σουδάριον). (**54**) For the standard spelling ܐܚܘܗ̄ܝ. (**55**) A ptc. complementing the verb ܩܪܒ: § 98 d. (**56**) On the position of the adjective, see § 91 a. (**57**) 'they had a discussion.' (**58**) 'one man' as against many, i.e. the whole nation: see § 91:3, 4. (**59**) On the resumptive suffix, see § 91 d. (**60**) 'of his own accord,' synonymous with ܡܢ ܨܒܘܬ ܢܦܫܗ. (**61**) 'openly' (παρρησίᾳ). (**62**) 'region, area' (χώρα). (**63**) 'to one another': § 12 b.

6. A Discourse on Fate by Bardaiṣan[1]

ܬܘܒ ܫܐܠܢܝܗܝ ܘܐܡܪܢ ܠܗ̇.[2] ܕܐܝܬ ܐܢܫ̈ܐ ܕܐܡܪܝܢ. ܕܡܢ
ܦܘܩܕܢܐ ܗܘ ܕܐܠܗܐ ܡܬܕܒܪܝܢ ܒ̈ܢܝܢܫܐ: ܒܝܢ ܒܝܫܐܝܬ ܘܒܝܢ
ܫܦܝܪܐܝܬ.[2a]

ܐܡܪ ܠܝ. ܐܦ ܐܢܐ ܐܘ ܦܝܠܝܦܘܣ.[3] ܘܒܪ ܡܟܐ ܝܕܥ ܐܢܐ
ܕܐܝܬ ܒ̈ܢܝ ܐܢܫܐ ܗܠܝܢ ܕܡܬܩܪܝܢ ܟܠܕܝ̈ܐ: ܘܗ̇ܢܘܢ ܐܢܫ̈ܐ ܕܠܗ̇[4]
ܠܗܕܐ ܐܝܕܥܬܐ ܕܐܘܡܢܘܬܐ ܪ̈ܚܡܝܢ: ܐܝܟܢܐ ܕܐܦ ܐܢܐ ܐܢܐ ܒܝܢ
ܙܒܢ ܗܘܝܬ ܠܗ̇. ܐܡܝܪ ܠܝ[5] ܓܝܪ ܒܕܘܟܬܐ ܐܚܪܬܐ. ܕܟܠܡܐ[6] ܗ̇ܝ
ܢܦܫܐ ܕܒܪܢܫܐ ܕܬܗܘܐ ܝܕܥܐ ܡܕܡ ܕܦ̈ܝܠܣܘܦܐ ܠܐ ܝܕܥܝܢ.
ܘܗ̇ܢܘܢ ܗܠܝܢ ܐܢܫܐ ܡܬܝܕܥܝܢ ܠܡܟܬܒ.[7] ܘܟܠ ܕܡܫܟܠܝܢ ܘܟܠ
ܕܥܒܪ ܒܟܪ̈ܝܢ: ܘܟܠܗܝܢ ܝ̈ܕܥܬܐ ܕܝܗ̈ܒܝܢ ܠܗܘܢ: ܒܝܘܬܪܐ
ܘܒܡܫܟܚܢܘܬܐ: ܘܒܡܘܗ̈ܒܬܐ ܘܒܣܘܟܠ̈ܐ ܘܒܣܘܪܗܒܐ ܕܦܓܪܐ:
ܡܢ ܕܘܒܪܐ ܗܘ ܕܗܠܝܢ ܒܟܘܟܒ̈ܐ ܕܡܬܩܪܝܢ ܫܒ̈ܝܚܐ[8] ܗܘ̈ܝܢ ܠܗܘܢ[9]
ܘܡܬܕܒܪܝܢ ܒܗܝܢ.[10] ܐܝܬ ܕܝܢ ܐܢܫ̈ܐ ܕܐܡܪܝܢ ܕܠܘܩܒܠܗܝܢ
ܕܗܠܝܢ.[11] ܐܝܟܢܐ ܕܗܕ̇ܐ ܐܘܡܢܘܬܐ[12] ܗ̇ܝ ܕܓܠܝܬܐ ܕܟܠܕܝ̈ܐ: ܐܘ
ܣܠܩܐ ܘܩܘܡܗ̇ ܠܐ ܐܝܬܘܗܝ. ܐܠܐ ܫܪܟܐ ܗܘ ܕܦܠܓܐ. ܘܒܟܠܗܝܢ
ܝ̈ܕܥܬܐ ܒܐܝ̈ܕܘܗܝ، ܗܘ ܕܒܪܢܫܐ ܗܝܟ[13] ܘܪܒܬܐ[14] ܘܕܪ̈ܘܫܬܐ.[15]
ܘܫܘܪܗܒܐ ܘܡܘ̈ܡܬܐ[16] ܕܦܓܪܐ: ܡܬܓܪܫ ܗܘ ܒܓܪܫܝܢ.[17] ܘܗ̇ܘܝܢ ܠܗ.
ܐܢܫ̈ܐ ܕܝܢ ܐܡܪܝܢ. ܕܟܠܡܕܡ ܕܥܒܕ ܒܪܢܫܐ. ܡܢ ܨܒܝܢܗ ܗܘ ܥܒܕ.
ܒܚܐܪܘܬܐ ܕܐܝܬܝܗ̇ ܠܗ. ܘܡܘܗ̈ܒܐ ܘܫܘܪܗܒܐ ܘܨ̈ܒܘܬܐ ܗ̇ܢܝܐܬܐ
ܕܝ̈ܗܒܝܢ ܠܗ̇ ܡܢ ܡܗܡܢ ܒܪܢܫܐ[18] ܗܘ ܡܦܟܠ ܠܗܘܢ ܡܢ ܐܠܗܐ. ܠܝ ܕܝܢ
ܐܝܟ ܡܣܬܒܪܢܘܬܝ، ܡܬܚܙܝܐ ܠܝ ܝ̈ܕܥܬܐ:[19] ܕܬܠܬܝܗܝܢ ܗܠܝܢ
ܗܪ̈ܣܝܣ.[20] ܒܡܕܡ[21] ܫܪ̈ܝܪܢ ܘܒܡܕܡ ܛ̈ܥܝܢ.[22] ܫܪ̈ܝܪܢ ܕܝܢ. ܡܛܠ
ܕܡܢ ܕܘܡܝܐ ܗ̇ܘ ܕܚܙܝܢ ܒ̈ܢܝ ܐܢܫܐ ܡܡܠܠܝܢ. ܘܕܐܦ ܗ̇ܢܘܢ[23]
ܒ̈ܢܝܢܫܐ: ܚܙܝܢ ܐܝܟܢܐ ܒܪ̈ܝܢ ܒܟܠܗܘܢ ܝ̈ܕܥܬܐ ܘܡܬܕܒܠܝܢ. ܡܛܠ
ܕܚܟܡܬܐ ܗ̇ܝ، ܕܚܙܝܢ ܫܟܚܬܐ ܕܐܠܗܐ: ܗ̇ܝ، ܕܐܝܬܝܗ̇ ܟܠܗ̇
ܘܒܪܬ ܐܢܫܐ ܘܦܠܚܘܬ ܡܕܒܪ̈ܢܐ:[24] ܘܝܗܒܬ ܠܟܠܗܘܢ ܝ̈ܕܥܬܐ
ܡܥܠܝܬܐ ܕܙܕܩܐ ܠܒܪܐ ܚܕܐ ܡܢܗܘܢ. ܐܡܪ ܐܢܐ ܕܝܢ
ܕܐܝܬܘܗܝ،[25] ܗ̇ܘ ܗܢܐ ܫܘܠܛܢܐ: ܠܐܠܗܐ ܘܠܡ̈ܠܐܟܐ
ܘܠܫ̈ܠܝܛܢܐ. ܘܠܡܕܒܪ̈ܢܐ ܘܠܐܣ̈ܛܘܟܣܐ.[26] ܘܠܒܢ̈ܝܢܫܐ ܘܠܚܝܘܬܐ.
ܘܒܟܠܗܘܢ ܗܠܝܢ ܬܓ̈ܡܐ[27] ܕܐܡܪܬ ܒܟܠܗܘܢ: ܠܐ ܗܘܐ ܒܟܠ[28]
ܝܗܝܒ ܠܗܘܢ ܫܘܠܛܢܐ. ܕܫܠܝܛ ܓܝܪ ܒܟܠ ܚܕ ܗܘ. ܐܠܐ ܒܡܕܡ

ܫܠܝܛܝܢ. ܘܒܡܕܡ ܠܐ ܫܠܝܛܝܢ. ܐܝܟܢܐ ܕܐܡܪܬ ܗܿܘܝܬ. ܕܒܗܿܘ
ܡܕܡ ܕܫܠܝܛܝܢ. ܬܬܚܙܐ ܛܝܒܘܬܗ ܕܐܠܗܐ. ܘܒܗܿܘ ܡܕܡ ܕܠܐ
ܫܠܝܛܝܢ. ܢܕܥܘܢ. ܕܐܝܬ ܠܗܘܢ ܡܪܐ. ܐܝܬ ܗܟܝܠ ܫܠܡܐ ܐܝܟܢܐ
ܕܐܡܪܬ ܟ̈ܠܗܝܢ. ܘܕܠܐ ܗܘܐ ܒܟܠܡܕܡ[30] ܡܨܒܝܢ ܗܿܘܐ. ܡܬܚܙܝܐ
ܨ̈ܒܘܬܐ ܗܕܐ. ܕܫܘܠܛܢܗܘܢ ܕܒ̈ܢܝܢܫܐ ܨܿܒܝܢ ܗܘܘ ܕܢܗܘܘܢ
ܒܬ̈ܪܝܢ ܘܡܫܠܛܝܢ ܥܠ ܣܥܪ̈ܝܗܘܢ ܘܕܢܗܘܘܢ ܫܠܝܛܝܢ ܒܦܓܪ̈ܝܗܘܢ
ܘܕܢܗܘܘܢ ܡܫܬܡܥܝܢ[31] ܠܗܘܢ ܨ̈ܒܘܬܐ ܐܝܟܢܐ ܕܐܪ̈ܥܝܢ.[32] ܘܠܐ
ܒܘܬܪܐ ܡܫܬܡܥܝܢ ܐܠܐ ܠܘܬ ܙ̈ܠܝܠܐ. ܘܠܐ ܡܫܠܛܘܬܐ ܐܠܐ ܠܘܬ

(**1**) Third century C.E. An extract from Drijvers 1965: 26-41. (**2**) In this text frequent use is made of the diacritical point: § 4 a. (**2a**) /bazvan ... bazvan/ 'now ... then.' (**3**) A disciple of Bardaiṣan. Likewise the following, Bar Jamma. (**4**) With a proleptic suffix: § 112 a. (**5**) On the syntagm <Ptc. pass. + ܠ>, see § 84. (**6**) 'it yearns for,' Pe Ptc. f. (**7**) 'they think to do' = 'they think they can do it'? (**8**) 'the seven planets.' (**9**) 'they (= ܒܟܠܗܝܢ ܨ̈ܒܘܬܐ) happen to them.' (**10**) = ܒܟܠܗܝܢ ܨ̈ܒܘܬܐ 'in all those situations,' not 'by them, i.e. the seven stars.' (**11**) 'as against these things, i.e. as against such a view.' On the proleptic structure, see § 112 e. (**12**) 'an art such as this': on the preceding qualifier, see § 91 b. (**13**) 'are placed,' Pe Ptc. pass. f.pl. (**14**) An irregular pl. (f.pl.) of ܪܒ. (**15**) /daqdqaaṯaa/ 'tiny.' (**16**) Synonymous with ܡܘܡ̈ܐ '(physical) defect.' (**17**) 'they happen but by way of accident, i.e. not by design.' On the syntax of the infinitive, see § 98 j, the enclitic pronoun is extraposing. (**18**) 'punishment,' lit. that which is placed (/msaam/, Af ptc. pass.) on head.' The following pronoun is extraposing, not the subject of the following ptc., 'he receives': the subject is understood (§ 106). (**19**) Lit. 'to me, according to my weakness, the matter seems to me,' i.e. 'in my humble opinion it appears to me that ...' (**20**) 'opinions.' On the suffix with the numeral, see § 91 c end. (**21**) Lit. 'in something,' i.e. 'in some respects; partly.' (**22**) /mašraan/ 'speaking the truth (Af Ptc. act. f.pl. of √ܫܪܪ) ... telling lies,' i.e. 'partly true and partly false.' (**23**) On the independent personal pronoun preceding the subject, see § 112 i. (**24**) 'those who guide,' a Pa nomen agentis: § 38 d. (**25**) On ܐܝܬ in a nominal clause, see § 109. (**26**) 'elements (constituting the universe)' (στοιχεῖον). (**27**) 'all these orders (τάγμα),' extraposed (casus pendens) and later resumed by ܠܗܘܢ. (**28**) The preposition is to be construed with ܫܘܠܛܢܐ 'power (over)': see ܫܠܝܛ ܒܟܠ in the following sentence. (**29**) 'one who has power': an antecedentless relative clause (§ 111). (**30**) The Dalath introduces a subject clause, 'the fact that not everything ...,' the subject of ܡܬܚܙܝܐ, which is reinforced by ܨ̈ܒܘܬܐ, 'the matter.' (**31**) /meštamʿaan/, 'to obey, be sub- ject to,' Ethpe Ptc. f.pl. of √ܫܡܥ). (**32**) A variant spelling of ܪ̈ܥܝܢ, m.pl. of ܪܥܐ /rʿe/ to be content, desirous.'

ܢ̈ܫܕܝܢܐ.[33] ܘܠܐ ܫܘܠܛܢܐ ܕܦܓܪܐ ܠܘܬ ܟܘܠܗܘܢ ܒ̈ܢܝܢܫܐ. ܘܠܐ
ܐܝܠܝܢ ܕܫܪܝܢ ܒܓܒܪܐܝܬ ܡܦܪܝܢ ܒܘܬܪܗܘܢ ܘܠܐ ܐܝܠܝܢ
ܕܡܫܠܛܝܢ ܡ̈ܫܬܡܥܝܢ ܠܗܘܢ[34] ܒܢ̈ܡܘܣܝܗܘܢ ܐܝܟܢܐ ܕܢܓܙܪܘܢ. ܘܒܢܝܢ
ܠܐ ܡܫܬܡܥܝܢ ܐܝܟܢܐ ܕܠܐ ܢܓܙܪܘܢ. ܘܒܢܝܢ ܚ̈ܬܪܝܢ ܒܚܬ̈ܪܝܢ ܬܚܘ̈ܪܐ ܐܝܟܢܐ
ܕܐܪ̈ܥܢ. ܘܒܢܝܢ ܡܬܡܬܡܢܝܢ ܐܝܟܢܐ ܕܠܐ ܐܪ̈ܥܢ. ܘܐܝܠܝܢ
ܕܒܡܕܝܢܬܐ ܡܬܡܢܝܢ ܐܝܟ ܚܕ̈ܬܝܢ ܐܝܟܢܐ ܕܠܐ ܢܓܙܪܘܢ. ܘܫܡܝܢ
ܒܒܠܒܐ ܐܝܟܢܐ ܕܠܐ ܬܚܝܢ. ܘܡܬܐܒܝܢ ܠܒܬ̈ܘܠܬܐ ܘܒܬܪ̈ܝܢ[35]
ܒܒܗܘܢ. ܘܦܓܥܐܐ ܒܡܠܕܝܢ ܒܢ̈ܝܐ ܘܠܐ ܡܬܒܝܢ. ܘܐܚܪ̈ܢܐ ܡܬܒܝܢ
ܘܠܐ ܡܟܕܝܢ. ܘܗܘܝܢ ܠܒܬܪܐ ܘܠܟ̈ܐܒܐ.
ܘܐܚܪ̈ܢܐ ܒܬ̈ܪܝܢ ܐܝܟܢܐ ܕܠܐ ܢܓܙܪܘܢ. ܘܡܬܒܪܗܘܢ ܐܝܟܢܐ ܕܠܐ ܢܓܙܪܘܢ.
ܘܐܚܪ̈ܢܐ ܡܫܬܠܛܝܢ ܐܝܟܢܐ ܕܢܓܙܪܘܢ. ܘܡܬܡܬܡܢܝܢ ܐܝܟܢܐ ܕܠܐ
ܢܓܙܪܘܢ. ܐܝܟ ܕܦܓܥܐ ܠܗܘܢ ܐܝܠܝܢ ܕܢܓܙܪܘܢ.[36] ܘܕܠܘ̈ܬܝܢ ܐܝܠܝܢ
ܕܠܐ ܢܓܙܪܘܢ. ܘܐܝܟ ܕܦܓ̈ܥܐ ܠܗܘܢ ܐܝܠܝܢ ܕܠܐ ܢܓܙܪܘܢ. ܘܕܠܘ̈ܬܝܢ
ܠܗܘܢ ܐܝܠܝܢ ܕܢܓܙܪܘܢ. ܘܗܟܢܐ ܡܬܚܙܝܐ ܒܢܘܬܐ:[37] ܕܢ̈ܟܣܐ[38]
ܘܐܡ̈ܪܐ ܘܫܘܠܛܢܐ ܘܒܗ̈ܘܢܐ ܘܟ̈ܝܢܐ: ܘܪܘܚܐ ܪܘܚܐ[39] ܕܐܬܚܙܝܬ[40]
ܫܠܡܐ ܗܢܘܢ: ܘܠܐ ܗܘ̇ ܕܫܘܠܛܢܐ ܕܝܠܝ.[41] ܐܠܐ ܒܐܝܠܝܢ ܕܗܘ̈ܝܢ[42]
ܐܝܟ ܡܐ ܕܐܬܒܝܢ.[43] ܡܬܒܪܝܢ ܚܝ ܒܗܝܢ ܘܢܫܝܢ. ܘܠܘܬ ܐܝܠܝܢ
ܕܠܐ ܐܬܒܝܢ ܒܗܝܢ ܡܬܬܢܦܠܝܢ ܡܢ ܦܠܓܐ. ܘܡܢ ܐܝܠܝܢ ܕܗܘ̈ܝܢ ܠܝ
ܒܪ ܠܐ ܬܒܝܢ. ܡܬܚܙܝܐ ܒܢܘܬܐ ܕܐܦ ܗܠܝܢ ܕܐܬ̈ܒܝܢ ܒܗܝܢ.
ܠܐ ܗܘܐ ܡܛܠ ܕܐܬܒܝܢ ܒܗܝܢ ܗ̈ܘܝܢ ܠܝ. ܐܠܐ ܒܠܝܢ ܗ̈ܘܝܢ ܐܝܟ
ܡܐ ܕܗ̈ܘܝܢ. ܘܒܡܒܪܗܘܢ[44] ܡܬܒܪܝܢ ܚܝ ܘܒܡܒܪܗܘܢ ܠܐ.
ܘܡܫܬܚܠܦܝܢ ܒ̈ܢܝܢܫܐ ܕܡܬܕܒܪܝܢ ܚܝ ܒܟܝܢܐ ܫܘܝܐܝܬ. ܘܚܠܦܐ
ܦܪܝܫܐܝܬ. ܘܚܐܪܘܬܗܘܢ ܐܢܫ ܐܝܟ ܡܐ ܕܢܦܩܐ. ܢܐܡܪ ܕܝܢ
ܡܟܝܠ: ܘܚܘܐ ܟܠ ܫܠܡܐ ܕܠܐ ܗܘܐ ܟܠ ܟܠ ܡܕܡ ܫܠܝܛ. ܡܛܠ
ܕܗܘ ܩܘܡܗ ܗܢܐ ܕܡܬܕܒܪܐ ܫܠܡܐ: ܠܫܡܝܐ ܗܘ ܕܡܬܕܒܪܬܐ:[45]
ܕܐܬܡܗܒܬ ܠܒ̈ܠܝܠܢܝܐ ܘܠܐܦ̈ܠܘܣܘܦܐ ܡܢ ܐܠܗܐ. ܘܒܠܡܕ[46] ܟܠ
ܗܕܐ ܡܬܕܒܪܐ ܘܠܫܡܝܐ ܫܠܡܐ ܡܕܒܪ̈ܐ. ܒܚܫ̈ܘܬܗܘܢ ܕܠܘܬ
ܢܦܫܐ. ܘܢܦܠܢ ܢܦܫܬܐ ܒܚ̈ܫܘܬܗܘܢ ܕܠܘܬ ܦܓܪܐ. ܘܗܘ̣ ܗܘܢܐ
ܡܫܠܡܢܐ:[47] ܡܬܕܒܪܐ ܫܠܡܐ ܘܒܝܬ ܠܒܝܐ:[48] ܕܗܕܐ ܒܝܫܘܬܐ
ܕܡܕܒܪܢܐ ܘܡܬܕܒܪܢܐ: ܠܒܕܪܝܐ ܕܗܘ̇ ܡܕܡ ܕܒܫܢܝܐ ܕܐܠܗܐ
ܘܒܠܒܘܬܐ: ܐܬܒܕܪܘ[49] ܘܡܬܒܕܪ ܒܕܡܝܐ ܠܫܘܠܡܐ ܕܟܠ.

ܡܬܕܒܪ ܗܟܝܠ ܦܓܪܐ ܒܟܝܢܐ:[50] ܟܕ ܐܦ ܢܦܫܐ ܚܫܐ[51] ܥܡܗ
ܘܡܬܪܓܫܐ. ܘܠܐ ܡܬܐܠܨ ܗ̣ܘ ܦܓܪܐ: ܘܠܐ ܡܬܕܒܪ ܡܢ ܗ̇ܘ
ܫܠܡܐ ܕܟܠܗܘܢ[52] ܨܒܘ̈ܬܐ ܕܒܒ̣ ܚܕܐ ܠܚܕܐ. ܠܐ ܓܝܪ ܓܒܪܐ[53]
ܗ̇ܘܐ ܐܒܐ ܡ̣ܢ ܡܕܡ ܫܟܝܚܣ̈ܐ ܫ̈ܠܝܢ. ܘܠܐ ܐܢܬܬܐ ܗܘܬ
ܐܡܐ ܡ̣ܢ ܡܕܡ ܬܠܬܠܡܣ̈ܐ ܫ̈ܠܝܢ. ܘܗܘܝܢ ܐܦ ܠܫܡܥܘܬܐ ܐܝܬ
ܒܚܘܣܐ. ܕܡܓܪ̈ܕܝܢ[54] ܢܫ̈ܐ ܡ̣ܢ ܡܠܕܐ. ܘܓܙܝܢ[55] ܓܒܪ̈ܐ ܡ̣ܢ ܒܢܝܐ
ܕܡܘܠܕܢܘܬܐ.[56] ܟܕ ܫܢ̈ܘܬܐ ܐܫ̈ܝܢܘܬܐ ܕܡܬܕܒܪ̈ܢ ܐܦ ܗ̣ܠܝܢ
ܒܚܝܠܗܝܢ. ܡ̣ܢ ܡܕܡ ܗܠܝܢ ܫ̈ܠܝܐ ܕܐܡܪܬ. ܠܐ ܗܘܐ ܡܘܠܕܘ[57]
ܒܠܚܘܕ ܬ̈ܚܘܠܢ: ܐܠܐ ܐܦ ܡܩܫ ܩܫ̈ܢ[58] ܡ̣ܢ ܕܠܡܘܠܕܘ.[58a] ܐܝܟܢܐ

(**33**) /ḥaḏḥḏaanee/, 'a handful,' a pl. formation by reduplication of ܚܕ. (**34**) The suffix pronoun resumes the preceding, extraposed constituent, ܐܝܠܝܢ ܕ. (**35**) /ʿaarqaan/, 'they run away from them, they elude them,' Pe Ptc. f.pl., the subject being ܨܒܘ̈ܬܐ. (**36**) 'there are those who have much with them that they desire': the first Dalath introduces an antecedentless relative clause, and ܐܝܠܝܢ ܕ has the preceding ܣ̈ܓܝܐܢ, f.pl. 'many things' as its antecedent. On the use of the f.pl. to refer to things, see § 69. Likewise the following ܕܩ̈ܠܝܠܢ /dallilaan/, 'few things.' (**37**) 'so is the matter found, that is then how the matter stands.' (**38**) /neksee/, 'possessions, wealth,' a plurale tantum: § 70. (**39**) 'every single desire': on the repetition of a noun in the st. abs. (< ܪܓܬܐ), see § 71 a. (**40**) The lengthy multiple subject seems to have led to the repetition of the uncalled-for conjunction, Dalath. (**41**) 'and they are not of our authority,' i.e. they are not subject to us.' The Pf. of the stative verb ܗܘܐ is used with the force of the present tense: § 81. The verb is 3f.pl., referring to things: § 69. (**42**) 'they (f.pl.) happen (ܗܘ̈ܝܢ).' On the gender of the Ptc., see the preceding note, and note the following ܨܒܝܢ. (**43**) Lit. 'as that which,' i.e. as we desire. (**44**) 'some of them': the preposition ܡܢ is partitive, and the initial prep. Beth goes with the verb ܡܬܕܒܪ̈ܢ. (**45**) /mardiṯaa/, 'the set course.' (**46**) With a proleptic suffix with a preposition: § 112 a. (**47**) /mḥalfaanaa/, Pa nomen agentis, 'one that transforms.' (**48**) ܒܝܬ ܝܠܕܐ /beeṯ yaldaa/, 'horoscope.' (**49**) Error for ܐܬܕܒܪ? (**50**) The preposition Beth is instrumental, though virtually a marker of an agent. (**51**) /ḥaaššaa/, 'it suffers,' Pe Ptc. f.sg. of √ܚܫܫ. (**52**) Apparently an error for ܕܟܠܗܝܢ. (**53**) 'for not a man ...': on the categorical negation, see § 93:7. (**54**) /mgardyaan/ Pa Ptc f.pl. (**55**) /gizin/, 'are deprived,' Pe Ptc. pass. from √ܓܘܙ. (**56**) /mawlḏaanuṯaa/, 'act of begetting,' Af action noun. (**57**) /mawlaaḏu/, Af inf. of ܝܠܕ 'to give birth.' On the syntax, see § 98 j. (**58**) 'they do grow old': a Pe Inf. of √ ܩܫܫ (/meqqaš/) plus a Ptc. f.pl. (/qaaššaan/). (**58a**) On the particle ܕ, see § 100: 'too old to bear.'

ܕܐܦ ܦ̈ܓܪܐ ܕܒ̈ܢܝܢܫܐ ܡܐ ܕܡܝܬܘ[59] ܠܐ ܡܬܒܠܝܢ. ܘܠܐ ܡܫܬܒܩ ܫܠܛܐ ܠܡܘܬܐ[60] ܠܗܘܢ ܥ̈ܠܡܐ: ܒܥܠܡܐ ܕܠܦܓܪܐ ܠܝܬ ܠܗ ܥܠܡܐ ܠܡܘܬܐ. ܘܐܦ ܠܐ ܬܘܒ ܡܫܒܩ ܗܘ ܫܠܛܐ ܕܠܐ ܡܐܟܠܐ ܘܕܠܐ ܡܫܬܝܐ: ܠܡܗܠܟ[61] ܦܓܪܐ ܕܒܪ̈ܢܫܐ ܒܚܝܘܬܐ. ܘܐܦܠܐ ܒܪ ܐܢܫ ܠܗ ܡܐܟܠܐ ܘܡܫܬܝܐ: ܠܡܘܬ ܠܗ ܕܠܐ ܢܡܘܬ. ܗܠܝܢ ܓܝܪ ܘܡܚܫ̈ܒܬܐ ܐܢ̈ܫܝܢܝܬܐ ܕܐܠܗ ܐܢܝܢ ܕܥܠܡܐ. ܐܠܐ ܐܡܬܝ ܕܥܠܡܝܢ ܘ̈ܟܠܗܘܢ ܘܕ̈ܝܠܗܘܢ ܕܥܠܡܐ: ܗܢܝܢ ܐܝܬܐ ܫܠܛܐ ܡܬܚܫܒܐ ܒܝܬ ܗܠܝܢ. ܘܟܕ ܢ̈ܦܫܬܐ ܕܦ̈ܪܘܫ ܫܪܐ ܡܢ ܫܪܐ.[62] ܘܒܗܝܢ ܡܕܒܪ ܠܗ ܠܥܠܡܐ ܘܡܫܡܠܐ. ܘܒܗܝܢ ܡܫܡܠܐ ܠܗ ܘܡܕܒܪ. ܘܡܢ ܥܠܡܐ ܗܘܐ ܬܪܥܝܬܐ ܘܡܫܡܠܝܐ ܕܦ̈ܓܪܐ. ܠܒܪ ܡܢ ܥܠܡܐ ܕܝܢ ܘܫܠܛܐ ܗܘܐ ܒܗܘ̈ܢܐ ܘܫܘ̈ܫܠܐ ܒܦ̈ܓܪܐ. ܡܢ ܥܠܡܐ ܗܘܐ ܡܫܬܘܬܦܘܬܐ ܕܕ̈ܒܪܐ ܘܕܢܩ̈ܒܬܐ. ܘܫܘܚܐ ܕܬ̈ܪܝܗܘܢ ܚ̈ܕܐ. ܡܢ ܫܠܛܐ ܕܝܢ ܗܘܐ ܗܢܐܬܐ. ܘܦܘܪܫܢܗ ܕܡܫܬܘܬܦܘܬܐ. ܘܡܠܟܗ ܠܡܫܘܚܬܐ ܘܢܣܝܘܬܐ.[63] ܗܝ ܕܒܥ̈ܠܬܐ ܕܡܫܬܘܬܦܘܬܐ ܗܕܝܢ ܒ̈ܢܝܢܫܐ ܒܪ̈ܬܗܘܢ. ܡܢ ܥܠܡܐ ܗܘܐ ܡ̈ܠܟܐ ܘܒ̈ܢܝܐ. ܘܡܢ ܫܠܛܐ ܒܗܝܢ ܡܬܚܫܠܝܢ ܡܠ̈ܟܐ: ܘܒܗܝܢ ܡܬܕܒܪܝܢ. ܘܒܗܝܢ ܡܫܟܚܝܢ[64] ܕܠܐ ܒܨܒܝܢܗܘܢ. ܡܢ ܥܠܡܐ ܗܘܐ ܗܒܒܘܬܐ ܒܡܫܬܘܬܦܘܬܐ ܠܒܝܬܗܘܢ ܦ̈ܓܪܐ. ܘܡܢ ܫܠܛܐ ܗܘܐ ܗܢܦܘܬܐ ܕܡܫܬܪܝܬܐ: ܘܐܘܠܨܢܗܘܢ ܕܦ̈ܓܪܐ. ܘܡܗܝܡܢܐ ܬܘܒ ܡܢܗ ܡܢ ܫܠܛܐ ܗܘܐ ܠܥܒܘܕܐ ܘܐܦܣܩܘܬܐ ܕܠܐ ܡܬܦܢܝܢܝܐ. ܒܝܢܐ ܦܩܕ ܕܢܗܘܘܢ ܕ̈ܢܝܐ ܩ̈ܫܝܫܐ ܠܬ̈ܠܡܝܕܐ: ܘܣ̈ܟܠܐ ܠܚ̈ܟܝܡܐ. ܘܢܗܘܘܢ ܕ̈ܫܝܐ ܫ̈ܒܠܝܬܐ ܠܬ̈ܚܝܬܐ: ܘܥ̈ܬܝܪܐ ܠܕ̈ܝܘܒܐ. ܫܠܛܐ ܕܝܢ ܚܒܪ ܕܢܗܘܘܢ ܓ̈ܒܪܐ ܕ̈ܫܝܐ ܠܩ̈ܫܝܫܐ: ܘܣ̈ܟܠܐ ܠܚ̈ܟܝܡܐ. ܘܢܚܦܘܢ ܒܪܒܝܐ ܕܐܘܪܚܐ ܬ̈ܚܝܬܐ ܠܥ̈ܠܝܬܐ. ܘܕ̈ܝܘܒܐ ܠܥ̈ܬܝܪܐ. ܘܦܫܝܩܐܝܬ ܕܒܗ: ܕܒܠܒܝܢ ܕܡܬܕܘܕ. ܒܝܢܐ ܡܢ ܬܪܝܢܘܬܗ. ܡܢ. ܒܠܬܐ ܗܘ ܕܫܠܛܐ ܗܘܐ ܕܘܕܗ. ܡܬܠܬܠ ܕܕܝܪܐ ܘܡܕܒ̈ܪܢܐ ܗܢܘܢ ܕܒܠܝܢܘܢ ܗܘܐ ܫ̈ܠܝܛܢܐ: ܗܘ ܕܡܬܕܘܪܐ ܒܝܬ ܡ̈ܠܟܐ. ܗܘܘܒܠܐ ܐܝܟ ܚܕ ܕܚܕ.. ܘܡܒܝܢܘܢ ܕܡܒܝܢܐ ܡܬܕܒܪܝܢ ܗܢܘܢ ܕܡܒܕܪܝܢ ܠܥܠܡܐ.[65] ܘܡܫܬܡܫܝܢ ܒܟܠ ܫܘܦܪܘܬܗ. ܐܡܬܝ ܕܡܕܒܪܐ ܠܗܘܢ ܡ̈ܕܒܪܢܐ. ܘܡܫܟܚܝܢ ܒܐܬ̈ܪܘܬܐ ܡ̈ܕܒܪܢܐ ܕܐܝܬ ܒܡܬܠܬܐ ܒܚ̈ܝܘܬܐ ܕܢܦܫܗܘܢ.[66] ܘܗܢܘܢ ܕܫܡܠܝܐ ܡܬܕܒܪܝܢ ܒ̈ܢܝܫܐ.[67] ܘܐܡܬܝ ܕܐܦ ܗܢܘܢ ܐܢܫ̈ܝܢ[68] ܐܬ̈ܪܘܬܐ ܕܪܘܚܐ. ܗܘܝܢ

ܗܘܦܟܐ ܠܟܝܢܐ. ܘܠܐ ܠܒ̈ܢܝܢܫܐ ܒܠܚܘܕ ܡܗܪܝܢ.[69] ܐܠܐ ܒܙܒܢ
ܙܒܢ ܐܦ ܠܚܝܘܬܐ ܘܠܐܝ̈ܠܢܐ ܘܠܦܐܪ̈ܐ: ܘܠܐܪ̈ܥܝܗ ܕܥܢܝܬܐ
ܘܠܟܘ̈ܟܒܐ ܕܫ̈ܡܝܐ. ܘܠܟܠܡܕܡ ܕܐܝܬ ܒܟܝܢܐ ܕܬܚܝܬ
ܡܕܒܪܢܘܬܗܘܢ. ܘܡܛܠ ܗܕܐ[70] ܦܠܓܘ̈ܬܐ ܘܗܪ̈ܣܝܣ ܕܐܝܬ ܒܝܢ
ܬܠܡ̈ܝܕܐ. ܐܝܬ ܒ̈ܢܝܢܫܐ ܕܣܒܪܘ. ܕܕܠܐ[70a] ܡܦܪܢܣܢܘܬܐ ܡܬܕܒܪ
ܥܠܡܐ. ܡܛܠ ܕܠܐ ܝܕܥܘ ܕܗ̇ܝ ܗܕܐ ܗܪ̈ܣܝܣ ܘܦܠܓܘ̈ܬܐ:
ܘܒܥܘܬܐ ܘܫܘܒܚܬܐ: ܡܢ ܕܘܒܪ̈ܐ ܗܘ ܕܐܝܬܝܗ ܒܡܐܪܘܬܐ ܡܢ
ܐܠܗܐ ܗܘ̇ܝܢ. ܕܐܦ ܗ̣ܢܘܢ ܥܒ̈ܘܕܐ[71] ܒܥܠܠܬ ܢܦܫܗܘܢ: ܐܘ
ܢܙܟܘܢ ܐܘ ܢܬܚܝܒܘܢ: ܐܝܟܢܐ ܕܚܙܝܢ[72] ܕܟ̣ܒܫ ܚܠܘܦܐ ܠܟܝܢܐ.
ܗܟܢܐ ܡܫܟܚܝܢ ܠܟܝܢܐ ܐܦ ܠܚܐܪܘܬܗ ܕܒܪܢܫܐ: ܟܕ ܕܒ̇ܢܐ ܠܗ
ܠܚܠܦܐ ܘܡܫܦܐ. ܠܐ ܕܝܢ ܒܟܠܡܕܡ. ܐܝܟܢܐ ܕܐܦ ܠܐ ܗ̣ܘ ܚܠܦܐ
ܒܟܠܡܕܡ ܕܒ̇ܢܐ ܠܟܝܢܐ. ܦ̇ܠܐ ܗܘ ܓܝܪ ܕܬܬܠܬܡܗܘܢ[73] ܨ̈ܒܝܘܬܐ:
ܕܟܝܢܐ ܘܕܚܠܦܐ ܘܕܚܐܪܘܬܐ: ܕܢܗܘܘܢ ܢܛܝ̈ܪܝܢ ܒܫܘܠܛܢܗܘܢ:
ܒܕܡܐ ܕܬܫܠܡ ܡܕܪ̈ܝܬܐ ܘܬܬܡܠܐ ܒܟܠܗܝܢ ܘܡܫܠܡܢܐ. ܐܝܟܢܐ
ܕܐܬܚܙܝ[74] ܡܕܡ ܗ̇ܘ ܐܝܢܐ ܕܦ̇ܩܕ.. ܐܝܟܢܐ. ܢܗܘܐ ܒܥܘܡܪܐ

(**59**) ܡܐ ܕ 'when' followed by a Pf. with reference to future: § 81. (**60**) /lmettal/, an irregular Pe Inf. of √ܢܬܠ 'to give': § 67. (**61**) /lemeṭṭar/, 'to keep, maintain,' Pe Inf. of √ܢܛܪ with the Nun assimilated (§§ 6M; 61). (**62**) /prišaan ḥd̲aa men ḥd̲aa/, 'different from one another': on the reciprocal expression, see § 12 b. (**63**) 'all impurity and immorality,' which appears to be part of the multiple subject together with the preceding ܣܢܝܘܬܐ ܘܦܘܪܢܣܗ ܕܙܢܝܘܬܐ, and the following pronoun ܗ̇ܝ /haay/, is in apposition to what immediately precedes it, 'that men practise on account of the matrimony in their passion.' (**64**) /maaytin/, 'they die,' a Pe Ptc m.pl. from √ ܡܘܬ. (**65**) 'Amongst them, those which assist the nature are called (those of) the right-hand...' (**66**) /bamnawaat̲aa dnafšhon/, 'sectors of their own.' (**67**) On the emph. state of the predicative adjective, see § 71 e. (**68**) /ʾaḥid̲in/,'they occupy, hold': on the passive participle with active meaning, see § 84. (**69**) /mahrin/, 'they harm,' Af Ptc m.pl. of √ܗܪܪ. (**70**) If the text be right, ܗܕ̇ܐ, f.sg., must be in apposition to the following two pl. nouns. (**70a**) ܕܠܐ 'without': the first ܕ introduces an object clause. (**71**) /ʿaavod̲ee/, 'docrs, actors,' a Pe nomen agentis: § 51. (**72**) /ḥaazeennan/, 'as we see.' (**73**) Strictly it should be ܬܬܠܬܡܗܝܢ, but see also ܢܗܘܘܢ and ܟܠܗܘܢ later. (**74**) /det̲ḥzi/, 'it appeared proper': on this meaning of the verb, cf. Dan 3.19 חֲזֵה, Mishnaic Hebrew רָאוּי, and Lk 1.3 where the Greek has ἔδοξε, which is rendered with the same Syr. form.

ܘܫܘܠܛܢܐ ܕܠܗܘܢ ܒܪ̈ܝܬܐ: ܘܩܝܡܐ ܕܠܗܘܢ ܐܪ̈ܝܬܐ ܘܒܢ̈ܝܐ܀
ܒܘܝܕܐ ܐܡܪ̇.[75] ܕܠܐ[76] ܗܘܐ ܡܢ ܟܝܢܗ ܡ̇ܫܟܚ ܒܪܢܫܐ:
ܐܬܦܝܣܬ[77] ܡܢ ܗܠܝܢ ܕܐܡܪܬ. ܘܕܠܐ ܗܘܐ ܫܘܐܝܬ ܡܬܕܒܪ̈ܝܢ
ܟܠܗܘܢ ܒܢ̈ܝ ܐܢܫܐ. ܟܢ ܕܝܢ ܐܦ ܗܕܐ ܬܫܟܚ ܠܡܚܙܘ: ܕܠܐ
ܗܘܐ ܡܢ ܚܝܠܐ ܘܦܘܩܕܢܐ ܡܫܟܚܝܢ ܐܝܠܝܢ ܕܡܫܟܚܝܢ. ܗܕܝܢ
ܗܘ ܦ̇ܠܐ ܠܡܗܝܡܢܘ. ܕܐܚܝܕ ܗܘ ܒܪ ܐܢܫܐ ܚܐܪܘܬܐ ܕܢܦܫܗ̇.
ܘܒܟܝܢܗ ܡܬܕܒܪ ܠܫܦܝܪ̈ܬܐ ܘܡܙܕܗܪ ܡܢ ܣܢ̈ܝܬܐ. ܘܡܛܠ ܗܢܐ
ܐܦ ܒܟܐܢܘܬ ܡܬܕܝܢܝܢ ܒܢܡܘܣܐ ܐܢܫܝܐ܀

ܒܪܕܝܨܢ ܐܡܪ̇. ܡܢ ܗܕܐ[78] ܕܠܐ ܗ̣ܘܐ ܫܘܐܝܬ ܡܬܕܒܪ̈ܝܢ ܟܠ
ܐܢܫܐ ܐܬܦܝܣܬ̇. ܕܠܐ ܗܘܐ ܡܢ ܟܝܢܗܘܢ ܡܫܟܚܝܢ. ܡܕܡ
ܐܠܝܨܐ ܠܟ ܒܥܘܬܐ ܕܬܬܦܝܣ.[79] ܕܐܦܠܐ ܡܢ ܚܝܠܗܘܢ ܓܡܝܪܐܝܬ
ܡܫܟܚܝܢ. ܟܢ ܐܫܟܚܢ ܠܚܣܝܘܬܗ ܕܠܐ ܫܘܐܝܬ ܡܕܒܪ ܓܙܪ
ܕܝܢܐ:[80] ܕܚܠ̈ܩܐ ܘܕܩܠܝܡ̈ܛܐ ܠܟܠܗܘܢ[81] ܒܢ̈ܝܢܫܐ: ܐܠܐ ܐܝܬܝܗ̇[82]
ܠܢ ܚܐܪܘܬܐ ܒܩܢܘܡܢ ܕܠܐ[83] ܢܥܒܕ ܚܝܠܐ ܕܦܘܣܝܣ. ܘܠܐ ܢܕܝܢ
ܕܘܒܪܐ ܕܩܠܝܡ̈ܛܐ܀

(**75**) This verb, when introducing direct speech as here and even in the past context as here, often takes the form of a participle. (**76**) The proclitic Dalath here introduces an object clause, a direct object of ܐܬܦܝܣܬ. On the negator /laa waa/, see § 93.9. (**77**) Ethpe Pf. 1sg. of ܦܝܣ 'to persuade, convince' (< πεῖσαι, Aorist of πείθειν 'to perusade'). The Tet instead of Taw is because the Greek π came over to Syriac speakers as more "emphatic" than the Semitic Pe, so that the Taw was assimilated to its emphatic counterpart: § 6M. (**78**) The demonstrative pronoun is a dummy for the following noun clause, 'on the basis of the fact that ...' The verb ܐܬܦܝܣܬ 'you have become convinced' is followed by an object clause ... ܕܠܐ. (**79**) 'therefore the matter is compelled to you that you should become convinced that ...,' i.e. you therefore have no choice but to accept that ...' (**80**) /gzaar dinaa/, 'verdict,' here synonymous with ܚܝܠܐ ܘܦܘܩܕܢܐ in the preceding paragraph, referring to a force beyond human control, and further specified by the following ܕܚܠ̈ܩܐ ܘܕܩܠܝܡ̈ܛܐ. The plural ܚܠ̈ܩܐ probably indicates concrete manifestations of Fate. (**81**) The preposition Lamadh here is an exponent of direct object: § 97a. (**82**) The use of the suffix pronoun signifies that the subject is determinate: 'we have that freedom (, of which we have been speaking).' See § 109. (**83**) The proclitic Dalath with an Impf. indicates a purpose: § 82.

7. The Odes of Solomon[1]

Ode 11

1 ܐܬܓܙܪ ܠܒܝ ܘܐܬܚܙܝ، ܒܘܦܥܗ
ܘܝܠܕܬ ܒܗ ܛܝܒܘܬܐ
ܘܥܒܕ ܦܐܪ̈ܐ ܠܡܪܝܐ.
2 ܡܪܝܡܐ ܓܝܪ ܓܙܪܢܝ ܒܪܘܚܗ ܩܕܝܫܐ
ܘܓܠܐ ܠܘܬܗ ܟܘܠܝ̈ܬܝ،
ܘܡܠܝܢܝ ܡܢ ܚܘܒܗ.
3 ܘܗܘܬ ܠܝ ܓܙܘܪܬܗ ܠܦܘܪܩܢܐ
ܘܪܗܛܬ ܒܐܘܪܚܐ ܒܫܠܡܗ
ܒܐܘܪܚܐ ܕܫܪܪܐ.
4 ܡܢ ܪܫܝܬܐ ܘܥܕܡܐ ܠܚܪܬܐ
ܢܣܒܬ ܝܕܥܬܗ،
5 ܘܐܫܬܪܪܬ ܥܠ ܟܐܦܐ ܕܫܪܪܐ
ܐܝܟܐ ܕܗܘ ܐܩܝܡܢܝ.
6 ܘܡ̈ܝܐ ܡܡܠܠܢ̈ܐ[2] ܩܪܒܘ ܠܣܦܘ̈ܬܝ،
ܡܢ ܡܒܘܥܗ ܕܡܪܝܐ ܕܠܐ ܚܣܡ.
7 ܘܐܫܬܝܬ[3] ܘܪܘܝܬ
ܡܢ ܡ̈ܝܐ ܚ̈ܝܐ ܕܠܐ ܡܝܬܝܢ.
8 ܘܪܘܝܘܬܝ، ܠܐ ܗܘܬ ܕܠܐ ܝܕܥܬܐ
ܐܠܐ ܫܒܩܬ ܣܪܝܩܘܬܐ.
9 ܘܐܦܢܝܬ ܠܘܬ ܡܪܝܐ ܐܠܗܝ،

(**1**) Harris and Mingana 1916-20: ܠ - ܠܒ, ܦܗ - ܦܘ; 265-71, 403-9. Most of the diacritical marks (§ 4) and ES vowel signs (but not the WS signs, which seem to be of secunda manus) appearing in the manuscript (H) have been reproduced here. Cf. also Charlesworth 1977, Lattke 1980, and Pierre 1994. (**2**) Though formally a noun indicating a profession (§ 36), /mallaalaa/ 'speaker,' it is functioning here as an adjective. (**3**) The form is Peal, not Afel: see § 64, n. 74. It is of ܚܕܝ type: § 64. So is the following verb.

ܘܓܒܪܬ ܒܢܓܘܗܒܬܗ.
10 ܘܫܒܩܬ ܠܫܠܝܘܬܐ ܢܕܝܐ[4] ܒܠ ܐܪܒܐ
ܘܫܠܝܬܗ[5] ܘܫܒܘܬܗ ܓܒܝ.
11 ܘܡܪܝܐ ܢܛܪܬܝ ܒܠܒܘܫܗ
ܘܥܒܕ ܒܢܘܗܪܗ.
12 ܘܓܕ ܠܒܠ ܐܢܫܝ ܕܠܐ ܚܙܠ
ܘܗܘܝܬ ܐܝܟ ܐܪܒܐ ܕܫܘܝܐ ܘܪܘܐ[6] ܒܓܐܪ̈ܝܗ.
13 ܘܡܪܝܐ ܐܝܟ ܫܡܫܐ
ܒܠ ܐܦ̈ܝܗ ܕܐܪܒܐ.
14 ܒܢ̈ܝ ܐܢܫܐ[7]
ܘܦܪ̈ܚܘܗܝ ܢܦܠ ܠܐܠܐ[8]
15 ܘܐܬܒܣܡܬ ܢܫܡܬܝ،
ܒܪ̈ܝܚܐ ܓܒܣܡܐ ܕܡܪܝܐ،
16 ܘܐܘܒܠܢܝ[9] ܠܦܪ̈ܕܝܣܐ
ܐܝܟܐ ܕܒܘܬܪܐ ܕܒܘܣܡܗ ܕܡܪܝܐ.[10]
17 ܘܣܓܕܬ ܠܡܪܝܐ ܡܛܠ ܬܫܒܘܚܬܗ
18 ܘܐܡܪܬ ܕܛܘܒܝܗܘܢ[11] ܡܪܝܐ ܠܐܝܠܝܢ ܕܢܨܝܒܝܢ ܒܐܪܥܟ
ܘܕܝܠܗܘܢ[12] ܕܐܝܬ ܠܗܘܢ ܐܬܪܐ ܒܦܪ̈ܕܝܣܟ
19 ܘܝܗܒܝܢ ܒܢܘܒܠܐ ܕܐܝ̈ܠܢܝܟ
ܘܫܢܝܘ ܡܢ ܚܫܘܟܐ ܠܢܘܗܪܐ،
20 ܗܐ[13] ܟܠܗܘܢ ܦܥ̈ܠܝܟ ܫܦܝܪܝܢ
ܕܥܒܕܝܢ ܒܥ̈ܒܕܐ ܠܛܒܐ
ܘܗܦܟܝܢ ܡܢ ܒܝܫܘܬܐ ܠܒܣܝܡܘܬܐ ܕܝܠܟ.
21 ܘܐܣܓܝܘ ܡܛܪ̈ܐ[14] ܕܐܝܠܢܐ ܡܢܗܘܢ
ܡܐ ܕܐܬܢܨܒܘ[15] ܒܐܪܥܐ ܕܝܠܟ.
22 ܘܗܘܐ ܒܠܒܘܡ ܐܝܟ ܫܪܒܐ[16] ܕܝܠܟ
ܘܕܡܪܝܐ ܕܠܒܠܡ ܕܥܒ̈ܕܝܟ[17] ܡܗܝ̈ܡܢܐ.[18]
23 ܗܐ ܗܘ̄ ܓܝܪ ܐܬܪܐ ܒܦܪ̈ܕܝܣܟ
ܘܟܠܗ ܒܗ ܡܕܡ ܕܓܠܒܠ

ܐܠܐ ܟܠܗܘܢ ܡܠܝܢ ܦܐܪ̈ܐ.

24 ܫܘܒܚܐ ܠܟ ܐܠܗܐ ܒܘܣܡܐ ܕܦܪܕܝܣܐ ܕܠܥܠܡ.
ܗܠܠܘܝܐ.

(**4**) This is an object complement, not a passive participle functioning as attributive adjective, which should be ܫܕܝܬܐ (in agreement with the noun head in the st. emph.): lit. 'I left the folly in an on-the-earth-cast state.' (**5**) This is a homonymous root √ܫܠܚ 'to strip off, undress.' (**6**) Both are regular verbs, Pe Ptc. f.sg.abs., with a consonantal Waw: ܥܒܘܐ ܘܙܗܘܪܐ 'flourishing and resplendent.' (**7**) The form is ambiguous: Af Pf 3f.pl. 'my eyes lit up' or 3m.sg. 'He illumined my eyes.' (**8**) Non-standard spelling for ܛܠܐ /ṭallaa/ 'dew.' (**9**) /awblan/ 'he transported me,' Af of ܝܒܠ + suf. (**10**) 'where (there is) the wealth of the Lord's suavity': on /ʾaykaa d-/, see § 77. (**11**) The proclitic /d-/ introduces direct speech in the manner of the Gk ὅτι recitativum, and on /ṭuvayhon l-/, cf. Ps 1.1 /ṭuvaw lḡavraa d-/ 'Blessed is the man who ...' and Mt 5.3 /ṭuvayhon lmeskeenee bruḥ/ 'Blessed are the poor in spirit.' The following /maaryaa/ is vocative. (**12**) This being parallel, or in apposition to the preceding ܒܐܝܠܝܢ, one would have expected ܒܗܠܝܢ. (**13**) This presentative particle introduces a long nominal clause which ends with the second ܕܒܟܝ in line 21: 'Behold, beautiful are all your labourers who do good works ...,' ܫܦܝܪܝܢ duly in the st. abs. as predicate (§ 71 e). (**14**) 'they divested themselves of bitterness': though here 'bitterness' is primarily meant in its ethical, moral sense, it is obviously part of the agricultural or horticultural imagery of this passage, for its plural form /mraaree/ means 'bitter herbs.' So is to be understood /bassimuṯaa/ 'benevolence, joy (Gk χρηστότης),' which is apparently a play on /besmaa/ 'perfume' produced, of course, from various fragrant herbs. (**15**) Here the syntagm </maa d-/ + Pf.> must refer to a past event: cf. § 81. (**16**) /šarkaanaa/ 'remainder.' Difficult. Error for ܨܒܝܢ̈ܐ 'desire, wish' or ܪܢܝܢ̈ܐ 'thought, design'? Cf. Gk θέλημα. (**17**) The diacritical dot below the Beth, not a rukkakha sign, distinguishes the noun /ʿavdaa/ 'servant' from its homograph /ʿvaaḏaa/ 'work, deed.' As a matter of fact, the main manuscript of this text, H, makes no use of a quššaya/rukkakha dot. (**18**) For the thought expressed in the second hemistich, cf. Mt 26.13 (with ܕܣܒܪܬܐ).

Ode 42

1 ܦܫܛܬ ܐܝܕܝ̈ ܘܐܬܩܪܒܬ ܠܘܬ ܡܪܝ
ܡܛܠ ܕܡܬܚܘܝܬܐ ܕܐܝܕܝ̈ ܐܬܘܗܝ ܗܘ[1]
2 ܘܦܫܝܛܘܬܝ ܩܝܣܐ ܦܫܝܛܐ[2]
ܕܐܬܬܠܝ ܥܠ ܐܘܪܚܗ ܕܬܪܝܨܐ.
3 ܘܗܘܝܬ ܕܠܐ ܢܚܫܘ[3] ܠܗܘܢ ܕܝܕܥܝܢ ܠܝ[4]
ܡܛܠ ܕܐܬܛܫܝܬ ܠܗܘܢ ܕܠܐ ܐܚܝܕܝܢ[5] ܗܘܘ ܠܝ.
4 ܘܐܗܘܐ ܠܘܬ ܗܢܘܢ ܕܪ̈ܚܡܝܢ ܠܝ.
5 ܡܝܬܘ ܟܠܗܘܢ ܪ̈ܕܘܦܝ[6]
ܘܒܥܐܘܢܝ ܗܢܘܢ ܕܣܒܪܘ ܒܝ ܡܛܠ ܕܚܝ ܐܢܐ.[7]
6 ܘܩܡܬ ܠܝ[8] ܘܐܝܬܝ ܥܡܗܘܢ.
ܘܐܡܠܠ ܒܦܘܡܗܘܢ.
7 ܐܣܠܝܘ ܓܝܪ ܠܐܝܠܝܢ ܕܪ̈ܕܦܝܢ ܠܗܘܢ.
ܘܐܪܡܝܬ ܥܠܝܗܘܢ ܢܝܪܗ ܕܚܘܒܝ.
8 ܐܝܟ ܕܪܥܗ ܕܚܬܢܐ[9] ܥܠ ܟܠܬܐ.
ܗܟܢܐ ܢܝܪܝ ܥܠ ܐܝܠܝܢ ܕܝܕܥܝܢ ܠܝ.
9 ܘܐܝܟ ܓܢܘܢܐ ܕܡܬܦܫܛ ܒܒܝܬ ܚܬ̈ܢܐ.[10]
ܗܟܢܐ ܚܘܒܝ ܥܠ[11] ܐܝܠܝܢ ܕܡܗܝܡܢܝܢ ܒܝ.
10 ܠܐ ܐܣܬܠܝܬ[12] ܐܦ ܐܬܚܫܒܬ.
ܘܠܐ ܐܒܕܬ ܐܦ ܪܢܘ ܥܠܝ.
11 ܫܝܘܠ ܚܙܬܢܝ ܘܐܬܕܘܝܬ
ܘܡܘܬܐ ܐܬܡܥܝ ܘܠܣܓܝ̈ܐܐ[13] ܥܡܝ.
12 ܚܠܐ ܘܡܪܪܐ ܗܘܝܬ ܠܗ.
ܘܢܚܬܬ ܥܡܗ ܥܡܩܐ ܕܐܝܬ ܗܘܐ ܒܗ ܒܥܘܡܩܐ.[14]
13 ܘܪ̈ܓܠܐ ܘܪܫܐ ܐܪܦܝ:
ܡܛܠ ܕܠܐ ܐܫܟܚܘ ܠܡܣܝܒܪܘ ܦܪ̈ܨܘܦܝ.
14 ܘܥܒܕܬ ܟܢܘܫܬܐ ܕܚ̈ܝܐ ܒܡܝ̈ܬܘܗܝ
ܘܡܠܠܬ ܥܡܗܘܢ ܒܣܦܘܬܐ ܚ̈ܝܬܐ.

ܡܛܠ ܕܠܐ ܢܗܘܐ ܒܛܠ ܦܬܓܡܝ.

15 ܘܪܗܛܘ ܠܘܬܝ ܗܢܘܢ ܕܡܝܬܘ.

ܘܩܥܘ ܘܐܡܪܘ ܚܘܢܝܢ[15] ܒܪܗ ܕܐܠܗܐ.

16 ܘܥܒܕ[16] ܥܡܢ ܐܝܟ ܒܣܝܡܘܬܟ.

ܘܐܦܩܢ ܡܢ ܐܣܘܪ̈ܐ ܕܚܫܘܟܐ.

17 ܘܦܬܚ ܠܢ ܬܪܥܐ ܕܒܗ ܢܦܘܩ ܠܘܬܟ.

ܚܙܝܢ ܓܝܪ ܕܠܐ ܡܬܩܪܒ ܠܟ ܡܘܬܢ.

18 ܢܬܦܪܩ ܐܦ ܚܢܢ ܥܡܟ.

ܡܛܠ ܕܐܢܬ ܗܘ ܦܪܘܩܢ[17].

19 ܐܢܐ ܕܝܢ ܫܡܥܬ ܩܠܗܘܢ.

ܘܣܡܬ ܒܠܒܝ ܗܝܡܢܘܬܗܘܢ.

(**1**) The enclitic agrees with the immediately preceding fem. noun. On the sense of the first two couplets, see Ode 27. The reference is to the posture of Jesus on the cross. (**2**) Double entente: 'streched' and 'simple, plain.' (**3**) The alternative pointing is /ḥaašḥu/. (**4**) From this verse to the end Christ is speaking. (**5**) 'had not comprehended me' (intellectually?). The participle is passive in form only: see § 84. (**6**) /raa*d*oofaa/ 'pursuer, persecutor,' Pe nomen agentis. (**7**) 'those who thought (ܣܒܪܘ Pe) of me that I was alive,' where one probably has to do with a calque of the Greek ὅτι, which is not only a causal conjunction, but also introduces an object clause. ܣܒܪ Pa 'to hope' takes either ܒ or ܠ, but not ܥܠ. This does not necessarily imply that our document is a translation from a Greek original. (**8**) A centripetal Lamadh: see Text 3, n. 4. (**9**) 'like the arm (/draaʿaa/) of the bridegroom' with a proleptic suffix. (**10**) 'in the bridal pair's home': the preposition Beth is often understood in local expressions. (**11**) The preposition retains the same force as in 7b, 8a, b. (**12**) 'I was despised' (Ethpe of Af ܐܫܛ): on Ethpe as reflexive-passive of Af, see § 49. (**13**) The Lamadh is a direct object marker. (**14**) 'as much as there was depth in it,' i.e. 'to its far end': on ܟܡܐ ܕ, see § 76. (**15**) 'have pity on us,' Impv Pe of √ܚܢ plus a suffix. The diacritical point ought to be above the letter: /ḥonnayin/. (**16**) Vocalise /waʿve*d*/, Impv., not Pf. /waʿva*d*/. (**17**) 'our saviour,' /paaroqan/, a Pe nomen agentis. The clause is an identifying nominal clause: '*You* are our saviour': see § 107b.

20 ܘܣܡܬ ܥܠ ܪܝܫܗܘܢ ܫܡܝ.
ܡܛܠ ܕܒܢܝ̈ ܚܐܪ̈ܐ ܐܢܘܢ ܘܕܝܠܝ ܐܝܬܝܗܘܢ.[18]
ܗܠܠܘܝܐ.

(**18**) 'and they are mine': an independent possessive pronoun (§ 16) and the copulaic use of ܐܝܬ (§ 109).

8. The Acts of Judas Thomas[1]

ܘܟܕ ܗܘܘ ܙܒܢܐ[2] ܒܐܘܪܫܠܡ ܫ̈ܠܝܚܐ ܟܠܗܘܢ: ܫܡܥܘܢ ܟܐܦܐ
ܘܐܢܕܪܐܘܣ: ܘܝܥܩܘܒ ܘܝܘܚܢܢ: ܘܦܝܠܝܦܘܣ ܘܒܪ ܬܘܠܡܝ:
ܘܬܐܘܡܐ ܘܡܬܝ ܡܟܣܐ. ܘܝܥܩܘܒ ܒܪ ܚܠܦܝ ܘܫܡܥܘܢ ܩܢܢܝܐ:
ܘܝܗܘܕܐ ܒܪ ܝܥܩܘܒ ܦܠܓܘ ܗܘܘ ܐܬܪ̈ܘܬܐ ܒܝܢܬܗܘܢ. ܐܝܟܢܐ
ܕܢܟܪܙ ܚܕ ܚܕ ܡܢܗܘܢ. ܒܐܬܪܐ ܕܡܛܝܗ ܘܒܐܬܪܐ ܕܫܕܪܗ
ܡܪܢ܀ ܘܢܦܠܬ ܒܦܣܐ ܘܒܦܠܓܘܬܐ: ܗܢܕܘ ܠܝܗܘܕܐ ܬܐܘܡܐ[3]
ܫܠܝܚܐ. ܘܠܐ ܨ̇ܒܐ ܗܘܐ ܕܢܐܙܠ: ܟܕ ܐܡ̇ܪ ܗܘܐ. ܕܠܐ ܡܫܟܚ
ܐܢܐ ܚܝܠܐ ܕܗܕܐ. ܡܛܠ ܕܟܪܝ̇ܗ ܐܢܐ. ܘܓܒܪܐ ܐܢܐ ܥܒܪܝܐ.
ܐܝܟܢܐ ܠܗ̈ܢܕܘܝܐ ܡܫܟܚ ܐܢܐ ܕܐܙܠ[4] ܀ ܘܟܕ ܗܠܝܢ ܡܬܪ̈ܥܐ
ܗܘܐ ܝܗܘܕܐ. ܐܬܚܙܝ ܠܗ ܡܪܢ ܒܚܙܘܐ ܕܠܠܝܐ ܘܐܡ̇ܪ ܠܗ. ܠܐ
ܬܕܚܠ ܬܐܘܡܐ. ܡܛܠ ܕܛܝܒܘܬܝ ܥܡܟ ܗ̄ܝ. ܗ̇ܘ ܕܝܢ ܦܝܣ ܠܐ
ܡܬܛܦܝܣ ܗܘܐ. ܟܕ ܐܡ̇ܪ. ܕܠܐܝܟܐ[5] ܕܨ̇ܒܝܬ[6] ܡܪܝ ܫܕܪܝܢܝ.
ܒܠܚܘܕ ܠܗܢܕܘ ܠܐ ܐܙܠ ܐܢܐ܀ ܘܟܕ ܗܠܝܢ ܡܬܪ̈ܥܐ ܗܘܐ
ܝܗܘܕܐ. ܓܒܪ ܬܓܪܐ ܚܕ [ܗܢܕ]ܘܝܐ ܒܐܬܪܐ ܕܬܡܚܝܢܐ ܡܢ ...
[ܕ]ܫܡܗ ܗܘܐ ܚ̇ܒܢ. [ܘܗܘ] ܡܠܟܐ ܓܘܕܦܪ ܡܫܕܪܗ[7] ܗܘܐ,
ܐܝܟܢܐ ܕܢܝܬܐ[8] ܢܓܪܐ ܐܘܡܢܐ[9] ܢܥܒܕ ܠܗ. ܘܚܙܝܗ ܡܪܢ ܟܕ
ܡܗܠܟ[10] ܒܫܘܩܐ ܘܐܡ̇ܪ ܠܗ. ܢܓܪܐ ܒܥܐ ܐܢܬ ܕܬܙܒܢ.[11] ܐܡ̇ܪ
ܠܗ ܐܝܢ. ܐܡ̇ܪ ܠܗ ܡܪܝ ܐܝܬ ܠܝ ܥܒܕܐ ܢܓܪܐ ܕܐܙܒܢ ܠܟ.
ܘܚܘܝܗ ܠܗ[12] ܡܢ ܪܘܚܩܐ ܠܬܐܘܡܐ. ܘܦܣܩ ܥܡܗ ܒܥܣܪܝܢ ܕܟܣܦܐ
ܕ̈ܡܘܗܝ. ܘܟܬܒ ܫܛܪܐ ܗܟܢܐ܀ ܝܫܘܥ ܒܪ ܝܘܣܦ ܢܓܪܐ ܕܡܢ
ܒܝܬܠܚܡ ܩܪܝܬܐ ܕܝܗܘܕ. ܡܘܕܐ ܐܢܐ ܕܙܒܢܬ ܠܝܗܘܕܐ
ܬܐܘܡܐ ܥܒܕܐ ܕܝܠܝ. ܠܚܒܢ ܬܓܪܐ ܕܓܘܕܦܪ ܡܠܟܐ ܀ ܀ ܘܟܕ

ܫܠܡܘ[13] ܐܫܛܪ̈ܘܗܝ. ܕܒܪܗ ܡܥܘܒ ܠܝܗܘܕܐ. ܘܐܙܠ ܠܘܬ ܚܒܢ
ܬܓܪܐ. ܘܚܘܝܗܝ ܚܒܢ ܘܐܡܪ ܠܗ. ܡܪܟ ܗܘ ܗܢܐ. ܐܡܪ ܠܗ
ܝܗܘܕܐ ܐܝܢ ܡܪܝ ܗܘ. ܐܡܪ ܠܗ ܚܒܢ ܬܓܪܐ. ܡܙܒܢܘ ܙܒܢܟ ܠܝ.[14]
ܘܝܗܘܕܐ ܫܬܩ ܠܗ[15] ܂܂ ܘܒܨܦܪܐ ܩܡ ܘܨܠܝ. ܘܒܥܐ ܡܢ ܡܪܗ
ܘܐܡܪ ܠܗ. ܗܐ ܡܪܝ ܐܝܟܢܐ ܕܨܒܝܬ ܢܗܘܐ[16] ܨܒܝܢܟ. ܘܐܙܠ
ܠܘܬ ܚܒܢ ܬܓܪܐ. ܟܕ ܡܕܡ ܠܐ ܫܩܠ[17] ܥܡܗ: ܐܠܐ ܗܘ ܕܡ̈ܘܗܝ.
ܒܗܘܒ ܗܘܐ ܐܠܘ ܠܗ ܠܚܕ ܡܪܝ. ܘܐܙܠ ܝܗܘܕܐ ܘܐܫܟܚܗ ܠܚܒܢ
ܬܓܪܐ ܟܕ ܡܣܩ[18] ܡܐܢ̈ܘܗܝ ܠܐܠܦܐ. ܘܥܠ ܗܘܐ ܕܢܣܩ ܥܡܗ ܂܂

(**1**) Wright 1871: I, pp. ܩܥܒ — ܩܥܗ. (**2**) 'for a while.' (**3**) We may have here an appellative meaning "twin" rather than the name Thomas, δίδυμος at Jn 14.21. See Klijn 1962:158f. (**4**) /ʔallef/ Pa Impf. 1sg. of ܐܠܦ. On the form and syntax, see § 62 f and 98 c respectively. (**5**) The proclitic Dalath introduces direct speech. (**6**) Simplified spelling for ܨܒܐ ܐܢܬ 'you want.' (**7**) /mšaddar/, Pa Ptc. pass., happening to be identical in form with its active form due to the *e* > *a* rule (§ 6B). The periphrastic construction indicates "he was on a mission" rather than "he had been sent." See § 84. (**8**) On this apparently redundant ܬܓܪܐ, see Joüon-Muraoka, § 131 *b*. (**9**) Another appositional combination: 'professional carpenter.' (**10**) On the syntax, see § 106. (**11**) The diacritical point below the Beth distinguishes the form as Peal ('to buy') from the one below with a point above the Beth as Pael ('to sell'). (**12**) ܚܘܝܗ ܠܗ Pa 'and he showed him him' where the direct object suffix attached to the verb refers to Habban, and the suffix of the preposition, which is proleptic (§ 112), to the following ܠܝܗܘܕܐ, the preposition of which is equally a marker of direct object. Cf. 2Sam 15.25 ܢܚܘܝܢܝ ܠܗ̇ 'he showed me it.' (**13**) Either Pe. '(the documents) were complete' or Pa. 'they completed (the documents).' The suffix of ܐܫܛܪ̈ܘܗܝ means 'pertaining to him.' (**14**) 'he has certainly sold you to me': on the syntax of the infinitive, see § 98 j. (**15**) A centripetal Lamadh: see § 133 *d*, but see also Joosten 1989. Cf. Gk ἡσύχαζεν 'he remained silent.' (**16**) This is a fully fledged verb, no copula: 'may your will come true!' (**17**) As against the diacritical dot below the word, which makes it Pf., a Participle seems to be more suitable: 'carrying nothing with him ...' (circumstantial clause, § 106), but cf. Gk κομισάμενος, an aorist ptc. (Bonnet 1903:103). (**18**) Both this /masseq/ and /nasseq/ on the following line are Afel forms of √ܣܠܩ (§ 61) where the dot above the Mem of the first indicates an *a* vowel whereas that below the Semkath of the second an *e* vowel.

ܘܟܕ ܫܠܡܘ ܘܝܬܒܘ. ܐܡܪ ܠܗ ܚܒܢ ܬܓܪܐ ܠܝܗܘܕܐ. ܡܢܐ ܗܝ
ܐܘܡܢܘܬܐ ܕܝܕܥ[ܬ] ܐܝܬ ܕܬܥܒܕ. ܐܡܪ ܠܗ ܝܗܘܕܐ ܢܓܪܘܬܐ
ܘܐܪܕܟܠܘܬܐ ܥܒܕܗ ܕܢܓܪܐ. ܐܡܪ ܠܗ ܚܒܢ ܬܓܪܐ. ܡܢܐ ܥܒܕ
ܐܢܬ ܕܬܥܒܕ. ܒܩܝ̈ܣܐ ܘܡܢܐ ܒܦܣܝ̈ܠܬܐ. ܐܡܪ ܠܗ ܝܗܘܕܐ.
ܒܩܝ̈ܣܐ ܝܠܦܬ ܕܐܥܒܕ. ܦ̈ܕܢܐ ܘܢܝ̈ܪܐ ܘܡ̈ܣܣܐ. ܘܐܠ̈ܦܐ
ܠܡ̈ܠܚܐ ܘܡܥܕ̈ܪܐ ܠܐܠ̈ܦܐ.[19] ܘܒܟܐܦܐ ܢܨ̈ܝܒܬܐ ܘܢܘ̈ܣܐ.
ܘܦ̈ܠܛܝܢ ܘܒܝ̈ܬܐ ܠܡ̈ܠܟܐ.[20] ܐܡܪ ܠܗ ܚܒܢ ܬܓܪܐ. ܐܦ ܐܢܐ
ܗ̇ܘ ܐܘܡܢܐ ܒܥܐ ܗ̇ܘܝܬ܀ ܘܕܒܪܗ ܗܘܐ ܠܒܪܐ. ܡܛܠ ܕܦܘܚܬ̇
ܗܘܬ ܠܗ̇ ܛܒܐ. ܘܒܫܠܡܐܝܬ ܪ̈ܕܝܢ ܗܘܘ. ܒܪܡܫܐ ܕܫܒܬܐ
ܠܣܢܕܪܘܟ ܡܕܝܢܬܐ. ܟܕ ܢܦܩܘ ܕܝܢ ܠܐܪܥܐ: ܘܥܐܠܝܢ ܗܘܘ
ܘܐܙܠܝܢ ܠܡܕܝܢܬܐ. ܫܡܥܘ ܗܘܘ ܩܠܐ ܕܙ̈ܡܪܘܬܐ ܘܕܗܕܪܘܠܐ[21]
ܘܙ̈ܡܪܐ ܫܦܝܪܐ. ܘܡܫܐܠ ܗܘܐ ܝܗܘܕܐ ܘܐܡܪ. ܕܡܢܐ ܗܝ
ܚܕܘܬܐ ܕܐܝܬ ܒܗܕܐ ܡܕܝܢܬܐ. ܐܡܪܝܢ ܠܗ. ܐܦ ܠܟ ܐܠܗ̈ܐ
ܐܝܬܝܟ ܕܬܚܕܐ ܒܗܕܐ ܡܕܝܢܬܐ. ܡܠܟܐ ܓܝܪ ܒܪܬܐ
ܝܚܝܕܝܬܐ ܐܝܬ ܠܗ.[22] ܘܠܓܒܪܐ ܝܗܒ ܠܗ̇.[23] ܘܝܘܡܐ ܗܢܐ ܕܚܕܘܬܐ
ܕܝܠܗ̇[24] ܗܘ ܕܡܫܬܘܬܐ. ܘܐܦ ܒܪ̈ܘܙܐ ܥܒܝܕܝܢ ܠܗ ܠܡܠܟܐ[25]
ܕܢܚܕܘܢ. ܕܟܠ ܐܢܫ ܢܐܬܐ ܠܡܫܬܘܬܐ. ܘܐܦ ܡ̈ܣܟܢܐ
ܘܥܬܝ̈ܪܐ ܘܥܒ̈ܕܐ ܘܒ̈ܢܝ ܚܐܪ̈ܐ. ܘܢܘܟܪ̈ܝܐ ܘܒ̈ܢܝ ܡܕܝܢܬܐ. ܘܟܠ
ܐܢܫ ܕܠܡܫܬܘܬܐ ܠܐ ܢܐܬܐ ܕܝܢܐ ܠܡܠܟܐ[26] ܢܚܘܒ܀ ܐܡܪ ܠܗ
ܚܒܢ ܬܓܪܐ ܠܝܗܘܕܐ. ܢܐܙܠ ܐܦ ܚܢܢ ܕܠܐ ܒܝܫܐܝܬ ܢܬܚܫܒ[27]
ܘܝܬܝܪܐܝܬ ܕܐܟ̈ܣܢܝܐ[28] ܚܢܢ. ܘܟܕ ܫܪܘ ܒܦܘܬܩܐ.[29] ܘܐܬܬܢܝܚܘ
ܩܠܝܠ ܐܙܠܘ ܠܡܫܬܘܬܐ. ܗ̇ܘ ܕܝܢ ܝܗܘܕܐ ܒܡܟܠܬܐ ܐܣܬܟܝ.
ܘܟܠܗܘܢ ܟܕ ܚܙܝܢ ܗܘܘ ܐܝܟ ܕܐܟܣܢܝܐ:[30] ܕܡܢ ܕܘܟܐ
ܐܚܪܢܐ ܐܬܐ. ܘܚܒܢ ܬܓܪܐ ܡܪܗ ܒܥܒܕܘܬܐ ܐܚܪܬܐ ܡܫܒܚܝܢ
ܗܘܐ. ܘܟܕ ܠܚܡܐ ܘܐܫܬܝܘ. ܡܕܡ ܡܢܗ ܠܐ ܛܥܡ ܗܘܐ.
ܐܡܪܝܢ ܠܗ ܗ̇ܢܘܢ ܕܠܘܬܗ. ܡܢܐ ܐܬܝܬ ܠܟܐ. ܟܕ ܠܐ ܠܡܐܟܠ
ܘܠܐ ܠܡܫܬܐ ܡܫܬܝ ܐܢܬ: ܐܡܪ ܠܗܘܢ ܝܗܘܕܐ. ܡܛܠ ܡܕܡ
ܗܘ ܕܡܝܬܪ ܡܢ ܡܐܟܠܐ ܘܡܢ ܡܫܬܝܐ ܐܬܝܬ ܠܟܐ. ܘܐܦ ܡܛܠ
ܢܡܘܣܐ ܕܡܠܟܐ ܘܕܐܒܠܗ ܓܒܝܢ. ܘܡܛܠ ܕܒܪ̈ܘܙܐ ܦܪܝܢ ܗܘܘ.
ܕܡܢ ܕܢܥܒܕ ܘܠܐ ܢܐܬܐ ܡܢܗ ܒܪܫܐ ܢܦܠ. ܘܟܕ ܠܚܡܐ ܕܝܢ
ܘܟܕ ܐܫܬܝܘ. ܐܦ ܡܫܚܐ ܘܡܟܘ̈ܠܐ ܐܝܬܝܘ ܠܗܘܢ. ܘܡܫܚܘ. ܐܝܬ
ܒܦܘܡܗܘܢ ܕܐܦ̈ܝܗܘܢ ܡܫܚܝܢ ܗܘܘ.[31] ܘܐܝܬ ܒܪܝܫܗܘܢ ܕܕܩ̈ܢܝܗܘܢ

ܘܐܝܬ ܕܙ̈ܘܡܪܬܐ ܐܢ̈ܫܬܐ. ܡܗܘܕܝܐ ܕܝܢ ܠܐܠܗܐ ܡܫܒܚ ܗܘܐ.
ܘܡܟܝܟܬ ܪܥܝܗ ܗܘܬ ܫܠܡ ܗܘܐ. ܘܒܫܘܒܚ̈ܗܘܢ، ܘܠܐ ܐܪܦܝܬ.
ܘܟܐ̈ܪܘܕܘܗܝ، ܫܡܥ ܗܘܐ. ܘܠܠܒܗ ܪܒܐ ܗܘܐ. ܘܟܠܠܐ ܕܐܦ̈ܐ
ܒܪܝܫܗ ܣܝܡ ܗܘܐ. ܘܫܒܛܐ ܕܡܠܟܐ ܒܐܝܕܗ ܐܚܝܕ ܗܘܐ܀[32]
ܗܝܕܝܢ ܙܡܪܬܐ ܕܐܝܬ ܗܘܬ ܒܝܢܬ ܣܡ̈ܟܐ. ܟܠ ܟܠܗܘܢ ܡܫܬ̈ܘܬܐ
ܗܘܬ. ܘܟܕ ܡܛܬ ܠܘܬ ܡܗܘܕܝܐ. ܩܝܡܐ ܗܘܬ ܘܠܟܠ ܚܕ ܡܢܗܘܢ ܙܡܪܐ
ܗܘܬ. ܗ̇ܝ ܕܝܢ ܙܡܪܬܐ ܒܥܒܪܝܬܐ ܗܘܬ. ܘܟܕ ܚܙܬ ܒܗ ܩܪܒܬ
ܠܟܠ ܚܕܝܗ. ܡܗܘܕܝܐ ܠܐ ܐܪܝܡ ܐܦܘ̈ܗܝ، ܠܟܠ: ܐܠܐ ܟܠ[33] ܟܐܪܥܐ
ܚܪ ܗܘܐ. ܘܐܚܕܐ ܚܕ ܡܢ ܗ̇ܢܘܢ ܫܩ̈ܘܬܐ.[34] ܐܪܝܡ ܐܝܕܗ ܘܡܚܠ
ܦܟܗ ܡܚܝܬܐ. ܡܗܘܕܝܐ ܕܝܢ ܚܪ ܒܗ ܘܐܡܪ ܠܗ. ܐܠܗܝ، ܢܫܒܘܩ ܠܟ
ܗܕܐ ܒܥܠܡܐ ܕܐܬܐ. ܒܗܢܐ ܕܝܢ ܥܠܡܐ ܢܚܘܐ ܐܝܕܐ ܕܡܚܬܗ ܒܝ،
ܐܝܕܐ ܕܡܚܬܢܝ. ܘܐܚܝܕܗ ܗܘ ܒܕ ܢܓܪ ܠܗ ܟܠܒܐ܀ ܘܩܒܪ، ܗܘܐ

(**19**) /qeeqnee wniree wmassaasee wliqee lfanṭoonee (Lat. *pontones*) wʿ??? lelfee/ 'ploughs and yokes and goads and oars for ferry-boats, and ... for ships.' (**20**) /wavk̲eefee nafšaat̲aa wnawsee (Gk *ναός*) whayklee wviraat̲aa dmalkee/ 'with stones, tomb-stones and shrines and palaces and fortresses of kings.' (**21**) /qaalaa dṣepponwaat̲aa (συμφωνία) wad̲hed̲rolee (ὕδραυλις)/ 'the sound of pipes and water-organs.' (**22**) A compound sentence: see § 113. (**23**) The context indicates the first Lamadh as marker of indirect object and the second as that of direct object. A pronominal direct object of a participle is always indicated by means of Lamadh: § 97 d. (**24**) The suffix is proleptic, anticipating the following ܡ̣ܫܝܚܘ̈ܬܐ. (**25**) On the syntagm ܡܛܠ ܠ of perfective force, see § 84. (**26**) The diacritical point distinguishes the word /malkaa/ from ܡܠܟ݁ܐ /melkaa/ 'advice, counsel.' (**27**) 'so that we may not get a bad report': the verb is an impersonal passive, lit. 'will be heard': see § 79. (**28**) The proclitic Dalath is weakly causal. (**29**) 'When they checked in at an inn.' The verb primarily means 'to loosen': its specific meaning here maybe had to do with the notion of a passenger loosening his donkey or horse at the end of a day's journey. The meaning "to begin" in Pa is also perhaps derived from the notion of releasing tension, letting go of. (**30**) On the syntax of the proclitic Dalath, see § 100. (**31**) 'there (were) some of them who ...,' 'some of them anointed ...' (**32**) A passive participle with active meaning: § 84. (**33**) ܥܕܢܐ /ʿeddaanaa/ is expected: 'all the while.' Or perhaps it means 'entirely,' i.e. 'solely.' (**34**) ܫܩܘ̈ܬܐ /šaaqawaat̲aa/, pl. of ܫܩܝܐ 'cup-bearer,' Pe ptc., though Af in meaning. Cf. ܐܣܝܐ 'physician' (pl. ܐܣܘ̈ܬܐ), though the verb 'to heal' is Pa, ܐܣܝ /ʾassi/. Likewise 'to pour drink' is Af ܐܫܩܝ.

ܗܘܕܪܐ ܕܢܒܝܪ ܙܡܝܪܬܐ ܗܕܪܐ. ܒܕܬ، ܒܪܬ ܢܗܪܐ. ܙܘܗܐ
ܕܬ̈ܠܬܐ ܐܝܬ ܠܗ. ܟܡܐ ܘܬܪ̈ܥܝܗ ܫܘܗ. ܡܐܐ ܘܡܪ̈ܟܒܬ ܒܒܠ
ܥܒܕ ܠܒ. ܠܒܥܠܝܗ ܠܦܩܣܐ ܕܟܗܢ ܕܦܢܝܢ ܘܟܗܢܝܢ ܪܫܘܥܘ.
ܒܪܝܫܗ ܥܕܪܐ ܟܠܒܐ ܘܐܓܪ ܠܟܡܘܪ̈ܘܗܝ، ܠܛܝܒܘܬ. ܘܡܫܬܐ ܒܪܝܫܗ
ܫܡܥܢ. ܚܕܘܬܐ ܒܬ̈ܚܠܝܗ ܡܕܝܠܐ. ܦܘܡܗ ܦܬܝܚ ܘܐܡܐ ܠܗ.
ܕܟܠ ܬܩ̈ܢܝܢ[35] ܒܗ ܐܘܪܐ. ܬܪ̈ܥܘܗܝ ܥ̈ܠܝܗܘܢ، ܕܒܪܐ ܘܬ̈ܥܒܝܢ
ܘܬܪ̈ܝܢ ܒܗ ܪܒܝܢ. ܠܥܠܡ ܢ̈ܦܫ ܬܪܥܐ. ܕܡܒܪܟ ܘܒܐܠ ܒܗܢܐ.
ܡܛܠܗ ܕܬܪ̈ܝܢ ܕܪ̈ܓܠܝ.[36] ܕܐܪܪܕܟܠܐ ܡܕܡܝܐ ܒܠܒܗ، ܐܢ̈ܕܪܗ
ܬܪ̈ܬܝܗܘܢ ܠܐܬܪܐ ܕܢ̈ܫܝܐ ܡܒܪ̈ܢ. ܘܒܗܘܢ ܪ̈ܒܒܬܗ ܬܪܒܐ ܕܥܡܡܐ
ܦܬܚ̈ܘ. ܒܝܬ ܓܢܘܢܗ ܢܗܝܪ. ܘܪܝܚܐ ܕܦܘܪܢܣܐ ܢܓܠܐ.[37] ܦܪ̈ܝܡܐ
ܓܒܘܗ ܡܬܘܡ. ܣܘܟܐ ܘܡܗܝܡܢܘܬܐ ܘܫܒܪܐ ܠܟܘܠ ܡܟܫܡ. ܡܢ
ܠܒܗ ܡܓܒܝܢ ܥܕ̈ܪܐ. ܬ̈ܪܒܝܗ ܒܦܫܬܐ ܡܓܒܠܝܢ. ܬ̈ܫܒܚܬܢܘܗ
ܚܕܪ̈ܝܢ[38] ܠܗ.[39] ܟܠܗܘܢ ܕܠܗܘܢ ܙܒܢܬ. ܘܬ̈ܫܒܚܬܢܘܬܗ ܩ̈ܕܝܫܬܐ
ܡܕܡܝܐ ܫܘܒܚܐ ܬ̈ܡܠܠܝܢ. ܡܫܒܚܝܢ ܡܕܡܝܐ ܢ̈ܫܐ.[40] ܘܚܝܪܝܢ
ܠܗܘܢܗܘܢ ܕܢܐܬܐ. ܘܗܒܝܢ ܒܫܘܒܚܗ ܢܗܪܘܢ.[41] ܘܢܗܘܘܢ
ܒܡܠܟܘܬܐ ܒܗܡ ܕܠܒܠܡ ܒܠܒܝܢ ܠܐ ܚܒܪܐ. ܘܢܗܘܘܢ ܒܫܘܒܚܐ
ܕܠܗ ܟܠܗܘܢ ܙܕ̈ܝܩܐ ܒܢܫܝܢ. ܘܢܗܘܘܢ ܒܒܘܣܡܐ. ܕܠܗ ܚܕ̈ܕܐ
ܒܐܠܝܢ. ܘܢܠܒܫܘܢ ܠܒܘܫ ܢܘܗܪܐ ܘܢܬܟܣܘܢ ܒܫܘܒܚܐ ܕܡܪܗܘܢ.
ܘܢܫܒܚܘܢ ܠܐܒܐ ܚܝܐ. ܕܫܠܚ ܢܘܗܪܗ ܠܟܢܫܐ. ܘܢܗܪܘ ܒܗ ܗܘ
ܕܡܪܗܘܢ. ܕܫܠܚ ܡܢ ܦܘܪܢܣܗ. ܕܐܦܘܣܩܐ[42] ܡܢ ܡܬܘܡ ܠܗ ܠܗ.
ܘܐܙܕܝܘ ܡܢ ܢ̈ܫܐ. ܕܡܠܗܘܢ ܘܡܪܗܘܢ ܠܐܬܢ̈ܝܗܘܢ.[43] ܘܫܒܚܘ
ܠܐܒܐ ܡܪܐ ܕܟܠ ܘܠܒܪܐ ܚܝܕܝܐ ܕܡܢܗ.[44] ܘܐܘܕܝܘ ܠܪܘܚܐ
ܚܒܝܒܬܗ܀ ܘܥܒܕ ܙܟܪ ܗܘܐ[45] ܗܕܐ ܕܡܛܪܬܐ. ܟܠܗܘܢ ܗܢܘܢ
ܕܠܘܬܗ ܒܗ ܢܦܩܝܢ ܗܘܘ. ܘܫܐܠ ܗܘܘ ܕܢܓܠܐ ܐܣܟܠܦ ܠܗ.[46]
ܡܒܝܢ[47] ܕܝܢ ܠܐ ܫܡܥܝܢ ܗܘܘ ܡܢܐ ܐܡܪ ܗܘܐ. ܡܛܠ ܕܗܘ
ܒܥܒܪܝܬ[48] ܐܡܪ ܗܘܐ. ܘܗܘܢ ܠܐ ܝܕܥܝܢ ܗܘܘ. ܙܓܪܬܐ ܕܝܢ
ܒܠܒܕܘܗ ܫܡܥܬܐ ܗܘܬ. ܡܛܠ ܕܥܒܪܝܬܐ ܗܘܬ. ܘܒܗ ܢܫܝܪܐ
ܗܘܬ܀ ܘܒܕ ܫܡܥܬ ܡܢ ܠܘܬܗ ܘܠܐܚܪ̈ܢܐ ܙܡܪܐ ܗܘܬ. ܬܘܒ ܒܗ
ܢܫܝܪܐ ܗܘܬ. ܘܐܫܬܒܚܘܗ ܗܘܬ ܐܝܟ ܕܠܟܒܪܐ[48a] ܒܪ ܐܬܪܗ. ܐܦ
ܒܚܘܗ ܫܦܝܪ ܗܘܐ ܡܢ ܟܠܗܘܢ ܗܢܘܢ ܕܐܝܬ ܗܘܘ ܬܡܢ. ܘܒܕ
ܙܓܪܬܐ ܫܠܝܚܬ: ܡܛܠܬ ܠܗ ܠܡܦܠܚܘ.[49] ܘܠܐ ܡܫܦܪܐ ܗܘܬ
ܬܟܠܬܗ ܡܢܝܗ. ܗܘ ܕܝܢ ܠܐ ܬܟܬܡ ܗܘܐ ܬܠܘܗ، ܘܠܐ ܢܦܩ ܗܘܐ

ܒܐܢܫ. ܐܠܐ ܥܠ[50] ܒܐܪܥܐ ܚ̇ܐܪ ܗܘܐ̇. ܟܕ ܢܦܘܩ ܘܢܦ̣ܛܪ ܡܢ
ܒܝܬ ܡܫܬܝܐ ܀ ܡܫܩܝܢܐ ܕܝܢ ܗ̇ܘ ܢܚܬ ܗܘܐ ܠܥܝܢܐ ܕܢܕܠܐ ܡ̈ܝܐ.
ܘܐܫܬܘܪ، ܬܡܢ ܐܪܝܐ ܘܬܒ̣ܪܗ ܘܗܕܡ ܗܕܡ[50a] ܦܣܩܗ ܗܘܐ܀
ܗ̇ܝܕܝܢ ܟ̈ܠܒܐ ܚܕ ܚܕ ܡܢ ܗ̈ܕܡܘܗܝ ܫܩܠܝܢ ܗܘܘ. ܟܠܒܐ ܕܝܢ ܚܕ
ܐܘܟܡܐ. ܐܝܕܗ ܕܡܫܩܝܢܐ: ܗ̇ܝ ܕܐܪܝܡ ܥܠ ܝܗܘܕܐ ܫܩܠ ܗܘܐ̣.
ܘܡܨܥܬ ܡܫܬܝܐ ܐܥܠܗ̇‥ ܘܟܕ ܚܙܐܘܗ̇ ܟܠܗܘܢ ܬܡܗܘ. ܘܟܕ
ܟܠܗܘܢ ܡܫܐܠܝܢ ܗܘܘ ܕܡܢܘ ܗ̇ܢܐ ܡܢܗܘܢ. ܐܫܬܘܕܥܬ ܐܝܕܐ
ܕܕܡܫܩܝܢܐ ܗ̇ܝ[51] ܗ̇ܘ ܕܡܚܝܗܝ ܗܘܐ ܠܝܗܘܕܐ܀ ܗ̇ܝܕܝܢ ܙܡܪܬܐ
ܬܒ̣ܪܬ ܐܒ̈ܘܒܗ̇ ܘܠܘܬ ܪ̈ܓܠܘܗܝ ܕܫܠܝܚܐ ܐܬ̇ܬ. ܘܝܬܒ̣ܬ ܘܐܡܪܐ
ܗܘܬ. ܕܗܢܐ ܓܒܪܐ ܐܘ ܐܠܗܐ ܗܘ ܐܘ ܫܠܝܚܐ ܕܐܠܗܐ. ܐܢܐ
ܓܝܪ ܫܡܥܬܗ ܒܥܒܪܐܝܬ ܡܕܡ ܕܐܡ̣ܪ ܠܗ̇ܘ ܡܫܩܝܢܐ. ܘܒܗ̇[52]
ܒܫܥܬܐ ܓܕܫ ܠܗ. ܐܡ̣ܪ ܠܗ ܓܝܪ: ܕܐܚܙܝܗ̇ ܠܐܝܕܐ ܕܡܚܬܢܝ. ܟܕ

(**35**) /tešbḥaan/, f.pl.abs. of ܬܶܫܒ̇ܘܚܬܐ 'praise.' (**36**) Lit. 'her neck is steps steps,' consists of several layers. On the distributive force of the repetition of a noun in the st. abs., see § 71 a. (**37**) The form must be vocalised as either /mlee/, an adj., or /maalee/, a Pe ptc. The diacritics are striking. (**38**) On the force of the passive participle, see § 84. (**39**) The diacritics are peculiar here, too: see n. 37 above. (**40**) ܚ̈ܝܐ /ḥayyee/ the living.' (**41**) The diacritical dot indicates a Pe form, /nenhrun/ 'they will light up' (intr.) as against Af ܢܢܗܪܘܢ /nanhrun/ 'they will illumine' (tr.). (**42**) = Gk ἀπουσία 'waste, excrement,' hence the food is wholly consumed? (**43**) /šaaṯyayhon/ 'its drinkers.' The possessive suffix is plural, referring to ܚ̈ܝܐ, a plurale tantum. (**44**) 'who is from Him': on the syntax of the proclitic, see § 91 h. 3. (**45**) The diacritic point over the Mem indicates a periphrastic progressive past tense, 'while he was singing,' which also agrees with the tense of the main verb (ܚܐܪܝܢ ܗ̇ܘܘ 'they were staring at him'), hence not 'when he had sung' (= /zmar waa/). (**46**) The preposition indicates an affected entity. (**47**) A structure similar to Heb. שָׁמֹעַ לֹא שָׁמְעוּ 'comprehend they did not': see § 98 j. (**48**) Adverbial: 'in Hebrew.' See § 47. (**48a**) On the ܕ, see § 100. (**49**) /lquvleeh/ 'opposite him.' On the alternation between /luqval-/ and /lquvl-/, see § 46. (**50**) See n. 33 above. (**50a**) 'tore him up limb by limb': on the repead st. abs., see § 71a. (**51**) 'the hand was found to be of the cup-bearer,' lit. 'the hand was found that it was of the cup-bearer.' The first Dalath of ܕܕܡܫܩܝܢܐ introduces a substantival clause, a clausal complement of ܐܫܬܘܕܥܬ, and the concluding ܗܝ is the subject of the embedded nominal clause with ܕܡܫܩܝܢܐ 'of the cup-bearer,' and not of ܐܫܬܘܕܥܬ. (**52**) On the force of the proleptic pronoun, see § 112 a.

ܓܝܪ ܠܗ̇ ܠܡܠܟܐ. ܘܗܘܐ ܚܕܝܘܬܢ ܐܡܝܢܐ ܓܪܗ̇ ܠܡܠܟܐ. ܘܡܢܗܘܢ
ܗܝܡܢܘ ܠܐܓܪܬܐ. ܘܡܢܗܘܢ ܠܐ ܡܗܝܡܢܝܢ ܗܘܘ. ܡܠܟܐ ܕܝܢ ܟܕ
ܩܒܠܐ[53] ܗܢܐ ܥܒܕ̣. ܐܓܪܬܐ ܘܐܫܕܪ ܠܗ ܠܡܗܘܕܥܐ. ܬܐ[54] ܒܥܕ
ܘܢܦܠܐ ܥܠ ܒܪܬܗ̇. ܡܛܠ ܕܡܫܝܪܬܐ ܗ̇ܝ ܠܝ. ܘܡܘܡܢܐ ܡܬܬܘܡ ܐܢܐ
ܠܗ̇. ܘܠܐ ܢܦܩܐ ܕܢܐܙܠ ܒܥܡܗ. ܡܛܠ ܕܠܐ ܒܕܒܠ ܐܬܘܢ، ܗܘܐ
ܠܗ ܡܢ ܒܪܗ ܐܬܪܐ܀ ܡܠܟܐ ܕܝܢ ܒܡܦܛܪܐ ܐܘܒܠܗ ܠܒܝܬ
ܓܘܢܐ. ܘܩܪܐ، ܗܘܐ ܕܢܦܠܐ ܘܢܐܡܪ ܡܒܢܐ. ܡܢ ܠܘܬܐ[55]
ܕܟܪ̈ܘܗܝ، ܘܗܕܝܐ ܘܡܒܪܟܝܢ ܕܐܝܠܝܢ ܕܡܗܝܡܢܝܢ ܒܗ. ܘܒܝܬ
ܓܘܣܐ ܘܢܝܚܐ ܕܐܠܗ̈ܝܐ: ܘܫܒܪܐ ܕܡܫ̈ܡܫܢܐ: ܘܦܪܘܩܐ ܕܡ̈ܚܝܠܐ.
ܘܡܐܣܝܢܐ ܕܟܐܒ̈ܬܐ ܒܪ̈ܝܬܐ. ܡܫܝܢܐ ܕܡ̈ܠܟܐ ܘܦܪܘܩܐ
ܕܒܪ̈ܝܬܐ. ܐܢܬ ܗܘ ܕܢܕܒ ܐܢܬ ܐܠܗܐ ܕܒܬ̈ܪܝ.[56] ܘܡܢ ܓܒܪܐ ܐܢܬ
ܠܗܝ. ܐܢܬ ܗܘ ܡܚܘܝܢܐ[57] ܕܐܪ̈ܙܐ ܟܣ̈ܝܐ. ܘܡܓܠܝܢܐ ܕܡ̈ܠܠܐ
ܫܬܝ̈ܩܬܐ. ܐܢܬ ܗܘ ܢܘܗܪܐ ܕܐܝܠܝܢ ܠܒܥܠܐ. ܘܡܐܒ̈ܝܪܝ ܒܠܗܘܢ
ܟܣ̈ܝܐ[58] ܗܘܘ. ܐܢܬ ܗܘ ܕܚܒܝܬ[59] ܒܟܠܗܘܢ ܟܣ̈ܝܐ ܘܡܬܝܕܥ
ܐܢܬ ܒܡܗܒܢܘܬܗܘܢ. ܡܥܕ ܒܪܐ ܡܫܠܡܢܐ ܕܪ̈ܚܡܐ ܡ̈ܫܠܡܢܐ:
ܘܩܘܡܬ ܡܚܣܢܐ ܘܠܒܫܬ ܠܒܪܢܫܐ ܘܡܣܒܪܐ. ܐܢܬ ܗܘ ܚܝܠܐ
ܘܚܟܡܬܗ: ܘܡܠܒܟܗ ܘܢܒܝܗ ܘܢܣܝܗ ܕܐܒܘܗܝ: ܕܒܦܫܬ ܒܗ
ܒܥܘܒܢܐ ܘܓܠܝܬ[60] ܒܗ ܒܒܥܘܕܘܬܟ. ܘܐܝܟ ܐܢܬܘܢ ܒܬܪ̈ܝܢ
ܫܡܗ̈ܝܢ. ܘܐܬܒܢܝܬ ܐܝܟ ܡܫܠܡ. ܘܡܫܕܪܘ ܒܠܝܟ ܫܪ̈ܝܝܢ.[61]
ܕܒܪܢܫܐ ܐܢܬ ܕܡܠܡ ܥܠ ܒܥܘܕܪܢܐ ‥ ܘܢܘܦܬ ܫܘܒܚܐ
ܕܐܠܗܘܬܟ ܒܢܐܓܪܬ[62] ܘܚܝܢ ܒܪ ܐܢܫܘܬܟ. ܒܗ̇ ܚܢܦܘܬܗ،
ܠܒܥܫܐ ܡܢ ܒܝܬܘܬܗ: ܘܦܪܝܬ ܒܥܠܝܢ ܠܬܟܠܬܐ ܘܚܝܐ. ܘܠܐܝܠܝܢ
ܕܢܒܝܢ ܘܡܗܒܪܝܢ ܒܝܢ. ܡܠܒܬ ܠܗܘܢ ܝܬܪܘܬܐ ܒܡܠܟܘܬܟ. ܐܢܬ
ܗܘ ܕܩܘܡܬ ܐܝܓܪܐ ܘܐܫܬܕܪܬ ܡܢ ܪ̈ܘܡܐ ܡ̈ܠܟܐ. ܡܛܠ ܕܐܢܬ
ܗܘ ܡܥܡܕ ܕܬܒܥܐ ܒܝܥܐ ܢܒܥܐ ܘܡܥܠܡܢܐ ܕܥܠܡܝܢ. ܥܡܝܢ
ܐܢܬ ܡܪܝ، ܒܫܠܝܢ. ܘܦܘܪܢܣܢ ܡܫܝܕܬܐ ܗܘ ܒܟܠܗܝܢ ܒܪ̈ܝܬܟ:
ܘܒ̈ܢܝܢܫܐ ܟܠܗܘܢ ܕܬܡܝܗ ܐܠܗܘܬܟ: ܘܐܫܪܝܬ ܠܐ ܡܥܡܕ
ܠܡܓܒܪ ܠܒܝܢܐ ܕܪܒܘܬܟ. ܘܠܐ ܕܢܩܘܡ ܥܠ ܦܘܡܟ ܐܡܝܢܐ
ܐܡܬܝ.[63] ܘܢܒܬܬ ܠܝ ܠܥܘܠ ܘܓܠܝܬ ܒܥܡܐ ܠܝܬܗ̇ ܘܦܩܕܬ
ܬܪ̈ܝܢܗ̇ ܘܐܫܬܡܥܬ ܢܒ̈ܝܥܝܢܗ̇. ܘܕܪܫܬ ܠܗܘܢ ܐܘܪܚܐ ܠܦܘܪܩܢܐ
ܒܥܘܡܩܗ̇ ܕܐܠܗܘܬܟ. ܐܝܟ ܡܪܝ، ܒܢܐ ܐܢܐ ܡܢܝ ܥܠ ܟ̈ܠܡܐ
ܗܠܝܢ. ܕܡܕܡ ܕܢܗܒ ܐܢܬ ܕܢܫܒܪ ܠܗܘܢ ܬܒܥܐ ܠܗܘܢ. ܘܗܕܡ

ܐܝܕܗ ܥܠܝܗܘܢ ܘܐܡܪ ܠܗܘܢ. ܡܪܢ ܢܗܘܐ ܥܡܟܘܢ. ܘܐܪܦ ܐܢܘܢ
ܘܢܦܩ. ܟܠܗܘܢ ܕܝܢ ܠܬܫܡܫܬܐ ܡܦܩܝܢ ܗܘܐ ܕܢܦܩܘܢ ܡܢ ܒܝܬ
ܓܢܘܢܐ. ܘܟܕ ܟܢܫܐ ܟܠܗ ܢܦܩ ܗܘܐ. ܘܬܪܥܐ ܕܒܝܬ ܓܢܘܢܐ
ܐܬܬܚܕ.[64] ܚܬܢܐ ܓܦ ܓܢܘܢܐ ܐܪܝܡ ܗܘܐ: ܐܝܟܢܐ ܕܠܟܠܬܐ
ܢܝܬܝܗ[65] ܠܘܬܗ. ܘܚܙܐ ܗܘܐ ܠܡܪܢ ܒܕܡܘܬܗ ܕܝܗܘܕܐ ܬܐܘܡ
ܗܘܐ ܘܥܡ ܟܠܬܐ ܡܡܠܠ ܗܘܐ. ܘܐܡܪ ܠܗ ܚܬܢܐ ܕܗܐ ܩܕܡܝܐ
ܢܦܩܬ ܗܘܝܬ ܠܟ. ܐܝܟܢܐ ܗܪܟܐ ܐܝܬ ܒܟܒܪ ܀ ܐܡܪ ܠܗ ܡܪܢ
ܐܢܐ ܠܐ ܗܘܝܬ[66] ܝܗܘܕܐ. ܐܠܐ ܐܚܘܗܝ ܐܢܐ ܕܝܗܘܕܐ ܘܬܒ
ܗܘܐ ܠܗ ܡܪܢ ܥܠ ܒܣܬܪܐ. ܘܐܦܣ ܗܘܐ ܠܗܘܢ ܠܬܠܡܝܕܐ ܕܢܬܒܘܢ
ܥܠ ܒܣܬܪܘܬܐ. ܘܐܡܪ ܕܢܐܡܪ ܠܗܘܢ. ܒܗܕܐ ܟܠ ܕܐܚܝ[67] ܡܠܠ
ܥܡܟܘܢ ܘܕܒܘ ܠܢܒܘ ܐܟܚܕܐ. ܘܕܒܘ ܕܡܫܝܚܐ ܕܡܬܦܪܩܝܢ
ܐܢܬܘܢ ܡܢ ܗܕܐ ܥܒܘܕܘܬܐ ܕܐܬܐ. ܘܗܘܝܢ ܐܢܬܘܢ ܢܩܦܐ ܕܚܢܐ.
ܘܡܬܦܪܩܝܢ ܐܢܬܘܢ ܡܢ ܚܫܐ ܟܣܝܐ ܘܓܠܝܐ.[68] ܘܡܢ ܝܩܠܬܐ

(**53**) The diacritical point indicates /ṭebbaa/ 'report' as distinct from ܛܒܐ /ṭaavaa/ 'good.' (**54**) /taa/ 'Come!', of the irregular verb ܐܬܐ: § 67. (**55**) This is the first of a series of agent nouns: /laawyaa/ 'companion' (Pe ptc.), /haadyaa/ 'guide' (ditto), /mdabbraanaa/ 'leader' (Pa nom. agentis), /paarooqaa/ 'deliverer' (Pe nom. agentis), /masyaanaa/ 'healer' (Pa nom. agentis from /ʾassi/), /maḥyaanaa/ 'life-giver' (Af nom. agentis from /ʾaḥḥi/). See § 51. (**56**) 'things to come': on the use of the f. pl. as neuter, see § 69. (**57**) Another series of agent nouns: /mḥawyaanaa/ 'discloser' (Pa nom. agentis), /mgalyaanaa/ 'revealer' (ditto), /naaṣovaa/ 'planter' (Pe nom. agentis). (**58**) The diacritical dot over the first letter indicates /ʿvaadee/ 'the works,' and not /ʿavdee/ 'the servants.' (**59**) /dakseet/ '*You* are the one who is hidden ...' ܕܟܣܝܬ is a short-hand for ܟܣܝܐ ܐܢܬ. (**60**) /gleet/ 'you are revealed': on the form, see the preceding note. (**61**) /ḥaazyayik/ 'those who saw you' from /ḥaazyaa/, a substantivised participle. (**62**) For the standard ܢܓܝܪܘܬ /naggiruṯ/ with an unusual vowel letter Alaf. If authentic, one possibly has to do with an alternative, synonymous form. (**63**) 'as you are.' The particle ܐܝܬ is here a mere copula: see § 109. (**64**) Ethpe Pf. of ܐܚܕ 'to shut': see § 62 e. (**65**) /naytee/ 'he shall bring,' Af Impf. of ܐܬܐ: § 67. (**66**) A Pf. with the force of the present tense: § 81. (**67**) The proclitic introduces an antecedentless relative clause: 'what my brother spoke ...' (**68**) /ḥaššee ksayyaa waḡlayyaa/ 'hidden and manifest sufferings.' The last two are the st. emph. pl. of /ksee/ and /glee/ respectively: on the ending, see § 21.

ܬܫܪܬܐ ܕܟ̈ܢܫܐ. ܗ̇ܢܘܢ ܕܫܪܬܗܘܢ ܒܡܬܐ ܗܝ ܡܕܝܢܬܐ.[69] ܘܐܦ
ܢܗܘܘܢ ܠܗܘܢ ܢ̈ܝܫܐ.[70] ܡܛܠܬܗܘܢ ܗ̇ܘܝܢ ܐܢܬܘܢ ܙ̇ܠܝܠܝܢ ܘܒܙܝܢ
ܘܒ̇ܣܝܢ ܠܝ̈ܬܡܐ. ܘܥܠܒܝܢ ܠܐܪ̈ܡܠܬܐ. ܘܡܫܬܥܠܝܢ ܐܢܬܘܢ ܥ̇ܠ
ܒܣܘ̈ܣܝܗܘܢ. ܣܘܓܐܐ ܓܝܪ ܕܟ̈ܢܫܐ ܒܢ̈ܝܫܐ ܦ̈ܓܥܐܐ ܗ̇ܘܝܢ
ܠܗܘܢ.[71] ܐܘ ܕܟܠܒܐ ܢܦܠ ܒܠܒܗܘܢ. ܐܘ ܕܒܪ ܐܓܪܐ ܐ̇ܚܕ ܠܗܘܢ.
ܐܘ ܕܦܠܓܐ ܢܦܠ ܒܠܒܗܘܢ. ܘܐܢ ܫܠܝܚܝܢ ܢܗܘܘܢ ܦܪܫܝܢ .. ܐܘ
ܒܓܘܪܐ ܐܘ ܒܓܢܒܘܬܐ. ܐܘ ܒܙܢܝܘܬܐ ܐܘ ܒܡܣܟܢܘܬܐ. ܐܘ
ܒܥܘܒܗܪܐ ܦܪܝܣܐ. ܘܒܗܠܝܢ ܦܘܪ̈ܥܢܐ ܡ̇ܬܒܥܝܢ ܐܢܬܘܢ ܒܗܘܢ.
ܐܠܐ ܐܢ ܬܬܦܢܘܢ ܠܝ ܘܬܬܒܪܘܢ ܢܦܫܟܘܢ ܕܚܛܝܬ ܠܐܠܗܐ.
ܢܗܘܘܢ ܠܗܘܢ ܦ̈ܓܥܐ ܢܝܫܐ. ܗ̇ܢܘܢ ܕܐܚܕ ܡܢ ܡ̈ܘܗܒܬܐ ܘܕܟܝܢܐ ܠܐ
ܦܪܥ ܠܗܘܢ. ܘܗ̇ܘܝܬܘܢ ܕܠܐ ܚ̈ܛܗܐ ܘܕܠܐ ܒܗܬܬܐ ܘܕܠܐ
ܒܪܘܢܬܐ. ܘܡܫܦܪܝܢ ܐܢܬܘܢ ܕܐܡܪܬ[72] ܛܒܝܢ ܡܫܬܘܬܐ ܗ̇ܝ
ܕܫܪܪܐ. ܘܬܬܩܘܢ ܒܗ̇ ܡܫ̈ܒܚܢܐ. ܘܬܬܒܢܘܢ[73] ܒܗ ܟ̇ܠ[74]
ܠܟܘܢܐ ܀ ܀ ܗ̇ܢܘܢ ܕܝܢ ܟ̈ܠܡܐ ܐܬܦܠܣܘ ܗܘܘ ܒܗ ܡܪܝ.
ܘܐܬܥܠܒܘ ܠܗ ܢܦܫܗܘܢ: ܘܐܬܦܪܥܘ ܗܘܘ ܡܢ ܥܘܠܬܐ. ܘܟܠ
ܕܘܒܪ̈ܬܗܘܢ ܐܓܠܘܗ[75].. ܘܡܪܝ ܢܓܡ ܡܢ ܠܘܬܗܘܢ ܘܐܡܪ ܠܗܘܢ.
ܬܗܘܐ ܠܘܬܟܘܢ ܫܠܡܘܬܗ ܕܡܪܢ܀ ܒܦܪܘܩܐ ܕܝܢ ܒܪ ܢܓܡܗ.
ܦܪܡ ܟܠܒܐ ܒܓܠܐ[76] ܦܬܘܪܐ. ܘܐܝܟ ܦܪܡ ܫܘܝܐ ܘܟܠܬܐ. ܘܐܫܟܚ
ܐܢܘܢ ܟܕ ܡܬܡܟܝܢ. ܚܕ ܠܘܩܒܠ ܚܕ . ܘܟ̈ܠܗܘܢ[77] ܐܦ̈ܝܗ ܕܟܠܬܐ
ܘܚܬܢܐ. ܘܐܦ ܫܘܝܐ ܦܪܝܣ ܗܘܐ ܠܒ. ܐܡܪܐ ܠܗ̇ ܐܡܗ̇
ܠܟܠܬܐ.[78] ܡܢܐ ܡܬܡܟܬ[79] ܗܟܘܬ ܘܠܐ ܒܗܬܬ. ܐܠܐ ܐܝܟ ܗ̇ܝ
ܕܗܘܐ ܙܒܢܐ ܣܓܝܐܐ ܘܒܬܘܠܬܐ ܕܡܬܒܬܐ ܐܝܬ ܠܟܝ. ܘܐܦ
ܐܚܘܗ̇ ܐܡܪ ܡܛܠ ܚܘܒܟܝ ܣܓܝܐܐ ܕܠܘܬ ܒܥܠܟܝ: ܘܐܦܠܐ[80]
ܡܬܚܦܝܐ ܡܬܚܦܝܬܝ[81] ܀ ܘܥܢܬ ܟܠܬܐ ܘܐܡܪܐ ܠܗ̇. ܫܪܝܪܐܝܬ
ܐܡܝ ܒܚܘܒܐ ܐܢܐ[82] ܣܓܝܐܐ ܘܠܒܪܝ ܡܬܒܥܝܐ ܐܢܐ ܕܐܡܘܐ
ܒܗܢܐ ܚܘܒܐ ܕܐܬܪܓܪܬ[83] ܒܗ ܒܗܢܐ ܠܠܝܐ. ܘܐܘܪܐ ܠܫܢܬܐ ܠܐ
ܡܬܚܫܒܢܐ[84] ܕܐܬܚܙܝ ܠܝ ܒܗܢܐ ܠܠܝܐ. ܘܕܠܐ[85] ܡܬܚܦܝܐ ܐܢܐ
ܡܛܠ ܕܬܚܦܝܬܐ ܕܣܟܠܐ ܡܢܝ ܐܫܬܩܠܬ. ܘܕܠܐ ܒܗܬܬܐ[86] ܐܢܐ.
ܡܛܠ ܕܥܒܕܐ ܕܒܗܬܬܐ ܡܢܝ ܐܬܪܚܩ ܠܗ. ܘܕܠܐ ܡܬܬܘܝܐ
ܐܢܐ. ܡܛܠ ܕܬܘܬ ܢܦܫܐ ܕܡܦܠܐ ܠܢܦܫܝ ܒܝ ܒܬܪܬ. ܘܕܦܨܝܚܐ
ܐܢܐ ܘܚ̇ܕܝܐ ܐܢܐ ܡܛܠ ܕܝܘܡܐ ܕܚܕܘܬܐ ܗܕܐ ܒܟܘܪܬܐ[87]
ܠܐ ܐܫܬܓܫܬ ܒܗ̇. ܘܕܐܬܬܫܝܛ ܠܝ[88] ܟ̇ܒܕܐ ܗܢܐ ܕܝܚܠܐ

ܘܫ̈ܠܠܐ[89] ܕܡܫܬܘܬܦܘܬܐ ܗܕܐ ܕܫ̈ܠܠܐ. ܡܛܠ ܕܠܡܫܬܘܬܦܘܬܐ ܗ̇ܝ
ܕܒ̈ܢܝܐ ܐܙܕܡܢܬ. ܘܕܠܐ ܐܙܕܘܓܬ[90] ܒܗ ܠܒܢ̈ܝܐ ܒܙܘܘܓܐ:
ܕܚܪܬܗ ܬܘܬ ܢܦܫܐ ܗܝ ܡܪܝܪܬܐ. ܡܛܠ ܕܠܒ̈ܢܝܐ ܗ̇ܘ ܕܒ̈ܢܝܐ
ܐܬܚܙܝܬ. ܘܐܦ ܦ̈ܘܠܓܢܘܬܐ ܕܠܗܠܝܢ ܕܩ̈ܕܡ ܐܡ̇ܪܬ ܗܘܬ ܀ ܗ̇ܢܝܢ
ܐܦ ܫܬܢܐ ܚܒ̣ܝܐ ܘܐܡܒ̣ܪ. ܡܘܕܐ ܐܢܐ ܠܟ ܐܠܗܐ ܒܚܕܬܐ:[91] ܕܚܒ̣ܝ
ܐܟܣܢܝܐ ܐܬ̣ܐ ܠܟܐ. ܢ̇ܟܣܝܢ ܐܢܐ ܠܟ ܐܠܗܐ ܕܚܒ̣ܝ ܠܒܪܐ
ܚܒ̣ܪܝܐ ܢ̇ܟܬܪܝ. ܗ̇ܘ ܕܐܪܫܝܡ ܡܢ ܫܚ̇ܠܐ: ܘܙܪ̇ܥ ܒܝ ܚ̈ܝܐ: ܗ̇ܘ

(**69**) 'those whose end is a bitter distress': the resumptive pronoun, /haannon/, refers to all the troubles just mentioned, but not /bnayyaa/. An enclitic subject often slips in as here (ܗܝ): see § 105. (**70**) Read ܒܢ̈ܝܐ with Gk: the proximity of the word to ܗܘܝܢ, mentioned in the preceding note, seems to have led to this error. (**71**) A compound sentence with ܒܢ̈ܝܐ ... ܣܘܓܐܐ 'many of the children' as topic and the rest as comment ('a lot of pain befalls them'). ܣܘܓܐܐ < * ܣܘܓܥܐ: § 6 K. (**72**) The proclitic Dalath here is probably somewhat akin to that which introduces direct speech: 'you would be hoping (asking yourselves) when you could be witnessing ...' (**73**) The diacritical dot indicates /teṯmnon/ 'you will be numbered,' an Ethpe as distinct from an Ethpa, /teṯmannon/ 'you will be appointed.' (**74**) 'those who are admitted to the wedding feast': a Pe ptc. m.pl.st.cst. of √ܥܠܠ 'to enter.' On the st. cst. followed by a prepositional phrase, see § 96 b. (**75**) /ʾaggah/ 'they spent the night,' Af of √ܢܓܗ. (**76**) /qaddem ... mlaa/ 'he set (lit: filled) the table early': on the asyndetic structure, see § 98 g. (**77**) /galyaan/ 'uncovered, exposed,' a Pe pass. ptc. f.pl.abs. of /glee/. (**78**) Very occasionally the preposition Lamadh may replace a st. cst. or a Dalath connection. (**79**) = ܡܬܒ̣ܥܝܐ ܐܢ̄ܬܝ. Similarly the following ܒܗ̄ܬ̈ܬܝ 'you are ashamed.' (**80**) ܘܐܦ = ܐܦ. (**81**) Shorthand for ܡܬܒܥܝܐ ܐܢ̄ܬܝ: see note 79 above. On the syntax of the infinitive, see § 98 j. (**82**) On the intervening enclitic, see § 104 end. (**83**) /ʾargšeṯ/ 'I feel,' a Pf. with the sense of the present tense, common with stative verbs: § 81. The following ܒܗ is proleptic, anticipating ܒܗܢܐ ܠܠܐ: § 112 a. (**84**) 'incorruptible bridegroom,' an Ethpa nomen agentis (ܡܬܚܒ̣ܠܢܐ) used as a plain adjective: § 51. (**85**) 'That I am not veiled is because ...' (**86**) Error for ܒܗܬܬܐ ? (**87**) 'this transient joy': ܥܒ̣ܘܪܬܐ , a Pe nom. agentis functioning as an adjective. See n. 84 above. (**88**) The preposition Lamadh is unlikely to mark the agent of a passive construction, but rather a kind of dative of interest: 'it has become contemptible to me.' (**89**) /šlaalee/ 'troubles, hassles' ? (**90**) /ʾezdawḡeṯ/, Ethpa of √ܙܘܓ (Gr ζυγόν, ζεῦγος), with partial assimilation (§ 6M). (**91**) /ḥaṯṯaa/ < /ḥaḏtaa/: § 6M.

ܕܦܪܩܢܝ ܡܢ ܒܘܗܪܢܐ ܕܡܚܒܠܬ ܗܘܐ ܒܝ ܠܒܠܡ: ܗܘ ܕܢܒܗ ܠܝ
ܢܦܫܗ. ܘܐܬܪܥܝܬ ܒܡܢܐ ܕܐܝܬܝ.[92] ܗܘ ܕܦܨܝܢܝ ܡܢ ܡܫܘܠܬܐ
ܘܠܡܬܬܘܪܬܐ ܫܘܫܛܢܝ. ܗܘ ܕܡܢ ܗܠܝܢ ܕܒܢ̈ܝܢ ܦܪܩܢܝ: ܘܠܗܠܝܢ
ܕܠܐ ܒܢ̈ܝܢ ܐܫܠܡܢܝ. ܗܘ ܕܐܫܬܘܕܥ ܒܕܡܐ ܠܒܢܘܪܬܗ، ܕܝܠܝ:
ܕܠܒܘܪܬܐ ܢܬܟܠܐ.[93] ܗܘ ܕܠܐ ܐܡܢܥ ܪ̈ܚܡܘܗܝ، ܡܢܝ ܕܐܒܝܕ ܗܘܝܬ.
ܐܠܐ ܕܐܚܘܐ ܢܦܫܗ ܣܥܪܢܝ. ܘܕܠܐ ܕܝܠܝ ܡܛܠ ܐܝܬܘܗܝ. ܗܘ ܕܒܪ
ܐܢܐ ܠܐ ܝܕܥ ܗܘܝܬ ܠܗ ܗܘ ܒܚܠܝ. ܗܘ ܕܒܪ ܐܢܐ ܠܐ ܐܬܒܥܝ
ܗܘܝܬ ܒܗ. ܗܘ ܐܫܬܘܕܥ ܠܝ، ܗܘ ܕܗܫܐ ܐܬܪܥܝܬ ܒܗ. ܘܠܐ
ܡܨܐ ܐܢܐ ܕܐܡܪ[94] ܡܕܡ ܕܠܐ ܝܕܥ ܐܢܐ. ܗܘ ܕܐܝܟ ܡܕܡ ܐܡܪ
ܐܢܐ ܒܡܪܚܘܬܐ ܚܠܦܘܗܝ، ܠܐ ܫܐܠܬ. ܡܛܠ ܚܘܒܗ ܗܘ[95] ܡܪܚ
ܡܪܚܢ ܐܢܐ. ܘܒܪ ܗܠܝܢ ܡܢ ܫܘܢܝܐ ܘܡܢ ܚܠܬܐ ܩܠܝܠܐ ܫܒܩ.
ܫܠܘܬܗ، ܩܡ. ܘܠܡܪ̈ܟܒܬܗ، ܐܡܪ ܗܘܐ. ܦܘܩ ܟܠ ܒܡܕܝܢܬܐ
ܚܠܢ. ܘܐܬܪܒܘ ܐܝܬܘ[96] ܠܝ ܠܚܒܪܐ ܗܘ ܢܫܐ: ܕܐܢܐ ܒܥܒܕ،
ܐܚܠܦܗ ܠܢܦܫܗ: ܘܟܠ ܒܪܬܗ، ܒܝܫܬ ܓܕܐ[97] ܐܡܪܬ ܠܗ ܕܢܬܠܐ.
ܚܒܪܐ ܕܢܚܝܘܗܝ ܘܢܝܬܘܢܗܝ، ܠܝ. ܟܠ ܕܢܫܐܠ ܐܬܠ[98] ܠܗ. ܘܐܙܠܘ[99]
ܡܬܒܥܝܢ ܗܘܘ ܒܬܪܗ. ܘܠܐ ܐܫܟܚܘܗܝ، ܡܛܠ ܕܢܦܩ ܗܘܐ ܠܗ.
ܘܐܙܠܘ ܠܦܘܬܐ ܕܬܪܥܐ ܗܘܐ ܒܗ. ܘܐܫܟܚܘܗܝ ܠܗ، ܘܐܡܪܬܐ ܒܪ
ܛܘܒܐ ܘܫܒܚܐ: ܥܠ ܕܠܐ ܕܒܪܗ ܒܚܡ. ܘܒܪ ܐܫܬܘܕܥܘ ܠܗ ܡܕܡ
ܕܗܘܐ. ܚܙܝܬ ܘܐܡܪܐ. ܐܫܟܚܬ ܠܝ ܢܦܫܐ ܗܪܟܐ. ܘܡܫܚܬ ܐܙܠܬ
ܠܘܬ ܗܘܢ ܬܠܡܝ̈ܕܐ. ܘܡܚܕܐ ܢܗܪܐ ܗܘܬ ܘܒܢܝܐ ܗܘܒܠܐ.
ܘܬܠܡܝܕܘ ܐܦ ܠܡܠܟܐ ܐܦ ܗܘܦܟܐ ܕܐܢܫܐ ܒܢܫܘ ܗܘܘ. ܒܪܡܫܐ
ܕܐܫܬܡܥ ܗܘܐ ܛܒܐ ܠܫܠܝܚܐ[100] ܒܗܢܕܘ ܡܕܝܢܬܐ: ܘܐܙܠܘ
ܠܘܬܗ ܘܐܬܟܢܫܘ ܠܘܬܗ.

(**92**) 'I perceived what I am, in what state I am.' (**93**) To be corrected to ܐܬܟܠܐ? (**94**) ܐܡܪ, Pe. Impf. 1sg., complementing the preceding ܡܨܐ /maaṣee/ 'I can.' (**95**) A focusing enclitic: 'it is because of his love that I do venture.' See § 110. (**96**) ܐܝܬܘ /ʾaytaw/ 'Bring,' Af Impv. m.pl. of ܐܬܐ. (**97**) /bišat gaddaa/ 'ill-fortuned': on the st. cst. of adjectives, see § 96 b. (**98**) /ʾettel/ 'I shall give': see § 67. (**99**) On the asyndesis, see § 98 g. (**100**) Most likely a preterital transform of the perfective syntagm ܫܡܝܥ ܠ (§ 84): 'in the end the apostle heard the news in India' rather than 'news was heard of the apostle (being) in the realm of India' (Wright 1871: II 159). On hearing the news Thomas sent for them.

9. Aphraates's sixth demonstration: On monks[1]

ܘ[2] ܩ̇ܠܝܐ ܗܝ ܡܠܬܐ ܗܝ ܕܐܡܪܢܐ. ܘܫܘܝܐ ܗܝ ܠܡܫܡܠܝܘܬܗ.[3]
ܕܢܬܬܥܝܪ[4] ܡܢ ܫܢܬܢ ܒܗܢܐ ܙܒܢܐ. ܘܢܫܩܘܠ ܠܒܢ ܥܡ ܐܝ̈ܕܝܢ ܠܘܬ
ܐܠܗܐ ܠܫܡܝܐ. ܕܠܡܐ ܡܢ ܫܠܝܐ ܢܐܬܐ ܡܪܗ ܕܒܝܬܐ. ܕܡܐ
ܕܐܬܐ ܢܫܟܚܢ ܒܥܝܪܘܬܐ. ܢܛܪ ܘܥܕܢܗ[5] ܕܡܐܬܝܬܐ ܥܬܝܕܐ. ܕܢܥܘܠ
ܥܡܗ ܠܓܢܘܢܗ. ܢܛܥܢ ܡܫܚܐ ܠܠܡ̈ܦܐܕܝܢ. ܕܢܦܘܩ ܠܐܘܪܥܗ
ܒܚܕܘܬܐ. ܢܚܕܪ ܘܩ̈ܕܪܐ ܠܐܘܠܝ. ܠܐܘܪܚܐ ܕܡܦܠܝܢܐ ܘܐܠܝܨܐ.
ܘܢܫܠܚ ܘܢܫܕܐ ܡܢܢ ܟܠܗ̇ ܨܐܘܬܐ. ܕܢܠܒܫ ܢ̈ܚܬܐ ܕܡܫܬܘܬܐ.
ܢܬܬܟܠ ܒܡܗܝܡܢܐ ܕܩܒܠ. ܕܢܬܦܪܐ ܒܬ̈ܪܐ ܒܥܝ̈ܪܐ. ܢܗܘܐ ܐܪ̈ܝܟܐ
ܟܠܘܬܐ. ܕܢܒܢܐ ܐܬܪܐ ܕܒܝܬ ܡܠܟܐ. ܢܒܥܐ ܠܗ ܡܢ ܒܘܠܐ.
ܕܢܫܐ ܠܒܢܐ ܒܐܒܘܗ. ܢܗܘܐ ܡܬܪܚܩܢܐ ܐܝܟ ܕܟܬܝܒ. ܕܢܛܥܢ
ܚܠܦ ܐܠܗܐ. ܢܗܘܐ ܫܠܝܐ ܒܡܢܬ . ܕܢܬܦܪܐ ܐܢ̈ܫܐ ܠܡܫܝܚܐ.
ܢܗܘܐ ܟ̈ܦܢܐ ܠܟܐܢܘܬܐ. ܕܢܣܒܥ ܡܢ ܦܬܘܪ ܡܠܟܘܬܗ. ܢܗܘܐ
ܡܠܝܐ ܕܫܪܪܐ. ܕܠܐ ܢܗܘܐ ܡܟܠܬܐ ܠܣܘܐ. ܢܪܒܐ ܙܪܥܢ ܡܢ
ܟܘ̈ܒܐ. ܕܢܬܠ ܦܐܪ̈ܐ ܚܕ ܒܡܐܐ.[6] ܢܗܘܐ ܒܢܝܢ ܥܠ ܫܘܥܐ. ܕܠܐ
ܢܬܬܙܝܥ ܡܢ ܪܘܚܐ ܘܓ̈ܠܠܐ. ܢܗܘܐ ܡܐ̈ܢܐ ܠܐܝܩܪܐ. ܕܢܬܩܒܠ
ܠܡܪܢ ܠܡܫܡܫܘܬܗ.[7] ܢܒܢܐ ܟܠܗ ܡܢܢ. ܘܢܗܘܐ ܠܗ ܡܪܟܒܬܐ ܕܢܬܒ.
ܢܗܘܐ ܡܫܟܚ ܒܥܡܠܐ. ܕܡܐ ܕܐܙܠ ܢܬܢܝܚ ܘܢܬܒܣܡ.[8] ܢܣܥܘܪ
ܠܡܪܢ ܒܐܣܝ̈ܪܘܗܝ.[9] ܕܢܩܪܝܢ[10] ܘܢܩܝܡܢ ܡܢ ܝܡܝܢܗ.[11] ܢܣܢܐ ܢܦܫܢ[12]

(**1**) Wright 1869 ܩܕ -- ܩܠ: ܬܚܘܝܬܐ ܕܒ̈ܢܝ ܩܝܡܐ. Cf. also Parisot 1894: 239-254. ܒܰܪ ܩܝܳܡܳܐ 'son of covenant,' i.e. covenanted person, monk who has taken a vow to religious life. (**2**) The Waw is the sixth letter of the Syriac alphabet. (**3**) Pa inf. with an object suf. 3f.sg. (**4**) The Dalath introduces a direct speech (§ 98 e, i), following ܐܳܡܰܪܢܳܐ 'I pronounce.' 'so that, when he comes, he will find us vigilant': the initial Dalath introduces a purpose clause with an Impf. (§ 82 end) and ܡܐ ܕ with a Pf. a temporal clause. 'Let us wake up from our sleep,' which is a quotation from Rom 13.11, is also the first of a very long series of exhortations, all Impfs. in the 1st person plural. (**5**) 'the appointed time (of arrival)' with a proleptic suffix. The Waw is no conjunction. (**6**) /ḥad̲ bamā/ 'a hundredfold.' Cf. BA חַד שִׁבְעָה 'sevenfold.' (**7**) Cf. 2Tim 2.21. (**8**) On the syntax, see note 4 above. (**9**) Cf. Mt 25.36. (**10**) 'in order that he would call us.' (**11**) 'at his right-hand side.' (**12**) 'Let us hate ourselves': on the reflexive force of ܢܦܫ-, see § 12 a.

ܘܪܕܦ ܠܡܫܝܚܝܐ. ܐܝܟ ܕܗܘ ܪܕܦ. ܘܐܫܬܠܛ[13] ܥܠ ܐܩ̈ܝܢ.[14] ܢܦܪ
ܠܪܘܚܗ ܕܡܫܝܚܝܐ. ܕܢܦܠ ܡܢܗ ܠܛܥܝܘܬܐ. ܢܗܘܐ ܡܢ ܥܠܡܐ
ܢܘܟܪ̈ܝܐ. ܐܝܟ ܕܡܫܝܚܝܐ ܠܐ ܗܘܐ ܡܢܗ. ܢܗܘܐ ܡܫܡ̈ܫܢܐ
ܘܪ̈ܗܡܣܐ. ܕܢܗܪܬ[15] ܐܪܒܐ ܕܫ̈ܢܝܐ. ܢܗܘܐ ܐܟܣ̈ܢܝܐ ܒܬܫܡܫܬܗ.
ܕܢܫܡܫܘܢ ܒܡܫܡܫܢܐ ܕܦ̈ܘܪܣܐ. ܢܝܠܐ ܠܘܬܗ ܒܕܒܚܘܬܐ. ܕܬܒܥܘܠ[16]
ܦܩܕ ܡܪܐ[17] ܪܒܘܬܐ. ܢܗܘܐ ܫܘܩ̈ܬܐ ܒܫܡܗ. ܕܗܒܝܐ ܐܦ
ܒܡܫܡܫܬܗ ܚܝܐ. ܢܫܘܠ ܪܘܫܡܗ ܥܠ ܦܓܪ̈ܝܢ. ܕܢܬܦܓܪܐ ܡܢ
ܪܘܓܙܐ ܕܐܬܐ. ܕܢܫܠ ܗܘ ܓܒܪ ܡܘܗܐ ܕܐܬܐ ܒܗ.[18] ܘܡܢܘ
ܡܫܟܚ ܡܫܡܫ[19] ܠܗ. ܐܟܘܬ ܗܘ ܘܫܡܡܢ[20] ܪܘܓܙܗ. ܘܡܘܒܕ.
ܠܟܠܗܘܢ ܪ̈ܫܡܐ. ܢܦܩ ܒܪܫ ܦܘܪܬܐ ܕܦܘܪܣܢܐ. ܕܠܐ ܢܟܠܒ
ܘܢܚܒܬ ܒܦܘܪܩܐ. ܢܫܘܦ ܣܦ̈ܪܝܢ ܒܙܪܙܐ. ܕܠܐ ܢܬܚܫܒ ܥ̈ܦܠܐ
ܒܐܓܘܢܐ. ܢܦܘܩ ܘܢܪܕܘܦܘܗܝ، ܠܡܫܝܚܝܐ. ܕܢܬܠܘܫ ܡܢ ܡܫ̈ܬܘܠܐ.
ܢܣܒ ܣܦܪܐ ܠܗܘܦܠ ܒܡܫܐ. ܠܛܘܪܐ ܕܣܪܬܗ ܕܦܪܘܩ. ܢܦܠ
ܡܢ ܡܪܝ ܫܘܠܛܢܐ. ܕܢܒܘܫ ܫܘܬ̈ܦܬܐ ܘܡܦܪ̈ܫܐ. ܢܢܫ ܡܢ
ܬܘܓܪܐ. ܒܗ ܒܠܗ̇ ܫܥܬܐ ܘܡܫܬܐ. ܘܫ̈ܒܝܬܐ[21] ܠܐ ܢܦܩ ܡܢ
ܦܘܡܝ. ܕܡܠܝܢ ܐܢܫܝܢ ܒܗ ܠܐܠܗܐ. ܠܐ ܢܗܘܐ ܠܬ̈ܠܐ. ܕܢܬܦܫܐ
ܡܢ ܠܘܛܬܗ ܕܢܡܘܣܐ. ܢܗܘܐ ܦܬ̈ܠܐ ܒܥܡܪ̈ܐ. ܕܢܬܒܥ ܐܓܪܐ
ܒܗ ܦܕ̈ܢܝܐ. ܢܫܩܘܠ ܡܘܦܪܗ ܕܡܘܗܪܐ. ܕܢܥܒܕ ܐܓܪܐ ܬܪܬܐ.
ܠܐ ܢܗܘܐ ܦܬܠܐ ܦܬ̈ܠܠܐ. ܕܗܐ ܡܢ ܐܓܪ[22] ܠܒܪܡܗ. ܢܬܦܠܓ
ܐܝܟ ܓܦ̈ܘܢܐ ܟܠܗ ܒܪܡܗ. ܕܗܘܘ ܒܪܡܐ ܕܫܪܪܐ. ܢܗܘܐ
ܓܦ̈ܘܢܐ ܓܠܝܬܐ. ܕܠܐ ܢܬܚܡܪ ܡܚܢܗ[23] ܡܢ ܒܪܡܐ. ܢܗܘܐ ܪܫܝܐ
ܒܫܡܝܐ. ܕܢܦܘܫ ܪܫܝ ܠܕܝܕܝ.[24] ܢܗܘܐ ܒܥܠܡܐ ܡܫܒ̈ܚܢܐ.
ܘܢܬܪ ܠܡܗܝ̈ܡܢܐ ܡܢ ܡܘܠܦܢܗ ܕܡܪܝ. ܐܡܪܐ ܠܐ ܢܦܪܐ ܠܝ
ܒܐܪܥܐ.[25] ܕܢܗܘܐ ܫ̈ܢܝܐ ܠܐܒܐ ܕܒܫܡܝܐ. ܒܪ ܡܕܡ ܠܐ ܢܗܘܐ
ܠܝ. ܒܟܠ ܡܕܡ ܐܣܝܪ ܫܠܝ. ܒܪ ܐܢܫ ܠܐ ܡܕܒܪ ܠܝ. ܕܡܠܝ ܡܕ̈ܒܪܝܢ
ܦܓܪ̈ܝܢ.[26] ܚܙܐ ܒܫܡܝ ܒܟܠܒܝ. ܕܚܙܐ ܡܢ ܫܡܝ ܘܦܪܘܩ.
ܢܕܘܢ ܢܦܫܝ ܒܐܝܬ ܘܚܝܒ. ܕܠܐ ܢܬܝ ܢܦ̈ܫܝ ܒܝܬ[27] ܕܢ̈ܫܐ.
ܕܡܬܒܥܝ ܥܠ ܒܘܪ̈ܣܘܬܐ ܘܕܝܠܝ ܥܪ̈ܒܬܐ. ܢܣܒ ܠܝ ܙܝܢܐ
ܠܬܒܬܘܫܐ. ܛܘܡܒܗ ܕܐܘܢܓܠܝܘܢ. ܢܦܘܫ ܒܬܪܥܐ ܕܫܡܝܐ.
ܕܢܬܦܫ ܡܕܡܝ ܘܢܒܘܠ ܒܗ. ܢܐܟܠ ܪ̈ܫܡܐ ܚܣܡܐܝܬ. ܕܢܫܒ
ܒܡܐ ܕܡܬܒܥܐ ܠܝ. ܢܒܥܐ ܡܠܒܘܬܗ ܘܕܡܘܬܗ. ܕܢܦܠ
ܒܐܪܥܐ ܬܘܫܒܚܬܐ. ܢܪܐ ܒܕܠܒܠ[28] ܒܫ̈ܬܐܣܬܐ. ܘܒܫܡܝ ܢܬܗܢܐ.

ܐܬܪ ܕܡܫܝܚܐ ܐܬܬܪܝܡ ܘܐܬܟܠ . ܢܫܒܘܩ ܕܝܢ ܒܠܒܐ ܕܠܐ
ܕܡܠܝ. ܕܢܚܣܢ ܠܐܬܪܐ ܕܐܙܕܡܢ ܠܗ. ܢܛܪ ܥ̈ܝܢܝܢ ܠܡܪܘܡܐ.
ܕܢܚܙܐ ܠܨܡܚܐ ܕܡܬܓܠܐ. ܢܪܝܡ ܓ̈ܦܝܢ ܐܝܟ ܢܫܪ̈ܐ. ܕܢܚܙܝܘܗܝ،
ܠܦܓܪܐ ܒܪ ܕܐܝܬܘܗܝ، ܢܥܬܕ ܩܘܪ̈ܒܢܐ ܠܡܠܟܐ. ܦܐܪ̈ܐ ܓ̈ܒܝܐ.
ܨܘܡܐ ܘܨܠܘܬܐ. ܢܛܪ[29] ܒܕܟܝܘ ܪܗܒܘܢܗ. ܕܢܗܡܝܢ ܟܠ ܟܠܗ
ܒܝܬ ܟܠܗ. ܐܝܟܢܐ ܓܒܪ ܕܡܙܕܠܠ ܒܪܗܒܘܢܗ. ܠܐ ܫܒܩܝܢ ܠܗ
ܠܡܥܠ[30] ܠܒܝܬ ܓܢܐ. ܢܙܗܪ ܒܦܓܪܗ ܕܡܫܝܚܐ. ܕܢܩܘܡܘܢ ܦܓ̈ܪܝܢ
ܒܟܠ ܥܕܢ. ܢܨܘܬ ܩܠܗ ܕܚܬܢܐ ܕܢܥܘܠ ܥܡܗ ܠܓܢܘܢܐ. ܢܥܬܕ
ܪܘܡܢܐ ܠܗܠܘܠܗ ܘܢܦܘܩ ܠܐܘܪܥܗ ܒܚܕܘܬܐ. ܢܠܒܫ ܠܒܘܫܐ
ܩܕܝܫܐ ܘܢܗܘܐ ܡܣܬܡܟܐ ܒܪܝܫ ܓ̈ܒܝܐ.[31] ܡܢ ܕܠܐ ܠܒܫ[32] ܠܒܘܫܐ
ܕܡܫܬܘܬܐ ܡܦܩܝܢ ܠܗ ܠܚܫܘܟܐ ܒܪܝܐ. ܡܢ ܕܡܫܬܐܠ ܡܢ
ܡܫܬܘܬܐ ܠܐ ܛܥܡ ܠܗ ܠܡܫܬܘܬܐ. ܡܢ ܕܙܒܢ ܩܘܪ̈ܝܐ[33]

(**13**) An Ethpe, which is in this case an *Eth*- form of Afel: § 49. The meaning is possibly reflexive, 'he gave himself up,' rather than passive 'he was delivered up, betrayed.' Cf. Eph 5..2, which is alluded to here: "just as Christ also loved us (ܐܚܒܢ) and gave himself up for our sake (ܐܫܠܡ ܢܦܫܗ ܚܠܦ ܐܦ̈ܝܢ)." (**14**) /ʿal ʾappayin/ 'for our sake.' (**15**) /nawrt̲an/ 'he would allow us to inherit': Af Impf. of ܝܪܬ. (**16**) /teʿʿol/, Pe of √ܥܠܠ . The subject is ܨܠܘܬܗ 'his prayer,' i.e. 'directed to him.' (**17**) ܦܐܪ, st. cst. of ܦܐܪ̈ܐ (historically of ܦܐܪ̈ܐ). (**18**) 'the day on which it [= the wrath] comes.' (**19**) Verb complementation by means of a participle: § 98 d. (**20**) /ʾakt̲aanu wḥammim/ 'vehement and intense.' (**21**) /ṣuḥyaat̲aa/, pl. of ܨܘܚܝܬܐ 'malediction.' (**22**) /ʾağran/ 'he hired us.' (**23**) Proleptic, anticipating the following ܒܪܡܐ ܡܢ (§ 112 a). (**24**) 'so that our fragrance would waft to those around us': prep. ܠ + independent relative pronoun ܕ + prep. ܚܕܪ. 'around': on the form, cf. § 46. (**25**) 'Let us call (nobody) father for ourselves, i.e. our father, on earth.' Cf. Mt 23.9. (**26**) 'those who know us are many': ܕܝܠܢ 'our' is emphatic and coterminous with the suffix of ܝܕ̈ܘܥܝܢ 'those who know us,' a Pe nomen actionis. (**27**) 'amongst,' a preposition. (**28**) 'Let us think of that which is above.' (**29**) ܢܛܪ /neṭṭar/, Pe Impf. 1pl. of √ܢܛܪ. (**30**) ܠܡܥܠ 'to enter,' Pe Inf. of √ܥܠܠ. (**31**) 'at the head of the chosen (guests)': ܓ̈ܒܝܐ /gvayyaa/, Pe Ptc. pass. pl. of √ܓܒܐ. (**32**) Here begins a long series of generalising pronouncements introduced by ܡܢ ܕ, 'he who ...' A compound sentence: § 113. (**33**) Irregular pl. of ܩܪܝܬܐ 'village.'

ܘܐܬܓܘܪܬܐ ܡܬܓܠܠ ܠܗ ܡܢ ܡܕܝܢܬܐ ܕܦܪ̈ܝܫܐ. ܡܢ ܕܠܐ ܡܗܒ
ܦܐܪ̈ܐ ܒܓܘ ܒܪܡܐ. ܡܬܒܩܪ ܘܡܫܬܕܪܐ ܠܬܫܢܝܩܐ. ܡܢ ܕܫܩܠ
ܚܣܦܐ ܡܢ ܡܪܗ. ܢܦܠܐ[34] ܠܡܘܗܒܗ ܒܡܘܬܪܢܗ. ܡܢ ܕܚܙܐ
ܕܢܘܗܪܐ ܬܓܪܐ. ܢܒܥ ܠܗ ܦܪܘܬܐ ܘܦܘܫܩܬܐ ܕܒܓܘܗ. ܡܢ
ܕܡܫܠ ܙܪܥܐ ܠܛܒܐ. ܢܒܥܐ ܐܪܥܗ ܡܢ ܒܢ̈ܝܐ. ܡܢ ܕܚܙܐ
ܕܢܘܗܪܐ ܙܥܪܐ. ܢܫܒܐ ܡܙܝܕܬܗ ܒܟܠ ܒܢ̈ܝ. ܡܢ ܕܡܬܪܒܐ
ܒܐܬܠܦܠܦܬܐ. ܡܢ ܒܠܒܐ ܢܓܪ ܢܦܫܗ. ܡܢ ܕܚܙܐ ܕܢܫܒ ܒܠܝܠܐ
ܢܗܓ ܒܐܓܘܢܐ ܐܝܟ ܢܚܘܫܐ. ܡܢ ܕܚܙܐ ܕܢܦܠ[35] ܒܐܘܦܢܝܐ
ܕܢܬܒܥ. ܢܗܘܐ ܥܠܦ ܠܡܦܠ ܒܟܠ ܕܪܗ. ܡܢ ܕܚܙܐ ܕܢܦܠ[36]
ܒܡܪܒܐ. ܢܫܒ ܠܗ ܙܢܝܐ ܕܢܬܒܥ. ܢܗܘܐ ܡܪܗ ܠܗ ܒܒܠܒ̈ܢ.[37]
ܡܢ ܕܫܩܠ ܕܡܘܬܐ ܕܬ̈ܠܐܒܐ. ܡܢ[38] ܟ̈ܠ ܐܢܫܐ ܢܗܘܐ ܢܘܟܪܝܐ.
ܡܢ ܕܢܫܒ ܢܡܪܐ ܕܦ̈ܪܝܫܐ. ܡܫܒܐ ܘܡܬܠܬܐ[39] ܢܚܘܫ ܡܢܗ. ܡܢ
ܕܢܦܫ ܒܒܐ ܕܢܡܪܐ. ܡܠܝܢ ܒܠܒܐ ܢܚܘܫ ܡܢܗ. ܡܢ ܕܐܚܕ ܒܡܬܐ
ܕܒܫܡܡܐ.[40] ܒܒܝܢ ܛܝܢܐ ܕܢܦܠ ܠܐ ܢܟܠ. ܡܢ ܕܡܣܒܐ
ܕܢܬܫܠܦ ܒܒ̈ܢܝܐ. ܙܒܘܢܐ ܡܙ̈ܢܬܐ ܠܐ ܢܒܙ ܠܗ. ܡܢ ܕܡܣܒܐ
ܠܡܫܬܘܬܐ ܕܫܬܝܐ. ܡܫܬܘܬܗ ܕܙܒܢܝܐ[41] ܠܐ ܢܐܫܦ. ܡܢ ܕܚܙܐ
ܕܢܬܒܣܡ ܒܡܫܬܘܬܐ ܢܦܓܪܐ.[42] ܢܥܫ ܡܢܗ ܪܘܓܙܬܐ. ܡܢ ܕܐܡܪ
ܢܦܫܗ ܠܫܡܫܘܬܐ. ܠܐ ܢܫܬܐܠ ܘܢܗܘܐ ܛܥܝܢܐ. ܡܢ ܕܢܦܠ ܒܗ
ܙܪܥܐ ܠܛܒܐ.[43] ܠܐ ܢܥܒܘܕ ܠܒܝܫܐ ܠܡܪܕ ܒܗ ܙ̈ܢܝܐ. ܡܢ ܕܫܪܝ
ܠܡܒܢܐ ܡܓܕܠܐ. ܚܫܘܒ ܐܢܫ[44] ܠܒܠܗܝܢ ܢܦ̈ܩܬܗ. ܡܢ ܕܒ̇ܢܐ
ܗ̇ܠܐ[45] ܠܗ ܠܡܓܒܪ. ܕܠܐ ܢܗܘܐ ܓܘܫܒܐ ܠܒܢ̈ܝ ܐܘܪܚܐ. ܡܢ
ܕܡܐܡܪ ܒܢܝܢܗ ܒܠ ܫܘܒܐ. ܢܒܢܘ ܫܬܐܣܘ̈ܗܝ . ܕܠܐ ܢܦܠ ܡܢ
ܓ̈ܠܠܐ. ܡܢ ܕܚܙܐ ܠܡܒܢܝܘ ܡܢ ܫܘܒܐ. ܢܗܠܟ ܒܗ ܐܝܬ ܠܗ
ܢܗܘܪܐ. ܡܢ ܕܕܚܠ ܕܠܐ ܢܒܢܘܢ ܒܫܘܬܐ[46] ܡܢ ܩܠܝܠ ܢܒܥܬ.
ܢܦܫܗ. ܡܢ ܕܠܒܫܐ ܡܣܒܐ ܠܟܒܠ. ܢܓܡܪ ܠܗ ܠܫܘܒܬܐ ܢܦ̈ܩܬܗ.
ܡܢ ܕܚ̇ܒܐ ܡܢ ܡܪܗ ܫܘܒܩܢܐ. ܢܥܒܘܕ ܐܦ ܗܘ ܠܚܒܪܗ. ܡܢ
ܕܠܐ ܬܟܒ ܡܟܐ ܕܢܒ̈ܝܢ. ܪܒܘ ܒܒ̈ܢܝܢ ܫܒܘ ܠܗ ܡܪܗ. ܡܢ ܕܪܗܒܐ
ܒܫܦ ܡܪܗ ܒܠ ܦܬܘܪܐ[47] ܠܐ ܡܬܡܪܐ ܒܒܪܐ ܒܡܫܐ. ܡܢ ܕܪܫܡ
ܡܒܡܒܬܗ ܗܘܐ[48] ܪܘܬܐ ܒܐܪܒܐ ܕܢ̈ܫܐ. ܡܢ ܕܚܙܐ ܕܢܒܒܪ
ܫܠܡܐ ܗ̇ܘܐ ܡܢ ܒܢ̈ܫܐ ܕܐܠܗܐ.[49] ܡܢ ܕܡܕܪ ܙܒܢ ܡܪܗ ܢܒܒܪ
ܙܒܢܝܗ ܕܠܐ ܢܒܠܥ ܗܘܢ. ܡܢ ܕܡܒܪܐ ܠܗ ܡܢ ܢܒܠܐ. ܠܡܠܟܐ
ܒܡܦܪܗ ܢܗܘܝܢ ܒܢ̈ܝܗ̇ . ܡܢ ܕܡܫܒܠ ܪܘܚܗ ܕܡܫܝܚܐ. ܢܙܒܬ

ܒܪ ܐܢܫܗ ܓܘܝܐ. ܡܢ ܕܐܬܩܪܝ ܗܝܟܠܗ ܕܐܠܗܐ. ܢܕܟܐ ܦܓܪܗ
ܡܢ ܟܘܠܗ̇ ܛܢܦܘܬܐ. ܡܢ ܕܡܚܝܣ ܠܪܘܚܗ ܕܡܫܝܚܐ. ܡܢ ܒܥ̈ܘܬܐ
ܠܐ ܡܪܝܡ ܪܫܗ. ܡܢ ܕܢܦܠ ܦܓܪܗ ܕܡܫܝܚܐ. ܢܛܪ ܦܓܪܗ ܡܢ
ܟܠܗ̇ ܛܢܦܘܬܐ. ܡܢ ܕܫܠܚ ܠܒܪ ܐܢܫܐ ܥܬܝܩܐ. ܬܘܒ ܠܐ
ܢܗܦܘܟ ܠܥܒ̈ܕܬܗ ܩܕ̈ܡܝܬܐ. ܡܢ ܕܠܒܫ ܠܒܪܢܫܐ ܚܕܬܐ. ܢܛܪ
ܢܦܫܗ ܡܢ ܟܘܠܗ̇ ܓܐܘܬܐ. ܡܢ ܕܠܒܫ ܙܝܢܐ ܡܢ ܫ̈ܡܝܐ. ܠܐ
ܢܫܠܘܚ ܙܝܢܗ ܕܠܐ ܢܬܚܝܒ ܠܗ.[50] ܡܢ ܕܫܩܠ ܩܪܒܐ ܠܘܩܒܠ ܒܝܫܐ.
ܢܛܪ ܢܦܫܗ ܡܢ ܓܐܪ̈ܐ ܕܒܝܫܐ ܒܗ. ܡܢ ܕܡܬܡܛܠܒܐ ܠܗ.[51] ܠܐ
ܓܒܐ ܒܗ ܡܪܗ. ܡܢ ܕܪܢܐ ܒܢܡܘܣܐ ܕܡܪܗ. ܒܡܪ̈ܢܝܬܐ ܕܒܠܒܐ.
ܗܢܐ ܠܐ ܢܬܕܘܕ.. ܡܢ ܕܡܬܗܓܐ ܒܢܡܘܣܐ ܕܡܪܗ. ܠܐܝܠܢܐ
ܡܬܕܡܐ ܕܢܨܝܒ ܥܠ ܡܝ̈ܐ. ܡܢ ܕܬܘܟܠܢܗ ܗܘܐ ܥܠ ܡܪܗ.

(**34**) *Pace* Parisot 1894:248 the verb is better taken as Pa, not Af, cf. 1Kg 20.34 Peshitta. See also Text 11, n. 14a. (**35**) /neppel/, Pe Impf. 3ms. of √ܢܦܠ, here in the sense of 'to descend.' (**36**) On the meaning of the verb, see the preceding note. (**37**) The habitual aspect of the syntagm <ܗܘܐ + Ptc> (§ 86) is reinforced by ܒܟܠܥܕܳܢ /bk̲olᶜeddaan/ 'at all times.' (**38**) The preposition hints at the underlying passive structure: 'he will be treated by people as alien.' Cf. Gk πάσχειν ὑπὸ 'to suffer at the hands of' as at Isocrates 3.61 ἃ πάσχοντες ὑφ᾽ ἑτέρων ὀργίζεσθε, ταῦτα τοὺς ἄλλους μὴ ποιεῖτε 'that which you get done by others and makes you angry, do not do that to others.' (**39**) /masvaa wmatlaa/, lit. 'taking and giving,' i.e. commercial negotiation, business transaction. Cf. Heb. מַשָּׂא וּמַתָּן. (**40**) On the attributive prepositoinal phrase introduced by ܕ, see § 91 h, 3. (**41**) 'his temporal banquet': the suffix is hardly proleptic. (**42**) /maštyaa nṭiraa/ 'preserved, i.e. good-quality drink.' Cf. Is 25.6. (**43**) Cf. Mt 13.8 where a certain group of audience of the divine teaching is compared to good soil. (**44**) A proleptic object pronoun: § 112 c. (**45**) /waale/ 'it is fitting for him, he ought to.' (**46**) Cf. Mt 24.20: "Pray that your flight may not be in winter ..." (**47**) 'the table (of moneychanger, banker)': cf. Mt 25.27. (**48**) Ptc. with the force of the future: see § 83. (**49**) 'will beocme (one) of the children of God.' (**50**) The verb is probably impersonal (§ 79), and the preposition is that of disadvantage: 'in order that it may not be defeated to him,' i.e. 'he may not be defeated.' (**51**) ܐܶܬܡܰܛܠܒܰܬ ܠܶܗ 'he was tired, disheartened,' Ethpa 3f.s. used impersonally. The relative clause beginning with /man/ is in casus pendens, resumed by the suffix pronoun of ܒܗ: see § 113.

ܠܐܠܝܢܐ ܬܘܒ ܕܡܟܐ. ܕܡܣܒܪܪ ܥܠ ܡܥܠܐ. ܗܢܘܢ ܕܡܬܬܟܠ ܥܠ ܒܪ ܐܢܫܐ. ܡܩܒܠ ܠܗܘܢ[52] ܠܠܘ̈ܛܬܗ ܕܐܪܡܝܐ.[53] ܗܢܘܢ ܕܐܙܕܡܢ ܠܚܬܢܐ.[54] ܢܚܬܪ ܢܦܫܗ. ܗܢܘܢ ܕܐܢܫܪ ܫܪܟܗ. ܠܐ ܢܫܡܥܘܢܝܗܝ ܕܢܕܚܘܢ. ܗܢܘܢ ܕܡܫܡܥܐ ܠܡܠܬܐ. ܢܫܒ ܠܗ ܡܫܝܚܐ ܒܡܐܢܗ. ܗܢܘܢ ܕܢܛܪ ܬܪܥܐ ܢܫܡܥ ܠܒܪܗ. ܗܢܘܢ ܕܪܚܡ ܒܬܘܠܘܬܐ. ܢܬܕܡܐ ܠܐܠܝܐ. ܗܢܘܢ ܕܫܦܠ ܢܦܫܐ ܕܡܕܒܪ̈ܐ. ܢܬܒ ܘܢܫܬܘܘܢ ܠܗ. ܗܢܘܢ ܕܪܚܡ ܫܠܝܐ ܢܫܡܥ ܠܒܪܗ ܠܫܒܪܐ ܕܫܢ̈ܝܐ.

(**52**) The preposition, which is proleptic, marks the direct object: see § 112 c. (**53**) Cf. Jer 17.5 "Cursed are those who trust in mere mortals." (**54**) 'one who has been proposed to become bridegroom' (?).

10. Ephrem's commentary on Genesis 22[1]

. [1] ܢܣܝ ܬܘܒ ܐܠܗܐ ܠܐܒܪܗܡ ܘܐܡܪ ܠܗ. ܕܕܒܪ[2] ܠܒܪܟ
ܘܙܠ ܠܐܬܪܐ ܕܐܡܘܪ̈ܝܐ. ܘܐܣܩܝܗܝ ܥܠܬܐ[3] ܥܠ ܚܕ ܡܢ ܛܘܪ̈ܐ
ܕܐܡ̇ܪ ܠܟ. ܕܠܐ ܕܝܢ ܢܐܡܪܘܢ[4] ܕܡܬܘܗܘ ܐܬܘܗܘܗܝ:[5] ܐܘܪܟܢ ܠܗ
ܬܠܬܐ ܝܘܡ̈ܝܢ܀ ܘܩܕܡ ܐܒܪܗܡ ܘܨܠܚ ܩ̈ܝܣܐ. ܘܕܒܪ ܠܬܪ̈ܝܢ
ܥܠܝ̈ܡܘܗܝ ܘܠܐܝܣܚܩ ܘܐܙܠ. ܠܛܘܪܐ ܕܝܢ ܕܠܐ ܓܠܐ. ܡܛܠ ܕܐܦ
ܠܐ ܐܬܦܢܝ ܕܢܓܠܐ ܗܘܐ.[6] ܒܪܡ ܐܦ ܡܦܣܝܐ ܗܘܬ ܠܗ ܕܬܐܙܠ
ܘܬܫܬܘܬܦ ܒܕܒܚܬܗ̇. ܐܝܟܢܐ ܕܫܘܬܦܗ̇ ܒܡܘܠܟܢܐ ܕܝܠܗ. ܘܕܠܐ
ܬܘܒ ܢܥܘܩܘܢ ܠܗܘܢ ܥܠܘܗܝ، ܒܥܒ̈ܕܐ، ܒܡܠܬܗ. ܘܢܛܠܩܘܢ ܠܗܝܢ
ܬ̈ܠܠܝܬܐ ܒܡܫܒܚܬܗ. ܘܢܬܒܥܘܢ ܒܥܒ̈ܕܐ، ܐܬܪܐ. ܘܢܒܕܘܢܝܗܝ
ܠܛܠܝܐ ܡܢܗ. ܐܘ ܢܬܗܘܢܘܢ ܒܗ ܡܘܡܐ ܕܕܒܚܐ. ܐܝ ܟܡܐ
ܐܦܠܐ ܠܬܪ̈ܝܢ ܕܕܒܪ ܥܡܗ ܐܦܣ ܠܛܘܪܐ ܡܛܠ ܕܕܚܠ. ܟܕ
ܩܛܠܐ ܒܥܕܢܐ ܕܚܠ ܗܘܐ.[7] ܗܘ ܕܠܬܪ̈ܝܢ ܡܛܠ ܡܢܬܗ ܠܐ
ܐܪܓܫ ܕܢܓܠܐ ܗܘܐ܀
[2] ܟܕ ܡܬܬܠܝܢ ܕܝܢ ܫܐܠ ܐܝܣܚܩ ܥܠ ܕܒܚܐ. ܘܐܬܢܒܝ ܐܦ
ܒܡܫܐܠܬܗ ܕܛܠܝܐ. ܐܝܟ ܕܐܬܢܒܝ ܠܥ̈ܒܕܐ ܕܢܗܦܘܟ ܒܗܦܘܟ
ܛܠܝܐ. ܟܕ ܦܬܪܗ ܕܝܢ ܠܐܝܣܚܩ ܘܣܡܗ ܥܠ ܥܠܬܐ ܘܢܣܒ
ܥܠܘܗܝ، ܣܟܝܢܐ. ܘܥܠܘܗܝ، ܡܠܐܟܗ ܕܡܪܝܐ. ܕܠܐ ܢܣܒ ܠܗ
ܐܒܪܗܡ ܕܒܪܗ ܩܪܝܒ ܘܐܫܠܡܗ ܠܩܘܪܒܢܗ. ܐܡܪ ܠܗ. ܕܗܫܐ

ܐܘܕܥܬ[8] ܕܕܚܠܗ ܐܢܬ ܕܐܠܗܐ. ܒܗܢܐ ܓܝܪ ܕܚܣܟܬ ܠܝ ܒܪܟ ܟܠ:
ܐܬܒܕܪ ܣܘܥܟ ܕܝ̈ܢ ܡܪܐ ܟܠ܀

ܒܬܪ̈ܬܝܢ[9] ܗܟܝܠ ܐܬܢܨܚ ܐܒܪܗܡ. ܕܦܠܓ ܠܒܪܗ ܐܦ ܟܕ ܠܐ ܦܠܓܗ. ܘܕܗܝܡܢ ܕܒܝ ܒܬܪ ܕܡܐܬ ܡܬܚܝܐ ܘܒܒܗ ܢܝܚ ܗܘܐ܀ ܫܪܝܪܐ ܗܘܬ ܠܗ ܓܝܪ ܕܠܐ ܡܕܓܠ ܗܘ̇ ܕܐܡܪ ܠܗ. ܕܒܐܝܣܚܩ ܬܬܚܙܐ ܠܟ ܐܡܪܐ܀

[3] ܚܙܐ ܕܝܢ ܐܒܪܗܡ ܕܒܪܐ ܒܐܝܠܢܐ. ܘܢܣܒ ܘܐܣܩܗ ܥܠܬܐ ܚܠܦ ܒܪܗ. ܕܠܝܬ ܗܘܐ ܕܝܢ ܬܡܢ ܕܒܪܐ.[10] ܫܘܐܠܗ ܕܐܝܣܚܩ ܕܠܐܡܪܐ[11] ܣܗܕ. ܘܕܠܝܬ ܗܘܐ ܬܡܢ ܐܝܠܢܐ. ܘܩܝ̈ܣܐ ܕܥܠ ܟܬܦܗ ܕܐܝܣܚܩ ܡܫܬܥܝܢ. ܛܘܪܐ ܓܙܐ ܠܐܝܠܢܐ. ܘܐܝܠܢܐ ܠܕܒܪܐ. ܕܒܕܒܪܐ[12] ܕܒܐܝܠܢܐ ܬܠܐ[13] ܗܘܐ. ܘܠܕܒܚܐ ܚܠܦ ܒܪ ܐܒܪܗܡ ܗܘ̣ܐ[13a] ܗܘܐ ܢܬܬܟܪ ܗܘ̣ܐ ܒܝܘܡܗ. ܗܘ̇[14] ܕܟܠ ܩܘܡܐ ܐܡܝܢ ܕܒܪܐ ܡܬܬܠܐ ܗܘܐ. ܘܒܡܘܬܐ ܚܠܦ ܥܠܡܐ ܟܠܗ ܛܥܡ ܗܘܐ܀

---

1) Tonneau 1955: 83f. (Syr. text); 69f. (Lat. tr.). Cf. Brock 1981, and Janson and Van Rompay 1993: 121-23. (**2**) The conjunction Dalath introduces direct speech: § 98 e, i. (**3**) 'Offer him (as) an offering ...,' an object complement (§ 98 f). The Peshitta reads: ܠܥܠܬܐ. (**4**) The purpose clause introduced by a Dalath precedes the main clause with ܐܘܪܟ /ʾawreḵ/. (**5**) 'he had greatly alarmed him': the Af infinitive functions as an internal object (§ 98 j). (**6**) On the compound tense, see § 88. (**7**) 'how much would he have dreaded?': on the use of the compound tense in an apodosis of a conditional clause, see § 86. (**8**) On the implications of this remarkable translation, whether 1st or 2nd person, of the Hebrew text (יָדַעְתִּי 'I know, have learned'), see Brock 1981:5f. (**9**) 'in two ways.' (**10**) 'that there was, however, no ramb there': a noun clause serving as direct object of ܣܗܕ 'testifies.' Likewise the following ܕܠܝܬ ܗܘܐ ܬܡܢ ܐܝܠܢܐ. (**11**) 'Isaac's question concerning lamb': on the prepositional phrase introduced by the conjunction Dalath, see § 91 h, 3. (**12**) The conjunction Dalath introduces a purpose clause with ܢܬܬܟܪ ܗܘܐ as its verb: on the compound tense, see § 88. The ܗܘܐ *before* ܢܬܬܟܪ appears to be redundant, unless one has to do with a compound tense, /hwaa waa/. ܠܕܒܚܐ ... ܐܒܪܗܡ ܗܘܐ is the second of two nominal clauses which constitute the relative clause with ܕܒܪܐ of ܕܒܕܒܪܐ as its antecedent: '... and served as a sacrifice instead of ...' (**13**) ܬܠܐ, a Pe passive Ptc. (**13a**) ܗܘܐ -ܠ 'to become (something).' (**14**) One expects ܕܗܘ̇ /dhaw/, 'his day, i.e. of one who ...'

ܘܐܡܰܪ ܠܗ ܕܬܰܪ̈ܬܶܝܢ ܙܒ̈ܢܝܢ.[15] ܕܒܝ ܝܡܝܬ ܐܡܰܪ ܐܠܗܐ.
ܕܡܫܠܡܘ ܐܫܠܡܬ[16] ܠܒܪܟ. ܘܢܬܒܪܟܘܢ ܒܙܪܥܟ ܕܐܬܝܘܗܝ
ܡܫܝܚܐ. ܟܠܗܘܢ ܥܡ̈ܡܐ ܕܐܪܥܐ܀

(**15**) Lit. 'of two times,' i.e. 'for a second time,' though not that the angel repeated the same message, but that it was his second address to the patriarch.
(**16**) On the syntax with the infinitive, see § 98 j.

11. Jacob of Serugh on the Apostle Thomas[1]

ܐܡܰܪ[2] ܣܒܢ ܠܐ ܡܗܝܡܢ ܐܢܐ ܡܛܠ ܦܬ̈ܓܡܐ:
ܒܡܐ ܕܡܗܝܡܢ[3] ܐܢܬ ܗܒ ܠܝ ܒܡܫܐ ܘܐܫܠܡ ܒܒܪܐ܀
ܐܝܟ ܗܢ ܗܘ ܠܐ ܐܢܫ ܡܗܝܡܢ ܫܡܥܬ[4] ܦܬ̈ܓܡܘܗܝ :
ܠܐ ܓܝܪ ܐܝܬ ܠܗ ܦܬ̈ܓܡܐ ܠܒܒܪܐ ܕܠܒܫ[5] ܘܡܫܬܐ܀
ܫܦܝܪܐ ܢܬܘܒ ܘܒܚܡܐ ܕܢܿܓܡܬ[6] ܗܒ ܠܝ ܦܬ̈ܓܡܐ:
ܒܒܪ ܒܪܓܠܫܐ ܘܗܒ ܠܝ ܕܗܘܐ ܒܡܐ ܕܢܚܫ ܠܝ܀
ܡܛܠ ܕܢܬܟܬܒ ܗܿܘ ܕܟܬܒ ܗܘܐ ܠܘ̈ܚܐ ܠܡܘܫܐ:
ܘܠܒܬܪ ܦܢܝܐ ܗܿܝ ܡܫܝܚܐ ܕܬܬܠܬ ܦܓܪ̈ܐ܀
ܫܡܗ[7] ܢܦܫܗ ܒܪ ܢܓܪܐ ܡܪܐ ܒܪܝܬܐ:
ܘܕܢܓܪܐ ܗܘ ܐܟܘܬ ܬܡܢ ܒܪ ܒܠܗܐ܀
ܒܦܓܪܢܘܬܗ ܐܡܪ، ܬܡܢ ܒܪ ܐܠܗܐ:
ܘܠܫܡܐ ܕܫܘܠ ܡܢ ܒܝܬ ܕܘܝܕ ܐܟܘܬ ܠܘܩܕܡ܀
ܠܐ ܟܬܒ ܬܡܢ ܕܐܢܐ ܝܫܘܥ ܒܪ ܐܠܗܐ:
ܐܠܐ ܝܫܘܥ ܘܒܪܗ ܕܝܘܣܦ ܘܕܡܢ ܢܨܪܬ܀
ܐܢܐ ܝܫܘܥ ܘܒܪܗ ܕܝܘܣܦ ܒܪ ܢܓܪܐ:
ܗܐ ܡܘܕܐ ܐܢܐ ܕܡܪܝ ܐܢܐ ܒܡܫܐ ܠܬܐܘܡܐ܀
ܘܒܡܬܪ̈ܬܐ ܢܗܒ ܐܢܐ ܠܗ ܒܒܪܐ ܠܝܕܝ:
ܘܡܪܝ ܐܢܐ ܘܡܫܠܡ ܐܢܐ ܠܗ ܢܡܘܣܐܬ܀
ܐܢܐ[8] ܢܓܪܐ ܘܒܪ ܢܓܪܐ ܘܪܫ ܢܓܪ̈ܐ:
ܘܚܝܠܬ[9] ܒܒܪܐ ܠܢܓܪܘܬܐ ܠܓܘܪܦ ܡܠܟܐ܀
ܐܢܐ ܟܬܒ ܐܢܐ ܘܡܪܝ ܐܢܐ ܐܦ ܡܣܗܕ ܐܢܐ:
ܕܒܒܪܐ ܗܘ ܬܐܘܡܐ ܘܡܗܝܡܢܘܬܐ ܢܗܪ ܠܟܐ ܗܘ܀
ܠܓܘܪܦ[10] ܦܠܐ ܘܣܡ ܙܢ ܘܐܢܐ ܡܙܝܢ:
ܒܒܪܐ ܦܠܐ ܕܠܒܘ̈ܒܗ، ܢܣܒ ܒܢܝ܀

ܢܡܘܣܐܝܬ ܙܒܢ ܘܙܒ̇ܢ ܗ̇ܘ ܡܫܝܚܐ:
ܕܣܡ ܢܡܘܣܐ ܬܐܘܡܐ ܠܡܪܗ ܘܠܐ ܟܦܪ ܠܗ܀
ܝܗܒ ܒܪܓܡܐ ܘܥܡܠ ܦܓ̈ܪܐ ܘܐܫܬܥܒܕ ܒܒܥܝܐ:
ܘܫܘܐ ܬܐܘܡܐ ܦܓ̈ܪܐ ܙܒܢܘܗܝ ܘܥܒܕ ܒܥܝܬ ܠܗ܀
ܚܐ ܕܒܥܬ ܠܗ̇ ܬܘܒ، ܘܥܡܠ ܡܢ ܦܓ̈ܪܘܗܝ :
ܘܡܫܟܠ ܕܙܒܢܘܗܝ ܐܝܟ ܒܪ ܪܚܝܠ[11] ܒܪ ܐܘܪܚܐ܀
ܙܒ ܒܥܠܬܘܢܐ ܘܡܚܐ ܘܐܡܚܪ ܠܚܘ̈ܒܬܗ:
ܘܡܚܐ ܡܢܗܘܢ ܕܢܒܥܘܢ ܒܠܗܘܢ ܡܢ ܦܘܪܩ܀
ܐܢܫ ܠܐ ܘܡܚܐ ܕܡܚܐ ܒܠ ܐܢܫܝܢ:
ܕܗܐ ܡܙܒܢ[12] ܐܢܐ ܥܒܕܐ ܠܫܝܢ ܘܬܘܒ ܠܡܪ̈ܝ܀
ܐܝܟ ܕܠܡܪܝܐ[12a] ܗܘ ܦܪܥ ܐܢܐ ܡܢ ܙܒܢܝܢ:
ܠܐ ܬܬܒܥܘܢ ܐܝܟ ܕܠܡܚܝܬܐ[12a] ܕܒܥܐ ܙܒܢܗ[13]܀
ܐܝܟ ܐܕܕܝܥܠܐ ܗܘ ܢܫܬ ܐܢܐ ܠܐܬܪܐ ܒܡܪܐ:
ܙܠܘ ܕܐܒܥܢܐ ܒܐܬܪܐ ܒܪ̈ܘܚܐ ܠܚܠܒܐ ܕܗܢܘ܀
ܐܬܚܫܒܘ ܒܗܝ ܕܠܐ ܢܘܒ ܒܢܝܢ ܡܢ ܡܫܝ̈ܚܠܐ:
ܘܠܐ ܢܒܘܢܗܝ ܬܠܠܐ ܥܒ̈ܕܝܐ ܕܡܢ ܙܪ̈ܘܦܐ܀
ܐܝܟ ܡܠܝܢܐ ܗܘ ܢܫܬ ܐܢܐ ܠܐܬܪܐ ܕܗܢܘ:
ܙܠܘ ܕܐܠܦܐ ܠܐ ܬܬܠܒܝ[13a] ܒܡܢܬ ܬ̈ܠܠܐ܀
ܥܒܕܘܢ ܪܥܐ ܘܪܒ ܬ̈ܠܠܢܐ[14] ܒܗܝ ܒܠ ܬܐܘܡܐ:
ܘܐܚܘܗܝ ܒܚܝܢ ܘܒܢ̈ܝ ܘܒܝ ܒܗ ܦܠܩܘܣ܀
ܘܐܢܬ ܒܪ ܬܐܘܠܝ ܐܦܩܘ ܠܒܪܐ ܕܢܬܠܐ ܠܝ:
ܘܡܐܬ ܒܚܝܢ ܘܡܢܝܐ ܒܗ ܒܪ ܫܠܦ܀

(1) Strothmann 1976:198-209. The poem is typically in couplets, each line with twelve vowels. (2) This Pe ptc. is often used to introduce direct speech. (3) For the standard spelling ܡܚܒ, an Af act. pass., 'love, like,' < √ ܚܒܒ. (4) ܡܫܟܚ 'can' complemented by a participle: § 98 d. (5) A stative passive Pe ptc., 'clothed': § 84. (6) /ṣaaveet/ = ܨܒܐ ܐܢܬ. On the conjunction Dalath, see § 76. (7) 'he named,' Pa Pf. (8) For the sake of metre, the pronoun is /naa/. Otherwise there would be 13 vowels. So two lines below. (9) The performative Pf, "I hereby sell ...": § 81. (10) The metre indicates /gudfar/ rather than /gudaphar/. So three lines above. (11) 'Rachel's son,' i.e. Joseph. (12) /mzabban/, a Pa pass. ptc. (12a) On the particle Dalath, see § 100. (13) /zavneeh/ 'his time.' (13a) On the spelling, see § 54, n. 64. (14) /ʿallaanee/, 'disciple,' pl. of ܥܠܢܐ /ʿallaanaa/: cf. ܣܡ̈ܡܢܐ /sammaanee/ 'drugs, herbs,' pl. of ܣܡܐ.

ܘܐܢܬ ܒܪ ܡܟܘܒ ܚܘܐ ܚܘܒܝܟ ܡ̣ܢ ܗܕ̈ܡܝܟ:
ܕܬܗܘܐ ܡܫܪܬܗ ܕܒܪܐ ܪܗܛܐ ܘܡܬܢܨܚܢܐ ܒܝ܀
ܒܠܒܟ ܐܝܟ ܙܠܘ ܘܟܒܘ ܒܠ ܐܣܘܒܟ:
ܕܒܡܬܪܢܐ ܢܦܩܐ[14a] ܒܒܪܐ ܠܡܪܐ ܒܥܘܡܐ܀
ܠܐ ܬܣܘܪܘܢ ܒܝ ܐܝܟ ܕܒܥܘܕܐ ܕܦܪܥ ܡܢܝ:
ܕܠܘ ܐܒܘܬܗ ܦܠܫܬ ܚܘܠܐ ܓܝܪ ܦܪܘܩܝ܀
ܐܦ ܕܢܠܬ ܐܝܟ ܒܪܢܫܐ ܡܢ ܥܘܒܪܢܐ:
ܗܐ ܓܠܐ ܐܢܐ ܘܠܐ ܚܦܐ ܐܢܐ ܠܡܪܝ ܘܠܥܒܕܝ ܀
ܗܐ ܓܠܐ ܐܢܐ ܒܒܪܐ ܠܗܢܘ ܕܝܗܒ ܐܠܗܝ :
ܙܠܘ ܕܐܬܒܪ[15] ܢܝܪܗ ܕܒܫܢܐ ܕܒܪܝܟ ܒܗ܀
ܠܐܬܪܐ ܒܥܘܡܐ ܗܐ ܐܫܬܠܬ ܕܐܥܒܪ ܒܗ:
ܡܠܘܬܟ ܬܥܘܠܐ ܒܓܘܗ[16] ܗܡܝܢܘܬܐ܀
ܪܕܝܐ ܓܠܘܬ ܕܐܬܪܐ ܒܐܪܥܐ ܕܡܠܝܐ ܒܘܒܐ:
ܡܠܘܬܟ ܬܥܘܠܐ ܒܠܠܬܐ ܘܣܓܝܐ ܡܪܗ܀
ܒܥܘܡܐ ܦܠܠܬ ܕܓܙܠ ܐܪܥܐ ܒܠ ܦܘܪܬܐ:
ܒܐܒ̈ܦܐ ܢܦܬܐ ܠܡܪܐ ܒܒ̈ܪܐ ܒܥܡ̈ܘܡܝܟ܀
ܒܗܠܝܢ ܟ̈ܠܗ ܕܒܡܘܬܐ ܘܣܓ̈ܝܬܐ:
ܡܥܘܡ ܗܘܐ ܬܐܘܡܐ ܒܪ ܦܪܥ ܗܘܐ ܡܢ ܓܝܪ ܐܣܘܦܗ܀

(**14a**) Pa. with ܓܒܪܐ, a fem. noun as its object (*pace* Strothmann 1976:207. (**15**) The vowel count indicates /deṯbar/ (Pe) rather than /dettabbar/ (Pa). (**16**) /bḡawweeh/ = /bḡaw/ 'within, inside' plus a m.sg. suffix.

12. Some juridic decisions (7th c.?)[1]

(ܐ) ܒܪܐ ܒܪ ܒܙܒܢ ܚܝ ܐܒܘܗܝ : ܡܛܠ ܬܫܡܫܬܐ ܘܝܩܪܬܐ ܕܠܗ. ܠܐ ܢܬܬܒܥ܀

(ܒ) ܠܐ ܐܢܫ ܕܢܦܩ ܡܢ ܒܝܬܐ ܡܕܡ.[2] ܡܬܐܠܝ ܒܡܬܚܫܚܢܘܬܐ ܕܝܠܗ. ܐܠܐ ܗܘ ܕܡܫܪܪ ܠܗ ܠܡܒܝܬܐ. ܡܢ ܗܪܟܐ ܠܐ ܡܙܝܐ[3] ܗܘ ܕܦܪܥ ܕܢܐܠܦ ܠܗ ܕܡܬܦܪܥܐ ܠܚܫܘܫܘ ܗܠܝܢ ܕܐܬܝܗܒ ܗܦ̈ܟܠܬܐ[4] ܠܗܠܝܢ ܕܗܘ ܕܐܡܪ ܘܡܫܪܪ܀

(ܓ) ܗܘ ܕܬܣܬܬܒ ܐܘܠܨܢܐ ܐܝܬܝܗ ܕܐܒܘܗ. ܐܝܟ ܕܬܬܟܘܒ ܡܪܗܛܐ ܕܒܥܬܗ: ܐܒܘܗ ܢܬܠܒܝܢ ܕܝܬܒܝܬܐ.[5] ܣܠܩ[6] ܡܢ ܒܝܬܐ ܗ̇ܝ

ܕܐܬܬ ܠܘܬܗ ܡܢ ܒܥܠܘܬܐ. ܡܛܠ ܕܡܢ ܗ̇ܝ، ܡܕܝܢܬܐ ܐܚܪܬܐ ܕܠܐ
ܒܕܝܠ ܐܬܬܩܕܡܬ.[7] ܕܐܢ ܠܘܬܗ ܡܛܠܬ: ܢܬܬܒܥ ܢܟܠܝܐ.[8] ܐܦ
ܗܠܝܢ ܕܐܬܪܐ. ܐܘ ܒܪ ܡܫܠܡ ܠܒܝܬܐ ܕܝܠܗ ܢܐܒܝ[9]܀
(ܚܢܢ) ܠܐ ܡܬܝܒ ܕܐܓܒܘܬܐ ܡܕܡ ܡܢ ܕܐܢܬܬܐ ܬܫܬܘܠ ܐܡܝܢ
ܕܠܡܫܒܩܢܐ ܣܠܩ ܫܘܒܬܐ ܕܟܒܪܐ ܕܝܠܗ. ܘܐܦܠܐ ܕܬܬܬܒܥ: ܣܠܩ
ܬܫܪܘܬܐ ܕܟܒܪܗ܀

(**1**) Selb 1990:34, 40, 42. (**2**) 'some matter': on the use of ܡܕܡ, see § 91 d. (**3**) An auxiliary verb, "can," is complemented by the following ܕܐܠܨܝܢ 'to compel.' (**4**) /saquvlaayaaṯaa/, the f.pl.emph. of the adjective ܣܩܘܒܠܝܐ used substantivally, 'things which are the opposite of.' (**5**) /dšaaʿṯaa/ 'at once.' (**6**) 'on account of,' originally 'in return for,' possibly under the influence of Gk. ἀντί. (**7**) Impersonal 3f.sg., 'it has not been established yet.' Hence the grammatical subject of this 3f.sg. verb is not the preceding ܡܕ̈ܝܢܬܐ, but rather the following Dalath clause. (**8**) Error for ܢܐܟܝܢܐ or ܢܟܝܢܐ /nekhyaanaa/ 'damage.' This word, however, is not the grammatical subject of ܢܬܬܒܥ, but rather 'he,' i.e. her father. Cf. Selb 1990:66 ܦܠܓܐ ܕܝܠܗܘܢ ܡܬܬܒܥܐ 'she shall be made liable to (repay) half of them.' (**9**) An obscure word.

13. Job of Edessa on sleep (early 9th cent.)[1]

ܟܠ ܫܢܬܐ ܕܡܛܠܠܢܐ ܗܘܬ݀ ܘܐܝܟ ܗ̇ܘܝܐ
ܡܛܠܠܢܐ ܗ̇ܘܬ݀ ܫܢܬܐ ܡܢ ܟܠܗܘܢ ܐܕ̈ܫܐ ܕܪ̈ܓܫܘܬܐ ܠܒܪܢܝܐ
ܠܢܦܫ ܘܐܝܟ ܗ̇ܘܝܐ ܡܢ ܟܠܗܘܢ ܐܕ̈ܫܐ ܕܪ̈ܓܫܘܬܐ ܡܬܪܓܫܢܝܬܐ.[2]
ܒܪܢܝܐ ܠܢܦܫ ܩܢܐ[3] ܣܘ̈ܟܠܐ ܘܣܘܠܘܓܝܣܡܘܣ[4] ܘܒܘܗܕܢܐ
ܘܦܢܛܣܝܐ[5] ܘܗܠܝܢ ܒܟܘܢܐ ܡܬܬܟܠܝܢ ܕܡܛܠ ܗܕܐ ܡܬܪ ܢ̇ܒܠ
ܒܟܘܢܐ ܕܒܪܢܝܐ ܕܒܪܢܝܐ[6] ܡܬܪ ܡܢ ܕܪ̈ܓܫܘܬܐ. ܐܚܪ̈ܢܝܬܐ.
ܘܡܛܠ ܢ̇ܒܠܐ ܢ̇ܒܕ ܦܘܪܫܢܐ ܠܪܓܫܘܬܐ ܕܒܗ ܡܬܪ ܡܢ
ܕܪ̈ܓܫܘܬܐ ܐܚܪ̈ܢܝܬܐ. ܘܟܠ ܗܕܐ ܡܬܥܒܕ ܫܠܝܐ ܟܠ ܢ̇ܦܫܐ

(**1**) Mingana 1935: ܥܐ - ܥ, pp. 70-71. (**2**) /meṯrağšaanyaaṯaa/, an Ethpe nomen agentis, f.pl., 'capable of feeling.' (**3**) Prob. /qnee/ 'possesses,' i.e. a Pe ptc. pass.: see § 84. (**4**) 'reasoning' (Gk συλλογισμός). (**5**) 'imagination' (Gk φαντασία). (**6**) An erroneous dittography. So also the following ܡܬܪ.

ܘܕܢܬܦܪܓܠ.[7] ܕܒܓܢ[8] ܗܘܐ ܠܗ ܫܢܬܐ ܘܡܬܢܝܚܐ ܠܗ ܘܡܬܦܪܓܠܢܐ
ܠܗ. ܒܝܕ ܗܝ ܕܢܕܕܡܟ[9] ܡܬܬܢܝܚ ܡܘܣܝܐ ܒܗ ܟܠܗܘܢ[10] ܠܡܘܫܟܐ
ܐܦ ܡܬܦܪܓܠ. ܗܘܐ ܓܝܪ ܡܢ ܕܠܐ ܗܘܝܐ ܫܢܬܐ ܡܬܦܪܓܠܝܢ ܠܗ
ܠܡܘܣܝܐ ܒܕܡܘܬܐ ܕܬܡܘܬܐ. ܒܡܘܣܝܐ ܓܝܪ ܡܬܦܪܓܠܝܢ ܒܢܝܫܐ ܕܫܡܪܐ
ܘܐܦ ܒܗܝܡܢܘܬܐ ܕܫܢܬܐ ܐܝܟ ܕܒܡܘܣܝܐ.[11] ܘܡܛܠ ܟܠܗܝܢ
ܗܕܐ ܗܘܬ ܫܢܬܐ ܒܐܕܫܐ ܕܒܪܢܫܐ. ܐܡܪܢܐ ܓܝܪ ܗܘܐ ܐܝܬ
ܒܡܘܫܟܐ ܦܓܪܢܝܬܐ ܒܢܝܫܬܐ ܗܝ ܕܪܒܝܥܐ ܒܡܪܝܡܐ. ܘܗܝ ܗܪܐ
ܦܠܘܓܐ ܠܡܘܣܐ ܘܥܪܩܐ ܠܡܫܝܘܬܐ ܗܝ ܕܗܘܬ ܘܒܪ ܫܪܩܐ
ܘܡܬܬܩܐ ܠܗ ܠܡܫܡܫܢܘܬܐ ܡܘܢܝܐ ܠܗ ܡܫܡܫܢܘܬܐ ܓܝܪ ܚܒܪܐ
ܗܝܐܘܬܐ ܘܠܐ ܡܫܡܫܢܘܬܐ ܚܫܐ ܘܗܢܘܢ ܢܦܫܐ ܡܒܪܕܐ ܠܗ
ܠܦܓܪܢܘܬܐ. ܒܗ ܕܥܠܝܐ ܠܫܠܝܐ ܕܦܓܪܐ ܕܢܦܫܘ ܠܐܬܪܐ ܒܪܝܐ
ܘܢܒܪܘ. ܒܪܡܫܐ ܕܢܣܒܐ ܢܫܐ ܘܡܫܡܫܘܬܐ ܬܬܦܪܓܠ. ܘܠܗܢܐ
ܫܘܠܦܐ ܕܗܝܡܢܘܬܐ ܕܪܫܝܐ ܒܡܘܣܐ ܡܫܡܫܗܝܢ ܠܗ ܫܢܬܐ.
ܢܗܒ ܕܝܢ ܡܘܣܐ ܡܢܗ ܕܗܝܡܢܘܬܐ ܒܝܕ ܦܓܪܐ ܠܟܠܗ ܠܡܘܫܟܐ
ܘܐܦ ܫܪܝܬܐ ܕܒܬܚܠܝܢ ܢܦܫܢ. ܘܐܢܫܝܢ ܕܐܢܫ ܢܐܡܪ ܕܐܦ ܫܢܬܐ
ܐܫܪܝܬܐ ܕܐܚܕ ܡܛܠ ܕܡܬܚܫܝܢ ܕܒܫܪܝܢ ܐܠܐ ܠܘ ܫܢܬܐ
ܐܝܬܝܗ. ܐܠܐ ܢܝܫܐ ܡܕܡ ܕܗܘܝܐ ܠܡܘܫܟܐ ܘܗܕܐ ܠܒܫܐ
ܚܕܪܐ ܠܫܦܝܪܬܐ ܡܬܐܪܟܬ ܡܢ ܕܒܡܫܠܐ ܗܘ ܓܝܪ ܗܘܝܢ ܒܫܪܐ
ܡܦܩܝܢ ܕܠܐ ܗܕܝܢ ܠܗܕܐ ܘܠܐ ܣܐܬܝܢ ܒܢܝܫܐ ܓܝܪ. ܘܠܐ ܣܪ ܡܘܡ
ܡܫܡܫܪ ܕܠܐ ܫܢܬܐ ܘܠܐ ܡܪܟܐ ܕܒܗ ܒܠܒܕܝܢܗ ܢܐܢܫܐ. ܗܝ ܓܝܪ
ܕܚܫܝܘܬܐ ܕܡܫܘܬ ܫܢܬܐ ܗܝ ܐܡܒܢܐ ܕܒܢܝܫܐ ܗܘ ܕܢܦܫ ܘܗܘ
ܕܢܒܙ ܘܠܘ ܗܘ ܒܪ ܗܘ ܐܝܟܘ.[12] ܢܒܪܝܢ ܫܒܬܐ ܕܐܪܫܐ ܕܒܪܢܫܐ
ܐܝܬܝܗ ܡܛܠ ܐܝܟܢ ܕܗܘܝܢ.

(**7**) The proclitic Dalath, followed by an Impf., introduces a second complement of ܗܝܡܢ. (**8**) Error for ܒܓܝܢ 'that is why' (Gk γοῦν). (**9**) /bya<u>d</u> haay dne<u>d</u>ma<u>k</u>/ 'on account of that that he sleeps,' i.e. 'because he sleeeps.' (**10**) Error for ܟܠܗ. (**11**) 'as in general.' (**12**) = ܐܝܟܘܬܗ, and ܗܘ ܒܪ ܗܘ means 'the same.'

14. Ishoʿdad of Merv on John 11[1]

ܗܘ[2] ܕܐܬܟܪܗ ܒܒܝܬܐ. ܒܥܘܪܝܗ ܕܝܢ. ܐܟܘܬ[3] ܗܘ ܕܢܩܒܬ ܡܢ ܟܠ

ܝܗܘܕܝܐ ܕܐܦ ܠܐ ܡܐ ܕܚܙܘ ܗܕܐ ܠܬܕܡܘܪܬܐ ܡܗܝܡܢܝܢ. ܡܠܘܢ[4] ܕܝܢ ܡܬܚܣܕܝܢ ܠܡܫܝܚܗ. ܘܐܦ ܠܠܥܙܪ ܩܛܠܗ. ܗܘ ܕܥܒܕܘܗܝ ܟܠ ܡܥܒܕܢܘܬܐ ܕܪܘܚܐ ܗܘ ܕܡܫܪܐ ܠܗ: ܕܒܗ ܡܫܬܕܥ ܗܘܐ ܘܢܕܥ ܐܝܟ ܕܠܐܢܫ. ܕܡܢܐ ܓܝܪ ܗܕܐ ܠܗܘ ܕܟܠ ܝܗܘܕܐ. ܕܐܬܚܘܝ ܠܗܘܢ ܘܐܡܪ. ܕܚܕ ܡܢܟܘܢ ܗܘ ܡܫܠܡ ܠܝ.[5] ܘܠܗܘ ܕܕܡܝܐ ܠܐܡܬܝ ܐܗܘܐ ܠܘܬܟܘܢ ܘܐܣܝܒܪܟܘܢ ܘܕܫܪܟܐ.[6] ܡܛܠ ܕܐܝܟܐ ܦܩܬܘܢܝܗܝ. ܠܘ ܟܕ ܠܐ ܝܕܥ. ܐܝܟܢܐ ܓܝܪ ܠܗܘ ܕܟܕ ܦܬܚ ܘܝܕܥ ܟܠ ܡܘܬܗ. ܗܕܐ ܥܠܝܐ ܗܘܬ ܠܗ.[7] ܐܠܐ ܥܠܬܐ ܕܟܪ ܠܡܘܪܝܗ ܕܦܘܠܚܢܐ. ܕܠܐ ܢܬܦܠܓ. ܕܡܫܡܗܪܐ ܟܕ ܠܬܕܡܘܪܬܐ. ܗܘ ܕܐܬܐ ܗܘ̈ܐ ܕܡܥܗܘ ܕܡܘܬ. ܘܗܐ ܟܠ ܕܬܐܕ ܗܘܐ ܕܢܬܡܪܗܘܢ ܠܬܪܥܬܐ ܗܘܬ ܕܝܕܥ. ܐܠܐ ܚܕܐ: ܠܡܘܕܝܐ ܚܬܝܬܐ ܕܦܘܡܐ ܐܝܟܢܐ ܕܡܢܝ.[8] ܠܝܬ ܓܝܪ ܠܗ ܠܐܠܗܐ ܕܩܕܡܐ. ܕܬܩܠܝ: ܕܢܣܒ ܡܥܘܚܬܐ ܕܐܠܦܐ ܕܟܠ ܡܐܬܐ ܕܕܡܝܐ ܠܡܥܒܪܐ ܢܕܥ. ܘܟܕܘ: ܘܠܐ ܢܬܟܠܠ ܒܥܡܬܐ ܕܠܐ ܒܝܠܐ. ܬܘܒ: ܡܕܡܕ ܟܠ ܕܝܘܬܗ ܘܬܫܘܒܘܬܗ ܕܚܝܝ. ܕܚܕ ܟܐܢܐ ܐܡܪܐ ܘܡܥܘܟܐ ܡܟܠܐ ܐܬܟܪܝ ܒܥܘܪܐ. ܟܐܢܐ ܥܦܠܐ ܘܣܟܠܐ ܐܬܬܚܬܝ ܒܝܕܥܗ ܘܕܫܪܟܐ. ܐܚܪ̈ܢܐ[9] ܠܘ ܠܗ ܕܚܫܐ[10] ܗܘܬ ܕܡܟܬܗ ܕܡܪܢ. ܐܠܐ ܡܠܦܢܝܬܐ.[11] ܘܕܝܕܥ ܕܝܢ ܗܘܐ.[12] ܠܥܙܪ ܠܡ ܪܚܡܢ ܫܟܒ. ܐܠܐ ܐܘܦ ܘܕܫܪܟܐ. ܡܢܘ ܡܢܢ ܟܐܒ ܠܗ[13] ܥܠ ܪܚܡܐ ܕܕܡܟ. ܕܒܬܪ ܥܠܠ ܡܫܚܐ ܕܢܥܒܕܘܢܗܝ܁ ܠܥܙܪ ܬܐ ܠܒܪ. ܘܟܕ ܡܛܐ ܚܙܐ ܗܘ: ܕܡܚܙܩ[14] ܡܗܠܟ ܗܘܐ. ܬܗܪܐ ܒܬܗܪܐ. ܒܦܣܩܝܬܐ ܐܦܣ̈ܝ ܗܘܐ

(**1**) Gibson 1911: ܡܕ - ܡܕܗ (Syr. text); Gibson: 1911:253-55 (Eng. tr.). (**2**) ܗܘ ܕ introduces a lemma in a commentary. (**3**) ܐܵܬ݂ܵܐ 'a sign.' (**4**) Gk μᾶλλον 'rather.' (**5**) Jn 13.21. (**6**) Mt 17.17. ܘܲܕ݂ܫܲܪܟܵܐ /wad̲šarkaa/ 'et cetera.' (**7**) 'How could this have escaped him?' On the hypothetical force of the compound tense, see § 86. (**8**) 'the human nature that (he had taken) from us.' (**9**) '(According to) other (scholars).' (**10**) 'that of suffering': the weeping of our Lord was not that of suffering. (**11**) /malfaanit̲aa/, a Pa f.sg. nomen agentis from √ ܐܠܦ: see §§ 38d, 20. (**12**) 'As is evident, so they say (ܠܡ), from this, i.e. the following scripture [Jn 11.11].' (**13**) A compound clause: 'Who amongst us, does it grieve him ...?' i.e. 'who amongst us grieves over a friend who is asleep?' See § 113. ܕܡܟ is a resultative Pe passive ptc.: § 84. (**14**) /mḥazzaq/, a Pa pass. ptc., 'girded round.'

ܩ̈ܒܠܐ. ܘܟܠ ܡܬܟܠܝ̈ ܗܘܘ ܨܝܕ ܘܟܠܐ. ܟܕ ܗܘܐ ܠܒܪ ܗܘ
ܕܡܚܝܠ[15] ܡܢ ܗܘ ܕܡܥܕܪ. ܘܐܝܟ ܗܘ ܕܟܬܝܒ ܗܘܐ ܕܢܥܒܕ ܗܠܝܢ
ܡܕܡ ܗܘܐ. ܐܠܐ ܒܟܠ ܝܘܡ ܠܡܣܟܢܘܬܗ ܡܫܡܫ. ܒܡܘܫ̈ܚܬܐ[16]
ܘܒܬܚܘ̈ܡܐ. ܘܕܢܫܬܘܬܦ[16a] ܒܚ̈ܫܐ ܕܚܒܪ̈ܐ. ܚܕܝ. ܒܕ ܥܡܕ
ܕܒܪܗ. ܘܒܟܐ ܥܡ ܐܒܐ ܕܢܣܘܗܝ. ܟܕ ܕܡܛܐ ܠܗ ܟܕ ܠܗ[17]
ܒܕܒܐ ܢܦܫܐ ܘܫܢܝ ܕܐܝܟܐ ܫܡܥܬܘܢܘܗܝ܀ ܗܘ ܕܫܩܠܘ[18] ܟܐܦܐ ܗܕܐ.
ܦܩܕ ܕܟܐܦܐ ܗܢܘܢ[19] ܫܩܘ. ܒܐܝ̈ܕܝܗܘܢ ܠܬܠܡܝ̈ܕܘܗܝ. ܐܝܟ ܕܟܠ ܢܗܘܐ
ܠܗܘܢ ܠܡܫܡܫܘ ܐܢܬ. ܐܪܐ[20] ܗܘ ܕܐܚܝ ܡܝܬܐ ܘܐܦܝ ܢܦܫܐ
ܘܕܒܪܟܐ. ܠܐ ܡܨܐ ܗܘܐ ܡܟܢܐ ܠܡܦܬܚ: ܘܟܐܦܐ ܠܡܬܓܠܠܘ
ܒܡܠܬܐ. ܘܗܘ ܕܐܡܪ ܠܬܠܡܝ̈ܕܐ ܕܢܫܪܘܢ ܗܘܐ ܟܠܗܘܢ ܗܝܡܢܘܬܐ ܐܝܟ
ܦܪܕܬܐ ܕܚܪܕܠܐ. ܠܬܝܢ ܛܘܪ̈ܐ: ܘܗܘ ܕܒܡܠܬܗ ܒܘܠܦܢܐ ܟܐܦܐ
ܘܡܟ̈ܬܐ ܢܦܩ ܘܕܒܪܟܐ܀ ܐܠܐ ܡܟܟ ܕܪܝܫܗ ܗܘܐ ܒܟܠܘܢ: ܐܡܪ
ܕܦܠܚܘ ܩܣܪܐ. ܕܝܢܐ ܪܚܡ ܦܪܘܫܐ ܟܐܦܝ̈ܗܘܢ. ܘܡܪܐܘܗܝ ܐܠܗܝ
ܕܐܬܟܫܦܘܬܗܘܢ ܕܒܬܫܒܘܚܬܗܘܢ ܟܕ ܐܬܪ̈ܝܟܘܢ: ܘܟܕ ܗܘܐ ܟܕ
ܡܐܢ. ܠܐ ܫܡܥܬ ܢܦܫܗ ܠܡܢ: ܕܠܐ ܢܡܪܘܢ ܕܠܗܘܢ ܫܡܘ
ܒܢܬܗܘܢ܀ ܐܪܡ ܒܢܝ̈ܗܘܢ ܠܟܠ ܡܢܟܢ ܠܬܠܬ ܬ̈ܟܠܢ܀[21] ܚܕܐ: ܕܝܢ
ܢܠܦ ܡܘܟܟܐ. ܕܠܐ ܥܠ ܢܦܫܢ ܢܬܬܟܠ. ܐܠܐ ܥܠ ܐܠܗܐ.
ܕܬܫ̈ܒܚܢ: ܕܢܣܒܐ ܕܦܓܪܐ ܕܢܝܚ ܠܒܝܬ ܗܘܐ: ܕܬܠܬܐ: ܕܢܘܕܥ:
ܕܒܬܘܗܝ ܫܘܒܚܐ ܠܐܠܗܐ. ܐܒܡܐ ܕܪܢܝ ܝܗܘܒܠܗ܀ ܗܘ ܕܒܡܐ
ܟܡܟܐ ܪܡܐ ܕܟܠܘܪ ܠܐ ܠܟܪ. ܠܗ ܠܡܣܟܢܐ ܢܟܣ ܗܘܐ ܡܟܠ. ܐܠܐ
ܕܢܕܒܘܢ ܗܢܘܢ ܕܐܡܝܢ ܕܢܦܫܐ ܒܪܘܚܐ ܐܠܗܝܐ ܗܘܬ ܡܢ ܦܓܪܗ.
ܘܠܘ ܟܕܘ ܡܟܢܐ ܒܡܗ. ܠܗܘܢ: ܕܝ. ܦܟܠܬܐ ܨܐܪ ܗܘܐ ܕܗܘ ܡܟܠ
ܕܡܪܢܐ ܐܢܫܝܬܐ. ܡܠܟܝ ܕܝܢ ܠܗ ܠܡܟܠܐ ܕܡܪܝ ܐܡܪ. ܕܡ̈ܝܬܐ ܠܡ
ܫܡܫܘ ܠܒܪ. ܘܒܪܦܦ ܟܢܐ ܡ̈ܝܬܐ ܡܬܐܣܝܢ. ܘܫ̈ܢܐ ܡܬܚܕܬܝܢ.
ܟܗܝ[22] ܕܐܚܘܢܐ ܕܟܠ ܥܘܠܡ ܟܠܡܐ: ܡܢ ܚܘܪܒܗ ܕܐܘܪܫܠܡ
ܥܕܪ. ܗܢ ܘܟܠ ܡܢܬܐ ܟܟܝܬܐ ܡܢ ܗܝ ܕܠܟܘܪ. ܐܬܬܐ ܠܡ
ܥܕܬܐ ܟܣܪܬܐ ܘܐܦ ܗܥܐ ܟܕ ܠܟܘܪ ܐܬܝܘ. ܐܡܬܝ ܕܡܝ̈ܬܐ
ܢܥܡܕܘܢ ܥܠܗ ܕܟܪܗ ܕܐܠܗܐ: ܘܕܒܪܟܐ. ܡܟܠܡܝ[23] ܕܢܡܕܪܐ ܚܙܐ
ܠܟܘܪ ܘܡܬܪܡܝ ܗܘܐ ܐܦܣܩܘܦܐ.

(**15**) /mḥayyel/, a Pa ptc., 'empowers.' (**16**) /mušḥaaṯaa/, pl. of ܡܫܘܚܬܐ 'measure.' (**16a**) Here an Impf. 1pl. (**17**) ܟܕ ܠܗ: probably to be omitted. (**18**) /šaqqel/, a Pa Impv., possibly a variant of Pe ܫܩܘܠ in the Peshitta.

(**19**) 'they themselves,' emphatic: § 74. See also the position of the following ܒܐܝ̈ܕܝܗܘܢ 'with their own hands.' (**20**) = Gk ἆρα, a particle introducing a rhetorical question. (**21**) /ʿellaan/, pl. of ܥܠܬܐ 'reason.' (**22**) ܒܕ = ܒܝܕ ܕ 'because.' (**23**) ܡܫܠܡܝܢ, an Af ptc. 'they transmit,' tradition has it that ...

15. Some light-hearted stories[1]

(468) ܐܢܫܐ ܡܢ ܡܠ̈ܟܐ ܐܢܬܬܐ ܩܢܐ[2] ܗܘܐ ܫܦܝܪܬ[3]
ܚܙܘܐ. ܘܡܛܠ ܕܠܐ ܩܐܡ ܗܘܐ ܒܣܢ̈ܝܫܘܬܗ. ܒܐܘܡܢܘ ܒܟܫܠܐ
ܗܘܝܢ ܗܘܘ. ܘܚܙܐ ܡܢ ܡܦ̈ܘܡܬܐ ܚܕ ܕܬܠܝ ܠܓܒܪܐ ܗܘ ܐܬܦܪܫ
ܡܢܗ ܢܡܘܣܐܝܬ ܘܡܛܒ ܠܗ ܡܗܪܗ ܘܐܣܩܗ ܡܢ ܡܫܒܢܗ. ܘܐܙܠ
ܠܟܠܐ ܕܡܠܟܗ[4] ܘܕܫܟܪܗ ܠܘܬ ܡܠܟܐ. ܘܐܬܪܬܪܢ ܠܗ ܘܫܕܪ
ܠܘܬܗ ܕܢܫܡܝܗ. ܗܝ ܕܝܢ ܐܡܪܬ. ܕܠܐ ܫܠܡܐ ܠܡܠܟܐ ܐܠܐ ܒܬܪ
ܕܦܩܕ ܕܢ̈ܬܟܐ ܟܠ ܡܪ̈ܟܒܬܐ. ܘܗܘ ܓܒܪܗ ܘܪܡܟܐ ܢܦܩ ܠܗ.
ܘܦܩܕ ܡܠܟܐ ܕܗܟܢܐ ܢܗܘܐ. ܘܟܕ ܐܙܠܝܢ ܗܘܘ ܒܐܘܪܚܐ ܐܦܩܬ
ܕܝܢܐ ܘܐܪܡܝܬ ܠ ܐܪܒܐ ܘܐܡܪܬ ܠܗܘ ܕܒܠܗ ܗܘܐ ܒܝܢ
ܘܢܚܬ ܗܘܐ ܡܪܟܒܬܗ. ܕܐܘܫܛ ܠܝ[5] ܙܘܢܐ ܕܢܦܠ ܡܢܝ. ܘܟܕ ܫܪ
ܟܠ ܐܪܒܐ ܐܫܟܚܗ ܠܕܝܢܐ. ܘܐܡܪ ܠܗ. ܕܠܘ ܙܘܢܐ ܗܘܐ. ܐܠܐ
ܕܝܢܐ. ܐܡܪܐ ܠܗ ܗܝ. ܕܒܪܝܟ[6] ܗܘ ܡܪܝܐ ܕܒܬܪ ܕܙܘܢܐ
ܐܘܒܕܬ. ܕܝܢܐ ܝܗܒ ܠܝ ܐܠܗܐ ܕܐܫܟܚ. ܒܗ ܟܠܗܘܢ ܕܐܘܒܕܬܗ
ܘܟܠ ܡܠܟܐ ܕܐܫܟܚܬܗ ܪܡܝܐ ܗܘܬ܀
(515) ܚܕܐ ܡܢ ܢ̈ܫܐ ܫܐܠܬ ܠܥܒܕܬܗ. ܡܛܠܡܢܐ ܠܒܪܐ
ܫܠܡܬ ܠܗ[7] ܕܢܒܚ ܠܗ ܐܡܬܐ ܘܢܕܡܝ ܒܡܗ ܘܢܒܕ ܒܠܒܐ
ܕܢ̈ܟܐ ܘܐܬܬܐ ܠܐ ܫܠܡܬ ܠܗ ܕܬܒܕ ܡܕܡ ܡܢ ܗܠܝܢ ܟܡܢ
ܒܠܒܐ[8]. ܘܗܝ ܐܡܪܬ ܠܗ. ܡܛܠ ܕܒܠܒ̈ܐ ܘܕܢ̈ܐ ܘܦܫ̈ܪܐ

(**1**) Budge 1897: 97 (Syr.) [= 120f. Eng.]; 110 (Syr.) [= 136 Eng.]; 143f. (Syr.) [= 171f. Eng.]. (**2**) /qnee/, a Pe pass. Ptc. with resultative meaning, 'having acquired,' i.e. 'in possession of': see § 84. (**3**) A st. cst. of the adjective, 'beautiful of look, good-looking': see § 96 b. (**4**) 'her news,' i.e. 'the story about her.' (**5**) 'Stretch out (ܐܘܫܛ, Af. Impv.) (your hand, and get) for me.' (**6**) A Pe Ptc., though in the rest of the conjugation the verb in this sense, "to bless," is used in Pael. (**7**) A compound sentence with ܒܪܐ in casus pendens: § 113. Hence ܒܪܐ is not the grammatical subject of ܫܠܡܬ, which is impersonal. Cf. the following sentence: ܐܬܬܐ ... ܫܠܡܬ ܠܗ ܕ ...

ܢܡܘ̈ܣܐ[9] ܟܬ̈ܒܐ ܗܘܘ. ܘܡ̈ܢܗܘܢ ܠܢܡܘܣܗܘܢ ܒܒܝܬ ܣܢܐܓܪܘܬܐ[10]
ܘܠܝܠܕ̈ܐ ܠܡܠܦܘ܀

(669) ܐܚܪܢܐ ܡܢ ܥܢ̈ܝܐ ܝܬܒ ܥܠ ܦܬܘܪܐ ܘܐܟܠ ܗܘܐ. ܘܦܫ ܪܘܚܐ ܕܒܥܠܕܒ̈ܒܘܗܝ ܠܒܪ ܒܥܘܬܐ. ܘܐܬܐ ܡܫܒܚܐ ܘܬܒܥ ܠܥܠ ܒܥܠܝܐ. ܘܡܦܝܣ ܐܢܬܬܗ ܕܬܬܠ ܠܗ. ܘܗ̣ܝ ܐܡܪܐ ܒܠܚܡܗ̇ ܘܠܐ ܥܒܕܬ ܕܬܬܠ. ܘܗܝ ܐܡܪܐ ܕܢܚܘܬ ܠܗ. ܘܢܦܠ ܡܢ ܪܫܗ ܕܡܫܠܡܢܘܬܐ ܘܡܝܬ. ܘܪܗܛܬ ܐܢܬܬܗ ܒܠܒܟܐ ܕܗܘܢܐ ܗܘܐ. ܘܡܦܝܣܬ ܠܚܝܬ ܐܒܘܗ̇. ܘܫܪܝܬ ܕܬܦܠܓ ܠܠܒܘ̈ܫܐ ܕܬܝ̈ܒܐ ܕܒܒܝܬܗ. ܘܐܡܪܬ ܗܘܐ ܠܗܘܢ[11] ܒܗܕܝܐ ܚܕ. ܗܟܢ ܒܬܘܡܐ ܘܚܙܐ ܡܢ ܡܟ̈ܬܒܐ ܚܝܬ ܕܗܕܝܐ ܚܕ. ܘܡܦܝܣܬܗ ܠܗ. ܘܐܡܪܬ ܗ̇ܘ ܕܗܕܝܐ ܘܦܩܕ ܠܒܢ̈ܝܐ ܐܚ̈ܘܗܝ ܕܢܝܬܘܢ ܗܘܐ ܠܒܗܕܝܐ. ܘܐܡܪ ܠܗܘܢ ܒܟܘܗ̇ ܐܠܦܐ ܕܝ̈ܢܪܐ ܕܕܗܒܐ. ܘܢܣܒ ܐܢܘܢ ܘܚܒܪ ܠܗ ܠܒܘܫܐ ܠܒܘܫܐ ܥܦܝܪܐ ܘܝܬܒ ܒܥܘܡܐ ܕܒܪ̈ܝܐ. ܘܐܡܪ ܠܡܫܟ̈ܢܬܐ ܕܚܙܝܢ ܠܗ ܐܢܬܬܐ ܕܢܒܥܘܪ. ܘܐܙܠܬ ܚܕܐ ܡܢܗܝܢ ܘܐܫܟܚܬܗ̇ ܠܗ̇، ܕܡܗܒܝܬ ܗܘܬ ܠܗ ܠܒܗܕܝܐ. ܘܐܬܬ ܘܐܡܪܬ ܠܗ ܕܗܐ ܐܫܟܚܬ ܚܕܐ ܐܪܡܠܬܐ ܥܦܝܪܬܐ. ܒܪܡ ܘܛܠܝܠܬܐ ܘܕܚܠܬ ܠܐܠܗܐ. ܘܐܬܝܬܗ̇ ܕܡܝܬܪܬ ܡܢ ܒܟܠܗ̇. ܡܪܕܝܐ ܡܠܐܐ ܪܒܐ. ܘܐܝܟܠܒ ܟܬܒܐ ܗ̇ܘ ܡܫܪܐ ܠܗ̇ ܫܪ̈ܟܐ ܘܢܣܒܗ̇. ܘܟܕ ܗܘܬ ܐܟܕܗܘܢ، ܘܬܘܠܝܬ ܫܪܟܗ̇ ܘܫܘܪܒܐ ܕܡܫܟܢܐ ܕܬܒܥ ܒܥܠܝܐ ܘܡܫܒܚܬܐ ܕܒܟܠܗ̇. ܘܬܘܒ ܗ̣ܘ ܫܪܟܐ ܕܒܗܕܝܐ ܐܫܬܘܕܥ ܠܫܪ̈ܝܐ. ܘܫܒܚܘ ܠܐܠܗܐ ܕܝܗܒ ܠܡܫܟܢܐ ܗ̇ܘ ܒܝܬܗ ܘܡܢܝܬܗ ܘܐܢܬܬܗ ܕܗ̇ܘ ܕܢܦܩ ܠܗ ܡܠܠ ܒܥܠܝܐ܀

(**8**) /ʿeen baḡlaa/ 'openly.' (**9**) /saaymay naamosee/, a Pe ptc. m.pl.cst. of ܣܡ 'to put,' legislators. (**10**) /sneegrutaa/ 'office of advocate (συνήγορος).' (**11**) Error for ܒܗܘܢ?

16. Bar Hebraeus's Syriac grammar[1]

ܦܫܘܩܐ ܣܡܥܢܐ ܡܠܬܐ ܦܘܪܫܢ ܒܥܘܪܐ ܘܣܡܘܚܐ
ܣܡܥܐ ܐܝܟ ܗܠܝܢ. ܡܠܬܐ. ܡܩܘܢܬ ܒܥܘܪܐ. ܘܐܣܝܪܬ ܣܡܘܥܐ. ܐܝܟ

(**1**) Moberg 1922:40f., 45f. (Syriac text). Cf. Moberg 1907-13: 86f., 97f. (German translation).

ܢܩܫܐ ܐܘܟܝܼ ܢܘܚܐ (Mt 1.11). ܘܗܘܪܐ ܡܪܝܡܘܬ ܒܗܘܢ ܢܩܫܐ ܒܒܘܪܘܬܐ
ܠܗ ܢܘܚܐ. ܘܐܚܪܢܝܬ ܢܘܚܐ ܫܩܘܫܩܘܬܐ. ܕܬܪܝܢ.[2] ܦܘܪܫܐ ܗܘܒܠܐ. ܟܕ ܡܰܪܝܡ
ܒܒܘܪܐ ܘܟܕ ܐܣܪܝ. ܡܪܝܡܐ ܡܶܢ[3] ܐܝܟ ܘܣܒܠܬܗ ܪܓܠܗ ܕܒܠܥܡ ܠܐܣܬܐ (Nu
22.25).[4] ܗܘ[5] ܐܠܐ ܠܓܠ. ܘܫܕܝܬܗ ܠܥܦܪܗ ܒܢܚܠܐ (Dt 9.21).[6] ܘܐܝܢܩܘ ܬܕ̈ܝ
ܐܡܪ̈ܝ (Ct 8.1).[7] ܘܫܕܪ ܗܪܘܕܣ ܦܣܩܗ ܪܫܗ (Mt 14.10).[8] ܘܫܩܠܗ
ܐܕܢܗ (Mt 26.51 etc.).[9] ܘܐܙܠܬ ܛܫܝܬܗ ܟܟܪܟ (Mt 25.25).[10] ܡܪܝ ܐܦܪܝܡ.[11] ܐܠܐ
ܗܘܐ ܘܡܬܠܐ ܡܪܢܝܬܐ ܘܠܐ ܓܠܝܐ ܠܠܐ ܐܘܡܟܝܬܐ. ܐܡܪܢܐ ܕܝܢ ܐܝܟ ܐܠܗܐ ܠܐ ܚܙܐ ܐܢܫ
ܡܢ ܡܡܬܘܡ (Jn 1.18)[12] ܗܘ ܐܢܫ ܠܐ ܚܙܐ ܠܐܠܗܐ ܗܘ. ܕܠܡܠܬܐ. ܦܘܪܫܐ ܒܪܬ
ܩܠܐ[13] ܒܒܗܘܢ ܠܐܬܘܬ ܫܩܘܫܩܘܬܐ. ܐܝܟ ܐܒܪܗܡ ܐܘܠܕ ܠܐܝܣܚܩ (Mt 1.2).[14]
ܘܚܪ ܡܪܝܐ ܒܐܪܥܐ ܘܙܥܬ (cp. Ps 104.32).[15] ܕܐܪܥܐ. ܕܒܪܘܬܐ ܘܡܡܕܘܬܐ. ܐܝܟ
ܡܚܒܠܝܢ ܐܡ̈ܘܬܐ[16] ܢܟܦܬܐ. ܘܡܬܢܒܠܝܢ ܬܪ̈ܝܐ ܒܣܝ̈ܡܬܐ ܫܘܥܝܬܐ ܒܝ̈ܫܬܐ (1Cor
15.33).[17] ܒܗܠܝܢ ܓܝܪ. ܕܒܪܘܬ ܡܚܒܠܝܢ ܠܢܟܦܬܐ ܒܒܘܪܘܬܐ ܢܘܚܐ.
ܘܡܡܕܘܬܐ ܕܡܬܢܒܠܝܢ ܠܫܘ̈ܥܝܬܐ. ܕܒܝܫܐ. ܫܚܩܘܬܐ ܘܚܒܘܫܐ. ܐܝܟ ܒܪܡܐ ܒܩܒܠ
ܐܘܟܝ. ܘܒܩܒܠ ܒܪܡܐ ܢܦܘܩ. ܘܒܗܠܝܢ ܐܘܒ ܫܪܝܘܬ ܐܘܟܝ ܠܒܪܡܐ
ܒܒܘܪܘܬܐ ܡܪܝܡܐ. ܘܒܫܥܘܬ ܫܦܘ ܠܒܩܒܠ

ܨܡܚܐ[18] ܐܝܬ ܐܝܠܐ ܕܒܦܠܓܘܬ[19] ܗܘܐ ܦܘܪܫܐ ܒܝܢ ܒܒܘܪܐ ܠܢܩܫܐ. ܐܝܟ
ܕܦܠܓܘܬ. ܠܗܘܐ ܓܝܪ ܐܒܐ. ܚܬܡ ܐܠܗܐ (Jn 6.27). ܡܢ ܗܘܐ[20] ܓܝܪ ܐܡܪܢ

(**2**) 'second': § 44b. (**3**) = Gk μέν corresponding to δέν (= ܕܶܝܢ, four lines below, in ... ܐܡܪܢܐ ܕܶܝܢ). (**4**) 'And it (= the she-ass) pushed Bileam's leg to the wall.' (**5**) = ܗܘ ܕܝܢ 'that is to say, i.e.' (**6**) 'I threw his dust into the wadi.' (**7**) 'My breasts suckled my lambs.' (**8**) 'And Herod sent (someone) and beheaded him.' (**9**) 'And he removed his ear.' (**10**) 'And I went away and hid your talent.' (**11**) 'Ephrem': ܡܳܪܝ lit. 'my lord' is a conventional title borne by a Syrian ecclesiastic. (**12**) 'Nobody has ever seen God.' (**13**) 'phonetic,' an adj. derived from a construct phrase ܒܪܰܬ ܩܳܠܳܐ 'sound.' (**14**) 'Abraham begat Isaac.' (**15**) 'The Lord looked at the earth and it shook.' (**16**) Pl. of ܐܘܡܬܐ 'nation.' (**17**) 'Bad stories ruin pleasant thoughts.' (**18**) ܨܶܡܚܳܐ /ṣemḥaa/ 'ray' or 'twig,' hence the title of the treatise ܟܬܳܒܳܐ ܕܨܶܡܚܶܐ. (**19**) ܐܺܝܬ ܐܺܝܠܳܐ, 'it sometimes happens that ...' (**20**) The word ܗܳܝ probably refers to the same word in the quoted text rather than meaning 'this sentence' (so Moberg: "dieser Satz").

ܡܫܡܠܝܐ ܐܝܬ ܠܡܫܬܡܠܝܘ. ܚܕ ܡܢ ܕܐܝܬ ܠܗ ܫܘܪ. ܕܐܠܗܐ ܐܠܗܘܬܗ ܗܝ. ܬܪܝܢ
ܕܝܢ ܕܐܠܗܐ ܡܢ ܫܘܪ. ܕܐܝܬ ܐܠܗܘܬܗ ܗܝ. ܘܬܪܝܢܐ ܡܩܕܡܐ ܗܘܝܘ ܚܠܝܬ

ܦܣܘܩܐ ܠܡܠܬܐ ܡܬܠܠ ܡܬܚܒܫܬ ܫܘܪܝܐ ܘܬܢܝܐ[1]

ܫܘܪܝܐ ܩܕܝܡ ܗܘ ܒܟܝܢܐ ܠܬܢܝܐ. ܐܝܟ ܩܨܡܐ ܚܘܒ ܡܟܒܫܐ (1Sm 15.23).[2]
ܘܕܚܠܬܟ ܗܝ ܗܝ ܣܟܠܘܬܟ (Job 4.6).[3] ܘܐܠܗܢ ܚܢܢ ܢܘܪܐ ܗܘ ܐܟܠܬܐ (Heb
12.29).[4] ܘܝܗܘܕܝܐ ܗܘܐ ܠܗ ܡܠܟܐ (Dn Bel v. 28)[5] ܗ̄ ܕܝܠܢ ܕܝܗܘܕܝܐ ܗܘ ܗܘ
ܐܬܡܠܟ. ܘܐܢܗܘ ܕܒܗܘܢ ܛܠܐ ܢܩܕܝܡ. ܒܗܘܝܐ ܬܪ̈ܬܝܢ[6] ܫܘܪܝܐ ܡܩܕܡ. ܐܝܟ
ܩܘܪ̈ܝ ܠܗܘܐ ܡܕ̈ܝܢܬܐ (Is 42.11).[7] ܘܫܪܓܐ ܗܝ ܡܠܬܟ ܠܪ̈ܓܠܝ (Ps 119.105).[8]
ܘܫܪܓܗ ܕܡܪܝܐ ܢܫܡܬܐ ܗܝ ܕܒܢܝ̈ܢܫܐ (Pr 20.27).[9] ܘܢܘܪܐ ܕܝܩܕܐ ܢܕܥܟܘܢ
ܡ̈ܝܐ (Sir 3.30).[10] ܘܪܘܚܐ ܗܘ ܓܝܪ ܐܠܗܐ (Jn 4.24) ܗ̄ ܩܘܪ̈ܝ ܠܗܘܐ ܡܕ̈ܝܢܬܐ.
ܘܡܠܬܟ ܫܪܓܐ ܗܘ̇ ܠܪ̈ܓܠܝ. ܘܢܫܡܬܐ ܕܒܢܝ̈ܢܫܐ ܫܪܓܐ ܗܝ ܕܡܪܝܐ. ܘܡ̈ܝܐ
ܢܕܥܟܘܢ ܢܘܪܐ ܕܝܩܕܐ. ܘܐܠܗܐ ܪܘܚܐ ܗܘ

ܙܒܢܐ ܐܝܬ ܐܝܟ ܕܦܬ̈ܓܡܐ ܣܓܝ̈ܐܐ ܒܗ ܫܘܪܝܐ ܠܬܢܝܐ ܢܬܩܕܡ.
ܐܬܘܠܘܓܘܣ.[11] ܗܘ ܡܠܬܐ ܐܠܗܐ. ܗ̇ܘ ܕܩܕܡ ܥܠܡܐ. ܠܐ ܡܬܚܙܝܐ. ܗ̇ܘ ܕܠܐ
ܫܘܡ.[12] ܡܢ ܫܘܒܚܗ ܐܚܪܢܐ ܡܚܝܠܐ. ܕܦܪܝܪ. ܐܢܫ[13] ܡܢܗ ܛܠܐ ܕܗܘܘ ܒܗ
ܓܘܡܐ ܕܢܒܗ ܐܬܐ

ܙܒܢܐ ܒܦܪܨܘܦܐ ܛܠܐ ܡܢ ܫܘܪܝܐ. ܐܝܬ ܐܝܟ ܕܡ̈ܛܠܬܐ[14] ܛܠܐ ܡܕܝܢܐ. ܐܝܟ
ܠܬ̈ܓܡܐ[15] ܕܟܕܝܐ. ܐܝܬ ܕܐܬܝܠܕܬ ܡܢ ܒܬܘܠܬܐ. ܒܟܘܡܪܐ ܘܠܐ ܫܘܫܘܦܬܐ.
ܠܛܠܛ ܡܬܘܡ ܕܦܫܛ ܟܕ ܡܕܝܢ ܐܝܬ ܛܒܠܬ ܡܫܝܚܐ[16] ܗ̄ ܠܬ̈ܓܡܐ ܕܟܕܝܐ.
ܐܝܬ ܝܠܕܐ ܕܒܬܘܠܬܐ ܛܒܠܬ. ܟܕ ܠܫܘܒܬܐ ܕܦܫܛ ܡܕܝܢ ܐܝܬ ܐܝܟ ܕܒܡܫܚܐ[17]

ܙܒܢܐ ܐܝܬ ܐܝܟ ܕܫܘܪܝܐ ܡܬܬܚܡܐ[18] ܒܡܡܠܠܬܐ. ܐܒܐ ܕܟܕ ܐܡܪ ܠܟܘ
ܢܟܪܘ ܡܐ ܛܟܘ. ܘܬܦܫ ܢܟܝܬܐ. ܟܕ ܐܢܐ ܢܟܝܬܐ ܗܘܝܘ ܦܘܫ. ܘܐܝܬ ܐܝܟ
ܕܛܠܐ. ܐܒܐ ܕܟܕ ܬܫܬܐܠ. ܡܢ ܠܐܢܬܘ ܘܬܦܫ ܫܡܥܘܢ. ܟܕ ܫܡܥܬܘܢ ܠܐܬ̈ܘ
ܗܘܝܘ ܦܘܫ. ܘܠܐܬܪ̈ܘܟܒܘܢ (Mk 13.29). ܕܒܗ ܕܡܬܡܠܠ ܗܘ. ܫܘܪܝܐ ܡ̇ܠܗܡ̇ ܗ̄
ܣܪܬܐ ܡܬܡܠܠ ܗܘ

ܙܒܢܐ ܒܚܕ ܫܘܪܝܐ ܢܬܦܪ ܡܢ ܚܕ ܛܠܐ ܣܘܓܐܐ. ܐܝܟ ܗܢܐ. ܚܕ ܡܟܝܠ ܢܦܫܐ.[19]
ܐܬܘܠܘܓܘܣ. ܪܘܚܐ. ܠܐܝܬܐ. ܢܫܡܐ. ܡܕܝܢܐ ܫܠܝܚܐ. ܦܪܘܫܐ

(**1**) Loan translation of Arabic *mubtada*ʾ and *ḫabar* respectively. (**2**) 'Divination is a grave sin.' (**3**) 'And your fear is your fault.' (**4**) 'And our God is a consuming fire.' (**5**) 'And the Jew became king.' (**6**) So in Martin 1872:45

contra Moberg 1922:45 ܥܒܪܬ. The form is a Pe Perf. 3fs. of √ ܥܒܪ used with the force of the present: see §81. (**7**) 'Kedar shall be a meadow.' (**8**) 'Thy word is a lamp for my feet.' (**9**) 'The soul of men is the lamp of the Lord.' (**10**) 'Water puts out a burning fire.' (**11**) 'theologian,' the reference being to Gregory of Nazianzus. (**12**) 'He, the Word, God, one who is invisible before the worlds, one who is incorporeal.' (**13**) 'thereafter, then' (Gk εἶτα). (**14**) A Pe Inf.; on the syntax, see § 98 j. (**15**) /gvayyaa/, a Pe Ptc pass m.pl.emph. of ܓܒܐ. (**16**) 'O Christ, you who were born from a virgin immersed the chosen of the heroes in the depths of the non-suffering whilst cleansing the three portions of the soul.' (**17**) 'as in water': on the conjunction Dalath, see § 100. (**18**) /mettahmee/ 'gets omitted,' an Ettaf Ptc of √ ܗܡܐ. Contrast ܡܗܡܝܢ, an Af pass. Ptc. later emphasising the state 'omitted': see § 50. (**19**) 'This is sweet (and) sour.'

GLOSSARY

[Verbs are arranged by roots, but other words alphabetically. The vowels of the Perfect and Imperfect in Peal are indicated like *a/e*: e.g., ܙܒܢ Pe *a/e*, which means Pf. ܙܒܢ /zvan/ and Impf. ܢܙܒܢ /nezben/.

Some of those words which occur only very rarely in the chrestomathy texts have simply been translated in footnotes, but not listed in the Glossary.]

ܐܠܦ

ܐܒܐ *m* (§ 43) father
ܐܒܕ *a/a* Pe (*Impf.* ܢܐܒܕ) perish; ܐܒܝܕ lost; Af (ܐܘܒܕ) = *caus* Pe, exterminate
ܐܒܘܒܐ flute
ܐܒܠܐ *m* grieving, mourning
ܐܓܘܢܐ *m* contest (ἀγών)
ܐܓܘܪܣܐ farm (ἀγρός)
ܐܓܪ *a/o* Pe hire
ܐܓܪܐ *m* reward, wages
ܐܓܪܐ roof; ܒܪ ܐ' demon
ܐܕܢܐ *f* ear
ܐܕܫܐ *m* produce, fruit; species
ܐܘ or
ܐܘܟܡ black
ܐܘܠܨܢܐ *m* constraint
ܐܘܡܢܐ *m* artisan, craftsman
ܐܘܡܢܘܬܐ *f* art, craftsmanship
ܐܘܢܐ *m* dwelling-place
ܐܘܢܓܠܝܘܢ *m* gospel (εὐαγγέλιον)
ܐܘܪܚܐ *f* way, road
ܐܘܪܥܐ *m* encounter; ܠܐܘܪܥ- to meet (a guest)
ܐܙܠ Pe *a/a* go, depart (§ 67)
ܐܚܐ *m* brother
ܐܚܕ Pe *a/o* capture, arrest; comprehend; retain; withhold; shut; Ethpe be shut
ܐܚܬܐ : see under ܚܬܐ
ܐ̄ܚܪܝ *adj* last; latter
ܐ̄ܚܪܝܘܬܐ *f* posteriority, post-position (*Nachstellung*)
ܐܚܪܝܬܐ *f* end
ܐ̄ܚܪܢ another, other
ܐܝܕܐ *f* (§ 43) hand
ܐܝܙܓܕܐ *m* envoy
ܐܝܚܝܕ *adj* only, sole
ܐܝܟ like, as (of similarity); ܐܝܟ ܕ *conj* just as
ܐܝܟܐ where?
ܐܝܟܢܐ, ܐܝܟܢ : how?; ܐܝܟܢܐ ܕ *conj* just as (of similarity); in order that
ܐܝܠܟܐ where?
ܐܝܠܢܐ *m* tree
ܐܝܡܡܐ *m* daytime
ܐܝܢ yes, indeed
ܐܝܢܐ which?; what!
ܐܝܩܪܐ (√ ܝܩܪ) *m* honour, fame; glory
ܐܝܬ there is; *copula in a nominal clause* (§ 109)
ܐܝܬܝ /ʾayti/ Af (√ܐܬܐ) bring
ܐܝܬܝܐ *m* substance, being
ܐܟܘܬ in the manner of (§ 46)
ܐܟܢܐ ܕ just as
ܐܟܚܕܐ together
ܐܟܡܐ *conj* as, just as
ܐܟܡܐ ܕ in order that ...
ܐܟܣܢܝܐ *m* foreigner (ξένιος)
ܐܠܐ but
ܐܠܗܐ *m* god
ܐܠܗܘܬܐ *f* divinity

ܐܠܘ if (of unreal condition)
ܐܠܝܨ strait
ܐܠܦ Pa teach
ܐܠܦܐ *f* ship
ܐܠܦܐ thousand (§ 44 a)
ܐܠܨ Pe *a/o* compel; oppress; Ethpe = *pass* Pe
ܐܡܐ *f* mother
ܐܡܝܢ constant, diligent
ܐܡܝܢܘ *f* constancy: ܒܐܡܝܢܘܬܐ constantly, incessantly
ܐܡܪ Pe *a/a* say; verbally indicate; mention; Ethpe (= *pass* Pe)
ܐܡܪܐ *m* lamb
ܐܡܬܐ *f* maid-servant, female slave
ܐܡܬܝ when?; ܐܡܬܝ ܕ- when, whenever
ܐܢ if
ܐܢܐ *pron* I
ܐܢܗܘ ܕ = ܐܢ 'if'
ܐܢܚܢ we
ܐܢܫ somebody; ܠܐ ܐܢܫ not a man, nobody; ܐܢܫܐ people, some people
ܐܢܫܘܬܐ *f* humanity; population
ܐܢܫܝ human
ܐܢܬ, ܐܢܬܝ you (*sg*)
ܐܢܬܬܐ *f* woman; wife
ܐܣܐ myrtle

ܐܣܘܛܘܬܐ *f* intemperance (ἀσωτία)
ܐܣܘܪܐ *m* chains
ܐܣܛܕܝܢ stadium (στάδιον)
ܐܣܛܘܐ *m* portico (στοά)
ܐܣܪ Pe *a/o* tie, bind
ܐܥܦܐ double
ܐܦ also
ܐܦܐ *f* face; ܥܠ ܐܦܝ for the sake of, on behalf of
ܐܦܕܢܐ *f* palace
ܐܦܝ̈ *m sg*. curtain; also ܐܦܝ̈ ܬܪܥܐ curtain
ܐܦܠܐ nor
ܐܦܢ even if, though (< ܐܦ ܐܢ)
ܐܦܝܣܩܘܦܐ *m* bishop (ἐπίσκοπος)
ܐܪܒܥ four
ܐܪܕܝܟܠܐ *m* architect
ܐܪܕܝܟܠܘܬܐ *f* architecture
ܐܪܝܐ *m* lion
ܐܪܟ Af prolong, delay
ܐܪܡܠܬܐ *f* widow
ܐܪܥܐ *f* land, country
ܐܫܛܪܐ (also ܫܛܪܐ) *m* deed (legal document)
ܐܫܬܘܕܝ: see under ܝܕܝ
ܐܬܐ (§ 67) Pe come; Af (ܐܝܬܝ) bring
ܐܬܐ *f* (*pl* ܐܬܘܬܐ) sign
ܐܬܘܬܐ *f* letter (of alphabet)
ܐܬܠܝܛܘܬܐ *f* fortitude

ܐܰܬܳܢܳܐ *f* she-ass
ܐܰܬܪܳܐ (*pl* ܐܰܬܪ̈ܘܳܬܳܐ) *m* place;
ܒܰܪ ܐܰܬܪܳܐ compatriot

ܒܝܬ

ܒ *prep* in; with [of instrument]
ܒܓܰܘ *prep* in, within: see under ܓܰܘ.
ܒܰܕܓܽܘܢ /ba<u>d</u>gun/ therefore
ܒܕܩ Pa inform, confirm
ܒܕܪ Pa disperse
ܒܰܢܝܳܚܳܐܝܬ gently
ܒܗܬ Pe *e/a* feel shame
ܒܶܗܬܬܳܐ *f* shame
ܒܘܣܳܡܳܐ *m* suavity, delight
ܒܘܫܳܠܳܐ *m* cooked food
ܒܬ (√ ܒܘܬ) Pe pass the night
ܒܙ (√ܒܙܙ) Pe *a/o* rob
ܒܙܳܙܳܐ *m* linen-draper, cloth-merchant
ܒܰܛܺܝܠ meaningless, useless
ܒܛܠ Pe *e/a* be idle
ܒܰܛܺܝܠ meaningless; transient, ephemeral; lazy
ܒܶܝܢܳܬ, ܒܶܝܢ *prep* amongst, between
ܒܺܝܫ bad, evil
ܒܺܝܫܳܐܝܬ badly
ܒܺܝܫܽܘܬܳܐ *f* badness; wickedness
ܒܰܝܬܳܐ *m* (*pl* ܒ̈ܳܬܶܐ) house
ܒܟܳܐ Pe cry, weep; Af = *caus* Pe

ܒܰܠܚܽܘܕ alone; only
ܒܠܥ Pe *a/a* be struck, wounded; Ethpe be carried away
ܒܢܳܐ Pe build
ܒܶܢܝܳܢܳܐ *m* building, edifice
ܒܶܣܳܕܳܐ *m* pillow, cushion
ܒܰܣܺܝܡ fragrant, sweet
ܒܰܣܺܝܡܽܘܬܳܐ *f* benevolence; joy, delight
ܒܶܣܝܳܐ *m* contempt, negligence
ܒܣܡ Pe *e/a* be merry, rejoice; Pa delight; Ethpa be made sweet; enjoy (ܒ)
ܒܥܳܐ Pe seek; look for; ask for; request (ܡܶܢ); beseech; Ethpe = pass Pe; be required (by ܠ); ܒܶܥܽܘܝܳܐ necessary
ܒܰܥܠܳܐ *m* husband
ܒܥܶܠܕܒܳܒܳܐ *m* enemy
ܒܨܺܝܪ weak, inadequate
ܒܰܪ outside; ܠܒܰܪ ܡܶܢ outside of
ܒܪܳܐ Pe create; Ethpe = *pass* Pe
ܒܪܳܐ *m* [*pl* ܒܢܰܝܳܐ § 43] son; (+ ܫܢܺܝܢ + card. num.) ... years old; ܒܰܪ ܐܢܳܫܳܐ, ܒܰܪܢܳܫܳܐ a human (pl. ܒܢܰܝ ܐܢܳܫܳܐ, ܒܢܰܝܢܳܫܳܐ)
ܒܳܪܳܝ *adj* outside
ܒܪܺܝܬܳܐ *f* (*pl* ܒܪ̈ܝܳܬܳܐ) creature; creation
ܒܪܶܟ Pa bless; Ethpa = *pass* Pa
ܒܪܰܡ *conj* but, however

ܒܪܢܫܐ *m* man
ܒܪܬܐ *f* daughter; ... years old
ܒܬܘܠܘܬܐ *f* virginity
ܒܬܘܠܬܐ *f* virgin
ܒܬܪ, *prep* after [of place]; ܡܢ ܒܬܪ *prep* after [of time]; ܒܬܪܟܢ thereafter; ܡܢ ܒܬܪ ܕ *conj* after

ܓܡܠ

ܓܐܐ (ܓܐܝܐ) glorious, lofty
ܓܐܪܐ *m* arrow
ܓܒܐ *m* side, bank (of river)
ܓܒܐ Pe choose
ܓܒܪܐ *m* man, male; husband
ܓܕܐ /gaddaa/ *m* control; fortune
ܓܕܫ Pe *e/a* happen; happen to be
ܓܘ : ܒܓܘ *prep* within, in the midst of (+ *suf.* ܒܓܘܗ); ܠܓܘ into; ܡܢ ܠܓܘ *adv* inside, within
ܓܘܚܟܐ *m* laughingstock
ܓܘܝ *adj* internal, inward
ܓܘܝܐ *m* inhabitant, resident
ܓܘܢܐ *m* colour
ܓܘܣܐ : ܒܝܬ ܓܘܣܐ refuge
ܓܘܪܐ *m* adultery
ܓܘܫܡܐ *m* body
ܓܙܐ : ܒܝܬ ܓܙܐ treasury
ܓܙܘܪܬܐ *f* circumcision
ܓܙܝܪܐ *m* lictor
ܓܙܪ Pe *a/o* circumcise; Ethpe = *pass* Pe
ܓܝܪ *conj* for
ܓܠܐ Pe reveal, uncover; Ethpe reveal itself, appear
ܓܠܠܐ, ܓܠܐ *m* wave
ܐܬܓܠܙ Ethpe deprive oneself (of ܡܢ), lose
ܓܡܝܪܐܝܬ *adv* completely
ܓܡܪ Pe *a/o* accomplish, complete; abolish, annul
ܓܢܒ Pe *a/o* steal
ܓܢܒܘܬܐ *f* theft
ܓܢܒܪܐ /gabbaaraa/ *m* hero
ܓܢܘܢܐ *m* bridal chamber (= ܒܝܬ ܓ'), canopy for wedding ceremony
ܓܥܐ Pe belch out
ܐܓܥܠ Af entrust, commit
ܓܦܐ *m* wing
ܓܦܬܐ *f* (*pl* ܓܘܦܢܐ) vine
ܓܪ (√ܓܪܪ) Pe *a/o* drag
ܓܪܒܝ northern
ܓܪܕ Pa cease (from ܡܢ)

ܕܠܬ

ܕ the fact that (Jn 11.13); in order that [+ *Impf.*]; because; *joins two nouns* (*of*); introduces direct speech (§ 96 e i); ܕܠܐ without

ܕܶܒܚܳܐ *m*, ܕܶܒܚܬܳܐ *f* act of offering a sacrifice

ܕܒܰܪ Pe *a/a* take, fetch; Pa govern, guide; Ethpa = *pass* Pa or *refl* conduct oneself, live

ܕܰܓܶܠ Pa lie, defraud (ܒ)

ܕܰܓܠܬܳܐ *f* lie

ܕܰܗܒܳܐ *m* gold

ܐܶܬܕܘܝ Ethpa be devastated

ܕܘܒܳܪܳܐ *m* guidance

ܐܶܬܕܘܕ Ethpa be troubled

ܕܘܳܪܳܐ *m* deviation

ܕܰܘܝܘܬܳܐ *f* misery, wretchedness

ܕܘܟܪܳܢܳܐ *m* remebrance, memory; record

ܕܘܟܬܳܐ *f* (*pl* ܕܘܟܝܳܬܳܐ) place; ܒܕܘܟܝܢ at places, occasionally

ܐܕܝܠ Af (√ܕܘܠ) move, stir oneself

ܕܘܡܝܳܐ *m* image

ܕܳܢ (√ܕܘܢ) Pe bring suit; judge; Ettaf be judged

ܕܳܫ (√ܕܘܫ) Pe trample

ܕܚܳܐ Pe force back

ܕܚܝܠ *adj* fearful, frightful

ܕܚܶܠ Pe *e/a* fear

ܕܝܠ + *suf* 'my, his' etc. (§ 16).

ܕܶܝܢ now, by the way; however

ܕܰܝܳܢܳܐ *m* judge

ܕܺܝܢܳܪܳܐ *m* denarium

ܕܰܝܳܪܬܳܐ *f* (female-)resident

ܕܟܶܐ (ܕܰܟܝܳܐ) *adj* pure

ܕܰܟܺܝ Pa vindicate, clear the name of; cleanse; clear, remove; Ethpa be purified

ܕܰܟܝܳܐܝܬ purely

ܕܰܟܝܘܬܳܐ *f* purity

ܕܶܟܪܳܐ *m* ram; a male

ܕܶܟܪܘܬܳܐ *f* masculine gender

ܕܰܠܺܝܠ few

ܕܰܠܡܳܐ in order that ... not, in case

ܕܡܳܐ Pe resemble (+ܠ); = Ethpa

ܕܡܘܬܳܐ *f* likeness, image

ܕܡܰܝܳܐ /dmayyaa/ *m pl* price

ܕܡܶܟ Pe *e/a* sleep

ܕܡܰܥ Pe *a/a* shed tears; Pa shed many tears

ܕܶܡܥܬܳܐ *f* (*pl* ܕܶܡ̈ܥܶܐ) tear

ܕܥܶܟ Pe *e/a* go out (of light)

ܕܰܩܢܳܐ *m* beard

ܕܰܪܳܐ *m* contest; ܒܥܶܠ ܕܪܳܐ protagonist, opponent

ܕܳܪܬܳܐ *f* hall

ܕܰܪܓܳܐ *m* step (of flight)

ܕܪܳܥܳܐ *m* arm

ܕܪܶܫ Pe *a/o* (or Pa) trail (a path)

ܗܐ

ܗܳܐ behold; here (I am)

ܗܓܳܐ Ethpa enter into a legal dispute (with ܥܰܡ); ponder (about ܒ)

ܗܳܕܶܐ this [§ 13]
ܗܰܕܳܝܳܐ /haddaayaa/ *m* guide
ܗܰܕܳܡܳܐ *m* limb
ܗܰܘ that (*dem. pron.*)
ܗܘܐ Pe be, become; [+ܠ] have; come into being, emerge, happen; end up as (ܠ)
ܗܰܘܢܳܐ *m* mind, reason
ܗܳܝܕܶܝܢ *adv* thereupon, then
ܗܰܝܟܠܳܐ *m* temple, shrine
ܗܝܡܢ Pa believe; entrust, put in charge (over ܥܠ)
ܗܰܝܡܳܢܽܘܬܳܐ *f* faith, belief
ܗܳܟܰܘܬ *adv* thus, so
ܗܳܟܺܝܠ *adv* therefore
ܗܳܟܰܢ, ܗܳܟܰܢܳܐ *adv* thus
ܗܳܠܶܝܢ these
ܗܠܟ Pa walk; walk along, walk about
ܗܰܠܶܠܽܘܝܳܐ Hallelujah
ܗܡܐ Af take no notice of
ܗܳܢܳܐ *m.sg.* this
ܗܶܢܽܘܢ *m.pl.* they
ܗܳܢܽܘܢ *m.pl.* those
ܗܰܢܝܳܐܽܘܬܳܐ *f* pleasantness
ܗܘܦܛܝܐ consulship (ὑπατεία)
ܗܦܟ Pe *a/o* return, turn round (*intr*); go against, contravene (ܒ); Ethpa spend time together; Af divert
ܐܰܗܰܪ Af (√ܗܪܪ) harm
ܗܳܪܟܳܐ *adv* here
ܗܪܣܝܣ *f* difference (αἵρεσις)

ܗܳܫܳܐ *adv* now

ܘ

-ܘ and
ܘܳܠܶܐ fitting, proper
ܘܰܥܕܳܐ *m* appointed time

ܙ

ܙܳܒܽܘܢܳܐ *m* buyer
ܙܒܺܝܢܽܘܬܳܐ *f* purchase
ܙܒܢ Pe *a/e* buy; Pa sell
ܙܶܒܢܳܐ / ܙܒܳܢܳܐ *m* purchase
ܙܽܘܒܳܢܳܐ /zubbaanaa/ *m* sale
ܙܰܒܢܳܐ *m* time (opp. space) [ܒܟܽܠܙܒܰܢ always]; ܙܒܰܢ at times; once, formerly; *f* time (of frequency) [ܙܒܰܬܳܐ /zvattaa/]
ܙܰܕܺܝܩ righteous, just
ܙܕܩ Pa attribute, confer
ܙܳܕܶܩ right, appropriate
ܐܶܙܕܗܰܪ Ethpe keep away from (ܡܶܢ); beware, watch over (ܒ)
ܐܶܙܕܰܘܰܓ Ethpa be joined, have (sexual) intercourse
ܙܘܳܕܳܐ *m* food (for a journey)
ܙܽܘܘܳܓܳܐ *m* coitus
ܙܳܢ (√ܙܘܢ) Pe feed
ܙܳܥ (√ܙܘܥ) Pe shake (*intr*); Af move (*tr*); Ettaf be moved, shaken

ܙܘܥܐ *m* movement
ܙܝܘܐ *m* splendour
ܙܝܙܢܐ *m* tares
ܙܝܢܐ *m* weapon
ܙܟܐ Pe be declared innocent; win a case; Pa defeat
ܙܟܘܬܐ *f* innocence
ܙܡܝܪܬܐ *f* song
ܙܡܢ Pa invite; Ethpa = *pass* Pa
ܙܡܪ Pe *a/a* sing
ܙܡܪܐ *m* singing
ܙܡܪܬܐ *f* songster, (female) singer
ܙܢܐ *m* mode
ܙܢܝܘܬܐ *f* fornication
ܙܥܘܪ little, slight
ܙܥܘܪܘܬܐ *f* littleness
ܐܙܥܩ Af shout (at ܥܠ)
ܙܥܪ Pa diminish (= Af)
ܙܩܝܦܐ *m* cross
ܙܪܥ Pe *a/a* sow (seed)
ܙܪܥܐ *m* offspring

ܚܝܬ

ܚܐܪ free; ܒܪ ܚܐܪܐ a free person (not slave)
ܚܐܪܘܬܐ *f* freedom
√ܚܒܒ Af (ܐܚܒܒ) love
ܚܒܝܒ *adj* dear
ܚܒܠ Pa destroy, corrupt; Ethpa *pass* Pa
ܚܒܠܐ *m* corruption, ceasing to exist
ܚܒܪܐ *m* colleague, friend
ܚܒܫ Pe *a/o* tie up, bind
ܚܕ, ܚܕܐ one
ܚܕܕܐ each other, one another
ܚܕܘܬܐ *f* joy, merry-making
ܚܕܚܕ̈ܢܐ some
ܚܕܝ Pe be glad, rejoice
ܚܕܝܘܬܐ *f* singular number, singularity
ܚܕܪ Pe *a/o* surround
ܚܕܪ *prep* around
ܚܕܬ Pa renew; Ethpa = *pass* Pa
ܚܕܬ (ܚܕܬܬܐ) new
ܚܒ (√ܚܘܒ) Pe become liable to; Pa condemn, pronounce guilty; Ethpa = *pass* Pa
ܚܘܒܐ *m* love
ܚܘܒܬܐ *f* debt; dues
ܚܘܝ Pa show, demonstrate
ܚܘܝܐ *m* (*pl.* ܚܘܘܬܐ) snake
ܚܘܠܡܢܐ *m* health
ܚܘܣܪܢܐ *m* need
ܚܪ (√ܚܘܪ) Pe *u* gaze at (ܒ); look forward to (ܠ)
ܚܘܪܒܐ *m* desolation, devastation
ܚܘܫܒܐ *m* thinking
ܚܘܫܚܐ *m* use
ܚܙܐ Pe see, spy; see to; Ethpe appear, seem; become visible, make appearance
ܚܙܘܐ *m* vision; appearance, look

ܚܙܩ Pe *a/o* gird, gird up; depart, set off; Pa gird round
ܚܛܗܐ *m* sin
ܐܬܚܛܦ Ethpe be snatched
ܚܝ *adj* alive, living
ܚܝܐ Pe (*Impf* ܢܚܐ: § 67) live, survive; become alive; Af quicken, restore life
ܚܝ̈ܐ *m* life
ܚܝܒܐ *m* debtor
ܐܬܚܝܒ Ethpa be declared guilty; be defeated
ܚܝܒܘܬܐ *f* guilt
ܚܝܘܬܐ *f* (*pl* ܚܝ̈ܘܬܐ) animal; life, vitality
ܚܝܠ Pa empower
ܚܝܠܐ *m* strength
ܚܝܠܬܢ mighty, strong; capable of
ܚܟܝܡ wise; expert
ܚܟܡܬܐ *f* wisdom
ܚܠܐ *m* sand
ܚܠܐ *m* vinegar
ܚܠܐ, ܚܠܝܐ sweet
ܚܠܘܠܐ *m* feast
ܐܬܚܠܛ Ethpa join (ܥܡ)
ܚܠܝܡ healthy
ܚܠܝܨ valiant
ܐܬܚܠܡ Ethpe (or Ethpa) become healthy
ܚܠܦ Pe *a/a* change (*intr*)
ܚܠܦ *prep* instead of; for the sake of

ܚܠܩܐ *m* fate
ܚܡܝܥ sour
ܚܡܝܫܝ fifth
ܚܡܪܐ *m* donkey
ܚܡܫ, ܚܡܫܐ five
ܚܡܫܝܢ fifty
ܚܡܫܡܐܐ five hundred
ܚܡܫܬܥܣܪ fifteen
ܚܡܬܐ *f* fury (at ܥܠ)
ܚܢܝܓ /ḥnig̱/ doleful
ܚܢ Pe *a/o* (√ܚܢܢ) show pity
ܚܢܘܬܐ *f* shop
ܚܢܢܐ *m* compassion, mercy
ܚܢܩ Ethpe to suffocate (*intr*), drown
ܚܣܝܪ *adj* less
ܚܣܟ Pe *a/o* spare, withhold
ܚܣܡܐ *m* jealousy, suspicion
ܚܦܐ Pa cover, bury out of sight; Ethpa cover oneself, put on a veil
ܚܨܐ *m* loins
ܚܨܝܦܐܝܬ shamelessly
ܚܪܕܠܐ *m* mustard
ܚܐܪܘܬܐ *f* liberty
ܚܪܫܐ *m* magician, sorcerer
ܚܪܬܐ *f* end
ܚܫ (√ܚܫܫ) Pe *a/a* suffer
ܚܫܐ *m* pain, suffering
ܚܫܒ Pe *a/o* calculate; Pa = Pe; Ethpa deliberate
ܚܘܫܒܢܐ = ܚܘܫܒܐ *m* ' ܥܠ ܚ on account of

ܚܫܘܟܐ *m* darkness
ܚܫܘܫܐ *m* [grammatical t.t.] patient, passive
ܚܫܘܫܘܬܐ *f* status of patient; suffering
ܚܫܚ Pe *a/a* be needed, necessary; useful
ܚܫܚܘܬܐ *f* usefulness
ܚܫܚܬܐ *f* (*pl* ܚܫܚ̈ܬܐ) need, necessity
ܚܫܡܝܬܐ *f* meal
ܚܬܐ *f* (pl. ܐܚ̈ܘܬܐ) sister
ܚܬܝܬ correct
ܚܬܡ Pe *a/o* sign; seal; Pa confirm
ܚܬܢܐ *m* bridegroom

ܛܝܬ

ܛܒ good; *adv* exceedingly, very
ܛܒܐ *m* news, report; [grammatical t.t.] predicate
ܛܒܥ Pe *a/o* immerse; Ethpa be sunk
ܐܛܝܣ Af let fly
ܛܘܝܒܐ *m* preparation
ܛܘܪܐ *m* mountain
ܛܝܒ Pa prepare; provide
ܛܝܒܘܬܐ *f* goodness
ܛܝܡܐ *m* price (τιμή)
ܛܝܢܐ *m* mud, clay
ܛܟܣ Pa set in order; appoint
ܛܟܣܐ *m* order, rule
ܛܠܝܐ *m* child
ܛܠܡ Pe *a/o* wrong, oppress; Pa negate, deny
ܛܢܦܘܬܐ *f* impurity
ܛܥܐ Pe be missing; err; forget
ܛܥܡ Pe *e/a* eat, taste
ܛܪܦܐ *m* leaf
ܐܬܛܫܝ Ethpa hide oneself

ܝܘܕ

ܝܐܝܐ comely, pretty
ܐܬܝܐܒ Ethpa desiderate
ܐܘܒܠ Af transport
ܝܒܠܐ *m* stream
ܐܬܝܒܫ Ethpa become dry
ܒܐܝܕ : ܒܝܕ *prep* through, by (instrumental, agency), because of
ܐܘܕܝ Af confess, declare, acknowledge; admit (ܒ); thank; praise; Eštaf (ܐܫܬܘܕܝ) confess; promise
ܝܕܥ Pe know; Ethpe become known; Af (ܐܘܕܥ) make known; Eštaf (ܐܫܬܘܕܥ) perceive, recognise
ܝܕܥܬܐ /yiḏaʿṯaa/ *f* knowledge
ܝܗܒ Pe (§ 67) give
ܝܗܘܒܐ *m* giver
ܝܘܠܦܢܐ *m* doctrine, teaching
ܝܘܡܐ (*pl* ܝܘܡ̈ܬܐ, ܝܘܡ̈ܐ) *m* day

ܝܘܡܢܐ today; nowadays
ܝܘܩܪܐ *m* weight, burden
ܝܘܪܬܢܐ *m* inheritance
ܝܘܬܪܢܐ *m* increment, interest
ܝܚܝܕܝ *adj* only, sole
ܐܘܠܕ (ܝܠܕ) Af procreate, beget; Ethpe be born
ܝܠܕܐ *m* child-bearing, birth
ܝܠܠܬܐ *f* (*pl* ܝܠܠܬܐ) howling, wailing
ܝܠܦ Pe *e/a* learn
ܝܡܐ Pe swear, take an oath
ܝܡܐ *m* sea
ܝܡܝܢܐ *f* the right-hand
ܐܘܣܦ Af add; Ettaf = *pass* Af.
ܝܥܐ Pe sprout, grow; Af (ܐܘܥܝ) produce
ܝܥܢܬܐ *f* crenel, battlement
ܝܥܢܘܬܐ *f* avarice
ܝܩܪ Pa honour
ܝܪܘܬܐ *m* heir
ܝܪܚܐ *m* month
ܝܪܬ Pe *e/a* inherit; Af = Pe *caus*
ܝܫܛ Af (ܐܘܫܛ) extend
ܝܬܒ Pe *e/e* (*Impf* ܢܬܒ) settle, dwell; sit, take a seat
ܝܬܝܒ seated
ܝܬܝܪ excessive; superfluous; more abundant; ܝܬܝܪ ܡܢ more than
ܝܬܝܪܐܝܬ especially
ܝܬܡܐ *m* orphan

ܟ

ܟܐܒ Pe *a* (ܢܟܐܒ) hurt, be painful
ܟܐܒܐ *m* pain
ܟܐܢܐܝܬ justly
ܟܐܦܐ *f* stone, rock
ܟܥܪ Pa disfigure
ܟܒܪ perhaps
ܟܕ when
ܟܕܒ Pa tell lies
ܟܕܘ enough
ܟܦܬ Pe *a/o* tie, bind
ܟܗܢܐ *m* priest
ܟܘܒܐ *m* thorn
ܟܘܟܒܐ *m* star
ܟܘܠܝܬܐ *f* kidney
ܟܘܪܗܢܐ *m* sickness
ܟܘܪܣܝܐ *m* (*pl* ܟܘܪܣܘܬܐ) chair, seat
ܟܝܠܬܐ *f* measure
ܟܝܢܐ *m* nature, natural character
ܟܟܪܐ *f* talent
ܟܠ every, all
ܟܠܐ Pe stay someone's hand; Ethpe be impeded; be suspended, stopped
ܟܠܒܐ *m* dog
ܟܠܝܠܐ *m* garland, crown
ܟܠܠ Ethpa be adorned
ܟܠܡܐ = ܟܠ ܡܐ all that ...
ܟܠܡܕܡ everything

ܟܠܢܝ *adj* general, universal
ܟܠܬܐ *f* bride
ܟܡܐ how much?; how!;
ܟܡܐ ܕ as much as
ܟܘܡܪܘܬܐ /kumr-/ *f* priesthood
ܟܐܢܐܝܬ justly
ܟܢܘܫܝܐ *m* plural number, plurality
ܟܢܘܫܬܐ *f* congregation
ܟܐܢܘܬܐ *f* righteousness (also spelled ܟܢ')
ܟܢܝܫܘܬܐ *f* plurality; confluence
ܟܢܫ Pe *a/o* assemble (both *tr* and *intr*); Ethpa come together (for a meeting); be brought together
ܟܢܫܐ *m* crowd, group of people
ܟܢܬܐ (*pl* ܟܢܘ̈ܬܐ) *m* colleague
ܟܣܐ (ܟܣܝܐ) hidden
ܟܣܦܝܠܐ coral (?)
ܟܣܦܐ *m* silver
ܟܦܢ, ܟܦܢܐ hungry
ܟܦܪ Pe *a/o* deny (ܒ)
ܟܪ *conj* where
ܟܪܘܙܐ *m* herald
ܐܟܪܙ Af proclaim (the gospel), evangelize; Ethpe = *pass* Af
ܟܪܛܝܣܐ *m/f* paper, document (χάρτης)
ܟܪܝ Pe ܟܪܝܬ ܠܗ he was sad
ܟܪܝܗ *adj* sick (the He is pronounced)

ܟܪܝܘܬܐ *f* sorrow, grief
ܟܪܡܐ *m* vineyard
ܟܪܣܐ *f* belly; womb
ܟܪܣܛܝܢܐ Christian
ܐܬܟܪܟ Ethpe go round
ܟܫܝܪ competent, able
ܟܫܠܐ *m* loggerheads
ܐܬܟܫܦ Ethpa supplicate
ܟܬܝܒܘܬܐ *f* writing, document
ܟܬܒ Pe *a/o* write; Ethpe = *pass* Pe; be enrolled, registered; Af record, write down
ܟܬܦܐ *f* shoulder
ܟܬܪ Pa remain
ܐܬܟܬܫ Ethpa contest

ܠܡܕ.

ܠ *prep* to; for; *marker of direct object*
ܠܐ not; ܠܐ ܗܘܐ *negating a word other than a verb*
ܠܒܐ *m* heart; mind
ܠܒܘܫܐ *m* clothing, garment
ܠܒܟ Pe *a/o* seize; Ethpe be taken to court, sued
ܠܒܪ outside of
ܠܒܫ Pe *e/a* wear; Af clothe
ܐܠܗܒ Af inflame thirst
ܠܗ not
ܐܬܠܘܝ Ethpa accompany (ܠ)
ܠܘܚܐ *f* tablet
ܠܘܛܬܐ *f* curse

ܠܘܝܐ *m* companion
ܠܘܩܒܠ *prep* against; facing
ܠܘܩܕܡ /luqdaam/ *adv* first
ܠܘܬ *prep* beside, by; towards
ܠܚܘܕ *adv* alone, only
ܠܛܝܐ m curser
ܠܝܬ there is not
ܠܟܐ hither
ܠܠܝܐ *m* night
ܠܡܦܐܕܐ *m* lamp, torch (λαμπάς)
ܠܥܘܣܘܬܐ *f* gluttony
ܠܥܝܢ *prep* in full view of
ܠܥܠ: upwards; ܠܥܠ ܡܢ *prep* over; ܡܢ ܠܥܠ *adv* above; from above
ܠܥܣ Pe *e/a* (or: /*o*) to eat
ܠܫܢܐ tongue

ܡܝܡ

ܡܐܐ *f* hundred
ܡܐܟܘܠܐ *m* food; eating
ܡܐܢܐ *m* wares; vessel, utensil
ܡܐܣܝܢܐ *m* healer
ܡܒܘܥܐ *m* fountain, spring; source
ܡܓܕܠܐ *m* tower
ܡܕܒܚܐ *m* altar
ܡܕܒܪܐ *m* wilderness
ܡܕܒܪܢܐ *m* guide, leader
ܡܕܒܪܢܘܬܐ *f* guidance, control
ܡܕܝܢ therefore
ܡܕܝܢܬܐ *f* region; city, town
ܡܕܡ something; (+ neg.) nothing
ܐܬܡܣܟܠ Ethpa understand, interpret
ܡܕܥܐ *m* mind; knowledge; understanding, comprehension
ܡܗܝܡܢ faithful
ܡܘܗܪܐ *m* dowry
ܡܘܗܒܬܐ *f* gift
ܡܘܪܩܥܬܐ *f* firmament
ܡܘܚܐ *m* brain
ܡܘܟܟܐ *m* humility
ܡܘܟܠܐ *m* lock, bolt (μόχλος)
ܡܘܠܟܢܐ *m* promise
ܡܘܡܐ *m* defect
ܡܘܥܒܬܐ *f* growth, shoot
ܡܘܬܐ *m* death
ܡܚܐ Pe strike, hit
ܡܚܕܐ: ܡܚܕܐ ܕ- as soon as
ܡܚܕܬܢܐ *m* renovator, innovator
ܡܚܘܙܐ *m* port
ܡܚܝܠ weak
ܡܚܝܠܘܬܐ *f* weakness
ܡܚܝܢܐ *m* life-giver
ܡܚܫܘܠܐ *m* storm, tempest
ܡܚܬܬܐ (√ܢܚܬ) *m* descent
ܡܛܐ, ܡܛܝ Pe reach, arrive at (ܠ, ܠܘܬ); Pa attain (ܠ)
ܡܛܟܣܘܬܐ *f* arrangement, syntax (τάξις)
ܡܛܠ, ܡܛܠܬ *prep* because of;

concerning, about; ܡܛܠ ܕ conj because; in order that (+ *Impf.*)

ܡܛܠܡܢܐ why?

ܡܛܪܐ *m* rain(fall)

ܡܝܐ *m* water

ܡܝܬ (*Impf* ܢܡܘܬ) Pe to die

ܡܝܬ *adj* dead

ܡܝܬܪ superior

ܡܝܬܪܘܬܐ *f* better state

ܡܟܐ from here, henceforward

ܡܟܘܠܬܐ *f* food (also spelled ܡܐܟ')

ܡܟܝܟ humble

ܡܟܝܟܘܬܐ *f* humility

ܡܟܣܐ *m* tax-collector

ܡܟܪ Pe *a/o* marry; Ethpe get engaged

ܡܠܐ (ܡܠܝܐ) full

ܡܠܐ Pe be full; fill (ܡܠܐ ܠܒ- to comfort); Ethpe be filled

ܡܠܐܟܐ *m* messenger; angel

ܡܠܘܐܐ *m* wealth

ܡܠܚܐ *f* salt

ܡܠܚܐ *m* seafarer, sailor

ܡܠܟ Pe *a/o* promise; Ettaf be made king

ܡܠܟܐ *m* king

ܡܠܟܘܬܐ *f* kingdom; reign, rule

ܡܠܠ Pa speak

ܡܡܠܠ *m* speaker, speaking

ܡܠܦܢ educative, instructive

ܡܠܬܐ (*pl.* ܡܠܐ) f word, term

ܡܡܠܠܐ *m* sentence; utterance

ܡܢ who?; ܡܢ ܕ one who

ܡܢ *prep* from, out of; than (in comparison); ܡܢ ܕ- when, after

ܡܢܐ what?; why?

ܐܬܡܢܝ Ethpe be counted, reckoned

ܡܢܝܢܐ *m* counting; number

ܡܢܝ Pa bring, lead

ܡܢܬܐ *f* (*pl* ܡܢܘܬܐ) portion, sector

ܡܣܟܢ poor, indigent

ܐܬܡܣܟܢ Ethpa become poor

ܡܣܟܢܘܬܐ *f* poverty

ܡܣܒ: ܡܣܒ ܒܐܦ̈ܐ peanlty

ܡܣܩܐ *m* ascent

ܡܥܒܕܢܘܬܐ *f* working, action

ܡܥܠܝ exalted, lofty

ܡܥܠܢܐ *m* entrance

ܡܥܡܪܐ *m* residence

ܡܥܪܬܐ *f* cave

ܡܥܪܒܝ western

ܡܦܘܠܬܐ *f* fall

ܡܦܪܢܣܢܘܬܐ *f* leadership

ܡܨܐ be able (to)

ܡܨܝܕܬܐ *f* net, trap

ܐܬܡܨܥܝ Ethpa intervene

ܡܨܥܬܐ *f* middle

ܡܪܐ *m* (*cst* ܡܪܝ) master

ܡܪܓܢܝܬܐ *f* pearl (μαργαρίτης)

ܡܪܕܝܬܐ *f* course
ܡܪܗܛܐ *m* property, possession
ܡܪܘܡܐ *m* height, high place
ܐܡܪܚ Af venture, act audaciously
ܡܪܚܘܬܐ *f* boldness, audacity
ܡܪܝܐ God (of Israel), Lord (w. ref. to Jesus)
ܡܪܝܡ exalted
ܡܪܝܪ bitter
ܡܪܟܒܬܐ *f* carriage
ܡܪܢܝܬܐ *f* thought
ܡܪܩ Pe *a/o* polish
ܡܪܪܐ *m* bitterness
ܡܫܒܚܢܐ *m* praiser
ܡܫܘܚܬܐ *f* (*pl* ܡܫܘܚ̈ܬܐ) measure; ܒܡܫ- moderately
ܡܫܚܐ *m* oil
ܡܫܝܚܐ *m* messiah, Christ
ܡܫܟܢܐ *m* tabernacle, tent; dwelling place; pledge, pawn
ܡܫܠܛܢܘܬܐ *f* power
ܡܫܠܡ perfect
ܡܫܬܘܬܐ *f* banquet; wedding feast
ܡܫܬܝܐ *m* drink; drinking
ܡܬܘܡ : ܡܢ ܡܬܘܡ ever
ܡܬܝܚܐ *m* act of extending
ܡܬܚܘܝܢܘܬܐ *f* demonstration

ܢ

ܢܓܝܪܘܬܐ *f* length; ܢܓܝܪܘܬ ܪܘܚܐ patience
ܐܬܢܒܝ Ethpa prophesy, foretell
ܢܓܕ Pe *a/e* draw
ܢܓܗ Pe (*Impf* ܢܢܓܗ) ܢܓܗܬ the dawn broke; Af (ܐܢܓܗ) spend the night
ܢܓܪܐ /naggaaraa/ *m* carpenter
ܢܓܪܘܬܐ *f* carpentry; carpentership
ܢܗܪ Pe *a/a* shine; Af light up (*tr*), kindle
ܢܗܝܪ illumined, light; informed, well versed; *noun* light
ܢܘܓܪܐ *m* a long time
ܢܘܗܪܐ *m* light
ܐܢܝܚ (√ܢܘܚ) Af give rest; put away; Ettaf have rest
ܢܘܟܪܝ foreign, alien
ܢܘܪܐ *f* fire
ܢܚܝܪܐ *m* nostril
ܐܬܢܚܡ Ethpa be resurrected
ܢܘܚܡܬܐ *f* resurrection
ܢܚܬ Pe *e/o* (*Impf* ܢܚܘܬ) descend
ܢܚܬܐ *m* robe
ܢܛܪ Pe *a/a* keep, maintain; watch out for; guard
ܢܝܚܐ *m* satisfaction; resting place; rest
ܢܝܣܢ Nisan = April

ܢܝܪܐ *m* yoke
ܢܟܝܢܐ *m* injury, blemish
ܢܟܠܐ *m* deceit
ܢܟܣ Pe *a/o* slaughter
ܢܟܣܐ *m* wealth
ܢܡܘܣܐ *m* law (νόμος)
ܢܡܘܣܐܝܬ legally
ܢܣܒ Pe *a/a* take (in hand)
ܢܣܝ Pa test
ܢܦܠ Pe *a/e* (*Impf* ܢܦܠ) fall; fall upon, harass
ܢܦܩ Pe *a/o* (*Impf* ܢܦܘܩ) exit; Af (ܐܦܩ) bring/take out
ܢܦܩܬܐ /nfaq-/ *f* (*pl* ܢܦ̈ܩܬܐ) expenses
ܢܦܫܐ *f* (*pl* ܢܦ̈ܫܬܐ) soul; tomb; (with a *pron. suf.*) -self, -selves
ܢܨܒ Pe *a/o* plant; Ethpe = *pass* Pe
ܐܬܢܨܚ Ethpa distinguish oneself
ܢܨܝܚ *adj* illustrious, glorious; victorious
ܢܩܒܘܬܐ *f* feminine gender
ܢܩܒܬܐ *f* a female
ܐܩܦ Af (√ ܢܩܦ) add, join
ܢܩܫ Pe *a/o* hit, knock (ܒ)
ܢܫܡܬܐ *f* breath
ܢܫܪܐ *m* eagle
ܐܬܢܓܕ Ethpa become drawn, attracted
ܢܬܠ Pe *Impf* 'he shall give' (§ 67)

ܣܡܟܬ

ܣܒܠܬܐ /sebbel-/ *f* ladder, flight of stairs
ܣܒܥ Pe *a/a* be satiated
ܣܒܥܘܬܐ *f* satiety
ܣܒܪ Pe *a/a* think; Ethpe = *pass* Pe; Pa hope (in ܒ / ܥܠ); evangelise, preach the gospel
ܣܒܪܐ *m* hope
ܣܒܪܬܐ /svartaa/ *f* gospel
ܣܒܬܐ *f* old woman
ܣܓܐ Pe increase (*intr*); Af increase (*tr*); assist
ܣܓܕ Pe *e/o* worship
ܣܓܝ /saggi/ much, many, abundant
ܣܓܦ Pa harm
ܣܕܩ Pe *a/o* rip, tear up
ܣܕܪ Pe *a/o* arrange
ܣܗܕ Pe *e/a* testify; Af = Pe
ܣܘܓܐܐ *m* multitude; majority
ܣܘܟܠܐ *m* meaning, sense
ܣܘܟܠܝ pertaining to meaning (ܣܘܟܠܐ)
ܣܘܟܬܐ *f* branch
ܣܘܥܪܢܐ *m* action; event
ܣܘܪܚܢܐ *m* defect; wrongdoing; damage
ܣܚܦ Pe *a/o* overthrow, expel
ܣܝܒܘܬܐ *f* old age
ܣܝܒܪ Pa bear, endure

ܣܝܒܪܬܐ *f* food
ܣܡ (√ܣܝܡ) Pe place; Ethpe be located; be issued
ܣܝܡܬܐ *f* treasure
ܣܟ at all; altogether
ܣܟܝ Pa expect, look forward (to ܠ)
ܣܟܝܢܐ *f* knife
ܐܣܟܠ Af do, act foolishly; err, sin
ܣܟܠ, ܣܟܠܐ foolish
ܣܟܪܐ *f* shield
ܐܣܠܝ Af think nothing of, despise; Ethpe = Af *pass*
ܣܠܩ Pe *e/a* (*Impf.* ܢܣܩ) ascend; Af (ܐܣܩ) = *caus* Pe load; take up
ܣܡܝܐ (ܣܡܝܬܐ) *adj* blind
ܣܡܟ Pe *a/o* reach; ܣܡܝܟ seated at a dinner-table; Ethpe seat oneself at a table for a meal; Af, Pa support
ܣܡܟܐ *m* banquet; ܒܝܬ ܣ' banquet hall
ܣܡܠܐ *f* left-hand
ܣܢܐ Pe hate
ܣܢܝܐ *adj* (ܣܢܝܬܐ) hateful
ܣܢܐܬܐ *f* dislike
ܣܢܘܪܬܐ *f* helmet
ܣܢܝܐܝܬ badly
ܣܢܝܩ in need of (ܠܘܬ)
ܣܢܝܩܘܬܐ *f* lack
ܣܥܪ Pe *a/o* do, practise; visit
ܣܦܩ Pa empty out
ܣܦܪܐ *m* document
ܣܦܪܐ *m* scribe
ܣܦܬܐ *f* (*pl* ܣܦܘܬܐ) lip; edge, rim
ܣܩܒܠ Pa present
ܣܩܘܒܠܐ opposed
ܣܩܘܒܠ opposed, adverse
ܣܪܚ Pe *a/o* do wrong, sin; damage (+ܒ)
ܣܪܝܚܘܬܐ *f* stink
ܣܪܝܩ empty, vain
ܣܬܘܐ *m* winter
ܣܬܪ Pe *a/o* hide

ܥ

ܥܒܕ Pe *a/e* make, manufacture; do; bring about (a situation)
ܥܒܕܐ *m* servant, slave
ܥܒܕܐ *m* product; work, deed; incident
ܥܒܘܕܐ *m* actor, doer; [grammatical t.t.] active, agent
ܥܒܘܕܘܬܐ *f* status of agent; performance
ܥܒܝܕܬܐ *f* work, deed
ܥܒܪ Pe *a/a* pass away; get past; overstep; pass by
ܥܒܪܝ Hebrew
ܥܓܠ Pa roll off (*tr*)
ܥܓܠ /ʿgal/ fast, quickly
ܥܕ whilst

ܐܥܕܝ Af wrest, snatch

ܥܕܟܝܠ /ʿdakkeel/ up to then; up to now, still

ܥܕܠܐ *conj* before

ܥܕܡܐ /ʿdammaa/ *prep*
ܥܕܡܐ ܠ as far as, up to;
ܥܕܡܐ ܕ- *conj* until

ܥܕܢܐ /ʿeddaanaa/ *m* time;
ܒܟܠܥܕܢ at all times

ܥܐܕܐ *m* festival

ܥܕܪ Pa help; Ethpa = *pass* Pa

ܥܕܬܐ *f* church

ܥܗܕ Pe *a/a* remember

ܥܘܕܪܢܐ *m* help

ܥܘܗܕܢܐ *m* memory; mentioning

ܥܘܪܪܐ *m* agitation

ܥܘܠܐ *m* iniquity

ܥܘܡܩܐ *m* depth

ܥܘܡܪܐ *m* existence

ܥܘܦܝܐ *m* flower

ܐܥܝܩ Af (√ܥܘܩ) distress

ܥܘܬܩܘܬܐ *m* seniority, antiquity

ܥܘܬܪܐ *m* richness

ܥܫܝܢܘܬܐ *f* strength

ܥܛܠܐܝܬ with difficulty

ܐܬܥܛܦ Ethpe to put on, clothe oneself

ܥܝܕܐ *m.* custom

ܥܝܢܐ *f* eye; fountain

ܥܝܪܘܬܐ *f* wakefulness, vigilance

ܥܪ Af (ܐܥܝܪ) wake up (*tr*); Etta wake up (*intr*)

ܥܟܪ Pa hinder

ܥܠ *prep* on; because of; *conj*
ܥܠ ܕ- because

ܥܠ (√ܥܠܠ) Pe *a/o* enter; Af (ܐܥܠ) bring in

ܥܠܒ Pe *a/o* oppress

ܥܠܝ Pa lift; Ethpa = *pass* Pa; ascend

ܥܠܝ upper, elevated; supreme, highest

ܥܠܝܡܐ *m* youth; servant

ܥܠܠܬܐ *f* crop, harvest

ܥܠܡܐ *m* world; era; ܠܥܠܡ,
ܠܥܠܡ ܥܠܡܝܢ for ever;
ܕܠܥܠܡ eternal

ܥܠܬܐ *f* cause, reason

ܥܠܬܐ *f* burnt-offering

ܥܡ *prep* together with

ܥܡܐ *m* (*pl* ܥܡܡܐ) nation, people

ܥܡܘܪܐ *m* dweller, resident

ܥܡܠ Pe *a/a* labour; trouble onself (about ܒ)

ܥܡܠܐ *m* labour

ܥܡܩ Pa deepen

ܥܡܪ Pe *a/a* dwell, inhabit

ܥܡܪܐ (= ܥܘܡܪܐ) *m* existence

ܥܡܪܐ *m* wool

ܥܢܐ Pe reply

ܥܢܢܐ *f* cloud

ܥܣܩܐ, ܥܣܩ difficult

ܥܣܪܝܢ twenty

ܥܦܪܐ *m* dust
ܥܨܐ Pe resist, fight against
ܥܩܝܪ *adj* devastated, barren
ܥܩܪ Pe *a/o* to destroy; Ethpa be uprooted
ܥܩܪܒܐ *f* scorpion
ܥܩܬܐ *f* distress
ܐܬܥܪܒ Ethpe be mixed
ܥܪܣܐ *f* bed, couch
ܥܪܐ Pe *a/a* happen, befall (ܠ)
ܥܪܩ Pe *a/o* run away
ܥܫܝܢ powerful
ܥܫܢ Pe *e/a* (*intr*) to intensify
ܥܬܕ Pa get ready
ܥܬܝܕ be due to (do); future
ܥܬܝܩ old
ܥܬܝܪ rich
ܥܬܪ Pe *a/a* be/become rich; Af = *caus* Pe

ܦܐ

ܦܐܐ, ܦܐܝܐ beautiful
ܦܐܪܐ *m* fruit
ܦܓܪܐ /pag̱raa/ *m* body
ܦܓܪܢܝܘܬܐ *f* corporeality
ܦܚ (√ܦܘܚ) Pe *u* give out odour, smell
ܦܘܡܐ *m* mouth
ܦܘܢܝܐ *m* answer, reply
ܦܘܣܝܣ nature (φύσις)
ܦܘܣܩܢܐ *m* decision
ܦܘܪܓܣܐ tower (πύργος)
ܦܘܪܢܣܐ *m* food; administration, care
ܦܘܪܩܢܐ *m* salvation
ܦܘܪܫܢܐ *m* break-up; dislocation; distinction, differentiation
ܦܫ (ܦܘܫ) Pe remain
ܦܘܬܩܐ *m* inn (πανδοκεῖον)
ܦܚܡܐ *m* copy
ܦܛܪ Pe *a/a* leave (a place)
ܦܝܚ fragrant
ܦܝܣܐ *m* supplication
ܦܝܪܡܐ *m* censer
ܐܦܝܣ Af persuade; Ethpe (ܐܬܦܝܣ) become convinced; consent
ܦܟܐ *m* cheek
ܦܟܪ Pe *a/o* tie, bind
ܦܠܐܬܐ *f* simile, parable
ܦܠܓ Pa divide; distribute, give away
ܦܠܓܐ apoplexy
ܦܠܓܘܬܐ *f* division
ܦܠܚ Pe *a/o* do; work
ܦܢܐ Pe return; Pa turn (to ܠ) (*tr*); reply; return; Af restore; Ethpe turn (to ܠ) (*intr*)
ܦܢܝܬܐ *f* area, region
ܦܣܘܩܐ *m* section
ܦܣܝܠܬܐ *f* cut stone
ܦܣܩ Pe *a/o* dissect, dismember
ܦܣܩܝܬܐ *f* bandlet
ܦܣܬܐ *f* lot (cast)

ܦܠܚ Pe *a/o* do; labour; ܦܠܚܐ (Pe *ptc*) labourer; doer

ܦܨܝܚ happy

ܦܨܝ Pa save, rescue; Ethpa = *pass* Pa

ܦܩܕ Pe *a/o* issue an order, command; Ethpe = *pass* Pe

ܦܩܚ more advantageous

ܦܩܚܐ flower

ܦܪܕܬܐ *f* grain

ܦܪܕܝܣܐ *m* paradise

ܦܪܘܩܐ *m* saviour

ܦܪܘܫܐ *m* divider

ܦܪܙܠܐ *m* iron(works)

ܦܪܝܫܘܬܐ *f* separation

ܦܪܝܫ different

ܦܪܝܫܐ *m* Pharisee

ܦܪܝܫܐܝܬ severally, in a different way

ܦܪܨܘܦܐ *m* face (πρόσωπον)

ܦܪܩ Pe *a/o* rescue, set free; Ethpe = *pass* Pe; dissociate oneself

ܦܪܫ Pe *a/o* separate (*intr*); Eth be divorced

ܦܫܛ Pe *a/o* extend, stretch out

ܦܫܝܛܘܬܐ *f* act of streching out

ܦܫܝܩܐܝܬ clearly

ܦܬܓܡܐ *m* word; matter; scriptural passage

ܦܬܘܪܐ *m* (dining-)table

ܦܬܚ Pe *a/a* open [*tr*]

ܦܘܬܝܐ *m* width

ܨܕܐ

ܨܐܝܐ filthy

ܨܐܝܘܬܐ *f* filth

ܨܒܐ Pe desire (+ܒ); Ethpe consent; take a liking (to ܒ)

ܨܒܘܬܐ *f* (*pl* ܨܒܘܬܐ..) thing; matter

ܨܒܝܢܐ.. *m* will, desire

ܨܒܥܐ.. *f* (*pl* ܨܒܥܬܐ..) finger

ܨܒܬ Pa decorate

ܐܨܗܝ Af (or Pa ܨܗܝ) make thirsty

ܨܘܡܐ *m* fasting

ܨܪ (√ܨܘܪ) Pe *u* depict; Ettaf (ܐܬܬܨܝܪ) = *pass* Pe

ܨܬ (√ܨܘܬ) Pe *u* heed (ܠ)

ܨܚܘܬܐ *f* lewdness

ܨܝܕ.. *prep* beside, next to

ܨܝܕܐ *m* hunter

ܨܠܘܬܐ *f* (*pl* ܨܠܘܬܐ) prayer

ܨܠܚ Pa split, chop (wood)

ܨܠܐ Pa pray

ܨܠܡܐ *m* image

ܨܡܚܐ.. *m* radiance

ܨܥܪܐ *m* disgrace

ܨܦܪܐ *m* morning

ܨܦܬܐ.. *f* worry

ܨܪܝ Pa cleave, split

ܩܘܦ

ܩܐܪܘܐ *m* distress, adversity
ܩܒܠ Pa receive
ܩܒܪܐ *m* grave
ܩܒܘܪܐ *m* burial; ܒܝܬ ܩ' cemetery
ܩܕܝ Pa have permanent possession of
ܩܕܝܡܘܬܐ *f* placing before, fronting
ܩܕܝܫ sacred, holy
ܩܕܠܐ *m* neck
ܩܕܡ Pa act early; Ethpa be said *or* done first, precede
ܩܕܡ /qdem/ *adj* earlier
ܩܕܡ /qdaam/ *prep* before, ahead of; ܡܢ ܩ' prior to
ܩܕܡܝ *adj* first, former; ancient
ܩܕܫ Pa purify
ܩܘܝ Pa remain
ܩܡ (√ܩܘܡ) Pe *u* arise, stand up; be standing; take up a position; provide (for ܒ); Af raise, establish
ܩܘܪܒܢܐ *m* offering
ܩܘܫܬܐ *f* truth
ܩܛܝܢ narrow
ܩܛܝܪܐ *m* force: ܡܢ ܩܛܝܪ, ܒܩܛܝܪܐ by force, against one's will
ܩܛܠ Pe *a/o* kill
ܩܛܪ Pe *a/a* arise (of clamor)
ܩܛܪܩܛܐ *m* (river) lock, sluice (καταῤῥάκτης)
ܩܝܛܐ *m* summer
ܩܝܡܐ *m* condition
ܩܝܡܬܐ *f* resurrection
ܩܝܣܐ *m* wood
ܩܠܐ *m* voice
ܩܠܘܛܐ *m* miser
ܩܠܝܠ little (of quantity)
ܩܢܐ Pe take possession of; acquire
ܩܢܘܡܐ *m* -self (§ 12a); nature
ܩܢܛܐ *m* fear, suspicion
ܩܢܝܐ *m* reed
ܩܢܝܘܬܐ *f* possessions
ܩܢܝܢܐ *m* possession, property
ܩܣܪ *m* emperor (of Rome)
ܩܥܐ Pe shout
ܩܥܬܐ *f* shout
ܩܦ (√ܩܦܦ) Pe *o* or *a* agree
ܩܦܢܐ *m* plough
ܩܪܐ Pe call; cry out; address, speak to (ܠ); Ethpe be named, called
ܩܪܒ Pe *e/o* approach (ܠ); touch, affect (ܠ) = Ethpa
ܩܪܒܐ *m* battle
ܩܪܝܒ *adj* near
ܩܪܝܬܐ *f* (*pl* ܩܘܪܝܐ) village; field (§ 43)
ܩܪܡ Pe *a/o* to cover over
ܩܪܢܐ *f* (*pl* ܩܪܢܬܐ) horn
ܩܫ (√ܩܫܫ) Pe *a/a* be (grow)

old (of age)
ܩܰܫܝܫ *adj* elderly

ܪܝܫ

ܪܐܙܐ *m* mystery
ܪܰܒ *adj* (*pl* ܪ̈ܰܘܪܒܝܢ) great; *noun* teacher; ܪܰܒ ܟܳܗ̈ܢܶܐ chief priest
ܪܶܒܘ *f* (*pl* ܪ̈ܶܒܘܳܬܐ) myriad
ܪܰܒܘܬܳܐ *f* majesty, greatness
ܪܒܝ Pa raise (child); Ethpa grow up
ܪܶܓ̈ܝܓܳܬܐ *f* desire, passion
ܪܓܙ Pe *e/a* get angry
ܪܓܝܓ attractive, desirable
ܪܓܝܫ perceptive, sensible
ܪ̈ܶܓܠܐ *f* foot
ܪܓܝܠܬܐ *f* rivulet, tributary
ܪܓܡ Pe *a/o* stone
ܐܬܪܓܪܓ Ethpa lust (after ܠ)
ܐܪܓܫ Af feel, sense (ܒ); notice
ܪܕܐ Pe proceed, sail
ܪܳܕܽܘܦܳܐ *m* pursuer
ܪܕܦ Pe *a/o* chase, persecute
ܪܗܒܘܢܐ *m* down payment (ἀρραβών < Heb עֵרָבוֹן)
ܪܗܘܡܝ Roman
ܪܗܛ Pe *e/a* run
ܪܗܝܒ timid
ܪܘܓܙܐ *m* anger, wrath
ܪܘܚܐ *f* spirit; wind
ܪܘܚܩܐ *m* distance

ܪܘܝ Pe be intoxicated
ܪܰܘܝܘܬܳܐ *f* intoxication
ܪܳܡ (√ܪܘܡ) Af (ܐܰܪܺܝܡ) lift; Ettaf = *pass* Af
ܪܰܘܡܳܐ *m* height
ܪܘܗܒܢܐ *m* gift, marriage gifts
ܪܘܫܡܐ *m* sign; signature, signing
ܪܰܚܝܩ *adj* far
ܪܚܡ Pe *e/a* love, care for; ܪܳܚܡܳܐ friend; Pa show mercy (to ܥܠ)
ܪ̈ܰܚܡܐ *m* (often *pl*) love, mercy
ܐܪܚܩ Af remove, keep away; Ethpa = *pass* Af
ܐܪܛܒ Af (= Pa ܪܛܒ) moisten; Ethpa become moist
ܪܰܛܝܒܘܬܳܐ *f* moisture, humidity
ܪܺܝܚܐ *m* smell, odour
ܪܺܫܐ *m* head
ܪܺܫܝܬܳܐ *f* beginning
ܪܟܘܒܐ *m* vehicle
ܐܪܟܢ Af lower, let drop
ܪܳܡ *adj* high
ܪܡܐ Pe cast; Af (+ ܥܠ) saddle; = Pe
ܪܡܙ Pe *a/o* hint (at ܥܠ)
ܪܟܝܟ gentle
ܪܢܐ Pe think (of ܒ)
ܐܬܪܢܝ Ethpa take into consideration; plan; think, ponder
ܐܬܪܢܝ (ܪܢܐ II) Ethpa have

satisfaction from (ܒ)
ܪܗܘܡ sad
ܪܢܝܐ *m* thought; mind
ܪܥܡ Pe *e/a* thunder, roar
ܐܪܦܝ Af let go of; leave
ܪܦܦܐ *m* movement; ܪܦܦ ܥܝܢܐ instant
ܪܫܐ Pe accuse; Ethpe = *pass* Pe
ܪܫܝܢܐ *m* opprobrium
ܪܫܝܥ wicked
ܪܫܡ Pe *a/o* make a sign
ܪܫܡܐ = ܪܘܫܡܐ
ܪܝܫܢܐ *m* nobleman
ܪܝܫܢܝ foremost, prominent

ܫ

ܫܐܠ Pe (*Impf* ܢܫܐܠ) ask for; Pa ask (a question); Ethpe excuse oneself; Ethpa = *pass* Pa
ܫܒܒܘܬܐ *f* vicinity; neighbourhood
ܫܒܒܬܐ *f* (female) neighbour
ܫܒܚ Pa praise, laud; Ethpa = *pass* Pa
ܫܒܝܚ praiseworthy, glorious
ܫܒܥܝܢ seventy
ܫܒܩ Pe *a/o* leave alone; permit; forsake; forgive; Ethpe be exempted
ܫܒܬܐ sabbath
ܐܫܬܓܫ Ethpe be perturbed
ܫܓܝܫ troubled, in turmoil
ܫܕܐ Pe cast; Ethpe be ejected, be born in miscarriage
ܫܕܦܐ gift given by bridegroom
ܫܕܪ Pa send, dispatch; Ethpa = *pass* Pa
ܫܗܪܐ *m* insomnia
ܫܘܐܠܐ *m* question, questioning
ܫܘܒܗܪܐ *m* boasting
ܫܘܒܚܐ *m* glory
ܫܘܒܩܢܐ *m* forgiveness
ܫܓ (√ܫܘܓ) Af (ܐܫܝܓ) wash
ܫܘܕܝܐ *m* declaration
ܐܫܬܘܕܥ Ethpa perceive, recognise (< √ܝܕܥ)
ܫܛ (√ܫܘܛ) Pe *u* treat with contempt; Ethpe (ܐܬܫܝܛ) become contemptible
ܐܫܘܝ Af deem worthy of (ܠ); Pe *ptc* ܫܘܐ worthy, deserving
ܫܘܝܐܝܬ equally, in the same way
ܫܘܠܛܢܐ *m* power
ܫܘܠܡܐ *m* completion, consummation
ܫܘܡܗܐ *m* attribute, epithet
ܫܘܡܠܝܐ *m* perfection
ܫܘܥܐ *m* rock
ܫܘܦܪܐ *m* beauty
ܫܘܩܐ *m* street; market
ܫܘܪܐ *m* wall, rampart
ܐܫܬܘܪܝ Ethpa come up against

ܫܘܪܝܐ *m* [grammatical t.t.] subject; beginning

ܫܘܫܒܝܢܐ *m* groomsman

ܫܘܫܒܝܢܬܐ *f* bridesmaid

ܫܘܫܛ Pa lead; Ethpa (ܐܫܬܘܫܛ) reach out

ܫܘܬܦ Pa associate, allow to take part (in ܒ); Ethpa (ܐܫܬܘܬܦ) take part

ܫܘܬܦܐ *m* one who shares (ܒ)

ܫܘܬܦܘܬܐ *f* (conjugal) union

ܫܚܠ Pe *a/o* flow, gush forth

ܐܫܬܚܠܦ Ethpa change (*intr*)

ܫܚܩ Pe *a/o* harass

ܫܛܝܘܬܐ *f* madness, folly

ܫܛܪܐ (also ܐܫܛܪܐ) *m* deed (legal document)

ܫܝܘܠ *f* Sheol, Hades

ܫܝܢܐ *m* peace

ܫܟܒ Pe *e/a* lie (down)

ܐܫܟܚ Af find; be able to; Ethpe be found

ܫܠܘܚܐ *m* sender

ܫܠܚ I Pe *a/o* (or: */a*) send a message; Ethpe be sent

ܫܠܚ II Pe *a/o* (or: */a*) strip, take off (clothing), divest

ܫܠܛ Pa lord it over (ܥܠ); Ethpa be allowed, authorised (to do)

ܫܠܝܐ *m* tranquility; ܡܢ ܫ' suddenly, unexpectedly

ܫܠܝܚܐ *m* apostle

ܫܠܝܛ *adj* entitled to (ܒ); permitted

ܫܠܝܛܢܐ *m* ruler

ܫܠܡ Pe *e/a* (a period of time) elapse; be complete; consent; Pa complete; accomplish; Ethpa = *pass* Pa; Af commit; hand, deliver; Ethpe deliver oneself up

ܫܠܡܐ *m* peace

ܫܡܐ *m* (*pl* ܫܡܗܬܐ, ܫܡܗܐ) name

ܫܡܗ Pa name

ܫܡܛ Pe *a/o* draw, pull out

ܫܡܝܐ *m* sky, heaven

ܫܡܝܢܝ heavenly

ܐܫܬܡܠܝ Ethpa be completed, performed

ܫܡܥ Pe *a/a* hear; take heed of; (+ ܒܩܠ) obey; Ethpe be subject

ܫܡܫ Pa serve, minister; make

ܫܡܫܐ *m* sun

ܫܢܝ Pa depart; remove (*tr*)

ܐܫܬܢܩ Ethpe (or Ethpa) be tormented

ܫܢܬܐ *f* (*cst* ܫܢܬ, *pl* ܫܢܝܢ) year

ܫܢܬܐ *f* sleep

ܐܫܬܥܝ Ethpa recount, narrate

ܫܥܬܐ *f* (*pl* ܫܥܐ) hour

ܫܦܘܠܐ *m* foot (of mountain)

ܫܦܝܪ beautiful; good, commendable

ܫܦܝܪܘܬܐ *f* beauty

ܫܦܠ /šfel/, ܫܦܝܠܐ frail
ܫܦܠܐ *m* low state, ignominy
ܫܦܥ Pe *a/a* to overflow
ܫܩܠ Pe *a/o* move (away); lift; take; carry; Ethpe = *pass* Pe
ܫܪ (√ܫܪܪ) Pe *a/a* be valid, true; ܫܪܪ Pa confirm; plant firmly; assert; secure, fasten; Ethpa be confirmed
ܫܪܐ Pe check in (at an inn); rest, nestle; lodge; free; Pa begin
ܫܪܒܐ *m* story
ܫܪܒܬܐ *f* tribe
ܫܪܓܐ *m* lamp
ܫܪܝܪ true; firm
ܫܪܝܪܐܝܬ truly
ܫܪܟܐ *m* remainder; ܘܫܪܟ' et cetera
ܫܪܪܐ *m* truth
ܫܬ, ܫܬܐ six
ܫܬܐܣܬܐ *f* (*pl* ܫܬܐܣܐ) foundation
ܐܫܬܝ /ʔešti/ Pe drink
ܫܬܩ Pe *e/o* be silent; Pa silence

ܬܘ

ܬܐܓܘܪܬܐ *f* business, commerce
ܬܒܥ Pe *a/a* ask for, demand; accuse (ܡܢ pers) of; Ethpe be made liable
ܬܒܥܬܐ /tvaʿṯaa/ *f* tax
ܬܒܪ Pe *a/o* (or: /*a*) tear; break
ܐܬܬܓܪ Ethpa conduct business
ܬܓܪܐ /taggaaraa/ *m* merchant
ܬܕܡܘܪܬܐ *f* wonder, miracle
ܬܗܝ Pa delay, withhold
ܬܗܪܐ *m* wonder
ܐܬܬܘܝ Ethpe repent
ܐܬܝܒ Af (√ܬܘܒ) return (*tr*)
ܬܘܒ again
ܬܘܗ Pe get alarmed, dismayed; Af = *caus* Pe
ܬܘܟܠܢܐ *m* trust, confidence
ܬܘܣܦܬܐ *f* increment
ܬܝܒܘܬܐ repentance
ܬܫܝܫܘܬܐ *f* helplessness, impotence
ܬܚܘܡܐ *m* border, limit
ܬܚܝܬ *prep* under
ܬܚܦܝܬܐ *f* veil
ܬܚܬ: ܠܬܚܬ /ltaḥt/ *prep* below
ܐܬܬܚܝܬ Ethpa be brought low
ܬܝܡܢܐ *m* south
ܬܝܡܢܝ southern
ܐܬܬܟܠ Ethpe trust, rely (on ܥܠ)
ܬܟܬܘܫܐ *m* combat
ܬܠܐ Pe hang; Ethpe be erected, hanged
ܬܠܝܬܝ third
ܬܠܡܕ Pa instruct
ܬܠܡܝܕܐ *m* disciple

ܬܠܬ three
ܬܠܬܝܢ thirty
ܬܡܗ Pe *a/a* be astonished
ܬܡܢ there
ܬܡܢܝܐ eight
ܬܢܘܝ *f* agreement, contract; condition
ܬܢܝ Pa recount, narrate
ܬܢܢ here
ܬܩܠ Pe *a/o* weigh; Ethpe stumble
ܬܩܢܐ *m* safe place
ܐܬܩܢ Af set, place; prepare
ܬܪܒܝܬܐ *f* growth
ܬܪܝܨ straight, just
ܬܪܝܨܘܬܐ *f* straightness
ܬܪܝܢ, ܬܪܬܝܢ two
ܬܪܝܢ second
ܬܪܥ Pe *a/o* break through.
ܬܪܥܐ *m* gate, entrance
ܬܪܥܣܪ, ܬܪܬܥܣܪܐ twelve
ܬܫܒܘܚܬܐ *f* glory, praise
ܬܫܡܫܬܐ *f* ministry, service
ܬܫܢܝܩܐ *m* torture
ܬܫܥ nine
ܬܫܪܝ Tishri (see Text 1, n. 3)

PROPER NOUNS[1]

ܐܒܓܪ Abgar

ܐܒܪܗܡ Abraham

ܐܓܐ Agga

ܐܕܣܝ Edessene

ܐܕܣܐ Edessa

ܐܘܛܘܟܘܣ Eutychus Εὔτυχος

ܐܘܣܒܝܘܣ Eusebius

ܐܘܪܠܝܐ Aurelia

ܐܘܪܠܝܘܣ Aurelius

ܐܘܪܠܝܣ Aurelis

ܐܘܪܫܠܡ Jerusalem

ܐܝܣܚܩ Isaac

ܐܝܪܘܕܣ Herod

ܐܠܟܣܢܕܪܝܐ Alexandria

ܐܡܘܪܝ Amorite

ܐܡܬܣܝܢ Ammath-Sin

ܐܢܕܪܐܘܣ Andrew

ܐܢܛܘܢܝܘܣ Antonius

ܐܢܛܘܢܝܢܝܐ Antoniniana

ܐܢܛܝܘܟܘܣ Antiochus

ܐܢܝܘܣ Annius

ܐܦܪܝܡ Ephraim (place name); Ephrem (personal name)

ܐܪܝܢܘܣ (= ܐܪܝܢܘܣ ?) Arrianus

ܒܝܬܠܚܡ Bethlehem

ܒܝܬ ܥܢܝܐ Bethany

ܒܠܥܡ Bileam

ܒܠܫܘ Belshu

ܒܪܒܥܫܐ Bar-Ba'sha

ܒܪܕܝܨܢ Bardaisan

ܒܪ ܝܡܐ Bar-Yama

ܒܪܫܡܝܐ Bar-Samya

ܒܪ ܒܥܫܡܝܢ Bar-Ba'eshamen

ܒܐܪܫܒܥ Beersheva

ܒܪ ܬܐܘܠܡܝ, ܒܪ ܬܘܠܡܝ Bartholomew

ܓܘܕܢܦܪ Gudnaphar

ܓܘܕܦܪ Gudaphar

ܓܘܪܕܝܢܘܣ Gordianus

ܕܘܝܕ David

ܕܝܨܢ Daisan, river flowing through Edessa

ܕܢܝܐܝܠ Daniel

ܗܢܕܘ India

ܗܢܕܘܝ Indian

ܙܒܕܝ Zebedee

ܚܒܢ Habban

ܚܠܦܝ Alphaeus

ܚܦܣܝ Hafsai

---

[1] In many cases the vocalisation remains uncertain.

ܚܪܢܝ Harranaean

ܝܗܘܕ Judaea
ܝܗܘܕܐ Judas
ܝܗܘܕܝ Jewish, Jew
ܝܘܕܝ Jew
ܝܘܚܢܢ John
ܝܘܟܢܝܐ Jechoniah
ܝܘܣܦ Joseph
ܝܘܫܝܐ Josiah
ܝܥܩܘܒ Jacob, James
ܝܫܘܥ Jesus

ܟܐܦܐ Cephas
ܟܠܕܝ Chaldaean

ܠܘܩܣ Lucas
ܠܥܙܪ Lazarus

ܡܐܬܝ Matthew
ܡܘܫܐ Moses
ܡܥܢܘ Ma'nu
ܡܩܝܡܘ Moqimu
ܡܪܝܡ Mary
ܡܪܩܘܣ Marcus
ܡܪܩܝܐ Marcia
ܡܪܬܐ Martha
ܡܬܝ Matthew
ܡܬܣܝܢ Mathsin
ܡܬܬܪܥܬܐ Mat-Tar'atha

ܢܫ divine name (inscription)
ܢܨܪܬ Nazareth
ܣܒܣܛܘܣ Sebastus
ܣܘܝܪܘܣ Severus
ܣܢܕܪܘܟ Sandaruk

ܥܒܪܝ Hebrew
ܥܒܝܕܐ Avida

ܦܠܝܦܘܣ, ܦܝܠܝܦܘܣ Philip
ܦܦܘܣ Papus
ܦܪܝܫܐ Pharisee
ܦܪܣܝ Persian

ܩܕܪ Kedar
ܩܢܢܝ Canaanite
ܩܝܦܐ Caiaphas
ܪܗܘܡܝ Roman
ܪܗܘܡܘܣ Romus

ܫܡܢܒܪܙ Shamenbaraz
ܫܡܢܝ Shamnai
ܫܡܥܘܢ Simon
ܫܡܫܝܗܒ Shamashyab
ܫܪܕܘܚܐ (inscription)

ܬܐܘܡܐ Thomas
ܬܝܪܘ Tiro